The Transmission of Medieval Romance

Studies in Medieval Romance

ISSN 1479-9308

This series aims to provide a forum for critical studies of the medieval romance, a genre which plays a crucial role in literary history, clearly reveals medieval secular concerns, and raises complex questions regarding social structures, human relationships, and the psyche. Its scope extends from the early middle ages into the Renaissance period, and although its main focus is on English literature, comparative studies are welcomed.

Proposals or queries should be sent in the first instance to one of the addresses given below; all submissions will receive prompt and informed consideration.

Professor Corinne Saunders, Department of English, University of Durham, Durham, DH1 3AY

Boydell & Brewer Limited, PO Box 9, Woodbridge, Suffolk, IP12 3DF

Previously published volumes in the series
are listed at the back of this book

The Transmission of Medieval Romance

Metres, Manuscripts and Early Prints

Edited by

AD PUTTER and JUDITH A. JEFFERSON

D. S. BREWER

First published 2018
D. S. Brewer, Cambridge

ISBN 978 1 84384 510 2

D. S. Brewer is an imprint of Boydell & Brewer Ltd
PO Box 9, Woodbridge, Suffolk, IP12 3DF, UK
and of Boydell & Brewer Inc.
668 Mount Hope Ave, Rochester, NY 14620–2731, USA
website: www.boydellandbrewer.com

A CIP catalogue record for this book is available
from the British Library

This publication is printed on acid-free paper

Printed and bound in Great Britain by TJ International Ltd, Padstow, Cornwall

Contents

Figures

Jordi Sánchez-Martí: The Printed Transmission of Medieval Romance from William Caxton to Wynkyn de Worde, 1473–1535

Michelle De Groot: Compiling Sacred and Secular: *Sir Orfeo* and the Otherworlds of Medieval Miscellanies

Rebecca E. Lyons: The Woodville Women, Eleanor Haute, and British Library Royal MS 14 E III

Contributors

Michelle De Groot is Assistant Professor at Hollins University.

Judith A. Jefferson is Honorary Research Associate at the University of Bristol.

Rebecca E. Lyons is Teaching Associate in English at the University of Bristol.

Carol M. Meale is Senior Research Fellow at the University of Bristol.

Donka Minkova is Distinguished Research Professor at the University of California, Los Angeles.

Nicholas Myklebust is Assistant Professor at Regis University.

Derek Pearsall is Professor Emeritus at Harvard University.

Rhiannon Purdie is Reader in Medieval Literature at the University of St Andrews.

Ad Putter is Professor of Medieval English Literature at the University of Bristol.

Elizabeth Robertson is Professor of English Language at the University of Glasgow.

Jordi Sánchez-Martí is Associate Professor of English Literature at the University of Alicante.

Thorlac Turville-Petre is Professor Emeritus at the University of Nottingham.

Acknowledgements

This book began with a conference held at Clifton Hill House at the University of Bristol, in April 2014, the fourteenth in the biennial 'Romance in Medieval Britain' series. Most of the essays in this volume were given as conference papers, and we would like to thank everyone who contributed to the conference, speakers, musicians, and listeners. We would also like to thank the staff at Clifton Hill House, the University of Bristol conference office, and Samantha Barlow and her colleagues at the BIRTHA, the Bristol Institute for Research in the Arts and Humanities.

The long-standing 'Romance in Medieval Britain' conference series has been a driving force for research on Middle English romances, and we were delighted to host the conference in 2014 to mark the conclusion of a four-year research project on the Verse Forms of Middle English Romance. Both this project and the conference were generously funded by an award (AH/H00839X/1) from the Arts and Humanities Research Council. We are grateful for their support.

This book is not the only legacy of the conference. Two of the conference lectures, one by Linda Marie Zaerr, '"Gode is the Lay, Swete is the Note": Performing *Sir Orfeo*', and one by Rosamund Allen, '"… hir lemman on loft skrilles and skrikes: Reading Verse Romance as Drama', were recorded on a double CD entitled *Performing Middle English Romance* (Chaucer Studio, 2015). This CD also contains musical performances of *Sir Orfeo* by Linda Marie Zaerr (soprano) and Laura Zaerr (harp) and of selections of *Octavian Imperator*, *Sir Bevis of Hampton*, and *The Stanzaic Morte Arthur* by Ad Putter (tenor) and Frances Eustace (rebec and harp). The conference dinner was enlivened by musical romance interludes, and we would like to thank the performers, especially Linda Zaerr, Laura Zaerr, and Frances Eustace. We are also very grateful to the Chaucer Studio, and particularly to its co-director Paul Thomas, for recording the CD, and for taking an interest in this research project from the very start.

This book has not been quick in coming, and it would have taken longer still if it were not for the efficiency and good-naturedness of all our contributors and the editorial and production team at Boydell & Brewer. We would like to thank in particular Caroline Palmer, Rob Kinsey, Nick Bingham, Rebecca Cribb, Rohais Haughton, and the anonymous reviewers who reported on the initial book proposal and the full manuscript. In preparing the manuscript for the publishers and in compiling the index, we had excellent editorial assistance from Hatsuko Matsuda. We are pleased to acknowledge her help and the financial support of the Arts Faculty Research Fund of the University of Bristol.

A final word of thanks is due to the staff at the libraries and special collections that make academic research possible. We are grateful to them for looking after us so well, and also for granting permissions to reproduce images from manuscripts and early-printed editions. We would especially like to thank Michael Richardson, Special Collections Librarian at the University of Bristol. We are also grateful to the Neil Ker Memorial Fund of the British Academy for giving us an award which allowed us to reproduce various manuscript illustrations.

Abbreviations

BL	London, British Library
BMC	*Catalogue of Books Printed in the XVth Century now in the British Library (Museum)*, Parts 1–13 (vols 1–10, 12, London: British Museum; vol. 11, 't Goy-Houten: Hes and De Graaf, 1908–2007; vols 1–8 reprinted with corrections, 1963; vol. 9 reprinted with corrections, 1967)
BnF	Bibliothèque nationale de France
Bodl.	Bodleian Library, Oxford
CHBB II, III	*The Cambridge History of the Book in Britain*, 6 vols, ed. John Barnard, D. F. McKenzie, David McKitterick, and I. R. Willison (Cambridge: CUP, 1999–2011), *vol. II: 1100–1400*, ed. Nigel A. Morgan and Rodney M. Thompson (2008), *vol. III: 1400–1557*, ed. Lotte Hellinga and J. B. Trapp (1999)
CR	*Chaucer Review*
CUL	Cambridge University Library
CUP	Cambridge University Press
DOE	*Dictionary of Old English: A to H* online, ed. Angus Cameron, Ashley Crandell Amos, Antonette diPaolo Healey *et al.* (Toronto: Dictionary of Old English Project, 2016) at https://tapor.library.utoronto.ca/doe/
Duff	*Printing in England in the Fifteenth Century*, E. Gordon Duff's Bibliography with supplementary descriptions, chronologies and a census of copies by Lotte Hellinga (London: The Bibliographical Society/The British Library, 2009)
EETS o.s.; e.s.; s.s.	Early English Text Society, original series; extra series; supplementary series
ELL	*English Language and Linguistics*
ES	*English Studies*
FB	*French Vernacular Books: Books Published in the French Language before 1601*, ed. Andrew

	Pettegree, Malcolm Walsby and Alexander Wilkinson (Leiden and Boston: Brill, 2007), 2 vols
GJ	*Gutenberg-Jahrbuch*
GW	*Gesamtkatalog der Wiegendrucke*, vols 1–7 (Leipzig: K. W. Hiersemann, 1925–40), from vol. 8 (Stuttgart: A. Hiersemann, 1968–), online at www.gesamktkatalogderwiegendrucke.de
HLQ	*Huntington Library Quarterly*
ILC	*Incunabula Printed in the Low Countries: A Census*, ed. Gerard van Thienen and John Goldfinch (Niewkoop: De Graaf, 1999)
IPMEP	*Index of Printed Middle English Prose*, ed. R. E. Lewis, N. F. Blake and A. S. G. Edwards (New York: Garland, 1985)
JEBS	*Journal of the Early Book Society*
JEGP	*Journal of English and Germanic Philology*
Kok	Ina Kok, *Woodcuts in Incunabula Printed in the Low Countries* (Houten: Hes and De Graaf, 2013), 4 vols
LAEME	*A Linguistic Atlas of Early Middle English, 1150–1325*, compiled by Margaret Laing [http://www.lel.ed.ac.uk/ihd/laeme2/laeme2.html]. Edinburgh: Version 3.2, 2013, © The University of Edinburgh
MÆ	*Medium Ævum*
MP	*Modern Philology*
MWME	*A Manual of the Writings in Middle English 1050–1500*, 10 vols (New Haven, CT: Connecticut Academy of Arts and Sciences, 1967–98)
N&Q	*Notes and Queries*
NK	W. Nijhoff and M. E. Kronenberg, *Nederlandsche Bibliographie, 1500–1540* ('s-Gravenhage: M. Nijhoff, 1923–71), 3 vols
NLS	National Library of Scotland, Edinburgh
NLW	National Library of Wales, Aberystwyth
NM	*Neuphilologische Mitteilungen*
NRS	Edinburgh, National Records of Scotland
OED	*Oxford English Dictionary*
OUP	Oxford University Press
PBSA	*The Papers of the Bibliographical Society of America*
PQ	*Philological Quarterly*
RES	*Review of English Studies*
SAC	*Studies in the Age of Chaucer*

SB	*Studies in Bibliography*
SP	*Studies in Philology*
STC	*A Short-Title Catalogue of Books Printed in England, Scotland, & Ireland, and of English Books Printed Abroad, 1475–1640*, ed. A. W. Pollard and G. R. Redgrave, 2nd edn rev. by W. A. Jackson, F. S. Ferguson and Katherine F. Pantzer (London: The Bibliographical Society, 1976–91), 3 vols
TEAMS	Consortium for the Teaching of the Middle Ages

Introduction: Forms of Transmission of Medieval Romance

Judith A. Jefferson and Ad Putter

For a long time, the main problem associated with the study of the romances that were read in medieval England seemed to be their popularity, a characteristic invoking such negative reactions that it seemed as if the word 'popular' was perhaps being used not with its current meaning of 'intended primarily to entertain, please, or amuse',[1] but instead with what the *Oxford English Dictionary* characterises as the obsolete meaning of 'vulgar, coarse, ill-bred'.[2] However, the defence of the study of Middle English popular romance no longer seems quite so necessary: it has already been ably undertaken, perhaps most successfully – and certainly most forcefully – by Nicola McDonald in her 'Polemical Introduction' to *Pulp Fictions of Medieval England.*[3] The collection of essays edited by McDonald in that volume is itself evidence of scholarly interest in such romances, as is the collection edited by Putter and Gilbert,[4] and more generally the Studies in Medieval Romance volumes published in the last two decades by Boydell and Brewer. As Cory Rushton observes on the final page of one of these last, 'the journey of the popular romance has been from the centre to the margins and then back again'.[5]

However, while medieval romance has been rehabilitated, the genre still poses many problems, and these are not the kinds of problems that beset scholars dealing with, for example, Chaucer, Gower, Hoccleve and others.

1 *Oxford English Dictionary*, s.v. popular, *adj.* and *n.* 7.b.

2 *Oxford English Dictionary*, s.v. popular, *adj.* and *n.* 3.c. For interesting and revealing discussions of the meaning of 'popular' as it applies to romances, see the Introduction to *A Companion to Medieval Popular Romance*, ed. Raluca L. Radulescu and Cory James Rushton (Cambridge: D. S. Brewer, 2009), pp. 1–8, at pp. 5–7; Jane Gilbert, 'A Theoretical Introduction', in *The Spirit of Medieval English Popular Romance*, ed. Ad Putter and Jane Gilbert (Harlow: Pearson, 2000), pp. 15–38; and the essay by Myra Stokes in the same volume (pp. 56–77): '*Lanval* to *Sir Launfal*: A Story Becomes Popular'.

3 Nicola McDonald, *Pulp Fictions of Medieval England: Essays in Popular Romance* (Manchester: Manchester University Press, 2004), pp. 1–21.

4 *The Spirit of Medieval Romance*, ed. Putter and Gilbert.

5 Cory James Rushton, 'Modern and Academic Reception of Romance', in *A Companion to Medieval Popular Romance*, ed. Radulescu and Rushton, pp. 165–79, at p. 179.

This volume focuses on two key issues, first the material forms in which these romances survive, and second the verse forms in which poets composed them and scribes handed them down. The two issues, as we shall see, are closely related, and to combine analyses of manuscripts with those of metre, as this volume does, is to unite perspectives that are often mutually illuminating. Both perspectives are important for our understanding of medieval romance. As Rosalind Field observes, what sets the majority of Middle English verse romances of the thirteenth and fourteenth centuries apart from the poems of Chaucer and others like him is that they are 'textually fragile, anonymous, and lack clear cultural and social contexts'.[6] A two-pronged approach that considers, on the one hand, the codicological history of such romances – the manuscripts and early printed books in which they have come down to us – and, on the other hand, the verse forms in which these romances have been transmitted, provides a practical way of dealing with such challenges.

Manuscript study is particularly useful when it comes to addressing gaps in our knowledge of the cultural and social context of romances, and it is not surprising that it has come to the fore in recent research. The appearance in the 1970s of various manuscripts in facsimile editions,[7] together with the publication of a catalogue of romance manuscripts,[8] reflected the growing interest in the codicological contexts of medieval romances and stimulated further research in this area. Since then material philology has figured prominently in the biennial Romance in Medieval Britain conference series, and in the volumes resulting from these. As many scholars have already demonstrated, information about those who commissioned romance manuscripts, who later owned them, where they lived, their social contacts, can tell us much about the reception (sometimes the changing reception) of romances. This information has slowly weaned criticism away from the idea that medieval romances must be bad because they were read by the lower orders, by the 'emergent bourgeoisie' and by 'social aspirants' who 'lack understanding' of their 'social superiors'.[9] We now know that many Middle English romance manuscripts were owned by landowning gentlemen like Robert Thornton. Following the lead of Raluca Radulescu and others, Michael Johnston has put the landed gentry on

6 Rosalind Field, 'Popular Romance: The Material and Its Problems', in *A Companion to Medieval Popular Romance*, ed. Radulescu and Rushton, pp. 9–30, at p. 9.

7 See, for example, *The Thornton Manuscript: Lincoln Cathedral MS 91*, intro. D. S. Brewer and A. E. B. Owen (London: Scolar Press, 1975); and *The Auchinleck Manuscript: Edinburgh, National Library of Scotland Advocates' MS 19.2.1*, intro. Derek Pearsall and I. C. Cunningham (London: Scolar Press, 1977).

8 Gisela Guddat-Figge, *Catalogue of Manuscripts Containing Middle English Romances* (Munich: Fink, 1976).

9 Quotations are from the pithy summary of critical opinion by McDonald, 'A Polemical Introduction', in *Pulp Fictions of Medieval England*, p. 9 (with references on pp. 19–20, notes 25 and 26).

the map as patrons and owners of Middle English romances,[10] finding in the production of manuscripts such as the Ireland manuscript from Lancashire (Princeton, University Library Taylor 9, associated with the manor of Hale) and the Findern manuscript (Cambridge, CUL Ff.1.6), compiled by a Derbyshire gentry family, support for his view that romances including *The Avowing of Arthur*, *Sir Amadace* and *Sir Degrevant* had special relevance for the provincial gentry, and were read both as dealing with their particular problems (and offering them comfort in respect of these problems), and as confirming their position in society as people who, like the aristocracy, had romances written about them.

Of course, some romance manuscripts clearly are to be associated with 'bourgeoisie',[11] but as the focus has shifted from town merchants to regional gentry it has become apparent that Middle English romances were popular not in the derogatory sense of being liked by 'socially inferior' people, but simply in the sense of being popular with people who could read (and with those who had stories read to them). And as literacy spread, the readership of medieval romances expanded to encompass an ever greater variety of social groupings.[12]

The essays in this collection bear this out. Two essays, by Carol Meale and Rebecca Lyons, take us higher up the social ladder. Carol Meale reminds us of the existence of a number of deluxe manuscripts of Middle English romances. As Meale observes, leaving aside *Sir Gawain and the Green Knight* only four manuscripts containing Middle English romances have illustrations: the Auchinleck manuscript (Edinburgh, National Library of Scotland Advocates MS 19.2.1); the portion of Bodl. MS 264 containing *Alexander B*; New York, Pierpont Morgan Library MS M 876, containing *Generides* (the couplet-version); and BL MS Harley 326, which contains *The Three Kings' Sons*.

All these manuscripts appear to have been bespoke productions. The place or origin of the Auchinleck manuscript is not problematic: it was almost certainly produced in London, where there were large numbers of scribes engaged in copying a wide variety of texts, both secular and religious, as well

10 Raluca Radulescu, 'Literature', in *Gentry Culture in Late-Medieval England*, ed. Raluca Radulescu and Alison Truelove (Manchester: Manchester University Press, 2015), pp. 100–18; and Michael Johnston, *Romance and the Gentry in Late Medieval England* (Oxford: OUP, 2014), in particular chapters 2 and 3 (pp. 48–127).

11 An interesting example is Longleat House, MS 55 (containing *Arthur*) which is to be connected with Bath's mercantile community rather than with the Cathedral Priory: Gareth Griffith and Ad Putter, 'Linguistic Boundaries in Multilingual Miscellanies', in *Middle English Texts in Transition: A Festschrift Dedicated to Toshiyuki Takamiya*, ed. Simon Horobin and Linne R. Mooney (York: York Medieval Press, 2014), pp. 116–24, especially pp. 122–3.

12 See on this point Carol M. Meale, '"Good men / Wiues maydnes and alle men": Romance and Its Audience', in *Readings in Medieval English Romance*, ed. Carol M. Meale (Cambridge: D. S. Brewer, 1994), pp. 208–25.

as official documents. In the case of Auchinleck, five or six scribes wrote the texts, and a number of artists were responsible for decorations and paraphs.[13] The question of who commissioned this manuscript is, however, more complicated. The clientele for associated volumes included clerics, merchants, the civic elite of London and royalty, while a female rather than a male patron is certainly possible.

We have more information about the earliest owners of Bodley 264.[14] This is a composite manuscript. The earliest part contains a copy of the French *Roman d'Alexandre*, produced in Tournai in the 1340s, but a scribe mistakenly thought that the French version lacked an important episode, the exchange of letters between Alexander and Dindimus. To make good this perceived lacuna, he added a Middle English romance about this exchange, *Alexander and Dindimus*. The English romance originated in the West Midlands, but the manuscript copy itself was a professional production from London.[15] The case shows that commercial book producers in London had alliterative romances as part of their stock.[16] The volume is also closely linked with royalty: Thomas Duke of Gloucester may have owned the French *Roman d'Alexandre* (though he would probably have been dead by the time of the copying of the *Alexander and Dindimus* section), and by the mid-fifteenth century the manuscript was in the possession of Richard Wydville, first Earl Rivers and father-in-law to Edward IV.

The patron of Morgan M 876 has not been identified, and what suggestions there have been have proved impossible to verify, but it seems certain that the book found an early readership in East Anglia where it remained as part of the Tollemache collection at Helmingham in Suffolk. In the case of Harley 326, though evidence as to its commissioner is not forthcoming, we do know that the book was probably produced between the early 1470s and the early 1480s in London. Other work by the scribe and by the illustrator of Harley 326 can be identified in a number of manuscripts (in the case of the artist, in, for example, London, Lambeth Palace MS 265, and, in the case of the scribe, in Bodl. MS

13 *The Auchinleck Manuscript: New Perspectives*, ed. Susanna Fein (York: York Medieval Press, 2016), brings together state-of-the-art studies of the manuscript.

14 See Mark Cruse, *Illuminating the Roman d'Alexandre: Oxford, Bodleian Library, Bodley 264* (Cambridge: D. S. Brewer, 2011).

15 Kathleen Scott localises the manuscript there on the basis of the style of the illuminations: *Later Gothic Manuscripts, 1390–1490*, 2 vols (London: Harvey Miller, 1996), II, pp. 68–73. The London localisation is confirmed by the dialect of the scribe (which is different from the western dialect of the original poet): see Ad Putter, Myra Stokes and Judith A. Jefferson, *Studies in the Metre of Alliterative Verse* (Oxford: Medium Ævum, 2007), pp. 11, 230–1. An ownership note in the manuscript tells us that Lord Rivers purchased the manuscript in London.

16 Another example of an alliterative romance that formed part of the stock of London book producers is *The Siege of Jerusalem*. See Ralph Hanna, 'Contextualizing *The Siege of Jerusalem*', *Yearbook of Langland Studies* 6 (1992), 109–21.

Fairfax 4). Overall, the ownership of such manuscripts suggests a client-base made up of the upper echelons of London society. London, then, was clearly an important centre for the production of deluxe books, while the number and type of volumes in which the work of the Harley 326 scribe can be identified suggests that, in the period between the production of the Auchinleck manuscript in the early 1330s and that of Harley 326 in the latter part of the fifteenth century, the possibility of deriving a living from the production of secular books may well have increased. Illustration of such secular books was not, however, common, and it was only to become so with the advent of printing.

Rebecca Lyons is also interested in the ownership of manuscripts, in particular the fifteenth-century ownership and readership of BL Royal MS 14 E III, an impressive volume containing three of the five Arthurian prose romances of the Lancelot-Grail Cycle. The manuscript was compiled in northern France between 1315 and 1324 and was later owned by Charles V and Charles VI of France, and then by John Duke of Bedford. It then passed, Lyons suggests, to Humphrey Duke of Gloucester and then to Richard Roos, who inscribed it with his own *ex libris*. On his death in 1482, it passed to his niece, Eleanor Haute, who also signed it, and later (possibly, Lyons suggests, as a gift from Eleanor) to Edward IV's queen, Elizabeth Woodville. The book was then inscribed by E. Wydevyll – possibly Elizabeth herself, her eldest daughters, Elizabeth of York and Cecily, and her sister Joan (or Jane) Grey. The two younger women identify themselves in the book as the king's daughters, but Lyons suggests that they may have done so after Edward IV's death, possibly as an act of political defiance following Richard III's usurpation. In any case, these particular signatures must have been written by the beginning of January 1486, when the younger Elizabeth married Henry Tudor. The deaths of Jane Grey and Elizabeth Woodville in 1492 make it clear that their signatures must have been written before this date and, in fact, Lyons suggests that Joan's signature, which appears immediately beneath those of the two sisters, was probably added at the same time, i.e. between 1482 and 1486. It is conceivable that all four of the Woodville inscriptions were added during the period which the Woodville women spent in sanctuary at Westminster from 1 May 1483 to 22 January 1484. The book, containing as it does those of the Lancelot-Grail Cycle texts which centre on the Grail stories and which are both religious and sober in tone, may have provided the women with spiritual and emotional comfort, as well as a certain amount of escapism, while their inscriptions and annotations testify to their literary interests and personal self-interest.

Studies have shown that the company which romances keep in manuscripts can also suggest to us something about the way such romances were read and used.[17] The three extant copies of *Sir Orfeo* (in the Auchinleck manuscript,

[17] See, for example, Lynne S. Blanchfield, 'The Romances in MS Ashmole 61: An Idiosyncratic Scribe', in *Romance in Medieval England*, ed. Maldwyn Mills, Jennifer

Bodl. MS Ashmole 61, and BL MS Harley 3810), though widely separated in time and varying in form from the extravagant to the modest, are all apparently aimed at a bourgeois readership and all appear in manuscripts containing religious material. The intentions behind such combinations are often difficult to determine: was this a matter of choice on the part of the scribe or his patron, or was the selection simply a matter of what was readily available? Such questions may well be unanswerable, and Michelle De Groot chooses instead to take a more formal approach to these collections, concentrating not on the intentions behind them but on the reader's response. De Groot argues that the companion texts to *Sir Orfeo* can help to provide interpretations of that poem and, in particular, to define what 'secular romance' might mean in a bourgeois medieval context. Texts in such medieval collections are in constant conversation with one another. All the religious poems in these three collections deal with one particular topic: the intersection between the natural and the supernatural world. Secular romances share this interest in the disturbance of the natural order by the marvellous, in the case of *Sir Orfeo*, by Fairie. Links between the romance and the sacred are particularly revealing in the case of their treatment of the afterlife. The *Orfeo* description of the Fairie realm echoes descriptions of the New Jerusalem which appear elsewhere in both the Auchinleck manuscript and in Ashmole 61, while anxieties about the afterlife hinted at in more religious poems such as *Saint Patrick's Purgatory* can be more forcefully addressed in a non-religious poem like *Sir Orfeo*. *Sir Orfeo* suggests that something diabolical can seem to be heavenly but that intimations of the eternal may actually be found elsewhere, in music and human bonds of loyalty and matrimony. The divide between the religious and the secular is thus breached in *Sir Orfeo*, suggesting that the pursuit of salvation by believers living in the world is a matter of constant judgement in a multivocal environment, just as readers and re-readers of manuscripts engage in repeated interpretation and reinterpretation, with *Sir Orfeo* influencing readings of religious texts and religious texts influencing readings of *Sir Orfeo*.

Changes in the attitude to texts might be expected to arise with the coming of printing: as Jordi Sánchez-Martí observes, whereas manuscript books were largely produced to order, the printing business was, of its nature, largely speculative. What Caxton published was no longer a matter of the wishes of a particular patron but was the result, instead, of the business acumen – and sometimes

---

Fellows and Carol M. Meale (Cambridge: D. S. Brewer, 1991), pp. 65–87; and Raluca Radulescu, *Romance and Its Contexts in Fifteenth-Century England: Politics, Piety and Penance* (Cambridge: D. S. Brewer, 2013). Blanchfield argues that the combination of religious and romance texts found in MS Ashmole 61 implies that romances could be used in conjunction with more religious texts to evangelise the importance of family unity and piety, providing an entertaining element to balance more instructional texts, while Radulescu argues for the socio-political relevance of *Sir Gowther*, *Robert of Sicily*, and *Sir Isumbras* by examining these romances in their manuscript context.

the prejudice – of Caxton himself: he chose, for instance, to publish romances such as the *Morte Darthure* and (his own) translations of French romances, rather than what he considered to be the somewhat old-fashioned and trite traditional English romances. Nonetheless, this did not result in a very great change in reading habits. Caxton's printed romances were not particularly successful, and those who did read them were mainly the gentry, i.e. those who had always read the traditional English romances. After Caxton's death, Wynkyn de Worde succeeded in broadening this customer base, appealing to the common people as well as the gentry by such techniques of textual presentation as the use of woodcuts and by producing a cheaper product in quarto format, but he did not succeed in changing the tastes of his customers: the translated prose romances he continued to publish were still not popular and he eventually ceased their production, whereas the English verse romances which, unlike Caxton, he was happy to print, were far more successful.

Printing might be expected to have other effects on romances, in particular on the way in which such texts were transmitted. Once the printing presses were established, memorial transmission of romances might be thought unlikely. Indeed, not all scholars have been convinced that such texts were transmitted by memory even before the advent of printing, with the type of variation once seen as evidence of working from memory often viewed more recently as the result of scribal practice.[18] Nevertheless, as Rhiannon Purdie observes, there is a certain amount of evidence that learning by heart may have influenced the pre-printing transmission of such texts as *King Horn* and *Of Arthour and Merlin*, and she argues strongly in her essay on *King Orphius* and *Sir Orfeo* for memorial transmission as an explanation of the differences between the two post-printing late sixteenth-century copies of the Scottish *King Orphius*, a version plainly related to *Sir Orfeo*, but with a number of clear differences (e.g. the name of the country, the name of the Queen, and the fact that Orphius's nephew rather than his steward is left in charge in his absence). *Sir Orfeo* is itself a text which has often been cited in debates on memorial transmission, but the manuscript evidence has never been entirely conclusive. However, the discovery in the early 1970s of fragments of the late medieval *King Orphius*, together with Purdie's own discovery in 2010 of David Laing's nineteenth-century transcription of eighty-two lines of a different but related form of that poem, has provided exciting additional evidence to work with, particularly since both the fragments and Laing's exemplar appear to have been copied in Scotland in the 1580s, and possibly both in East Lothian. There are also later Scottish ballads related to *King Orphius*, something

[18] For the two sides of the argument, see Derek Pearsall, 'The Auchinleck Manuscript Forty Years On', in *The Auchinleck Manuscript: New Perspectives*, ed. Susanna Fein (York: York Medieval Press, 2016), pp. 1–25 (pp. 22–3); and Linda Marie Zaerr, *Performance and the Middle English Romance* (Cambridge: D. S. Brewer, 2012), p. 110.

which makes it clear that oral (and thus memorial) transmission has definitely been part of this story, but even more interesting is the relationship between the two *King Orphius* witnesses. These two copies are so close in time and space to one another that the radical differences between them (combined as they are with close agreement in the narrative and in some key phrases) simply could not have developed as a result of scribal copying. Such differences are, instead, of the type described by Albert B. Lord in his account of the individual performances of the same song by Yugoslavian guslars, or the type of interpolation (borrowing from other works) noted by Child in ballads.[19] The role of memorial transmission in the history of Middle English (or Older Scots) romance is thus, in this case at least, beyond argument.

Just as the study of manuscripts and early printed books has yielded obvious insights into questions of transmission, so the study of the rhyme and metre can offer valuable clues about the textual history of romance. In this area, however, scholarship on Middle English romance has a lot of catching up to do. For while the rhythms and rhyme schemes of Chaucer and Gower are well understood, and alliterative metre has received a great deal of attention in recent years, the same cannot be said of the verse forms of Middle English romances. Take, for example, the earliest Middle English romance, *King Horn*.[20] The French source, *The Romance of Horn* by 'mestre Thomas', is in the recognisable French verse tradition of the *chanson de geste*: mono-rhymed alexandrines grouped together in *laisses*. But what kind of verse is the English adaptation supposed to be? Consider the brief passage below:

> Hit was upon a someres day.
> Als ic you telle may,
> Muri, the gode king,
> Rod on his pleying
> Bi the se side,
> As he woned ride.
> He fond bi the stronde
> Arived on his londe,
> Shipes fiftene,
> With Sarazins kene. (29–38)[21]

[19] Albert B. Lord, *The Singer of Tales* (Cambridge, MA: Harvard University Press, 1960); Francis James Child (ed.), *The English and Scottish Popular Ballads*, 5 vols (Boston, MA: Houghton Mifflin, 1882–94; repr. New York: Dover, 1965).

[20] We follow the datings of *A Manual of the Writings in Middle English, 1050–1500. I: Romances*, gen. ed. J. Burke Severs (New Haven, CT: Connecticut Academy of Arts and Sciences, 1967), p. 13. *King Horn* is dated to c. 1225.

[21] *King Horn*, in *Of Love and Chivalry: An Anthology of Middle English Romance*, ed. Jennifer Fellows (London: Dent, 1993).

Certainly, the poem rhymes, but there is no consensus about anything else. Is this poem in short couplets or are these short lines actually to be understood as half-lines, as some scholars believe? Is there any regularity in the distribution of stressed and unstressed syllables? How many beats are there in each line (or is it half-line?). All these basic questions are still to be answered.[22]

With very few exceptions, verse form has been neglected in the study of romances, even though the exceptions show how illuminating this approach can be. For instance, Rhiannon Purdie in her book on tail-rhyme is able to shed light on the textual history of many romances, including *The Wedding of Sir Gawain and Dame Ragnell*. The surviving text of this romance was copied c. 1500, but as it stands in the manuscript (Oxford, Bodl. MS Rawlinson C.86) the romance is in a bad way: tail-rhyme stanzas (many missing one or more lines) give way to couplets and many rhymes no longer work. Some of this corruption may be the unintended by-product of the 'graphic tail-rhyme' format in which many tail-romances were transmitted in medieval manuscripts. In this format, the shorter tail-lines were set to the right of the couplet lines. In the case of *The Wedding*, the 'text's periodic degeneration into couplets is probably a legacy of a tattered tail-rhyme exemplar in which an outer column of tail lines has either become illegible or been cut off altogether in the process of binding'.[23]

The essays dealing with verse form in this collection seek to shine light into the dark corners of this neglected area. Ad Putter uses stanza form to address the question of transmission, arguing that textual references to music and singing, rather than being simply a way of creating atmosphere in what were basically written texts, should often instead be taken more literally. Robert Mannyng in his *Chronicle* lists the various ways in which the transmission of oral, rather than written, texts can fail, and uses *Sir Tristrem* as one example. The *Tristrem* stanza is also known to appear in one of Laurence Minot's political poems, and Putter points out that, in addition, it can be found in Mary's lament in the Towneley play of the Crucifixion, as well as in the *Alphabetical Praise of Women* and its French source, the *ABC a femmes*, both probably from the West Midlands, suggesting a widespread circulation of this form. The reason for the shared stanza form, Putter suggests, is that all these various poems were intended to be sung. The presence of a bob itself may hint at a musical connection (though clearly not all poems with bobs were intended to be sung). The bob is common in medieval carols, a genre with clear musical associations, and one where the bob itself is not uncommonly marked with the word 'chorus'. It seems likely, therefore, that Mannyng was correct when

22 See Ad Putter, 'The Metres and Stanza Forms of Popular Romance', in *A Companion to Medieval Popular Romance*, ed. Radulescu and Rushton, pp. 111–31, at pp. 114–16.

23 Rhiannon Purdie, *Anglicising Romance: Tail-Rhyme and Genre in Medieval English Literature* (Cambridge: D. S. Brewer, 2008), p. 71.

he asserted that *Sir Tristrem* was sung, and the same is probably also true of *King Horn* and of the tail-rhyme *Bevis of Hampton*, both of which go back to Anglo-Norman *chansons de geste* composed in *laisses*, a form for which there is ample evidence of song delivery. Music for neither of these poems survives, but fortunately there are tail-rhyme texts for which music is still extant, e.g. the Raising of Lazarus from the Fleury Playbook (c. 1200) and the first stanza of the Middle English song 'Ar ne kuth ich sorghe non', where the musical form goes back to that of the Marian lament *Planctus ante nescia*, attributed to Godfrey of St Victor. Each strophe has a different rhyme scheme and melody, but the first stanza is in tail-rhyme and the melody can easily be fitted to the text of *Bevis*. Such surviving music can offer us at least a glimpse of what medieval romance texts may have sounded like in performance.

Donka Minkova is also concerned with the oral links of the romance genre, but approaches this from a linguistic perspective. Minkova considers the extent to which the oral and informal aspects of the romance are reflected in the type of linguistic structure employed in the verse line, and whether romance works differ in this respect from poetry in other genres. Concentrating on adjectives used both in adjective-noun phrases and predicatively, Minkova analyses material drawn from a wide range of poetic texts, including *Sir Orfeo*, *The King of Tars*, various works by Chaucer and *Sir Gawain and the Green Knight.* She does not find that the use of the adjective-noun combination varies with genre and thus does not find that verse traditionally thought of as belonging to an oral tradition differs in its use of such combinations from more literary texts. She does, however, find evidence to support the view that metrical placement is closely linked to the semantic weight born by a particular item (more common adjectives, which bear less semantic weight, are less likely to take a beat) and she suggests that further investigations into such patterns would be profitable. Also profitable might be the study of the predicative use of adjectives. Recent research has suggested that an increase in such use reflects more informal interaction among intimates, and the study of the use of adjective in *The King of Tars* (where predicative use outweighs attributive use) might suggest that more informal use of language is characteristic of romances. However, a different pattern is evident in *Sir Orfeo*, and further work needs to be done before any firm conclusions can be drawn. This type of approach is applicable to a wide range of texts and should allow comparison between those traditionally thought to belong to the romance genre and other types.

Both Minkova and Putter show that analysis of formal features of romance such as versification and prosody can shed light on larger issues such as generic distinctiveness and musical performance. The study of metre is the second means of approaching romances adopted in this volume. The importance of metre to Middle English romance is evident from the very fact that, prior to the fifteenth century, such romances were invariably written in verse, in contrast to French romances which were often written in prose.[24] As is the case with manuscripts, information on the social and cultural associations of romances and their audience/readers can often be gleaned from the metre. Thorlac Turville-Petre argues in his essay that, in the case of the *Cheuelere Assigne*, certain characteristics of the metre may be a consequence of the intended audience. The metre of this particular poem is, to some extent, problematic, partly because of our preconceptions about alliterative verse. Thus, although the opening verse paragraph of the poem fulfils all our expectations as far as alliteration is concerned (i.e. most lines follow the classic aa/ax pattern), this pattern does not persist throughout the poem; overall only 14 per cent of lines are of this type. In the case of the *Siege of Jerusalem*, which immediately precedes the *Cheuelere Assigne* in BL MS Cotton Caligula A.ii, failure of alliteration results from systematic revision to appeal to a more southerly audience, but, if the alliterative irregularities of the *Cheuelere Assigne* have a similar cause, the revision must have been much more thoroughgoing, involving reordering of the line (alliteration often falls on the final beat) as well as the replacement of alliterating words with synonyms. In fact, as Turville-Petre argues, the complete lack of characteristic alliterative vocabulary in the poem, even in the scene of combat, suggests that the *Cheuelere Assigne* was never what might be termed a traditional alliterative composition. It is noticeable, however, that from the point of view of rhythm, the poem is in fact a perfectly satisfactory alliterative poem (the b-verses, for instance, follow the traditional pattern of having one and only one long dip), and Turville-Petre suggests that alliteration, though characteristic of the type of long line which we call the alliterative long line, is not in fact essential for this type of verse: it reinforces the rhythmic pattern but it is that pattern rather than the alliteration which forms the essence of the line. The *Cheuelere Assigne* is thus written in alliterative metre but without the traditional vocabulary and, as a result, often without the alliterative patterning. The reason for this, Turville-Petre argues, can be found in the nature of the poet's audience. The *Cheuelere Assigne* has sometimes been assigned to the North West Midlands, but Turville-Petre suggests dialect evidence cited in support of this placement is not convincing and that the poem was in fact written for a London and East Midlands audience, and that the traditional vocabulary was modified to meet the needs and expectations of this audience.

Metrical problems, and, in particular, those faced by poets writing in the earlier Middle English period, are also considered by Derek Pearsall. Much

24 See Corinne Saunders, 'The Romance Genre', in *A Companion to British Literature*, vol. I: *Medieval Literature, 700–1450*, ed. Robert Demaria Jr., Heesok Chan and Samantha Zacher (Chichester: Wiley-Blackwell, 2014), pp. 161–79, at p. 163; and Ad Putter, 'The Metres and Stanza Forms of Popular Romance', in *A Companion to Medieval Popular Romance*, ed. Radulescu and Rushton, pp. 111–31, at p. 111.

pre-Ricardian Middle English poetry seems to us metrically awkward, but Pearsall argues that there was often a degree of sophistication and self-awareness in the way in which particular metres and combinations of metres were used. We tend to expect poems to stick to one particular metre, but the Anglo-Norman poet Jordan Fantosme used metrical variation (decasyllabics and fourteeners in poems mainly written in alexandrines) for stylistic purposes, and similar types of variation were used for similar ends by the authors of the Latin *Physiologus* and the Anglo-Norman *Bestiaire*. Such practices may well have provided models for Middle English poets. In the case of the English *Bestiary* and that of the *Proverbs of Alfred*, for example, changes in metre are used to mark separate sections of the poems, while Laȝamon turns to the alliterative long line for battle scenes. Such sophistication is not, however, normally evident in poems written in the 'old long line', a line combining characteristics of the alexandrine and septenary with the four-stress alliterative line. The opening lines of the *Tale of Gamelyn*, for instance, are simply metrically confusing, lacking the regularity essential for poetic metre. The variability shown by the metrical structure of these lines seems unlikely to result from oral delivery, which, if anything, demands an increase in regularity. These opening lines are very difficult to scan, but something different seems to happen as the poem progresses: there seems to be an attempt to solve the incoherence of the metre by driving it in one particular direction and the dominant rhythm thus becomes that of the alliterative long line. A similar tendency to push the long line in one direction or another can be found in other poems of the period (e.g. in the *South English Legendary*, in *Ferumbras*, and in *Beryn*). The situation for poets in this period was confusing, faced as they were not only with different metres but with different *principles* of versification (syllabic, accentual-syllabic, accentual). Such poets nevertheless recognised the need for regularity and made attempts to impose it.

Prose began to be used for English romances during the fifteenth century, a change which post-dated a move by romance writers to employ more prestigious metres associated with Chaucer rather than traditional metres such as tail-rhyme or octosyllabic couplets.[25] Two of the essays in this collection, those by Elizabeth Robertson and Nicholas Myklebust, deal with this period of transition. Poems of this period, too, can often be metrically difficult. Myklebust sees the comparative neglect of John Metham's 1449 rhyme royal stanza poem *Amoryus and Cleopes* as resulting from its failure to fit neatly into either of the standard competing narratives about fifteenth-century metrics, the one a narrative of decline, the other a narrative of cunning and sophistication.

[25] Putter, 'Metres and Stanza Forms', p. 111. For the influence of Chaucer on fifteenth-century romances, see further Andrew King, 'Romance', in *A Companion to Fifteenth Century English Poetry*, ed. Julia Boffey and A. S. G Edwards (Cambridge: D. S. Brewer, 2013), pp. 187–98, at pp. 191–3.

Myklebust argues that the poem's instability of genre (it displays elements of chivalric romance, Christian miracle, *roman antique* and popular romance) is also reflected in its form and specifically in its prosody. This is a poem in which a given line can have between 8 and 19 syllables and between 4 and 8 beats. Working out how to read such lines can place considerable demands on the reader. Nevertheless, there are a number of rules and a larger number of tendencies to be discerned in Metham's prosody: the metre tolerates double off-beats but not missing off-beats; the norm is for there to be no more than one off-beat and the rule is for there to be no more than two; the norm is a five-beat or six-beat line, and the optimal syllable count is twelve. Of especial help to the reader is the fact that particular types of line show a tendency to appear in clusters and that the size of the gap between individual types of cluster is, to some extent, predictable, and the metre is thus more accessible than the overall variation in line pattern might suggest. This, in turn, suggests that Metham's metre is not simply careless, and further support for this view can be drawn from the pattern of Metham's five-beat line. Double off-beats are not unusual in Metham's prosody, but his five-beat line shows a tendency to avoid this pattern, to stick strictly, that is, to alternating off-beats and beats. Such lines appear to be deliberately designed to echo Chaucer's decasyllabic metre, but Metham echoes this metre only to turn away from it, ironising Chaucer's line and refusing to let it determine his own choice of metre. In doing so, he challenges the currently accepted, if conflicting, views of fifteenth-century verse.

The use of the rhyme royal stanza in romances in general is discussed by Elizabeth Robertson. As we have already seen, particular verse forms were often viewed as being suitable for particular genres or topics, others less so. As Robertson points out, rhyme royal, despite its versatility, is rarely the form of choice for romance, possibly because its syntactic complexity, combined with the pause created at the end of every stanza by the closing couplet, interferes with the sense of forward movement so characteristic of romance. Nevertheless, the rhyme royal stanza has been used for a handful of romances (the stanzaic *Generydes*, *Amoryus and Cleopes*, the *Roman de Parthenay* and, most noticeably, by Chaucer in *Troilus and Criseyde* and *The Man of Law's Tale*). Robertson argues that the way in which the rhyme royal stanza is used in *Generydes* and *Parthenay* is unsatisfactory (too much padding and too many end-stopped lines in the former; too little variation in the latter), but that, in *Amoryus and Cleopes*, Metham shows himself capable of making use of the form's potential for expansive thought and reflexivity. Chaucer exploits the meditative potential of the form most fully, using it to defamiliarise the romance form and to engage with philosophical questions, forcing a different type of engagement from the reader. Rhyme royal may not have been an ideal form for romance in general, but it suited Chaucer's purposes very well.

Much further work on the metre and the manuscripts/early printed editions of romance lies ahead, and in bringing these two approaches together we also hope to encourage further work that integrates these two approaches. For the study of textual tradition and that of verse form are often mutually informative. As several contributors show, metrical analysis can shed new light on textual transmission, by indicating, for instance, scribal corruption or potential lines of influence. To give some examples, it is possible, as Pearsall notes, that the poet of the *Tale of Beryn*, which was inserted as a second tale for the Merchant in a single manuscript of the *Canterbury Tales*, the Northumberland MS (Alnwick Castle, Duke of Northumberland MS 455), acquired his metrical habit of interspersing pentameters with longer lines from the *Tale of Gamelyn*, and reckoned that this could plausibly pass for Chaucerian metre because he had read it in a manuscript in which *Gamelyn* featured as one of the *Canterbury Tales*. As Rhiannon Purdie argues, the curious formatting of some fragmentary tail-rhyme stanzas of *Sir Isumbras* jotted down on a flyleaf of Oxford, University College MS 142, where a tail-line is run together with a couplet line, and two couplet lines are lineated as a single long line, suggests the text was not in this instance copied from a written exemplar but from memory. To take another example, the study of manuscripts has a role to play in confirming or disconfirming hypotheses about a poet's metrical understanding. As Ad Putter argues, some critics assume that Mannyng had a rather loose understanding of *ryme couwee* (= tail-rhyme), but the manuscripts of Mannyng's *Chronicle* suggest otherwise. Inserted into these manuscripts are various tail-rhyme songs. Although the songs are not laid out there in the traditional graphic tail-rhyme form, it is notable that the lines are carefully punctuated for metre and that the songs are explicitly picked out as *ryme couwee* by rubrics in the margin.

Medieval scribes and poets cared about form, and questions of form (how to organise texts in a miscellany; how to format a text for the page) occupied book producers just as they did poets. Scholars are increasingly beginning to realise that the formal features of verse texts often hold the key to understanding both the groupings and the *mise-en-page* of texts in medieval codices.[26] Manuscripts and metres present us with *forms* of transmission, and we still have much to learn by attending to both.

26 For further discussion and examples see *The Dynamics of the Medieval Manuscript: Text Collections from a European Perspective*, ed. Karen Pratt, Bart Besamusca, Matthias Meyer and Ad Putter (Gottingen: V&R, 2017), pp. 22–3. This book is openly accessible at http://www.v-r.de/_uploads_media/files/9783847107545_meyer_etal_dynamics_wz_083454.pdf.

1

King Orphius and *Sir Orfeo*, Scotland and England, Memory and Manuscript

Rhiannon Purdie

The Middle English romance of *Sir Orfeo* is frequently cited in the fitful debate over the place of memorial transmission in the history of medieval romance.[1] Its three extant manuscript copies span at least a century and a half – from the earlier fourteenth to the later fifteenth century – and show a degree of textual variation that is notable even for a Middle English romance. In 1954, *Sir Orfeo*'s editor A. J. Bliss was content to explain the divergences and gaps in the second copy, MS Harley 3810, as the result of memorial transmission: 'Probably the text was written down by a minstrel from memory: this would explain the steadily increasing omissions, the transpositions, and the generally advanced corruption of the readings.'[2] The question of how the variations arose amongst copies of *Sir Orfeo* was greatly enlivened by Marion Stewart's discovery, in the early 1970s, of fragments of a late-medieval Scottish retelling of the 'Orfeo' story (as opposed to the classical myth of Orpheus), copied in East Lothian in the early 1580s.[3] The differences between the Middle English *Sir Orfeo* and the Scottish *King Orphius* are far more extensive than amongst the copies of the Middle English *Orfeo* alone,

1 I have used the term 'memorial transmission', despite the fact that critical discussion is more often framed in terms of 'oral' versus written, because the means of transfer (oral) and storage (memory) are separable: it is possible to memorise a text directly from a written source, and likewise to perform a text from a written exemplar without storing it first in memory. Transmission via memory (rather than questions of authorship or performance) is the subject of the present argument.

2 *Sir Orfeo*, 2nd edn (Oxford: OUP, 1966), p. xvi (all *Orfeo* quotations will be from this edition). These remarks are unchanged from the 1954 edition, although Bliss made other updates in response to reviews (see Preface). See also his note on the change of the queen's name from *Heurodis* (Auchinleck) or *Erodys* (Harley) to *Meroudys* in Ashmole: 'the form Meroudys must be due to oral transmission, the *m* being transferred from the almost invariable *dame* which precedes the name' (note to l. 44: this is the only spelling of her name in Ashmole 61, recurring at ll. 53, 324, 587).

3 '*King Orphius*', *Scottish Studies* 17 (1973), 1–16.

involving as they do elements of plot as well as mere diction. There are additional and altered scenes: Orphius is king of 'Portingale' rather than Thrace (or even the 'Inglond' of the Auchinleck *Orfeo*); the queen is called 'Issabell' rather than 'Heurodis'; Orphius leaves his kingdom in charge of his nephew and heir rather than a steward (it is tempting to read into this a greater Scottish determination to maintain a stable royal line). There is nevertheless just enough correspondence between the texts to lure the eager textual scholar into searching for more evidence of a direct textual relationship. The impetus to engage in such textual sleuthing was further stoked in 2010 by the present author's discovery of David Laing's nineteenth-century transcription of another eighty-two lines of *King Orphius*, entirely independent of the first but also apparently copied in Scotland in the 1580s, possibly also in East Lothian.[4]

The purpose of this chapter is, first, to demonstrate the clear evidence for memorial transmission revealed by the two sixteenth-century copies of the Scottish *King Orphius*. From this evidence for an active literary culture of memorial transmission in 1580s Scotland – despite the self-evident availability of scribes, paper and even printed books – I will work backwards to consider what, if anything, it might be able to tell us about the relationship between the Scottish *King Orphius* and the Middle English *Sir Orfeo*, and finally about the medieval circulation of *Sir Orfeo* itself. First, however, this emphasis on memorial transmission needs some comment.

The scholarly climate has changed since Bliss's casual assumption of minstrel involvement in the transmission of *Sir Orfeo*.[5] Since the latter half of the twentieth century, the focus in textual studies has shifted strongly towards medieval scribal copying habits and the ownership and circulation of manuscripts. Long narrow manuscripts such as *Sir Orfeo*'s Ashmole 61, once dubbed minstrel 'holster books', were recognised as a standard late-medieval format which, though associated with the keeping of accounts, was used for quite a wide variety of purposes.[6] Much of the formulaic language and trivial

4 *Shorter Scottish Medieval Romances: Florimond of Albany, Sir Colling the Knycht, King Orphius, Roswall and Lillian*, ed. Rhiannon Purdie, STS 5th series 11 (Edinburgh, 2013), pp. 45–8 (edited in parallel with MS RH 13/35).

5 For a clear summary of the oral versus written debate in relation to Middle English romance, see Ad Putter, 'A Historical Introduction', in *The Spirit of Medieval English Popular Romance*, ed. Ad Putter and Jane Gilbert (Harlow: Longman, 2000), pp. 1–15.

6 See J. C. Hirsch, 'Additional Note on MSS Ashmole 61, Douce 228 and Lincoln's Inn 150', *NM* 78 (1977), 347–9; Lynne Blanchfield, 'Rate Revisited: The Compilation of Narrative Works in MS Ashmole 61', in *Romance Reading on the Book*, ed. J. Fellows et al. (Cardiff: University of Wales Press, 1996), pp. 208–20; Andrew Taylor, 'The Myth of the Minstrel Manuscript', *Speculum* 66 (1991), 43–73. D. F. Foxon, discussing the format for printed books, prefers the term 'long format' despite his title: 'Some Notes on Agenda Format', *The Library*, 5th series 8 (1953), 163–73. Gisela Guddat-Figge, *Catalogue of Manuscripts Containing Middle English Romances* (Munich: Fink, 1976) includes a section on 'Holster Books' (pp. 30–6): although she doubts the validity of

textual variation once attributed to minstrels was shown to be at least as likely to have arisen through written transmission.[7] As Murray McGillivray put it in *Memorization in the Transmission of the Middle English Romances*: 'There is nothing in the fact of intentional alteration itself that can tell us whether it was done pen in hand or harp on knee [...] There is no sure way, in summary, to tell scribal recasting from minstrel recasting, scribal introduction of formulas from minstrel introduction of formulas, scribal editing from minstrel alterations with the same effects.'[8] McGillivray was nevertheless arguing for the prevalence of memorial transmission and he went on to identify other features which signal it more reliably, principally the long-range transfer of lines or passages. Although he was swimming against the scholarly tide with this focus on memorial transmission, he was not entirely alone.[9] Rosamund Allen and O. D. Macrae-Gibson had independently concluded, over the course of mapping the textual histories of *King Horn* and *Of Arthour and Merlin* respectively, that some of their scribes were conflating written exemplars with versions of the text that they knew by heart.[10] This raises an important issue that we will return to in relation to the Scottish *King Orphius*: so much of the debate over

the term (p. 32), she carefully separates this from the question of what involvement minstrels had with the transmission of romance texts themselves (pp. 33–4).

7 Cf. the classic study by Albert C. Baugh, 'The Middle English Romance: Some Questions of Creation, Presentation, and Preservation', *Speculum* 42 (1967), 1–31. More generally, see George Kane's magisterial survey of medieval scribal copying habits in *Piers Plowman: The A Version* (London: Athlone Press, 1960), pp. 115–65.

8 (New York and London: Garland, 1990), p. 27. A year later – and thus probably without sight of McGillivray's work – Tim William Machan would conclude that the textual variants in the *Orfeo* tradition may 'recall differences inherent in improvisation', but that in such texts 'we can at best establish only the probability of the influence of orality, not the certainty': 'Editing, Orality, and Late Middle English Texts', in *Vox Intexta: Orality and Textuality in the Middle Ages*, ed. A. N. Doane and Carol Braun Pasternack (Madison: University of Wisconsin Press, 1991), pp. 229–45, at pp. 238, 230.

9 See for example Michael Chesnutt, 'Minstrel Reciters and the Enigma of the Middle English Romance', *Culture and History* 2 (1987), 48–67; Karl Reichl, 'The Middle English Popular Romance: Minstrel versus Hack Writer', in *The Ballad and Oral Literature* (Cambridge, MA: Harvard University Press, 1991), pp. 243–68; Nancy Mason Bradbury, 'Literacy, Orality and the Poetics of Middle English Romance', in *Oral Poetics in Middle English Poetry*, ed. Mark C. Amodio, assisted by Sarah Gray Miller (New York: Garland, 1994), pp. 39–69. See also J. A. Burrow's much-quoted dig at scholars who are too reluctant to acknowledge the oral dimension to medieval vernacular literature: 'if the "geestour" or "disour" was as unimportant a person as these writers suggest, it is hard to understand why the sources mention him so often': *Ricardian Poetry: Chaucer, Gower, Langland and the Gawain Poet* (London: Penguin, 1992), p. 13.

10 *King Horn*, ed. Rosamund Allen (New York and London: Garland, 1984), pp. 25, 31, 34; *Of Arthour and of Merlin*, ed. O. D. Macrae-Gibson, 2 vols, EETS o.s. 279 (Oxford, 1979), II, 52.

memorial versus written transmission hangs on the status of the minstrel that potential vectors other than such professional performers have been ignored.

The default position for modern scholars of medieval romance is to explain variants as far as possible – and preferably entirely – through established features of written textual transmission. Oral performance and memorisation have been largely reduced in the scholarly imagination to a series of individual dead-end offshoots from the written textual tradition. This is the case with Joyce Coleman's attractive coinage of the term 'aurality' which, she writes, 'is distinguished from "orality" – i.e., from a tradition based on the oral performance of bards or minstrels – by its dependence on a written text as the source of the public reading' (Coleman does explicitly exclude most romances from her study).[11] Overall, although the existence of the medieval minstrel or *disour* was never entirely denied,[12] his importance in the modern historiography of Middle English romance has very much given way to that of the scribe and his gentle readers. But scholarly recognition of the role of oral/memorial transmission persists, and may even be regaining some favour. Andrew Taylor demonstrates the continued vigour of oral literary tradition into Tudor times in his 2012 study of the minstrel Richard Sheale;[13] Douglas Gray's 2015 study *Simple Forms: Essays on Medieval English Popular Literature* aims to remind readers 'that underneath the written texts they read there

[11] *Public Reading and the Reading Public in Late Medieval England and France* (Cambridge: CUP, 1996), p. 28 and Preface, p. xi. Cf. also Simon Horobin and Alison Wiggins's study of apparent performance cues for amateur readers in the texts of Lincoln's Inn MS 150 (including romances) in 'Reconsidering Lincoln's Inn MS 150', *MÆ* 77 (2008), 30–53.

[12] Some scholars come close. Shuffelton argues that the medieval romances 'created the medieval minstrel long before the antiquarians did': 'Is There a Minstrel in the House? Domestic Entertainment in Late Medieval England', *PQ* 87.1–2 (2008), 51–76, at p. 53. Simon Horobin and Alison Wiggins write: 'from the extant evidence for minstrels, such as it is, it is unclear whether they had any involvement in the performance of texts at all': 'Reconsidering', p. 32. Michael Johnston likewise claims that 'manuscript studies has more or less debunked the romantic notion of travelling performers of romance': 'New Evidence for the Social Reach of "Popular Romance": the Books of Household Servants', *Viator* 43 (2012), 303–31, at p. 323. Paul Bracken demonstrates the misleading ambiguity of terms such as 'jongleur', 'ménestrel', 'joglar' and 'histrio' in historical records in the provocatively titled 'The Myth of the Medieval Minstrel: An Interdisciplinary Approach to Performers and the *Chansonnier* Repertory', *Viator* 33 (2002), 100–16.

[13] *The Songs and Travels of a Tudor Minstrel: Richard Sheale of Tamworth* (York: York Medieval Press, 2012). Ironically, Taylor is often claimed by the 'anti-minstrel' camp thanks to his earlier essay 'The Myth of the Minstrel Manuscript'. In fact, that article argues specifically against the unevidenced labelling of manuscripts as 'minstrel' property; he goes on to discuss several documented minstrels (pp. 65–7, 70–3) and his wry conclusion – 'the hope for direct access to medieval oral narrative must be postponed' – refers to the difficulty of researching medieval oral narrative, rather than denying its existence.

lies a vast substratum of oral literature which has now disappeared, leaving only traces'.[14]

King Orphius

The Scots romance of *King Orphius* seems likely to date from the fifteenth century.[15] A reference in the c. 1550 *Complaynt of Scotland* to 'Opheus kyng of portingal' provides an absolute *terminus ad quem*,[16] but its existence by the mid-fifteenth century is suggested by a detail in Robert Henryson's *Orpheus and Eurydice* that was overlooked in earlier scholarly arguments over whether Henryson knew an *Orfeo/King Orphius* version of the story.[17] In Henryson's version, it is a sobbing maid who breaks the news of the loss of Eurydice to a furious Orpheus:

> Scho said, 'Allace, Erudices ȝour quene,
> Is with the fary tane befor myne ene!'
>
> This noble king inflammit all in ire,
> And rampand as ane lyoun ravenus,
> With awfull luke and eyne glowand as fyre,
> Speris the maner, and the maid said thus ... (ll. 118–23)[18]

The intermediary maid occurs neither in the classical sources nor in *Sir Orfeo*, but is a memorable feature of a pair of scenes in *King Orphius*. In the first, Orphius is nonplussed to be told by a nervous lady that Queen Issabell cannot dine with him in the hall. Hurrying to her chamber, he finds the queen on her

14 *Simple Forms: Essays on Medieval English Popular Literature* (Oxford: OUP, 2015), p. 2. See also *Medieval Oral Literature*, ed. Karl Reichl (Berlin and Boston: De Gruyter, 2012), including an essay by Ad Putter on 'Middle English Romances and the Oral Tradition', pp. 335–52.

15 See Purdie, *Shorter Scottish*, pp. 30–3.

16 Priscilla Bawcutt, '*King Orphius* and "Opheus Kyng of Portingal"', *N&Q* 246, n.s. 48 (2001), 112–14.

17 See Kenneth R. R. Gros Louis, 'Robert Henryson's *Orpheus and Eurydice* and the Orpheus Traditions of the Middle Ages', *Speculum* 41 (1966), 643–55, at p. 652; John MacQueen, 'Neoplatonism and Orphism in Fifteenth-Century Scotland: The Evidence of Henryson's "New Orpheus"', *Scottish Studies* 20 (1976), 69–89, at p. 70; Carol Mills, 'Romance Convention and Robert Henryson's *Orpheus and Eurydice*', in *Bards and Makars: Scottish Language and Literature, Medieval and Renaissance*, ed. A. J. Aitken et al. (Glasgow: University of Glasgow Press, 1977), pp. 52–60; Emily Lyle, *Fairies and Folk: Approaches to the Scottish Ballad Tradition*, B.A.S.E., vol. 1 (Trier: Wissenschaftlicher Verlag, 2007), pp. 71–4; and *Robert Henryson: The Poems*, ed. Denton Fox (Oxford: OUP, 1981), p. cv and notes to lines 74, 119, 125 and 179. Fox dates Henryson's period of literary activity to 'the third quarter of the fifteenth century and perhaps the early part of the fourth quarter' (*Poems*, p. ix): *Orpheus and Eurydice* is no more precisely dateable than this.

18 All *Orpheus and Eurydice* quotations are from *The Poems*, ed. Fox.

bed 'grainand sair' ('groaning sorely', l. 30) and he demands angrily of another lady to know what has happened. This provokes the queen herself to beg that he 'vyd na ladyis of my deid' ('blame no ladies for my death', l. 47). In *Sir Orfeo*, although two maidens fetch knights and squires to help to carry the distraught queen back to her chambers from the orchard, they have no further role to play. Orfeo hears the news – from whom we are not told – and rushes to see his queen; he is distressed rather than furious; he questions Heurodis directly rather than addressing one of her ladies, and in Heurodis's reply there is no admonition to save her ladies from blame. Fox objects that 'fary' was a common medieval term for the classical gods and thus cannot be taken as evidence – as it has been by some – that Henryson was thinking of the romance here, but this does not address the other correspondences between *Orphius* and Henryson's 'bearer of bad news' scene.

In the light of this, another small similarity of wording between Henryson's *Orpheus* on the one hand, and both the Scots *Orphius* and the English *Orfeo* on the other, begins to look less generic and coincidental than it might first have appeared. When Orpheus first sees Eurydice in the Underworld she is described thus:

> Lene and *dedelike*, pitouse and *pale* of hewe,
> Rycht warsch and *wan* and walowit as the wede,
> Hir lily lyre was lyke vnto the *lede.* (ll. 349–5, italics mine)

In *Orphius,* Issabell is likewise described as death-like, wan and pale after the Fairy King's terrifying visitation:

> … And ay sensyne scho vas deidlyk.'
> And be þai had tellit þair taill
> Þe quein vas bayth *van* and *paill.* (ll. 43–5, RH 131/35 *Orphius*, italics mine)

The Auchinleck and Ashmole versions of the Middle English *Orfeo* similarly describe Heurodis/Merodys as being wan, pale and death-like (Au 107–10; Ash 95–8), but only the Harley version additionally describes her pallor as being like lead, as in Henryson but not in the extant Scots *Orphius*:

> Alas! þy rode, þat was so rede,
> Is as *wanne* as ony *lede*;
> Also þy fyngrys smalle,
> Þey ben al blody & *palle*. (ll. 105–8, italics mine)

The fact that Henryson's text appears to echo both Scots and English versions of the romance suggests that the *Orphius* he knew (if we accept the implications of all of these parallels) was slightly closer to the Middle English *Orfeo* than the version that would be copied a century later into MS RH 13/35. This suggestion in turn is consistent with the argument advanced here that *Orphius* not only evolved from *Orfeo*, but continued to evolve and change gradually as it passed through memorial transmission.

There are now two witnesses to the Scottish *King Orphius*. The first is Edinburgh, NRS MS RH 13/35, a scrappy, disintegrating bundle of papers which are all that remain of a collection of independent booklets copied by several different scribes between the 1560s and 1580s: the whole is associated with the Cockburn family of Ormiston, East Lothian.[19] One of these damaged booklets (fols 8–15, copied by a Thomas White) contains the two fragments of a once-complete copy of *King Orphius* (see Fig. 1.1) as well as the surviving complete text of the brief romance of *Sir Colling*; copies of two legal precepts among the other items date White's booklet to 1582–83. The *Orphius* fragments consist of a mere 51 and 103 lines respectively: the intervening folios have been lost. The first, acephalous fragment takes up the narrative when Issabell, as the queen is called in this version, awakes in distress from her sleep under a 'laurein' ('laurel tree', l. 41, replacing the 'ympe-tre' of *Orfeo*) and is carried back to her bed. It breaks off in the middle of her lament to Orphius that the King of Fairy will abduct her. The second fragment rejoins the story near the end, when the incognito Orphius and Issabell are lodging with a merchant in town. There is an amusing interchange in which the merchant doubts Orphius's right to travel with such a lady until Orphius speaks and reveals his own nobility (there is nothing like this in the briefer exchange between the English Orfeo and the beggar); Orphius hears the story of his own disappearance and how his regent nephew (not a steward, as in *Orfeo*) prays for his 'eim' ('uncle') publicly every day. He comforts the burgess and makes his way to court disguised as a harper, where the nephew recognises the harp, demands to know how he got it and is inconsolable when Orphius pretends to have found it 'besyd þe banis of ane ald man' (l. 115). There is general rejoicing when Orphius reveals his true identity, and the queen is brought home in triumph.

The second witness to *King Orphius* was found by the present author in 2010 amongst the unpublished papers of the Scottish antiquary David Laing at Edinburgh University Library. La.IV.27(54) consists of a carefully corrected transcription of eighty-two lines over five little notebook pages, which Laing entitles: 'Fragment of "Orpheus King of Portingaill" from a MS. written in the year 1586' (see Fig. 1.2). The narrative is roughly coterminous with the second fragment in MS RH 13/35, picking up the story when Orphius is staying incognito with the merchant and finishing with 'ffinis amene by m.... / cochrane'. Laing's date of 1586 (for which, frustratingly, he gives no source) places his exemplar to within a mere four years of the RH 13/35 *Orphius*.

19 See Emily Wingfield, 'The Familial, Professional and Literary Contexts of Edinburgh, National Archives of Scotland, Manuscript RH 13/35', *Textual Cultures* 7 (2012), 77–96; and Purdie, *Shorter Scottish*, pp. 33–43.

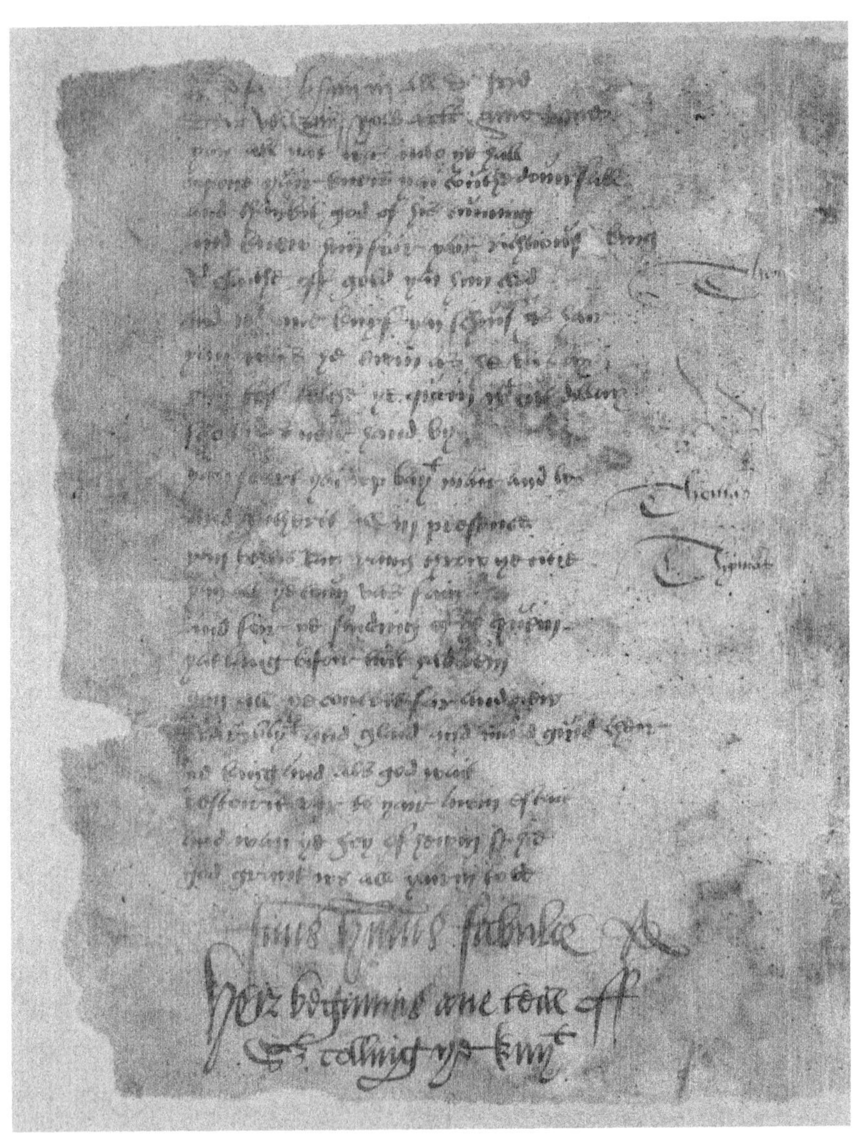

Fig. 1.1 Edinburgh, NRS RH13/35, fol. 12r (left): conclusion of King Orphius. Reproduced by kind permission of the National Records of Scotland.

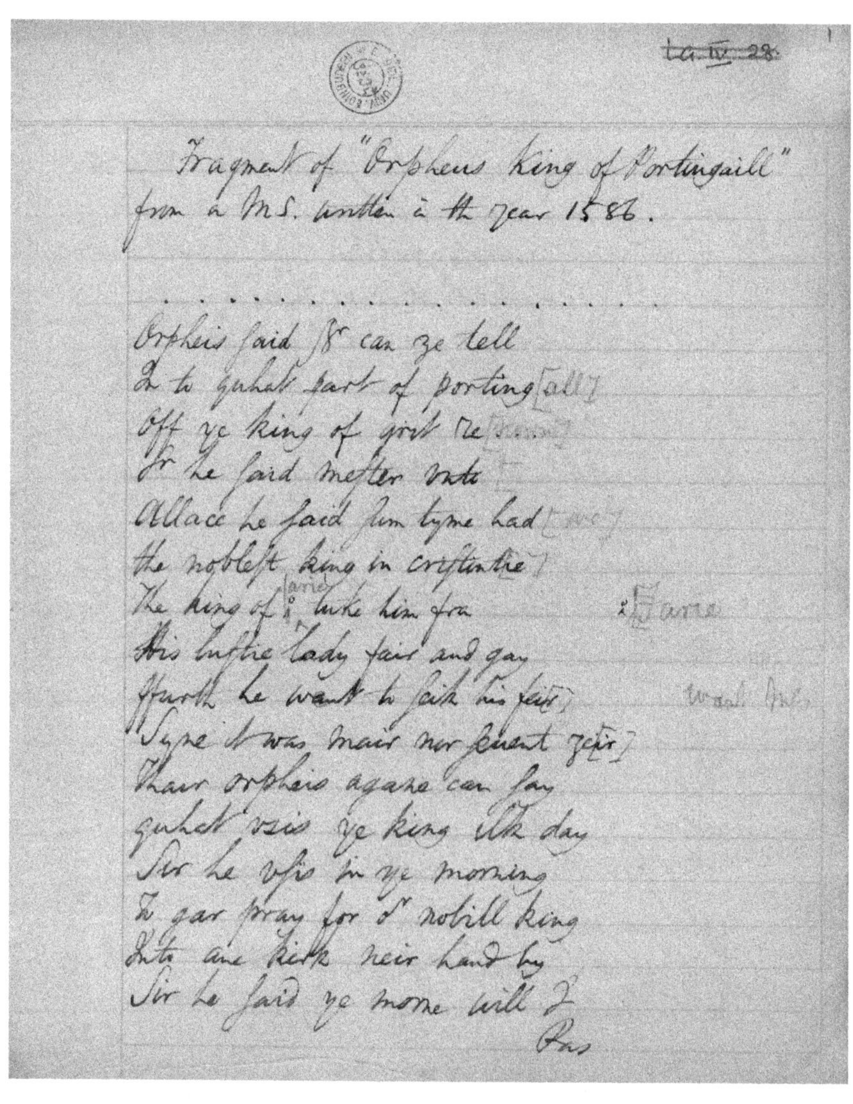

Fragment of "Orpheus King of Portingaill"
from a MS. written in the year 1586.

. . . .

Orpheis said Sr can ye tell
In to quhat part of porting[all]
Off ye king of grit re[nown]
Sr he said mester vnto
Allace he said sum tyme had [we]
the noblest king in cristinthe]
The king of [farie] tuke him fra : Farie
His lustie lady fair and gay
ffurth he want to seik his feir] want MS.
Tyme it was mair nor seuint ȝeir]
Thair orpheis agane can say
Quhat vsis ye king ilk day
Sir he vsis in ye morning
To gar pray for or nobill king
Into ane kirk neir hand by
Sir he said ye mone will I
Pas

Fig. 1.2 Edinburgh, Edinburgh University Library MS La.IV.27(54), p. 1: opening lines of Laing's transcription of a lost MS copy of 'Orpheus King of Portingaill'. Reproduced by kind permission of Edinburgh University Library.

Although 'cochrane' cannot be identified certainly as either author or scribe, it is a common form of scribal sign-off and a promising 'James Cochrane' can be identified in the wider circle associated with the Cockburn family in 1580s East Lothian, so the two copies of *Orphius* may well hail from the same East Lothian social circle as well as the same decade.[20] Laing had clearly hoped to publish this fragment. In notes recording his intention to produce a two-volume anthology combining his *Select Remains of the Ancient Popular Poetry of Scotland* from 1822, *Early Metrical Tales* from 1826 and a few additional texts, he lists item 2 of the proposed Volume II as 'King Orfeo – a fragment of Orpheus King of Portingall', evidently intending it as a replacement for the English *Sir Orfeo* which he had printed alongside primarily Scottish texts in *Select Remains* on the strength of the citation of 'Opheus [sic] kyng of portingal' in the c. 1550 *Complaynt of Scotland*.[21] In the event, no combined anthology would be published until after Laing's death.

The story of *King Orphius* would enjoy a long life in the oral literary tradition of Scotland: at least four renditions of a ballad of 'King Orfeo' were recorded in Shetland in the nineteenth and twentieth centuries.[22] Despite its brevity, a couple of details prove that this Shetland ballad is related to the Older Scots *Orphius* rather than the Middle English *Orfeo*: the queen is called 'Isabel' (or 'Lisa Bell'), and Orfeo's regent is his nephew rather than a steward. The status of ballads as oral literature, preserved primarily by memorial transmission, is not in doubt, and other ballads collected in the nineteenth century have links with romances preserved in medieval manuscripts.[23] This raises the question of whether the romances themselves were already in oral circulation – in some form or other – during the period in which they were copied, but the tremendous distances in both time and textual form normally prevent this from being anything more than idle speculation. The key piece of information supplied by the new fragment of the Older Scots *Orphius* is that this text – not a brief ballad but a romance of several hundred couplet lines – was *already* in oral circulation at the time that the two sixteenth-century copies were made.

20 Purdie, *Shorter Scottish*, pp. 47–8.

21 La.IV.27(63), fol. 41r, and see his original introduction to *Sir Orfeo* for *Select Remains* as reprinted in *Early Popular Poetry of Scotland and the Northern Border*, ed. David Laing, rev. W. Carew Hazlitt, 2 vols (London: Reeves and Turner, 1895), I, 60.

22 *The English and Scottish Popular Ballads*, ed. F. J. Child, 5 vols (New York: Dover, 1965), I, 215–17 [Ballad 19]; P. Shuldham-Shaw, 'The Ballad of "King Orfeo"', *Scottish Studies* 20 (1976), 124–6; Ian Spring, 'Orfeo and Orpheus: Notes on a Shetland Ballad', *Lore and Language* 3[10] (1984), 41–52.

23 See Emily Lyle, 'The Relationship between "Thomas the Rhymer" and "Thomas of Erceldoune"', *Leeds Studies in English*, n.s. 4 (1970), 23–30. On 'Hind Horn' and the romances of *King Horn* and *Horn Childe and Maiden Rimnild*, see Child, *Popular Ballads*, I, 193 [Ballad 17].

Such claims have been advanced, and then dismissed, so often for other medieval romances showing wide variation in their textual histories that this seems a bold statement to make now. The differences between the two copies of *Orphius* are, however, different in kind. The textual histories of many – perhaps most – Middle English romances illustrate free substitution of one formula for another, gaps, additions, rearrangements, changes in dialect and so on. As Derek Pearsall has observed, 'the surviving manuscripts of a poem like *Beves of Hamptoun* make it clear that each act of copying was to a large extent an act of recomposition',[24] and this scribal activity is compounded by the loss of untold numbers of intervening exemplars recording the text's evolution. What one finds in comparing the two copies of *Orphius*, however, is close agreement of the narrative and some key phrases coupled with such divergence in every other aspect – descriptive details, wording, and rhymes (only two couplets in the entire eighty-two-line fragment have the same rhyme as their RH 13/35 equivalents)[25] – that it is impossible to match them up, and this is not just due to textual lacunae in Laing:

RH 13/35	*Laing*
Syne wpone þe morne	Orpheis rois in þe morning
He met þe king þe streit biforne.	And furth he want to seik þe [king]
Orphius kneillit wpone his knie	Quhilk was cumit on þe cauld sey
And said, 'S*ir* king, for cheratie,	W*yth* kny*ch*tis stout and gay.
Gif ȝe pleiss I sall ȝow tell	Orpheis knelit vpon his knie:
Þat I may play into ȝour hall,	'Quhair is yowr dw[el]ling? Can ȝe?'
And now ane menstrall me to mak	'Sir, in the heicht of Portingall
Foir Orphius, ȝour eimis saik.'	[...]
Þe king command ane squyr	I am ane menstrell – I wald pl[ay]
To haif him to þe hall bot veir,	For Orpheis saik in yowr hall þis [day],

24 'Texts, Textual Criticism, and Fifteenth-Century Manuscript Production', in *Fifteenth-Century Studies*, ed. R. F. Yeager (Hamden, CT: Archon, 1984), pp. 121–36, at pp. 126–7.

25 Laing ll. 50–1 and RH 13/35 ll. 110–11, quoted above, and Laing ll. 64–5 and RH 13/35 ll. 126–7, the dramatic moment at which Orphius reveals his identity: 'He said, "Lat be and veip na mair: / I am þe man þow veipis foir"' (quoted from RH 13/35).

And he commandit v*ith* reverence	And na vþ*er* companie
Þat nain to [hi]m suld do offence.	Playand na menstrall þis day bot [me].'
Sone efter [þe] king vas set	The king said, 'ȝe, it sal be done,'
And he vas s*er*wit of his meit.	And to ane place haue þai him schon.
The menstrellis playitt and did no*ch*t ceis:	Effter mess þe king com hame,
'Sall na man play,' þe king said þan,	Thay bounit to denneir everie [an]e.
'Bot ȝone auld hairritt man.'	Menstrallis þan began to play,
Than Orpheus tuik his hairp in hy.	Þan þe king þ*er*to said, 'Nay,
Þe king beheld him fellonlie –	Sall nane play bot yon awld men.'
He knew þe hairp vondrus veill –	To tempeir his stringis than he began,
And said, 'Auld man, I haud sum feill!	Suth by singand and playand but dreid,
Þow tell me, foir þi vrisone,	The king than to the herp tuk heid,
Quhidder þow gat þi hairp in to[vr] or	Sayis, 'awld men, for vrisone,
toun.'	Gat thow þ*a*t herp in towr or town?'
(ll. 89–111)	(ll. 29–51)

Were these copies as distant from each other in time and space as, say, the copies of *Orfeo* from 1330s London (the Auchinleck manuscript) and late fifteenth-century Leicester (MS Ashmole 61), we could ascribe the dramatic textual variation to a century and a half's worth of lost intermediary copies and progressive scribal revision/recomposition. But these were copied within four years of each other at most – certainly in the small, interconnected literary world of 1580s non-Gaelic-speaking Scotland, and quite possibly in the smaller-still Reformist social circles of East Lothian. The temporal and geographical distances that exist between most manuscript copies of medieval romance are absent here, leaving no room in which to develop such radical divergences by scribal means. Rather, their loose textual relationship is very similar to what Albert B. Lord found between the individual performances of Yugoslavian *guslars* in his classic study *The Singer of Tales*. I will quote McGillivray's summary of Lord, because his own explanation of how this situation differs from that of most Middle English romances is very instructive:

> When the singer performs the same song on different occasions, the themes remain the same, but the words and formulas which are used to give them expression are not the same (*Singer*, 71–78) [...] Between two performances of a song by the same singer the differences are smaller, but still there is no verbal identity. The themes will remain the same from performance to performance, but they will be told with more or less elaboration (*Singer*, 113–19) [...] It is obvious that the techniques of composition and the kind of transmission – of story outline rather than fixed texts – described by Parry and Lord cannot have been used to produce the various versions of the Middle English romances. Although there is great variation between the different versions of a single romance the versions are not verbally distinct like the separate performances of the *guslar*. There is a general fixity of diction, of rhymes, of number of lines, and of degree of elaboration, though each of these may vary to some extent.[26]

But the two copies of *Orphius* clearly fit Lord's description of *guslar* poetry much better than McGillivray's description of the Middle English romances.

Once these texts are accepted as the products of memorial transmission, other 'memorial' features can be recognised in them. In the parallel *Orphius* passages quoted above, the initial couplets contain the same information about Orphius rising in the morning to meet the nephew-king in the street. The Laing copy, however, adds:

> Quhilk [i.e. the king] was cumit on þe cauld sey
> W*yth* kny*ch*tis stout and gay. (ll. 31–2)

There has been no mention of the sea until this point, no parallel to this in either RH 13/35 or the Middle English *Orfeo*, and indeed we have previously been told that the king prays in town every day for his lost uncle so he cannot really be 'arriving on the cold sea' with his entourage now. This intrusion looks very similar to something that P. R. Coss noted in the *Gest of Robyn Hode* in the episode of an indebted knight helped by Robin. In Fitt 2, we are unexpectedly told that the knight has been abroad 'ferre beyonde the see' (stanza 89) and when he appears at the abbey gate (where he has come with Robin's money to pay his debt to the abbot) he exhorts his retinue to dress in 'symple wedes / That ye brought fro the see' (stanza 97). Coss remarks:

> In fit 1 the knight explicitly lacked attendants and there was nothing at all to suggest that he had come from the sea. Indeed it is extremely unlikely. He had come through Barnsdale (probably from his home in Wyredale, Lancashire) and was heading for Blyth or Doncaster. Thus the story-line of

[26] McGillivray, *Memorization*, pp. 13–14, with references to Albert B. Lord, *The Singer of Tales* (Cambridge, MA: Harvard University Press, 1960).

> an earlier version where the knight earned his redemption through service overseas seems to come through loud and clear.[27]

Coss was arguing for the *Gest* as the work of an author who knitted together several originally distinct tales, generally with great care but occasionally slipping up, as here. *Orphius*, however, does not have the multiple narrative strands of the *Gest*, and the intrusive trope of 'coming from across the sea' is not an entire embedded story but a sign of the casual interbreeding that is such a common feature of balladry, a direct result of its oral circulation and memorial transmission.[28]

I have not thus far speculated on what forms the memorial transmission of *King Orphius* might have taken, and this is not the aim of this chapter. I would, however, like to remove a dependence upon the figure of the minstrel from the equation. There undoubtedly were professional performers of *King Orphius* in Scotland, but it seems to me a mistake to consider the memorial transmission of substantial poems to be their exclusive domain. McGillivray seems reluctant to believe that people other than professional minstrels might memorise lengthy romances. In response to Allen's and Macrae-Gibson's suggestions that their romance-scribes were occasionally conflating their exemplars with versions they knew by heart, he writes:

> Despite what Allen says, the memorization of long narrative poems is not something that can be accomplished without a great deal of effort, and especially not in the course of listening to one or two recitations [...] It is especially difficult to see why a scribe who had a written copy to hand, as both Allen and Macrae-Gibson assume, would take the trouble to get the text in it by heart.[29]

But this view seems anachronistic. Then and now, people will memorise things for pleasure. Unlike now, however, books and paper were still relatively scarce and expensive: an alternative method of collecting favoured texts

[27] 'Aspects of Cultural Diffusion in Medieval England: The Early Romances, Local Society and Robin Hood', *Past and Present* 108 (1985), 35–79, at pp. 70–1.

[28] Cf. Tristram P. Coffin, 'An Index to Borrowing in the Child Ballads of America', *The Journal of American Folklore* 62, no. 244 (Apr.–Jun. 1949), 156–61. Coffin compiled his index because 'flow of ballad material constitutes a problem that every ballad scholar has to face': one feature he records is the 'exchange of actual lines', although he has sometimes 'been unable to identify specifically the song from or to which the material has come or gone' (p. 156). The difficulties that Child faced in sorting hundreds of similar ballads into distinct groups for his *English and Scottish Popular Ballads* testifies to this fluidity on a larger scale.

[29] *Memorization*, p. 123, and cf. his introductory remarks on memorial transmission as the special provenance of minstrels: 'Since scribes would have no reason to memorize the texts but minstrels would, the widespread presence of memorial transfer shows that in many cases the texts which have come down to us are the texts which were published abroad by minstrels' (p. 6).

was to memorise them, for one's own benefit or to recite to others. Medieval and early modern education depended far more upon rote learning than ours does; those who had little education were perforce obliged to depend on their memories far more than we do: either way, the average modern capacity for memorisation cannot be taken as an accurate gauge of what was possible for medieval and early modern audiences.[30]

White and Cochrane may have had written exemplars for their copies of *Orphius*, although it seems extremely unlikely that there were two such different exemplars circulating in close proximity. They may, alternatively, have taken dictation from a professional performer, or an amateur one, or from their own memories. That people capable of writing down a text may nevertheless be inclined to memorise one seems to be demonstrated not only by Allen's and Macrae-Gibson's scribes, but by a scrap of *Sir Isumbras* copied onto a rear flyleaf of Oxford, University College MS 142 in a hand of perhaps the late fifteenth century. The lines are copied with unusually wide spacing and they end abruptly, mid-stanza and after only seventeen lines, with 'Amen'. The oddest feature is the lineation, which runs a tail-line and the first half of the following couplet together at ll. 3–4 (the romance is in tail-rhyme stanzas) and two couplet lines together at l. 6:

> All þat wyllyn þys romonse her
> of lordes þat be for ous wer
> and leued her yn lede Ihū c'st þat ys heuen kyng
> So grant ham all hys bessyng
> and heuene to her mede
> I woll ȝow tell of a knyȝt þat was herdy man and wyȝt
> And duȝty of hys dede (fol. 128r)

There is clearly no written exemplar behind the confused lineation here, but the abrupt halt mid-stanza also suggests that this is not someone taking dictation from a professional performer. It may indicate a failed, rather than successful, attempt to memorise *Sir Isumbras*, but the attempt is the key thing. We are already familiar with the scraps of memorised verse found scrawled in the margins of medieval manuscripts: this suggests that people other than professional performers thought it reasonable to memorise longer works too.

In MS RH 13/35, White finishes copying *King Orphius* on what is now fol. 12r(i) and squeezes the incipit for *Sir Colling the Knycht*, the other romance in his booklet, in at the bottom of the page (see Fig. 1.1). *Sir Colling* is the earliest known version of a text that reappears in the English Percy Folio manuscript of c. 1650 as 'Sir Cawline' and, like *King Orphius*, it also has descendants among the ballads collected in the nineteenth century: details in

30 See Karl Reichl, 'Plotting the Map of Medieval Oral Literature', in *Medieval Oral Literature*, ed. Karl Reichl (Berlin and Boston: De Gruyter, 2012), pp. 3–69, at pp. 22–9.

these late ballads agree with *Sir Colling* rather than the Percy Folio 'Cawline'.[31] The texts of the Percy Folio have a complex history of transmission, but memorial transmission somewhere along the line is strongly suspected for many of them.[32] *Colling* is in a loose version of ballad metre (alternating four- and three-stress lines rhymed *abcb*, though with much variation on this theme) and its text diverges frequently from 'Sir Cawline', whose garbled elements can often be resolved by reference to *Colling*. The way that White has run these two texts together may suggest a common exemplar, but the associations of both with memorial transmission raises the question, once again, of whether there was a written exemplar, an oral recitation, or whether both were drawn from his own memory.

King Orphius and *Sir Orfeo*

That *Orphius* derives from *Orfeo* somehow seems fairly clear. The story is essentially the same and events are narrated in the same order despite the fact that there are added scenes (Orphius at the banquet hearing of his wife's distress); altered scenes (the English beggar transformed into a courteous merchant), and changes to characters or things (Heurodis becomes Issabell; Orfeo of Traciens becomes Orphius of Portingale; the *ympe-tre* becomes a laurel; the steward is replaced by Orphius's nephew, his natural heir). The narrative parallelism is highlighted by flickers of actual verbal correspondence, some of which are reproduced in the table opposite.

The similarities support Dorena Allen Wright's contention that *King Orphius* does indeed derive ultimately from the Middle English *Orfeo*, rather than representing an entirely independent retelling of the story as Stewart had initially proposed.[33]

This claim is strengthened by additional agreements with the Laing copy, which was unknown to either Wright or Stewart. But there is no consistency to those correspondences which would allow us to identify one Middle English version as being closest to the 'original' that made it to Scotland.

In fact, the relationship between the texts of *King Orphius* and *Sir Orfeo* reveals a similar pattern to what we find in comparing the two copies of *Orphius*. This observation raises unanswerable questions about the form

31 See Purdie, *Shorter Scottish*, pp. 14–23; text edited at pp. 104–11. Originally published in Marion Stewart, 'A Recently Discovered Manuscript', *Scottish Studies* 16 (1972), 23–39. On the ballad connections see Lyle, *Fairies and Folk*, pp. 85, 101–2. For editions of the ballads see Child, *Popular Ballads*, II, 56–63 [Ballad 61]; and Lyle et al. (2002), 12–17.

32 See Gillian Rogers, 'The Percy Folio Manuscript Revisited', in *Romance in Medieval England*, ed. M. Mills, J. Fellows and C. M. Meale (Cambridge: D. S. Brewer, 1991), pp. 39–64.

33 'From *Sir Orfeo* to *King Orpheus*', *Parergon* 27 (1980), 9–11; Stewart, '*King Orphius*'.

Selected verbal correspondences between Scottish *Orphius* and English *Orfeo* texts

King Orphius (Laing)	*King Orphius* (RH 13/35)	*Sir Orfeo* (Auchinleck, Harley, Ashmole)
Orpheis **knelit** vpon his **knie** (33)	Orphius **kneillit** wpone his **knie** (91)	& loude he sett on him a crie (Au 511) He set hym dou*n* on his **kne** (Ha 462) And fell o*n* **kneys** wy*th* grete pyté (As 500)
After the nephew-king has silenced other minstrels: To **tempeir** his stringis than he began (47)	Than Orpheus <u>tuik his hairp</u> in hy (106)	*Orfeo waits till other minstrels fall silent:* He <u>toke his harp</u> & **tempred** schille (Au 526) He <u>toke his harpe</u> þat was schille (Ha 477) And <u>toke his herpe</u> & **temperde** schyll (As 517)
Sir, out throw ane <u>wod</u> I wand (52)	**Throw ane vildernes** com I (112)	Þurgh **a wildernes** as y 3ede (Au 536) In vnkouþe londe / By a <u>forest</u> (Ha 484–5) Thorow a wyld <u>forest</u> j 3ede (As 527)
Preistis and **prossessioun** did … Thair was grit **mirth** and be … (76–7, text defective)	(text defective)	& seþþen, wiþ gret **pr*o*cessioun**/ Þai brou3t þe quen in-to þe toun, / Wiþ al maner menstraci. / Lord! þer was grete melody! (Au 587–90) W*ith* **mer**þe, joy & **processioun /** Þey fet þe quene in-to þe towne (Ha 500–1) And sethin, wy*th* grete **pr*o*cessyoun** / The brou3t þe quen thorow þe tou*n*ne / – For þ*er* was **myrth** & melody, / Off yche man*er* my*n*stralsy. (As 582–5)

in which *Sir Orfeo* reached Scotland. Was *King Orphius* deliberately recast from a written text of *Orfeo*, or an *Orfeo* transmitted by memory and performance? Do we have a single *King Orphius*-poet at all, or did the Scottish text as represented by the sixteenth-century fragments evolve incrementally over the course of its circulation in Scotland? However satisfying it would be to be able to answer some of these questions, there is nothing more the surviving texts can tell us. Nevertheless, the clear evidence for the memorial transmission of *King Orphius* in late sixteenth-century Scotland is valuable for assessing the likelihood of earlier memorial transmission, because the complete *King Orphius* seems to have been of similar length to the Middle English *Sir Orfeo*.[34] It makes the memorial transmission of the earlier romance far more plausible, even if it can do nothing to prove it, and this in turn helps to reassert the crucial but so often invisible role of memorial transmission in the history of Middle English romance.

34 Purdie, *Shorter Scottish*, pp. 27–9. Some segments are longer than their Middle English counterparts but others much shorter, so it is impossible to arrive at an exact figure. It is unlikely to have been longer than the 604 lines of the Ashmole *Orfeo*, and something nearer the size of the 509-line Harley *Orfeo* seems more likely. Emily Lyle estimated *King Orphius* at 586 lines: 'Three Notes on *King Orphius*', *Scottish Literary Review* 1 (2009), 51–68, at pp. 56–7.

2

The Metre of the *Tale of Gamelyn*

Derek Pearsall

This essay is not 'work in progress', a phrase often used by scholars these days, but, more appropriately, a return to 'unfinished business'. In the book that I published in 1977 on *Old English and Middle English Poetry*, there are a number of poems, in fact whole tracts of thousands of lines of Middle English verse, the metre of which is categorised, in a confident-sounding way, as 'the old septenary/alexandrine couplet', with the powerful cadences of the native alliterative long line often said to lie behind the borrowed forms.[1] The *Tale of Gamelyn* is one of the poems so characterised. The purpose of this essay is to test whether significant differentiations can be made between metrical forms that are allowed to fall into such a rag-bag, and whether there are indications of developments within them.

There was justification for using the term, for there is a very plausible line of descent for the septenary/alexandrine couplet, as it appears in early Middle English poetry. That line of descent can be traced through the combination of Anglo-Norman and Latin metres already naturalised in English with the looser forms of the unrhymed alliterative long line as it appeared in both poetry and rhythmical prose in late Old English and early Middle English.[2] It is a period of both linguistic and metrical hybridity, in which what were to become the dominant forms and rhythms of Middle English verse were held for a while in suspension. Practice in early English verse was flexible and unformulated rather than chaotic, as it may seem from the retrospect of long-established fixed metres.

The septenary is the most readily recognisable ingredient in the mix. The Latin *septenarius* denoted a verse of seven feet, and the word was first adopted into English by nineteenth-century historians of verse and metre to describe the verse of Orrm, an Augustinian canon of the first half of the thirteenth

1 Derek Pearsall, *Old English and Middle English Poetry* (London: Routledge & Kegan Paul, 1977), pp. 96, 100, 103, 105, 117, 144 (*Gamelyn*), 151.

2 See Pearsall, *Old English and Middle English Poetry*, pp. 79–80; also N. F. Blake, 'Rhythmical Alliteration', *MP* 67 (1969), 118–24.

century. The *Orrmulum*, his only known work, provides almost more than one can bear as a specimen of the form, with a strict count of fifteen syllables and neither rhyme nor alliteration. The first line of the Preface will stand for all:

x / x / x / x / x / x / x / x
Þiss boc iss nemmnedd Orrmulum forrþi þatt Orrm itt wrohhte.[3]

Somewhat earlier there is the *Poema Morale* ('Moral Ode'), a verse-sermon written in accomplished septenary couplets without alliteration. The style of the poem is remarkably direct and personal, with effective use of gritty proverbs:

x / x / x / x / x / x / x / x
Þe wel ne doð þe hwile he mai ne sal he þan he wolde …
/ x x / xx / x / x / x / x / x
Wo wurðe soreȝe seue ȝier for seue nihte blisse.[4]

Later in the thirteenth century, perfect septenaries are still appearing in various mixes in the trilingual manuscript miscellanies often associated with the friars' preaching activities, though the poems themselves probably date from earlier in the century. It may seem surprising that a fairly recondite Latin metre should have such influence in English, but one of the poems in Trinity College Cambridge MS B. 14. 39 may provide an explanation. It is called *The Bargain of Judas*, and is written in readily recognisable though not regular septenaries, in the abrupt laconic style, with incremental repetition, that is recognised as characteristic of the popular ballad:

x / x / xx / x / / xx / x / x
'Þou comest fer i þe brode stret, fer i þe brode strete,
/ x / / x / / x / x / x
Summe of þin cunesmen þer þou meist imete.'[5]

The poem is often called the first English ballad, and helps to show how the septenary retained its hold in English: equipped with rhyme, it awakened echoes of the older pre-literate forms that came to be called 'ballad-metre'.

The alexandrine is a verse of six feet, so called because it was prominent in poems in French about Alexander the Great in the twelfth century. Perhaps

3 Quoted in *Early Middle English Verse and Prose*, ed. J. A. W. Bennett and G. V. Smithers, 2nd edn (Oxford: OUP, 1968), p. 174. Orrm's septenaries are usually explained as deriving from Latin hymns and goliardic poems: see Elizabeth Solopova, 'The Metre of the *Ormulum*', in *Studies in English Language and Literature: 'Doubt wisely': Papers in Honour of E. G. Stanley*, ed. M. J. Toswell and E. M. Tyler (London and New York: Routledge, 1996), pp. 423–39, at pp. 428–31.

4 Quoted from *Selections from Early Middle English*, ed. Joseph Hall, 2 vols (Oxford: OUP, 1920), I, 33, 39.

5 *The Bargain of Judas*, in *Religious Lyrics of the Thirteenth Century*, ed. Carleton Brown (Oxford: OUP, 1932), p. 38, lines 5–6.

particularly influential in the adoption of the name was the expanded compilation of poems on Alexander in twelve-syllable lines transmitted in the work of the happily named Alexandre de Paris. The French epics, or *chansons de geste*, in *laisses* of various lengths with rhyme or assonance, were at first written in ten-syllable lines, but from the late twelfth century the twelve-syllable line, or alexandrine, was for a time dominant, before giving way in turn to the octosyllabic couplet. In Anglo-Norman, as well as scribal copies of French *chansons de geste* made in England, there was the *Horn* of 'Mestre Thomas' in monorhymed *laisses* of alexandrines, *Boeve de Haumtone*, in a mix of decasyllabics and alexandrines in *laisses*, and other 'romance-epics' in a bewildering variety of metres, not just decasyllabics and alexandrines.[6] Alexandrines were also used in other genres, such as the Anglo-Norman *Romaunz de Temtacioun de Secle* (or 'Sermon en vers') written by a monk of Beaulieu priory about 1200 in *laisses* of rhymed alexandrines.[7] The alexandrine is prominent also in historical writing, most strikingly in the *Chronicle* of Jordan Fantosme, its subject the conflict between Henry II and his eldest son, 'the young Henry', in 1173–74. Fantosme writes in monorhymed *laisses* of alexandrines, but with passages in different metres (decasyllabics and 'fourteeners') deliberately intercalated. Legge points out that such mixing of metres is found also in the romance of *Aiol* and elsewhere.[8] Such practice has been seen further as a precedent for Layamon in its attempt 'to satisfy a taste for stylistic diversity within the single long vernacular work'.[9]

The evident presence of a considerable degree of sophistication and self-consciousness in the handling of metre by Anglo-Norman poets, with variation as a stylistic ornament in its own right, perhaps at times with ideological implications, gives reason to think that metrical variation in early Middle English poems was likewise the product of stylistic ambition and not of mere confusion. The *Proverbs of Alfred*, written in the late twelfth century, may not seem the likeliest candidate to be regarded as possessing such sophistication, for its metre is undoubtedly rough, but the difficulties of scribes with unfamiliar forms and perhaps an unfamiliar language may play some part in this. Sometimes the four-stress alliterative line without rhyme is used, sometimes a

6 See Melissa Furrow, '*Chanson de geste* as Romance in England', in *The Exploitations of Medieval Romance*, ed. Laura Ashe, Ivana Djordjević and Judith Weiss (Cambridge: D. S. Brewer, 2010), pp. 57–72, at p. 67.

7 See M. Dominica Legge, *Anglo-Norman Literature and Its Background* (Oxford: OUP, 1963), p. 137.

8 See Legge, *Anglo-Norman Literature*, pp. 77, 171.

9 Elizabeth Salter, *English and International: Studies in the Literature, Art and Patronage of Medieval England*, ed. Derek Pearsall and Nicolette Zeeman (Cambridge: CUP, 1988), p. 54 (see also pp. 59–60). Laura Ashe, in *Fiction and History in England, 1066–1200* (Cambridge: CUP, 2007), suggests that the mixing of forms 'alerts us to a difficulty, a fissuring in his representation' (p. 106).

two-stress or three-stress couplet, but the variation seems deliberate as a way of marking the different sections of the poem. Such differentiations within a compilation-poem of this kind are characteristic of the Latin *Physiologus* of Thetbaldus, though the Anglo-Norman *Proverbs of Solomon* of Sanson de Nanteuil, a possible model for the English poet, is in octosyllabic couplets. The English *Bestiary*, slightly later, is another compilation-poem, with the different sections (allegorising different animals) variously in the alliterative line, with or without rhyme, or in hexasyllabic or octosyllabic couplets in direct imitation of Anglo-Norman. The deliberate differentiation of form is seen in the following examples of alliterative verse (the ant):

x / x / x / x x / x
Đe mire is magti; mikel ge swinkeð
x / x x x / x x x / x x x / x x
In sumer and in softe weder, so we ofte sen hauen,
/ x / x / x x x / x
In ðe heruest hardilike gangeð,
x / x / x x x x / x x / x
And renneð rapelike, and resteð hire seldum (68–71)

and octosyllabic couplet (the whale):

/ x / x / x /
Cethegrande is a fis
x / x / x / x /
Đe moste ðat in water is,
/ x / x / x /
Đat ðu wildest seien get,
x / x / x / x /
Gef ðu it soge wan it flet. (141–4)[10]

The Latin *Physiologus* (a bestiary) is again an immediate model for this deliberate use of different metres (five in all), as is the Anglo-Norman *Bestiaire* of Philippe de Thaon, with hexasyllabic couplets abruptly, but with some fanfare ('Or voil jeo mun metre muer / Pur ma raison mielz ordener'), giving way to octosyllabics. Again, the copyist seems unfamiliar with the language. Speculating, one might see the two poems as part of the same hybrid culture, with monks, clerics and schoolmasters working with Latin school-texts in the two vernaculars in order to prepare their charges for the real work of learning Latin.[11]

10 *The Bestiary*, in *Early Middle English Verse and Prose*, ed. Bennett and Smithers, pp. 168, 171.

11 Lines 2889–90. See Legge, *Anglo-Norman Literature*, p. 23. For an excellent brief account of this neglected world of poetic practice, see G. T. Shepherd, 'Early Middle English Literature', in *The Sphere History of Literature: The Middle Ages*, ed. W. F. Bolton, 2nd edn (London: Sphere Books, 1986), pp. 81–117, at pp. 96–106. In the first

Layamon's *Brut*, towards the mid-thirteenth century, is the most important prize of the effort to recover a metrical rationale for early Middle English poetry. He writes good four-stress unrhymed alliterative lines, mostly following the looser structures of the later popularisations of the form, but quite often corresponding to more traditional forms, as if he might have known, unlikely as it may seem, some of the classical alliterative verse. But most often the lines are broken up into two hemistichs (both manuscripts are written throughout in these shorter lines), some preserving the old two-stress alliterative rhythm, but many assuming rhyme and assonance and as a consequence falling into syllabic rhythm with three or four stresses, partly imitating the octosyllabic couplets of Layamon's source in Wace's *Roman de Brut*. At times it has seemed possible to believe that there is a principle at work in the metrical variation of the poem, the alliterative line, complete with kennings and compounds and the traditional diction (but not the classical 'variation'), being used for battle-scenes and heroic passages, and the couplet for more routine narration. Some of the examples of the former seem powerfully to support such an argument:

> / x x / x / x x / x
> feollen þa uæie : uolden to grunde.
> x x x x / / x / x x x / x
> þer wes muchel blod-gute : balu þer wes riue.
> / x x / x / x x / x
> Brustlede scæftes : beornes þer ueollen.[12]

In an important essay, Rosalind Field has pointed out an important parallel between Layamon's practice as described here and the Anglo-Norman practice of lacing the new romance-epics in octosyllabics with the heroic language and phrases of the older *chanson de geste*. The decasyllabics and alexandrines in *laisses* of the older epic gave way towards the end of the twelfth century to the more fashionable octosyllabic couplets, but with 'the formulaic phrases of the *chansons* being retained, fragmented and adapted for the couplet form but still unmistakable, to embellish scenes of grandeur and heroism'.[13]

The view of Layamon's metrical practice, buttressed by Anglo-Norman parallels, as historically explicable is preferable to a diagnosis of utter confusion or of the kind of prosodic vertigo that George Saintsbury identified in

edition (1970), this section of Shepherd's chapter was memorably titled, in good Ivy Compton-Burnett style, 'Pastors and Masters'.

12 *Laȝamon's Brut*, ed. G. L. Brook and R. F. Leslie, 2 vols, EETS o.s. 250, 277 (1963, 1978), lines 10019–21.

13 Rosalind Field, 'The Anglo-Norman Background to Alliterative Romance', in *Middle English Alliterative Poetry and Its Literary Background: Seven Essays*, ed. David Lawton (Cambridge: D. S. Brewer, 1982), pp. 54–69, at p. 60.

fifteenth-century Chaucerian verse.[14] It is also preferable to the idea that his verse is at continual war with itself, an agonistic concept of metre which is always seeing battles of various kinds being fought out in metre – the alliterative line bravely resisting rhyme and shaking off the invasion of French syllabic verse, or the artificial and alien pentameter besieged by older native four-stress patterns in Lydgate and in the scribes of the Chaucer manuscripts. In opposition to this view, the example of Layamon encourages us to see a certain self-consciousness about metrical practice in early Middle English. The shift from short couplet to tail-rhyme in the Auchinleck manuscript of *Guy of Warwick* is an example (albeit from a different metrical system): it coincides with the shift from homicidal adventuring to Christian chivalry, to which tail-rhyme, with its more pronounced emotive colouring, is better suited.[15] Legge remarks on a similar change from octosyllabic couplet to tail-rhyme in the Anglo-Norman *Blancheflour et Florence* as 'giving more scope for development and reflexion'.[16] There are other English romances with switches of metre, including *Bevis*, *Roland and Vernagu* and *Richard Cour de Lyon*, though these may be simply the practical result of a fresh translator or versifier taking up his task. But the *Guy of Warwick* example fits in with the way we like to think about metre as explicable choice. One recalls too the unexpected sophistication and vehemence with which Robert Mannyng speaks of the plain couplet against *rime couwee* and other fancy metres in the Preface to his *Chronicle*.[17]

At the same time, a closer and more prolonged familiarity with Layamon's practice throughout his long poem reveals metrical inconsistencies and indeed confusions that cannot be ignored. Perhaps, to consolidate the gain that might have been made for metrical rationality, we might return to an earlier formulation concerning the sophistication of metrical variation in general in early Middle English, and praise Layamon more broadly for his 'compilation and modulation of multiple literary styles'.[18]

One would look in vain for much evidence even of the limited kind of metrical awareness that has been discussed above in the mass of verse written

14 George Saintsbury, *History of English Prosody*, 3 vols (1908, repr. New York: Russell & Russell, 1961), I, 218–34.

15 The Anglo-Norman *Gui de Warewic* has likewise a mix of metres, but not the same ones, nor in the same place (Legge, *Anglo-Norman Literature*, p. 171). Rhiannon Purdie, in *Anglicising Romance: Tail-Rhyme and Genre in Medieval English Literature* (Cambridge: D. S. Brewer, 2008), does not entirely agree with this distinction between the two parts of the English poem, but she does accept the characterisation of tail-rhyme (see p. 5).

16 Legge, *Anglo-Norman Literature*, p. 335.

17 Robert Mannyng of Brunne, *The Chronicle*, ed. Idelle Sullens (Binghamton: State University of New York at Binghamton, 1996), lines 75–88.

18 Salter, *English and International*, p. 48.

in the thirteenth and fourteenth centuries in what I must go on calling the old septenary/alexandrine long line. It was widely disseminated. There is an early thirteenth-century example in the biblical paraphrase of *Iacob and Iosep*, where the mix of rhymed alexandrines, septenaries and four-stress alliterative lines without alliteration seems to admit of no principle of discrimination. The poem opens with a run of alexandrines:

/ x x / x / x / / x / x
Wolle ʒe nou ihere words swiþe gode
x / x / x / x / x / x / x
Of one patriarke after Noees flode?
/ x / x / x / x / x / x
Nellic ʒou nouʒt tellen of þis flodes game,
/ x x x / x/ x / x / x / x
Bote of one patriarke, Iacob was his name.

The story of the brothers' visit to Egypt begins with an emphatic anaphora on 'Muche was' which seems to demand the four-stress line:

/ x x x / x x / x x / x
Muche was þe blisse þat hi þar iseye,
/ x x / x / x x / x
Bernes ful riche and mowen ful heye.
/ x x x / (x) / x x / x
Muche was þe blisse after here swinke
x / x x / x x / x x / x
Þat hi þare funden of mete and of drinke.

Immediately follow two septenaries:

/ x / x / x / x / x / x / x
Hem oftok a menestral, his harpe he bar a-rugge.
/ x / x / x / x / x x / x / x
'Whennes be ʒe, ʒunge men? Ich bidde þat ʒe me sigge.'[19]

It must be admitted that many of these lines could be scanned differently, and there is only the one instance (as noted) of any rationale for the choices suggested. Nevertheless, one has also to admit that the lines are vigorous and fast-paced, especially by contrast with the tedious octosyllabic couplets of the near-contemporary *Genesis and Exodus*, in the same genre.

Later, from about 1280, there comes the vast *South English Legendary*, by many writers, in over fifty manuscripts, continually revised and added to over a century and more, in which septenary/alexandrine lines, rhyming in couplets, are thoroughly mixed in with alliterative long lines, also in couplets.

[19] *Iacob and Iosep*, in *Early Middle English Texts*, ed. Dickins and Wilson, lines 1–4, 25–8, 29–30 (pp. 110–11).

Seeking any settled principle of choice between the different forms would be unrewarding, especially when scribes are so prone to error, and when the sounding of final *–e* seems so uncertain. There do at times seem to be what one might call 'runs' of one form or another, which is as one might expect, but nothing is sustained. Here, in lines from the Prologue, a brief run of shaky septenaries lasts barely four lines:

x / x / x x / x / x / x (/) / x
Men wilneþ muche to hure telle : of bataille of kynge
/ x / x x / x / x x / x x / x / x
And of kniȝtes þat hardy were : þat muchedel is lesynge
/ x / x / x x / x / x x / x / x
Wo so wilneþ muche to hure : tales of suche þinge
/ x / x x / x / x / x / x / x
Hardi batailles he may hure : here þat nis no lesinge
x x / x x / x x / x / x x x
Of apostles & martirs : þat hardy kniȝtes were
x / x / x x / x x x x / x / x / x
Þat studeuast were in bataille : & ne fleide noȝt for fere.[20]

The first four lines, with sounded *–e* for *bataille* in the first line and stress on *And* in the second, make plausible septenaries, but the fifth is a thumping four-stress alliterative line without alliteration and the sixth an alexandrine. Such irregularity is the norm. The claim often made that irregularities of this kind are characteristic of verse written with oral delivery in mind (such as the *Legendary*, possibly) seems mistaken. Such verse has to be more than usually regular. Two recent scholars of the *Legendary*, Oliver Pickering and Manfred Görlach, both speak of the metre of the *Legendary* as 'septenary couplets' (Pickering) or 'rhymed seven-beat couplets' (Görlach), without further qualification.[21] Pickering, it is true, is writing specifically of the *Southern Passion* (closely associated with the *Legendary*), which has signs of greater regularity, but his remarks refer to the *Legendary* generally. It is difficult to accept that there is a single principle of versification in the *Legendary*. But the authority of the two recent scholars who know this vast volume of verse better than anyone is persuasive of at least a recurrent tendency towards regularity such as has been and will be frequently noticed in this essay.

20 *The South English Legendary*, ed. Charlotte d'Evelyn and Anna J. Mill, 3 vols, EETS o.s. 235, 236, 244 (the last edited by D'Evelyn alone) (1956–59), Prologue, ll. 59–64 (I, 3).

21 O. S. Pickering, 'The "Defence of Women" from the *Southern Passion*', in *The South English Legendary: A Critical Assessment*, ed. Klaus P. Jankofsky (Tübingen: Francke, 1992), pp. 154–76, at pp. 155, 158; Manfred Görlach, *Studies in Middle English Saints' Legends* (Heidelberg: Universitätsverlag C. Winter, 1998), p. 27.

An odd intrusion is the appearance of two lines of good alliterative verse in the Life of St Kenelm, who was murdered by his sister and his body buried in the Clent Hills in Worcestershire. The event is recorded in a kind of 'commemorative snatch', which appears in other manuscripts, written on a little scrap of parchment, carried by a dove (the only witness to the event) to the Pope at Rome, on which were written two lines revealing where the martyred boy was buried:

x / / x / x / x x
In Clent Coubach Kenelm kinges bern
/ x x x / x / x x / x
Liþ under a [haȝ] þorn heued bireued.[22]

The passage is a reminder of the ever-present possibility that odd lines or phrases of genuine alliterative verse may surface late into the thirteenth century and so refresh ancient memories. It is of interest too that the quotation of the two lines is introduced with a specific comment, in alexandrines, on the absence of rhyme:

x / x x / x x / x / x / x / x
Þe writ was iwrite pur Engliss : as me radde it þere
x x / x x / x / x x / x / x / x
And to telle it wiþoute rime : þis wordes riȝt it were.

There is a suggestion here of some degree of metrical self-awareness in the midst of a vast unconscious. For no amount of straining of the accent and the syllable-count can reveal the presence of an intelligible principle of versification in the *Legendary*.

The 12,000-line *Chronicle* of Robert of Gloucester, a monk who wrote at least part of it, began to be composed in the late thirteenth century, mostly in alexandrines, with some septenaries and a little alliteration. The narrative occasionally draws on the *Legendary* and also on Layamon, and the alexandrines drive it on at a great pace. The dominance of alexandrines suggests that the authors were influenced by what they saw as the special suitability of that metre to historical writing in Anglo-Norman, as in the *Chronicle* of Fantosme, already mentioned. Striking confirmation of this association is provided by the Anglo-Norman Pierre de Langtoft, whose early fourteenth-century version of

[22] *South English Legendary*, ed. D'Evelyn and Mill, 'The Legend of St Kenelm', lines 267–8 (I, 288). The emendation is suggested by Bennett and Smithers (eds), *Early Middle English Verse and Prose*, p. 104, who also supply (p. 96) the descriptive phrase quoted above. See also R. M. Wilson, *The Lost Literature of Medieval England*, 2nd edn (London: Methuen, 1970), p. 99; and Derek Pearsall, 'The Origins of the Alliterative Revival', in *The Alliterative Tradition in the Fourteenth Century*, ed. Bernard S. Levy and Paul E. Szarmach (Kent, OH: Kent State University Press, 1981), pp. 1–24, at pp. 11–12.

Wace's *Roman de Brut* (itself also translated into English by Robert Mannyng) turns the octosyllabic couplets of the original into *laisses* of alexandrines, clearly of a mind that the latter was a more suitable medium for historical writing.

The old septenary/alexandrine line with some alliterative lines continued to be written in the late thirteenth century and well into the fourteenth, before being displaced by the short couplet, as in the *Cursor Mundi* and Mannyng's *Handlyng Synne*. But it still appears in trilingual miscellanies of about 1300 like Oxford, Jesus College MS 29 (which contains some much earlier poems), in Rolle, in the satirical poem of *The Simonie* in the Auchinleck manuscript, in popular Prophecies (where it sometimes strays into prose), in some of the political poems of BL MS Harley 2253, and in romances such as *Gamelyn*. It also threw off a kind of irregular hexameter couplet through the addition of internal rhyme and the division of the half-lines, as in the romance of *King Horn*, and often in Anglo-Norman. But it did not change its nature or become regularly metrical.

And so to *Gamelyn*. It is a 'Robin Hood' type of romance, its plot of the dispossessed younger son picked up by Thomas Lodge in his *Rosalynde*, the source of *As You Like It*. The story is romanticised, but it tells of land law and disputed inheritance and has its roots in actuality. John Scattergood has a very good essay in which he scours early fourteenth-century legal records and poems on contemporary events and finds many parallels for disputes about property in provincial gentry families, who take the law into their own hands to correct what they see as unjust laws and corrupt officials.[23] *Gamelyn* may read at times like a fantasy of violence, but it is often outdone by prosaic reality. The survival of the poem in twenty-five manuscripts, far more than any other romance, is due solely to its adoption by scribes of the *Canterbury Tales* to follow or replace the unfinished and rather rude tale of the Cook (everyone agrees that the Yeoman would have been a better choice as pilgrim-teller). It entered the textual tradition early, which suggests that it may have had some connection with Chaucer – perhaps, as Skeat says, it was found amongst his papers at his death and it was assumed that he contemplated recasting it.[24] The poem appears in none of the romance compilations of the fifteenth century,

[23] John Scattergood, '*The Tale of Gamelyn*: The Noble Robber as Provincial Hero', in *Readings in Medieval English Romance*, ed. Carol M. Meale (Cambridge: D. S. Brewer, 1994), pp. 159–94.

[24] See Walter W. Skeat, *The Complete Works of Geoffrey Chaucer*, 6 vols (Oxford: OUP, 1894, with an additional volume of *Chaucerian and Other Pieces*, 1894), III, 399. Skeat's edition of the poem is in an Appendix in IV, 645–67, with Notes in V, 477–89. For a full discussion of the position of *Gamelyn* in the Chaucer manuscript tradition, with conclusions similar to Skeat's, see A. S. G. Edwards, 'The *Canterbury Tales* and *Gamelyn*', in *Medieval Latin and Middle English Literature: Essays in Honour of Jill Mann*, ed. Christopher Cannon and Maura Nolan (Cambridge: D. S. Brewer, 2011), pp. 76–90.

perhaps a mark of the fashionable disdain in which its old-fashioned metre was held. So the tale has been punished for masquerading falsely as Chaucer's by not being read, like much of the Chaucer apocrypha.

This is unfair, because the poem has a good deal of vitality. It is full of sensational and violent incident, and is told with a saga-like sardonic relish. Gamelyn himself, though shrewd enough, is something of a thug, and only really happy when fighting against his older brother and beating his household to a pulp with his staff. The servants and workmen and porters flock to his aid on such occasions, one of the Robin Hood-like elements in the story, as does Adam the spenser, not an old greybeard, as in *As You Like It*, but a young fellow thug. When the sheriff arrives with his posse they all make off to the woods. There they join the 'maister outlawe' (line 688), as he is called (Robin Hood is not named), with his company of 'sevene score of yonge men' (628), 'mery men under woode-bough' (774). Gamelyn soon takes over as outlaw-king and later returns to face his elder brother in the sheriff's court. Impatient with the legal procedures, Gamelyn declares himself judge and has his brother and the sheriff and the sheriff's officers summarily hanged. He is then reconciled with the king. Stirring stuff, but the total absence of women, until Gamelyn gets married four lines from the end, makes it a questionable candidate for romance-hood.[25]

Here, then, as presumably representative of the metre of the poem, are the opening lines of *Gamelyn*, as they appear in Skeat's edition. The scansion is often doubtful: lines where it is particularly tentative are indicated by a question-mark at the end of the line.

/ x x / x x / x x /
Litheth, and lesteneth / and herkeneth aright,
x / x / x / x x x / x /
And ye schulle here a talking / of a doughty knight;
x / x x / x x x / x / x ?
Sire Iohan of Boundys / was his righte name,
x / x x / x x / x / x x / x
He cowed of norture y-nough / and mochil of game.
x / x x / / x x / x / x x /
Thre sones the knight hadde / that with his body he wan;
x / x / x / x / x / / x /
The eldest was a moche shrewe / and sone he bigan.
x / x / x / x / x x / x / x /
His bretheren loved wel here fader / and of him were agast,

[25] It is in the romance-anthology of *Middle English Verse Romances*, ed. D. B. Sands (New York: Holt, Rinehart and Winston, 1966); Scattergood's essay (cited above) is in a book of romance essays; and Nancy M. Bradbury makes a sub-category for 'romances of the greenwood' in her book, *Writing Aloud: Storytelling in Later Medieval England* (Urbana and Chicago: University of Illinois Press, 1998). *Gamelyn* is the only one.

x / x x / x x / x / x / x / x /
The eldest deserved his fadres curs / and had it at the last.
x / x / x / x / x x x / x
The goode knight his fader / livede so yore,
x / x / x x / x / x / x / x
That deth was comen him to / and handled him ful sore.
x / x / / x / x / / x / ?
The goode knight cared sore / syk ther he lay,
/ x / x / x / x / x x / ?
How his children scholde / liven after his day.
x / x x / x / x / x / x /
He hadde ben wyde-wher / but non housbond he was,
/ x / x x / x / x / x x /
Al the lond that he hadde / it was a verrey purchas.
/ x / x / x / x x / x / x
Fayn he wolde it were / dressed among hem alle,
x / x x / x / / x / x / x ?
That ech of hem hadde his part / as it mighte falle.
x / x / x / x / x / x / x
Tho sente he in-to cuntre / after wyse knightes,
x / x / x x / x x / x / x / x
To helpe delen his londes / and dressen hem to-rightes.
x / x / x / x x / x / x / x
He sente hem word by lettres / they schulden hye blyve,
x / x x / x x / / x / x / x ?
If they wolde speke with him / whyl he was on lyve.

With very little evidence to go on, Skeat dated the poem about 1340. He calls the metre 'very variable', but only emends when he sees an obvious grammatical fault, as with the final –e of the weak adjective preceding a noun and following the definite article or a demonstrative or a possessive, as in 'his righte name', or 'The goode knight', lines 3 and 9 in the extract.[26] It is something that Chaucer, fifty years later, scrupulously observes. Other emendations, of course, plausible if not so compelling, could be made in order to 'mend' the metre, as for instance in lines (such as line 11) where there are consecutive accents or clashing stress. Skeat comments on this practice, and recommends reading the poem half-line by half-line, with three or four stresses in the first half-line and three or possibly two in the second. He says the effectiveness of the metre must have depended a lot on recitation, and concludes 'This slippery matter I leave to the reader's discretion'. This is Skeat at his admirably pragmatic best. It should be remarked that the scribe of BL MS Harley 7334, which includes *Gamelyn*, and which Skeat chooses as his copy-text, is

[26] Skeat comments on the metre of the poem in his edition of Chaucer as cited above, III, 401–3.

one of the most dedicated 'improvers' of Chaucer, regularly 'correcting' and emending his exemplar to restore what he regards as regular pentameter. He, or his superior, clearly made no effort to improve *Gamelyn*.

Skeat's emphasis on the half-line is sensible, as is his decision not to scan individual lines, for line-by-line scansion, such as is attempted above, is confusing. The first line in the extract is an almost perfect four-stress alliterative line, surviving vigorously in the fossilised context of audience address. Similar lines appear at appropriately recurrent intervals in the poem, at line 169 ('Litheth, and lesteneth, and holdeth your tonge'), with another similar line following, and again in 289–90, and again in 341–4, with alliteration prominent. The distinctive structure of these lines, and the characteristic traditional use to which they are put, is a warning against reading the 'long line' in general as a degraded form of the alliterative line. In the rest of the passage quoted, alexandrines are dominant, though some, it must be said, strain unpleasingly against the natural speech-stress, and are barely scannable, or recognisable as alexandrines (for instance, lines 3, 12, 16, 20). One or two lines have very light second half-lines, as Skeat remarked, and are more like pentameters than anything (for instance, lines 2, 4 and 9). There is a little run of pentameters (lines 6–8), and others at lines 17 and 20. A tendency might be detected here for septenaries, with their persuasive ballad-like cadences, to run for a few lines, and also to close verse-paragraphs. This tendency will be noted in later examples. But, for the most part, confusion prevails.

This is most unsatisfactory. The first principle of poetic metre is regularity, which includes regular irregularity of variation in stanza-forms such as Spenser's, with an alexandrine as the final line of each nine-line stanza.[27] But no metre can be based on irregular irregularity, which seems to be the character of the lines quoted from *Gamelyn*. The second principle of metre is 'equal periodicity', or 'isochronous intervals' between accents.[28] This is a necessity of metre, but of course individual lines do not necessarily adhere to it, because of the influence of the rhythms of spoken English. These rhythms are pleasingly counterpointed against the strict metrical pattern. Robert Frost gives a poet's description of the process, with reference to blank verse:

> It is as simple as this: there are the very regular pre-established accent and measure of blank verse; and there are the very irregular accent and measure

[27] Dryden's use of alexandrines irregularly disposed among the heroic couplets is something that only he seems to have approved of. Pope thought it a very bad idea: 'A needless Alexandrine ends the song / That, like a wounded snake, drags its slow length along' (*Essay on Criticism*, lines 356–7).

[28] These are terms used by older theorists of metre such as William Thomson, *The Basis of English Rhythm* (Glasgow: Holmes, 1904), p. 11; and Coventry Patmore, 'English Metrical Critics', *North British Review* 27 (1857), 127–61, at p. 138. See also Paul Verrier, 'English Metric', *Modern Language Review* 7 (1912), 522–35.

> of speaking intonation. I am never more pleased than when I can get these into strained relation. I like to drag and break the intonation across the meter as waves first comb and then break stumbling on the shingle.[29]

Given the second principle of metre, traditional alliterative verse is, strictly speaking, not metrical, but that does not concern us here.

The earlier part of this essay concentrated on finding evidence of metrical sophistication, whether or not under the influence of Latin or Anglo-Norman, in early Middle English verse. There was evidence of a marked degree of awareness, but it seems not to have reached the 'old long line', except for an important tendency on the part of some writers to resolve its incoherence by driving it in one direction – four-stress, alexandrine or pentameter – and not another. If attention is diverted away from the opening lines of *Gamelyn*, as possibly not representative, to passages where the narrative has got fairly under way, something similar becomes evident:

x x / x / / x / x / x
Ther was noon with Gamelyn / wolde wrastle more,
x x / x x / x x / x x / x
For he handled the champioun / so wonderly sore.
x / x x x / x x / x x x / x
Two gentil-men ther were / that yemede the place,
/ x x / x x / x x x / x
Comen to Gamelyn / (god yeve him goode grace!)
x / x x x x / x / x x x /
And seyde to him, 'do on / thyn hosen and thy schoon,
/ x x x / x x / x x /
For sothe at this tyme / this feire is y-doon.'
x x / x / x x / x x / x
And than seyde Gamelyn / 'so mot I wel fare,
x / x x x / x / / x x / x
I have nought yet halven-del / sold up my ware.'
x / x x / x x / x x / x
Tho seyde the champioun / 'so brouke I my sweere,
x / x / x / x / x x / x / x / x
It is a fool that ther-of byeth / thou sellest it so deere.' (*Gamelyn*, 265–74)

There is no doubt that the dominant rhythm here is that of alliterative verse, with or without alliteration. These lines, which are representative, are a long way from the metrical tentativeness of the opening lines, where perhaps the author was trying to write 'poetry' in the traditional alexandrines. Here the verse falls into the familiar cadences of the four-stress line, alliteration no more than a memory or occasional decoration, and swings along with a fine

[29] *Selected Letters of Robert Frost*, ed. Lawrence Thompson (London: Jonathan Cape, 1965), p. 128: Letter to John Courmos, 8 July 1914.

bravado. Again, we may note, the passage quoted closes with a septenary. The tendency in *Gamelyn* as a whole is thus to draw, as in previous poems, towards some principle of regularity.

Two further lines of enquiry seem to offer some support for this view. The unique text of the romance of *Ferumbras* in Bodl. MS Ashmole 33 is one of three Middle English attempts to translate the Anglo-Norman *Fierabras*, the others being the Fillingham *Ferumbras* (BL MS Add. 37492) in a rough imitation of the alexandrines of the French, perhaps work in progress, and the *Sowdone of Babylone*, in accomplished alternate rhyming quatrains. The Ashmole *Ferumbras* is in tail-rhyme up to line 3411, with the rest in the *Gamelyn* mix of lines. There is the delightful added complication that 400 lines of a draft of this part of the poem survive written on the manuscript's parchment wrapper and elsewhere, and bits of a third version. Comparison of such drafts ought to be useful for metricists. Phillipa Hardman has tried to untangle this mess and her tentative observations are interesting in relation to *Gamelyn*.[30] One example that she gives suggests an attempt to convert alexandrines in the draft to septenaries in the final version, both with both internal and end-line rhyme. The revision is probably by the author, who would thus be seen drifting towards the regularity that can be detected elsewhere.

x / x / x / x / x / x / x
'Draft': As Charles stod by chance at conseil with his feris
/ x / x / x / x / x / x
Whiche þat wern of france his oȝene doȝeperes ...
x / x x / x / / x / x x / x / x
'Copy': As Charlys was in his greuance · stondyng among his feren
x / x x / x / x / x / x / x / x
And counsailede with þe grete of fraunce · and with ys doþþeperen ...[31]

But there are many counter-movements in the process of rewriting, including some which simply spoil the metre in the search for other effects, and Hardman concludes that the manuscript presents 'an inherently unstable accumulation of alternative and potential states of the text'.[32]

A clue to the later development of the old long line is to be found in a poem of about 1420, the *Tale of Beryn*. As well as being in the same metre

[30] Phillipa Hardman, 'Bodleian Library MS Ashmole 33: Thoughts on Reading a Work in Progress', in *Middle English Texts in Transition: A Festschrift Dedicated to Toskiyuki Takamiya*, ed. Simon Horobin and Linne Mooney (York: York Medieval Press, 2014), pp. 88–103. See also Stephen H. A. Shepherd, 'The Ashmole *Sir Ferumbras*: Translation in Holograph', in *The Medieval Translator*, ed. Roger Ellis (Cambridge: CUP, 1989), pp. 103–21.

[31] Lines quoted from Hardman, 'Bodleian MS Ashmole 33', p. 89. A similar example is cited on p. 91.

[32] Hardman, 'Bodleian MS Ashmole 33', p. 95.

as *Gamelyn*, it has, oddly enough, the same sort of textual history, having been inserted as a second tale for the Merchant in a single manuscript of the *Canterbury Tales*, the Northumberland MS (Alnwick Castle, Duke of Northumberland MS 455).[33] It is a moral tale, not a romance, very long, of clerical authorship, and best known for its lively Prologue, which describes the pilgrims arriving in Canterbury and bustling around the town to see the sights, and the Pardoner's evening adventures with a barmaid. The metre is not as confusing as the opening lines of *Gamelyn*, the individual alexandrines and pentameters both being clearly distinguished. The two types of line often come in runs of eight lines or more (for instance 185–92 in sevens, 2121–32 in sixes). The specimen given here is from early in the Prologue.

x x x / x / x / x / x / x
'Lo, here I ligg,' quod she, 'myselff al nyght al naked,
x x / x / x / / x / x x / x
Without mannes company, syn my love was dede.
/ x / x x / x / x / x / x / x
Jenkyn Harpour, yf ye hym know, from fete to the hede
x / x / x / x x / x / x / x
Was nat a lustier persone to daunce ne to lepe,
x / x x / x / x / x / x / x
Then he was, thoughe I it sey.' – And therewith she to wepe
x / x / x / x / x / x /
She made, and with hir napron feir and white i-wassh,
x / x / x / x / x x / x /
She wyped sofft hir eyen, for teres that she out lassh
x / x / x / x / x / x /
As grete as eny mylstone, upward gon they stert
x / x x / / x / x / x / ?
For love of hir swetyng that sat so nyghe hir hert.
x / x / x x / x / x x / x / x /
She wept and wayled and wrong hir hondes, and made much to done,
x / x / x x / x / x / x x / x /
For they that loven so passyngly, such trowes they have echon.
x / x / x x / x / x / x / x / x
She snyffeth, sigheth, and shooke hire hede, and made rouful chere.[34]

33 In a recent article, 'The *Tale of Beryn*: An Appreciation', *CR* 49 (2015), 499–511, John Burrow suggests that the author of *Beryn* encountered *Gamelyn* in one of the many manuscripts in which it occurs, and concluded that Chaucer himself countenanced the use of the old long line (p. 500). Burrow gives a succinct account of the metre of *Beryn*.

34 Quoted from *The Canterbury Tales: Fifteenth-Century Continuations and Additions*, ed. John M. Bowers, TEAMS (Kalamazoo, MI: Medieval Institute, 1992), *The Canterbury Interlude and the Tale of Beryn*, pp. 60–164, lines 28–39.

The passage is in alexandrines (except line 3), but closes with a series of septenaries, as if slowing down the tempo in a kind of coda *ritardando*. This might be taken as an indication of a desire to impart a more familiar pulse of regularity to the close of a passage in alexandrines.

Any conclusion must be tentative. Early Middle English verse, partly under the influence of Anglo-Norman and Latin, shows numerous signs of metrical sophistication, or at least metrical awareness. The exception is the 'old long line', variously based on alexandrines and septenaries, with admixture of four-stress 'alliterative' lines with or without alliteration. Poems in this form are often difficult to scan, which is understandable if we consider the confusing situation in which English poets found themselves, with not only different kinds of metre to cope with but also different principles of versification, ranging from the strictly syllabic (but non-quantitative) verse of Orrm to syllabic-accentual verse imitated from Anglo-Norman, and the dominantly accentual verse derived from native models. Poets working in the long line often recognised the unsatisfactoriness of such irregularity and showed a marked tendency, as we have seen in *Gamelyn* and elsewhere, to bring the line into conformity with some principle of regularity. These attempts were patchy and soon belated, as the centre ground for longer narrative poems was taken over by the Chaucerian pentameter, with all the further potential for confusion that it carried with it.

3

Rhyme Royal and Romance

Elizabeth Robertson

Rhyme royal, as is well known, is a seven-line stanza with a rhyme scheme of ababbcc introduced into English by Chaucer and employed by him effectively in his charming dream vision, the *Parliament of Fowles*, his great love poem, *Troilus and Criseyde*, and in his religious tales. In those tales, which consistently feature suffering religious heroines, the stanza serves well the themes of time, space and embodiment that are at issue in them. This versatile and philosophically expansive form was widely adopted by the Scottish Chaucerians and by Lydgate in the majority of his prolific writings. Despite the variety of genres in which rhyme royal was used, it rarely is the form of choice for the romance. Even Lydgate eschews rhyme royal when he writes his version of a romance, the *Troy Book*. There are a handful of romances written in rhyme royal, however, and it is to those that I shall turn my attention in this essay. I will argue here that rhyme royal is rarely chosen for romance because the form of the stanza itself mitigates against some of the aims and purposes of romance.

The romance is of course an elusive genre to define, and the genre appears in many different verse forms from the tail-rhyme to the bob and wheel structure although the most common form – especially on the continent – is the octosyllabic couplet. Yet, despite the variety of forms in which they appear, romances in general share some basic stylistic elements, as Eric Auerbach discusses in his paradigmatic essay on the romance, 'The Knight Sets Forth'. As the title suggests, a key feature of romance is forward movement. Auerbach focuses his attention on a long passage from Chretien de Troyes's *Yvain*, an octosyllabic romance in French he allows to stand for most romances in general. Of the style of the romance he writes:

> The narrative flows; it is light and almost easy. It is no hurry to get on, but its progress is steady. Its parts are connected without any gaps. Here too, to be sure, there are no strictly organized periods; the advance from one part of the story to the next is loose and follows no set plan; nor are the values of the conjunctions yet clearly established – *que* especially has to fulfil far

> too many functions so that many causal connections … remain somewhat vague. But this does not harm the narrative continuity; on the contrary, the loose connections make for a very natural narrative style, and the rhyme – handled very freely and independently of the sense structure – never breaks in obtrusively.[1]

He goes on to discuss the fairy-tale qualities of the romance form, its freedom from political purposiveness, its manifestation of class privilege, and its eschewal of the specificities of time and place. As he writes, 'indications of time are as reminiscent of fairy tale as the indications of place'.[2] Auerbach points to the thematic emphasis of the genre on 'feats of arms', and 'the dalliance of true love'.[3] Dalliance is a key thematic feature of romance – dalliance in love and dalliance in wandering – but dalliance may also be understood as an aspect of the leisurely but steady pace of the octosyllabic style of the romance with its potentially endless series of couplets, and its potential to allow for endless episodic adventures.

I suggest in this essay that poets writing romances rarely chose rhyme royal because the form does not lend itself easily to these predominant stylistic characteristics. The form of rhyme royal puts different pressures on narrative; above all, in its use of the closing couplet and in its characteristic syntactic complexity and variation, the form of the stanza breaks narrative flow. As we shall see, the closing couplet of rhyme royal demands a pause that functions in various ways but in general creates a self-consciousness about temporality that presses against the fairy-tale temporalities of the romance. The rhyme scheme, far from being unobtrusive as Auerbach suggests it is in octosyllabic romance, draws attention to the words that form rhyming pairs. It is perhaps for these and other reasons that those few poets who tried to write romance in rhyme royal had difficulty in doing so. We shall see in the few extant examples, poets who decide to tell their romances in rhyme royal are rarely committed to producing the iambic pentameter metre of the stanza, and, even if they faithfully hold to a regular metre, often fail to grasp fully the opportunities the form affords.

There is one poet, however, who clearly uses rhyme royal to advantage when writing a romance: Chaucer, in *Troilus and Criseyde* and *The Man of Law's Tale.* Chaucer uses the form with great versatility, such as for dialogue, pathos, irony, and philosophical reflection. Moreover, as Barry Windeatt observes, he uses the closing couplet with flexibility, often reserving the last lines

1 Eric Auerbach, *Mimesis: The Representation of Reality in Western Literature*, trans. Willard R. Trask (Princeton, NJ: Princeton University Press, 2003), pp. 127–8.

2 Auerbach, *Mimesis*, p. 130.

3 Auerbach, *Mimesis*, pp. 140, 132.

for 'sententious reflections, exclamations, oaths, prayers, and wishes'.[4] But are these poems really romances? Because they engage issues that are usually not central to romance, one could conclude that when rhyme royal is applied well to narrative we have moved out of the realm of romance into some other genre – a philosophical love poem in the case of *Troilus and Criseyde* and something approaching a saint's life in *The Man of Law's Tale* – or we might conclude that rhyme-royal romances are especially self-conscious instances of the romance genre. To begin to characterize the functions of rhyme royal, I will now turn to a brief summary of the origins of the form and some of the functions early critics assign to it. I shall then consider some sample stanzas of rhyme royal in romances in order to demonstrate the ways in which the form lends itself, first, to critical engagement with the narrative, second, to self-reflection and meta-discourse about its own creation, and third, to a heightened consciousness about both beginnings and renewal, all impulses that conflict with the onward movement of romance narrative that Auerbach describes.

Chaucer introduced the form of rhyme royal into English first in the 1380s in his *Parliament of Fowles*, and he exploited the potential of the form for both serious purposes and humour in *Troilus and Criseyde* before writing in rhyme royal the so-called religious tales of *The Canterbury Tales*, *The Man of Law's Tale*, *The Prioress's Tale*, *The Second Nun's Tale* and *The Clerk's Tale*. Rhyme royal became the preferred verse of Lydgate and Hoccleve as well as of later Scottish poets, though these poets do not usually compose romances. The form eventually petered out in the sixteenth century. It is clear that most writers of rhyme royal in English did so in imitation of Chaucer, in part, as James Goldstein has argued, in order to accrue some of his cultural capital.[5] In his view, writers of the rhyme-royal romance and the scribes who produce the usually lavish manuscript versions of those romances increased their own association with those of upper social status through the use of the form.[6]

We do not know much about the origins of the form or even of its name. The earliest extant reference to it as 'royal' is Gascoigne's when in 1575 he writes:

> Rhythme royall is a verse of tenne sillables, and seven such verses make a staffe, whereof of the first and thirde lines do aunswer (acrosse) in like

[4] See Barry Windeatt, *Oxford Guides to Chaucer: Troilus and Criseyde* (Oxford: OUP, 1992; repr. 2002), p. 356.

[5] See James Goldstein, 'A Distinction of Poetic Form: What Happened to Rhyme Royal in Scotland?', in *The Anglo-Scottish Border and the Shaping of Identity, 1300–1600*, ed. Mark P. Bruce and Katherine H. Terrell (New York: Palgrave Macmillan, 2012), pp. 161–80, at pp. 163–70. See also his '"Betuix pyne and faith": The Poetics of Compassion in Walter Kennedy's *Passioun of Crist*', *SP* 110 (2013), 482–505. I am grateful to James Goldstein for sharing with me both his unpublished and published work on rhyme royal.

[6] See Goldstein, 'A Distinction', p. 166.

> terminations and rime, the second, fourth and fifth do likewise answere each other in terminations, and the two last do combine and shut up the Sentence: this has been called Rithme royall, and surely it is a royall kinde of verse, serving best for grave discourses.[7]

This description of the stanza suggests that a rhymed pair sets a question, which is then answered. The couplet then closes the discussion. The imagery of 'shutting up the sentence' suggests, on the one hand, that the stanza – or a room, to specify the meaning of the Italian term – has a door or a window that needs to be shut; whatever ideas and emotions that are raised in the stanza are firmly closed in at its end. Furthermore, his phrase suggests that the dominant purpose of the stanza is a 'sentence', a kernel of wisdom that is finalized in its closing lines. We shall see the degree to which Gascoigne's understanding of the function of the couplet actually holds when we look at some sample stanzas later in the essay.

In 1584, George Puttenham contrasts Chaucer's use of rhyme royal with his use of couplets, concluding that 'His meter heroical of *Troilus and Cresseid* is very grave and stately, keeping the staff of seven, and the verse of ten; his other verses of *The Canterbury Tales* be but riding rhyme, nevertheless very well becoming the matter of that pleasant pilgrimage.'[8] Surely the term 'riding rhyme' would apply even more to the octosyllabic couplets of the romance with its predominant motif, as Auerbach says, of the knight 'setting forth'. Puttenham carries forward the idea that rhyme royal is associated with gravity, although he designates the form as heroic rather than royal. Given the variety with which Chaucer uses the rhyme-royal stanza, it is perhaps odd that these two critics share a view that the stanza lends itself to gravity, a word that, because of its association with death, suggests that the stanza in some senses transcends time. We shall see how skilfully Chaucer makes use of the potential of the form itself to draw attention to aspects of the temporal.

The royal designation has nothing to do with James I's later use of the form, as most poetry guides claim; the association with royalty may simply have emerged from its kinship with the French chant royal, although, as Derek Pearsall has pointed out, the two forms have little in common.[9] Martin Stevens observes that John Quixley used the term 'ballade royal' in 1400 to refer to a seven-line stanza with an ababbcc rhyme scheme, which he himself

7 Cited in Martin Stevens, 'The Royal Stanza in Early English Literature', *PMLA* 94 (1979), 62–76, at p. 62.

8 *The Art of English Poesy by George Puttenham: A Critical Edition*, ed. Frank Whigham and Wayne A. Rebhorn (Ithaca, NY: Cornell University Press, 2007), pp. 149–50.

9 Derek Pearsall, 'Rhyme Royal: Craft and Status', Manuscript of an unpublished lecture given at the University of Glasgow, November, 2010. See also the entry for chant royal in *The Princeton Encyclopedia of Poetry and Poetics*, ed. Alex Preminger et al. (Princeton, NJ: Princeton University Press, 1965), p. 115.

employed.[10] Stevens goes on to suggest that the name may be linked to the fact that the form was often used in addresses to royalty in poetry competitions known as *pui* or in ceremonial events involving royalty, such as John Lydgate's civic show in honour of Henry V's return to London in 1432 or the festive entry of Henry VII into York in 1486.[11]

The form surely emerges from Chaucer's acquaintance with a variety of both French and Italian forms. It has been suggested that Chaucer either regularized the ballade stanzas that Machaut and Deschamps used more variably or that he dropped the fifth line of the *ottava rima* stanza (abababcc), a form used by Boccaccio, or perhaps that he decided to drop line six (the fourth b rhyme) of the monk's tale stanza.[12] The fact that scribes were often especially careful when copying rhyme royal, sometimes presenting, in a wasteful use of vellum, only four or five stanzas per page, suggests, as Daniel Wakelin has argued, that the scribe considered the stanza itself to be a valuable constructed work of art worthy of visual display and thus one demanding care in writing it down.[13] The issues of temporality and spatiality that the material instantiations of rhyme royal involve thus reinforce what we can see as rhyme royal's structural availability for engaging ideas about time and space at a meta-level.

With the exception of Rhiannon Purdie's examination of the tail-rhyme romance and Susanna Fein's contextual analysis of the twelve-line *Pearl* stanza, very little work has been done on the history of the development of stanzaic forms in Middle English literature, and even less on their functions.[14] In the 1980s, Barbara Nolan suggested that rhyme royal was well suited to 'prayerful purposes', a description that does not quite suit the functions of the form in romance.[15] More recently, Pearsall suggested that, 'There is a sense of patterns being woven, of a meditative frame of mind, of thought being in

10 See Stevens, 'The Royal Stanza', p. 63.

11 See Stevens, 'The Royal Stanza', pp. 63–6.

12 See Pearsall, 'Rhyme Royal', p. 5. For a superb discussion of Chaucer's indebtedness to and departure from both Italian and French metres in his use of rhyme royal in *Troilus and Criseyde*, see Barry Windeatt's explanation of metre in his edition of Geoffrey Chaucer, *Troilus and Criseyde* (New York: Longman, 1984), pp. 55–64, and his discussion of Chaucer's style in his *Oxford Guides to Chaucer: Troilus and Criseyde*, pp. 314–59. See also Paull F. Baum, *Chaucer's Verse* (Durham, NC: Duke University Press, 1961), pp. 47–51 and esp. p. 48.

13 Daniel Wakelin, *Scribal Correction and Literary Craft* (Cambridge: CUP, 2014), pp. 234–45, 253–8.

14 See Rhiannon Purdie, *Anglicising Romance: Tail-Rhyme and Genre in Medieval English Literature* (Cambridge: D. S. Brewer, 2008); and Susanna Fein, 'Twelve-Line Stanza Forms in Middle English and the Date of "*Pearl*"', *Speculum* 72 (1997), 367–98.

15 Barbara Nolan, 'Chaucer's Tales of Transcendence: Rhyme Royal and Christian Prayer in the *Canterbury Tales*', in *Chaucer's Religious Tales*, ed. C. David Benson and Elizabeth Robertson (Cambridge: D. S. Brewer, 1990), pp. 21–38, at p. 23.

progress.'[16] In his study of Thomas More's use of the form, Robert Cummings comments on its intrinsic expansiveness, the space it makes for 'the cultivation of meditative postures'.[17] Meditative may be a misleading adjective, for, as we shall see, the form demands a much more active engagement from the reader than the adjective suggests. Indeed, the form creates expansive spaces in which a variety of unpredictable outcomes can occur, only one of which might be meditative.

How does Chaucer achieve the expansiveness both Pearsall and Cummings observe as characteristic of the form? In part, the decasyllabic length of the lines in the stanzaic form itself invites expansiveness. Extending the octosyllables he had used in his previous dream visions to decasyllables allows the poet ease of enjambment as well as the opportunity to develop and vary syntax. As Paul Fussell writes,

> What happens when the octosyllabic couplet is expanded to the heroic is that adjectives and adverbs come flocking in. Thus the two sorts of couplets deal in very different textures: the texture of the octosyllabic couplet, regardless of who is writing in it, is likely to be lean and clean, spare and logical, a texture supremely appropriate to sarcasm or solid virile reasoning; the texture of the heroic couplet, with its abundant modifiers and qualifications, is likely to be more shaded, subtle, and busy.[18]

Chaucer avails himself of the rhythmic potential of the longer line and is especially versatile in his play with metrical pauses, his varied use of enjambment across lines and across stanzas, and, as Goldstein and others have observed, in varying the placement of the caesura in each line and in setting syntactic structures and rhyme patterns in conversation with one another.[19]

Almost any stanza of *Troilus and Criseyde* (a poem to which I shall return at the end of this essay) makes use of at least one of these effects. Chaucer is masterful in his various uses of the form in this poem, as Windeatt has observed, from presenting a balanced witty dialogue in a single stanza such as in Book II, lines 134–40 to his extension of the narrative over several stanzas to create an almost lyric-like effect in Troilus's petition to Criseyde in Book III, lines 127–47.[20] His control of the interplay between syntactic variation and rhyme is brilliantly demonstrated in the opening stanza:

16 Pearsall, 'Rhyme Royal', p. 4.

17 Robert Cummings, 'The Province of Verse: Sir Thomas More's Twelve Rules of John Picus Earle of Mirandula', in *Elizabethan Translation and Literary Culture*, ed. Gabriela Schmidt (Berlin and Boston, MA: Der Gruyter, 2013), pp. 201–26, at p. 211. I am grateful to the late Robert Cummings for delightful conversations about rhyme royal.

18 Paul Fussell, *Poetic Meter and Poetic Form*, rev. edn (New York: Random House, 1975), p. 130.

19 See Goldstein, 'A Distinction'; Stevens, 'The Royal Stanza'; and Pearsall, 'Rhyme Royal'.

20 Windeatt, *Oxford Guides to Chaucer: Troilus and Criseyde*, pp. 357–8.

> The double sorwe of Troilus to tellen,
> That was the king Priamus sone of Troye,
> In lovynge, how his aventures fellen
> Fro wo to wele, and after out of joie,
> My purpos is, er that I parte fro ye.
> Thesiphone, thow help me for t'endite.
> Thise woful vers, that wepen as I write. (I. 1–7)[21]

Pearsall writes of this passage:

> It is a virtuoso performance: the inversion of the opening line, echoing the structure of the first line of the *Aeneid* (syntactical inversion is always a marker of the high style), the binding of the first five lines into a single continuous sentence through the enfolding inversion ending 'My purpos is', the daringly artificial rhyme of 'joie/fro ye', and the full advantage taken of the ending couplet with the two-line apostrophe to Thesiphone. The stanza declares the ambition, the emotionally expressive power, and the formal control of the poem.[22]

The end of the poem presents a series of stanzas that play with different aspects of its formal properties. The stanza that describes Troilus's ascent to the eighth sphere, for example, illustrates the ways in which adjectives 'flock in' to the form, as Fussell puts it:

> And whan that he was slayn in this manere,
> His lighte goost ful blisfully is went
> Up to the holughnesse of the eighthe spere,
> In convers letyng every element;
> And ther he saugh with ful avysement,
> The erratik sterres, herkenyng armonye
> With sownes ful of hevenyssh melodie. (V. 1807–13)

Chaucer often uses the couplet to close off the topic raised in the stanza, but here the shift into trisyllabic or dactylic adjectives opens up the space into the heavens, and the three adjectives, 'erratik', 'herkenyng' and 'hevenyssh', create sounds that contribute to the celebration of the harmony of the sphere to which Troilus tends.

Chaucer makes particularly effective use of enjambment in the next stanza:

> And down from thennes faste he gan avyse
> This litel spot of erthe that with the se
> Embraced is, and fully gan despise
> This wrecched world, and held al vanite

21 All quotations from Chaucer are taken from *The Riverside Chaucer*, ed. Larry Benson et al. (Boston, MA: Houghton Mifflin, 1987), and line numbers are indicated in parentheses within the body of the text.

22 Pearsall, 'Rhyme Royal', p. 6.

> To respect of the pleyn felicite
> That is in hevene above; and at the laste,
> Ther he was slayn, his lokyng down he caste; (V. 1814–20)

By allowing *se* to be the last word stressed in the second line (1815), the poet opens up the vision to the vastness of the sea whose power to contain the earth surprises us in the next line. In the next line, Troilus's new-found understanding of the vanity of human wishes is intensified when the object of his spite is withheld until the following line (1817).

Ultimately, by stopping the flow of the lines with a couplet, Chaucer creates an area or a space, a room in which to wander, that is, a stanza. In the *De Vulgari Eloquentia*, Dante describes the stanza as follows: 'stantia, hoc est mansio capax sive receptaculum totius artis. Nam quemadmodum cantio est gremium totius sententie, sic stantia totam artem ingremiat' ('a stanza ... [is] a capacious storehouse or receptacle for the art in its entirety. For just as the *canzone* is the lap of the whole of its subject-matter, so the stanza enlaps its whole technique').[23] Dante's words *gremium* and *ingremiat* might more specifically be translated as 'womb' and 'enwomb'. The metaphor of the stanza as a womb rather than a room emphasizes its expansiveness – that is, its nature as an expandable space for growth – and undermines the more static notion of a stanza as merely a container. The womb creates a contained but dynamic space, one in which the container enlarges in response to embryonic growth. Such reciprocity has its literary counterpart: form is an active principle that responds to content. The structure of the rhyme-royal stanza, which allows for extensive syntactic variation as well as enjambment itself, allows for such generative dilation. In his use of rhyme royal, Chaucer draws attention to such 'enlapping' or 'enwombing' qualities, ones that serve him well not only for the Christian meditations on embodiment that occur in the religious tales but also for the philosophical meditations on temporality that shape his versions of romance. Rhyme-royal stanzas, at least in Chaucer's use of them, are thus, as Dante suggests, capacious, and ultimately able to contain the whole world.

The rhyme-royal stanza is not only spatially expansive, but also bound and constrained, and the form asks the reader to engage those conflicting aspects. The two couplets interrupt the flow of thought and concentrate the mind. The first couplet gives us pause – and indeed, according to Wakelin, it is the fifth line, with its unexpected slowing produced by the couplet, that gives scribes the most difficulty.[24] Then the next couplet stops and, as Gascoigne says, 'shuts up the sentence', or as Dante would have it, enwombs us, forcing us back into the stanza as a whole and therefore immersing us into the bounded

[23] Dante, *De Vulgari Eloquentia*, ed. Steven Botterill (Cambridge: CUP, 2008), 2.9.2, p. 73.

[24] Wakelin, *Scribal Correction*, p. 255.

but expansive space of that room and allowing us to become hyper-aware of its contents. Going on to the next stanza requires entering a new space and therefore involves a recalibration of the imagination and often an engagement with the idea itself of beginning again.

The rhyming pattern of each stanza allows the poet to highlight constellations of ideas through juxtaposition of words whose different meanings are linked by sound. Like the Spenserian stanza and the sonnet the rhyme-royal stanza anticipates, the pattern is well suited for the development of an idea, or perhaps more accurately for what Jeff Dolven, when discussing the Spenserian stanza, has called a 'mimesis of thinking'.[25] Furthermore, as Patricia Parker has shown, when Spenser augments the form, he releases what she identifies as a particularly dangerous feminine dilatoriness one could say is latent in the rhyme-royal form, a characteristic intuited by Dante in his use of diction referring to the womb in his description of the stanza.[26]

The patterned stanza also draws on other non-semantic elements such as rhythm and metre and the musicality of rhyme to convey its alternations of mood and the movement of its energies or to contribute to what Derek Attridge designates as an aspect of form itself, 'mobilization'; as he writes,

> Form in the sense I am developing here includes the mobilization of meanings, or rather of the events of meaning: their sequentiality, interplay, and changing intensity, their patterns of expectation and satisfaction or tension and release, their precision or diffuseness. It does not include any extractable sense, information, image, or referent that the work lays before the reader. Through this mobilization of meanings the work's linguistic operations such as referentiality, metaphoricity, intentionality, and ethicity are staged.[27]

The different rhythms produced by varied syntax and the intensification of meaning produced by placing a given word at the end of the line in a rhyming position reinforce the different kinds of mental and emotional energies at play in each stanza. Finally, as a carefully constructed, bound container, both as a room and a womb, the verse form like all stanzas draws attention to itself as a made thing that is itself capable of making.

A particularly powerful example of Chaucer's use of such formal properties, including rhyming patterns, syntactic complexity, the non-semantic dimensions of sound, and the intellectual demands produced by the couplets, all of which create 'enwombing' effects, can be found in his recasting of Dante's *terza rima* prayer of St Bernard to the Virgin Mary in the prologue to the

[25] Jeff Dolven, 'The Method of Spenser's Stanza', *Spenser Studies* 19 (2004), 14–25.

[26] Patricia Parker, *Literary Fat Ladies: Rhetoric, Gender, Property* (New York and London: Routledge, 1987).

[27] Derek Attridge, *The Singularity of Literature* (New York and London: Routledge, 2004), p. 109.

Prioress's Tale.[28] The prioress's prayer in form and content as a whole powerfully engages the problem embodiment poses for those seeking transcendence. To focus here on just one of the stanzas in the prayer, consider how this passage from the prologue to the *Prioress's Tale* stresses the violent intensity of the speaker's relationship to God. Given that the topic of the stanza is enwombment – that is, the incarnation of Christ in Mary's womb – the way in which the stanzaic form creates an act of enwombment only deepens its subject matter. The Prioress begins with praise of Mary's paradoxical status as virgin and maid:

> O mooder Mayde, O mayde Mooder free!
> O bussh unbrent, brennynge in Moyses sighte,
> That ravyshedest doun fro the Dietee,
> Thurgh thyn humblesse, the Goost that in th' alighte,
> Of whos vertu, whan he thyn herte lighte,
> Conceyved was the Fadres sapience,
> Help me to telle it in thy reverence! (467–73)

The progression here from the nasal *m* to the plosive *b* in the next line which linguists have associated phonaesthetically with violence reinforces the expression in this stanza of the violent nature of the encounter between the human and the divine. Intensifying the paradox of a virgin mother and suggesting a powerful erotic encounter with the divine, the poet in his double use of chiasmus in the first two lines creates a verbal violence that places burning at its centre. By placing the word 'free' at the end of the line in a rhyming position, in contrast to Dante who places *liberamente* both later in his passage and at the beginning of the line, Chaucer emphasizes the infinite reach of Mary's generosity. The tortuous syntax of the next lines simultaneously obscures Mary's capacities as an agent and asserts her power, one found in humility, as one who ravishes or seizes – indeed rapes – in actively pulling God down to earth. That the third line is metrically awkward makes the odd verb *ravyshedest* central to this stanza.

Chaucer's choice of rhyming patterns further intensifies the poem's engagement with the female body's capacity for transcendence. A-rhymes of 'free' and 'dietee' link Mary's powers to that of God where b-rhymes bring together 'sight', 'alight', and 'light'. The fact that two of the b-rhymes are rich rhymes that draw attention to the polysemous dimensions of the word, light and light, reinforces the imagery of the light that comes from burning, a light that in both cases refers to the holy ghost's insemination of Mary, thus

[28] It is illuminating to compare and contrast the different effects Chaucer creates in translating this prayer twice, once in the prologue to the *Second Nun's Tale* and once in the prologue to the *Prioress's Tale*. I discuss these two different versions of Dante's Bernardian prayer in detail in a chapter of my forthcoming book, *Chaucerian Consent: Women, Religion and Subjection in Late Medieval England*.

intensifying the feminine erotic excess of Mary's union with God and the speaker's pleasure in it. The rich rhyme also creates a tension between a spirit that descends, 'alights', and the human one that ascends in being 'lighte', that is, set alight. Furthermore, that burning takes place in the human sphere, in the sight of Moses. In his creation of a particular pattern within the rhyme-royal scheme, Chaucer thus creates an interplay between the b-rhymes of vision and heat and the a-rhymes of beneficence and power.

C-rhymes modulate the erotic energies of the previous lines by asserting the wisdom and reverence of God the father. The couplet brings us back into the orbit of the clerically mediated divine in its use of rhymes of multisyllabic Latinate abstract words, 'sapience' and 'reverence'. The petition of the last lines reaches towards God, bringing the uncontrollable burning of human desire into the orbit of God's will. Yet, though the speaker asserts her praise of the father's wisdom, at the same time she grants Mary power as the rhyme pulls the wisdom of the father into the speaker's orbit who reveres that aspect of divine knowledge that is accessible through the senses, that is sapiential knowledge. The word *conceyved* concludes the stanza by joining conception as the consequence of ravishment with conception as a mental construction of the father's wisdom – another paradox allowed by the expansive size of the stanza: that the raped daughter produces the father's wisdom. Wisdom and reverence are thus recast and make room for burning and violence. The final couplet shapes – or enwombs – the uncontained energies of the earlier lines in that the metre makes the divine at one with the unruly energies of the body.

To turn now to rhyme royal and romance, it is difficult to assess its effectiveness as a form used for romance since only a handful of Middle English romances in rhyme royal have survived, most notably, the *Generydes*, and two close translations of their French sources, *Amoryus and Cleopes* and the *Roman de Parthenay*. One might argue that the *Kingis Quair* should be included in this list since it draws on romance conventions, but the poet's work is primarily a poetic autobiography rather than a romance. Generally speaking, most post-Chaucerian poets, concerned above all to imitate Chaucer, use rhyme royal for dream visions or religious poems. Interestingly, Lydgate turns away from his Chaucerian rhyme-royal model in choosing to tell his Troy legends in couplets instead, but, perhaps, finds the form indeed suited to 'prayerful purposes' when he composes his *Lyf of Our Lady* in rhyme royal. I shall consider sample stanzas from these three notable romances in order to explore the degree to which rhyme royal suits their romance purposes.

Of the three, only the late fourteenth-century *Generydes* follows both the metre and the rhyme scheme of the rhyme-royal form. Here are its beginning stanzas:

> In olde Romans and storys as I rede,
> Of Inde Sometyme ther was a nobyll king,

Ientill, curteys, full trew in worde and dede,
Wyse and manly prevyd in every thyng,
To his people full good and eke lovyng,
Myghty and ryche, a man of nobyll fame.
And Auferius this was the kynges name.

This worthy prince hadde weddyd in sertayne
A fayre lady, and comne of nobyll kynne
And what pleasure he cowde for her ordeyne,
That shuld be do, ther was noo lette therin;
In every thyng he dede hyr love to wynne,
He hade nomore to lese and that he knewe
ffor afterward she was to hym untrewe.[29]

The poem is based on a French original in octosyllabic couplets, and is also closely related to an octosyllabic English version (in the Helmingham manuscript), a form that would, I suspect, suit better its narrative drive. Rather than letting a variety of adjectives and adverbs flock in, the poet simply fills the line by doubling adjectives ('good and eke loving', 'myghty and ryche', etc.). Often for the sake of rhyme, he pads the line in other ways with romance tags such as 'as I rede' and 'in certayne'. In this poem, as Pearsall said once of Lydgate's use of rhyme royal in *The Fall of Princes*, too often 'chunks of verbiage like bags of sprouts pass as if on a conveyor belt before us stretching out to infinity'.[30] Rarely does the poet use the closing couplet to create the effects Dante describes of 'enwombing' or that Gascoigne describes of 'answering' or 'shutting' a thought. The last line of the second stanza does surprise us with the prediction of Auferius's wife's future infidelity, but this is a rare pause in the narrative, which then hurries on. As Pearsall concludes, in this poem,

> The end-stopped line is dominant with [little] enjambment ... The stanza is treated as a unit [...] Within the stanza, rhyme exercises a tyranny which can be overcome only by dilution of the sense and the use of tags; there is a marked reluctance to begin a new thought after the fourth line of the stanza, and the padding is often but thinly disguised [...] pith and point are sacrificed unhesitatingly to fluency of metre and stanzaic unity.[31]

In contrast, in his mid-fifteenth-century rhyme-royal romance, *Amoryus and Cleopes*, John Metham, while refusing to follow a regular accentual/syllabic metre, does at times profitably make use of rhyme royal's shape and rhyming patterns. Nicholas Myklebust argues in this volume that Metham's metrical irregularities may have been deliberate, and this argument accords

[29] *Generydes*, ed. W. Aldis Wright, EETS 55. 70 (London: Trübner, 1873, 1878), lines 1–14.

[30] Pearsall, 'Rhyme Royal', p. 8.

[31] Derek Pearsall, '*The Assembly of Ladies* and *Generydes*', *RES* 12 (1961), 229–37, at p. 233.

with my sense that there are more interesting effects in Metham's use of poetic form – both in his use of the rhyme-royal stanza and his use of metre – than have been acknowledged.[32] Although his line length is almost never uniform in length, and even though he does vary the rhyming pattern from time to time, Metham, on the whole, typically follows the standard ababbcc rhyming pattern of rhyme royal. Occasionally he, or his scribe, perhaps because of the pressures of layout, produces some stanzas of six or eight lines, despite the fact that the manuscript is always ruled for twenty-eight lines or four seven-line rhyme-royal stanzas.[33]

Metham's occasional use of the rhyme-royal stanza's potential for expansive thought and for self-reflexivity can be seen in this passage, a seemingly stock romance description of the heroine:

> As Phebus in bryghtenes alle planetys excedyth in general,
> Ryght so in beuté Cleopes yche erthly creature
> Precellyd in fayrenes; that yn the reme in specyal
> The fame of her beuté was spred, and of here stature.
> For so womanly was sche, so benygne to yche creature,
> That lusty yong knyghtys gret parte wold make
> To breke huge sperys fersly for Cleopes sake.
>
> And brevely this proces for to trase
> Qwat that Nature myght werke to beuté in ony creature
> Was wrought in the persone and in the lovely face
> Of this lady, for sche proporciond was in sqwych mesure
> That sche sempt be outeward apparens to pase nature,
> Hos beuté thus floryscyng I omyt, as of the douter of Venus,
> Contynwyng here fortunat fate undyr Mars furyus.[34]

In his choice of rhyme words for the b-rhymes, Metham brings together thoughts about making – creation ('creature'), nature ('nature') and measure ('mesure') – and the word 'make' is signalled in the couplet. His use of syntactic variation draws our attention to the idea of an overwhelming beauty, one that flourishes and expands even beyond the bounds of measure. Indeed, one might argue that Metham consciously exceeds measure here since the excessive number of syllables in the line is analogous to her excessive beauty. Metham does use the closing couplet effectively from time to time as he does here where the enjambed two-line closing couplet with no caesura reinforces formally the clash of spears

[32] See Nicholas Myklebust, 'The Problem of John Metham's Prosody', in this volume, pp. 149–169.

[33] See John Metham, *Amoryus and Cleopes*, ed. Stephen F. Page (Kalamazoo, MI: TEAMS, 1999), p. 17.

[34] *Amoryus and Cleopes*, ed. Page, lines 148–61. All further quotations from Metham's text will be taken from this edition and line numbers will be given in parentheses in the body of the essay.

the lines describe. Myklebust demonstrates a similar sophisticated play at work in the first stanza, which he calls an 'ironic *tour de force*'.[35]

While it is possible to find a reason for Metham's metrical choices here and in some places elsewhere, in many cases his irregular line lengths seem only to be random. Yet, even though Metham's syllable count may 'vary between eight and nineteen syllables and between four and eight beats', he does seem to aim to bring together clusters of lines that make use of a more or less regular pattern of accents, as Myklebust demonstrates.[36] One could argue that Metham consciously moves away from an accentual-syllabic line towards a more accentual one, as does Coleridge three hundred years later. As Coleridge writes in his preface to *Christabel*,

> the metre of the Cristabel is not, properly speaking, irregular, though it may seem so from being founded on a new principle: namely, that of counting in each line the accents, not the syllables. Though the latter may vary from seven to twelve, yet in each line the accents will be found to be only four. Nevertheless, this occasional variation in number of syllables is not introduced wantonly, or for the mere ends of convenience, but in correspondence with some transition, in the nature of the imagery or passion.[37]

Coleridge's movement away from accentual-syllabic to accentual verse has been seen as a break from the stranglehold of the iambic line and a movement towards the freer modern poetic line.[38] Perhaps Metham is reaching towards more modernist metrical effects in his use of metre. How fully in control Metham is of his metrical choices is a matter of debate, but there is no doubt that there is more conscious play with form and metre than has been recognized.

Metham is possibly the earliest poet to see within rhyme royal its potential as a basis for the creation of a sonnet. In one section of the manuscript, there appear significantly two rubricated stanzas of four lines followed by one of six lines, which Stephen Page has called the first sonnet in English:

> 'O, Fortune! Alas! qwy arte thow to me onkend?
> Qwy chongyddyst thow thi qwele causeles?
> Qwy art thow myne enmye and noght my frend,
> And I ever thi servant in al maner of lovlynes?
>
> 'But nowe of my lyfe, my comfort, and my afyauns
> Thowe hast me beraft; that causyth me thus to compleyn.

35 Myklebust, 'The Problem of John Metham's Prosody', p. 158.

36 Myklebust, 'The Problem of John Metham's Prosody', p. 168.

37 Samuel Taylor Coleridge, *The Complete Poems*, ed. William Keach (London: Penguin, 1997), p. 187.

38 See, for example, the discussion of poetic developments in Donald Wesling, *The New Poetries: Poetic Form since Coleridge and Wordsworth* (Lewisburg, PA: Bucknell University Press, 1985).

O bryghter than Phebus! O lyly! O grownd of plesauns!
O rose of beauté! O most goodely, sumtyme my lady sovereyn!

'But, O, allas! that thru summe enmye or sum suspycyus conjecte,
I throwyn am asyde and owte of my ladiis grace.
Sumtyme in faver but now fro alle creaturys abjecte
As oftyn sqwownyng as I remembyr her bryght face.
But now, adwe for ever, for my ful felycyté
Is among thise grene levys for to be.' (388–401)

The fact that this embryonic sonnet, one anticipating in its rhyme scheme (abab cdcd efefgg) that of Henry Howard, Earl of Surrey and also Shakespeare, appears in a poem predominantly written in rhyme royal reinforces the notion that rhyme-royal stanzas and the form of the sonnet are closely related to one another in their interest in expansive yet bounded thought. As Page points out, the sonnet, as it unfolds, does develop its ideas, presenting in the first two quatrains a lament to fortune, and then in the following sestet narrowing the focus by attributing the true cause of his pain to his unattainable beloved; the couplet concludes with the speaker's resignation.[39] While this sonnet is hardly as sophisticated as those produced by Surrey and Wyatt, it is extraordinary that this first version of a sonnet is so rarely commented upon in histories of the development of the sonnet form.

Rather than enhance the development of the plot of the romance, the rhyme-royal stanza seems best to serve the poet's overriding interest in a thematic focus outside the concerns of the romance, a meta-discourse about poetics. His frequent ekphrases and digressions on the nature of art and even on his own artistic choices as a writer of rhyme royal disrupt the onward flow of the narrative. The stanza that follows the above passage, for example, foregrounds the problems he faces in translating French octosyllabic couplets into English decasyllables:

But now of descrypcionnys I sese and forth this proces.
  As myn autor dothe wryte, ryght so wul I,
    Word for word, save only a lenger progres
    Yt nedyt in Englysch; for in Latyne he that wrytyth most schortly,
    Most ys comendyd; qwerfore that myn autour endytyth, in more and les,
    Compendyusly he pasyth; and so I, in termys fewe,
  The entent of myne autour I purpose bravely to schewe. (162–9)

His hypermetric line, one that follows two conventionally decasyllabic lines, reflects the content of the line in which he states that translation of Latin into English requires more words in lines. His use of metre here, if a conscious

39 See the discussion of the sonnet, *Amoryus and Cleopes*, ed. Page, pp. 17–19.

choice, might suggest he believed that line length should be responsive to content rather than to a rigid idea of form.

The anonymous author of the late fifteenth-century *Parthenay* also uses the form and his own awkward use of metre to comment on his status as a non-native speaker of English:

> For full fayne I wold do that myght you plese
> yff connyng I had in it to procede;
> To me wold it be grete plesaunce and ease,
> yff aught here might fourge to youre wyl in dede;
> But barayne is my soule, fauting connynghede
> Natheles in it wil I make progresse
> Evermore trustyng to youre gentilnesse.
>
> I not aqueynted of birth naturall
> With frenshe his verray trew parfightnesse,
> Nor enpreyntyd is in mynde cordiall;
> O word for other myght take by lachesse,
> Or peradventure by unconnyngnesse;
> For frenshe rimed or metred alway
> Ful oft is straunge in englishe to display.[40]

Although the author draws closer here to producing an iambic pentameter line, in not varying the medial pause and in not making use of enjambment, the author produces monotony. Finally he has not taken advantage of the opportunity to shift the discourse in the couplet. The couplet of the second stanza, in which he complains of the difficulty of translating French into English, is particularly metrically awkward – perhaps, as in Metham's passage above, deliberately so.

It is of course Chaucer who exploits most fully the potential of the form to expand and complicate his vision and to reflect upon his own discursive fields. Let us consider an example of two striking stanzas:[41]

> Criseyde, which that felte hire thus itake,
> As writen clerkes in hir bokes olde,
> Right as an aspes leef she gan to quake,
> Whan she hym felte hire in his armes folde.

[40] *The Romans of Partenay or of Lusignen: Otherwise known as the Tale of Melusine*, ed. W. W. Skeat, EETS o.s. 22 (London: Kegan Paul, Trench, Trubner, 1866), lines 1–14.

[41] Like the stanzas of *Parthenay* and *Amoryus and Cleopes*, many stanzas of *Troilus and Criseyde* are also translations of a source, the Italian *Filostrato*, although these particular passages are not in the Italian source. While Chaucer does in the poem reflect upon the difficulty of language change over time, he does not comment directly on difficulties he may have faced in translating Italian into English. For a discussion of Chaucer's use of his Italian source, see the section of Windeatt's introduction to his edition of *Troilus and Criseyde* entitled 'The "Troilus" as translation', pp. 3–24.

But Troilus, al hool of cares colde,
Gan thanken tho the bryghte goddes sevene;
Thus sondry peynes bryngen folk in hevene.

This Troilus in armes gan hire streyne,
And seyde, 'O swete, as ever mote I gon,
Now be ye kaught, now is ther but we tweyne!
Now yeldeth yow, for other bote is non'.
To that Criseyde answerde thus anon,
'Ne hadde I er now, my swete herte dere,
Ben yolde, y-wis, I were now nought here!' (III, 1198–211)

The first stanza's opening line, which brings us into the present moment of Criseyde's experience, is followed by an appositive in the next line that stops the flow of the narrative, taking us from the present moment back into a different time and space, the world of books and their scribes. That her seizure frightens her is reinforced by the a-rhymes 'take' and 'quake' and that this is a potentially deadly fear is reinforced in the b-rhymes of 'olde', 'folde' and 'colde'. In the next line, we return to the present, where the simile, although taking us into another domain, the domain of trees (the aspen leaf), paradoxically reinforces the immediacy of her experience. Criseyde's feelings are indeed folded into the stanza. The couplet, however, rather than closing the reader into Criseyde's experience, disrupts the register, once more taking us into the realm of the gods and the heavens ('goddes sevene'; 'hevene'). Thus the couplet moves us from a quotidian moment into a broader frame of reference with its 'sentence', its universal wisdom statement.

The a-rhymes of the second stanza, 'streyne' and 'tweyne', reinforce the idea that Troilus is forcing himself even closer upon Criseyde, with a temporal finality suggested in the b-rhymes, 'gon', 'non', 'anon'. The couplet, however, is a perfect example of the scope of Chaucer's use of the couplet in rhyme royal, for not only do the rhyme words 'dere' and 'here' bring us into a different present moment, a here and now of love rather than of threat, but also it forces us back not only to rethink the whole stanza but the whole narrative of potential rape hinted at by the machinations of both Pandarus and Criseyde up to this point. Here, Chaucer demonstrates the extraordinary range of the form of rhyme royal for romance.

One might object that the poem isn't really a romance after all – rather it could be said to engage larger philosophical questions about time and embodiment, for ultimately the love story, as many critics have observed, is as much about the progress of history as it is about two lovers, and ultimately this stanza is the quintessence of the poem's larger meditation on the potential of personal love to achieve transcendence.[42] Perhaps a poem that follows more

[42] For an extended study of the poem's engagement with history in what he calls its

readily the expected conventions of romance in which the protagonist sets forth, in this case a woman rather than a knight, might be *The Man of Law's Tale*, but even in this poem Chaucer's use of rhyme royal destabilizes its narrative impulses. In contrast to Metham's merely descriptive representation of Cleopes, Chaucer's representation of Constance is much more active:

> 'In hire is heigh beautee, withoute pride,
> Yowthe withoute grenehede or folye;
> To alle hire werkes vertu is hir gyde,
> Humblesse hath slayn in hire al tirannye,
> She is mirour of alle curteisye;
> Hir herte is verray chambre of hoolynesse,
> Hir hand ministre of fredam for almesse.' (162–8)

We might find this seemingly conventional blazon of Constance's stellar qualities in descriptions of any number of romance heroines, but Chaucer complicates these attributes by his syntactical variety and by his use of personification, metaphor and metonymy (for example, humility kills; she is a mirror; her heart is a chamber; her hand is a minister). Her virtues hardly seem her own; rather they have been put within her as if she were a container, act on her, or emerge from parts of her that are disengaged from her body. The effect of these shifting descriptions is to dismantle any notion of a unitary subject and to destabilize Constance's agency, the very topic of the poem as a whole.[43]

To conclude, what I have observed about the rhyme-royal stanzas I have cited in this essay is that they disrupt the forward movement of romance narrative better suited for octosyllabic couplets and for prose. These stanzas thus defamiliarize the inherited form of romance. Expanding across the page and down, the form makes room for syntactic variation, figurative language and tension between syntactic structure and rhyme scheme, thus allowing for dilation and lateral expansion. The stanza's closing couplet folds the reader back into the stanza, forcing the reader in an active mental engagement with time, space, and embodiment. Finally, the form contains within it, both in the form the poet writes and in the material object the scribe produces, a self-conscious awareness of its own artistry. As we have seen, these very features work against the predominant narrative drive of the romance genre and thus rhyme royal generally was not a felicitous choice of form for writers

---

'Theban recursiveness', see Lee Patterson, '*Troilus and Criseyde* and the Subject of History', in his *Chaucer and the Subject of History* (Madison, WI: University of Wisconsin Press, 1991), pp. 84–164.

[43] For a negative view of Constance's agency see Carolyn Dinshaw, 'The Man of Law and Its "Abhomynacions"', in her *Chaucer's Sexual Poetics* (Madison, WI: University of Wisconsin Press, 1989), pp. 88–112; and, for a contrasting positive view, see Elizabeth Robertson, 'The "Elvyssh" Power of Constance: Christian Feminism in Geoffrey Chaucer's *The Man of Law's Tale*', *SAC* 23 (2001), 143–80.

of romance.[44] That said, it should be noted that when Spenser comes to write a romance, his *Faerie Queene*, he invents a nine-line stanza (eight lines of iambic pentameter followed by a single alexandrine line in hexameter) that is not dissimilar to rhyme royal in its use of a couplet and internal rhymes in the rhyme scheme: ababbcbcc. One might say that Spenser succeeds in using a rhyme-royal-like stanzaic form for a romance only because his stanzas become the vehicle through which he probes the very heart of the romance form at a meta-level, dalliance. But the influence of the rhyme-royal stanza on Spenser is the subject of another essay.

[44] I am grateful to Ad Putter for encouraging me to think about rhyme royal and romance, Joyce Coleman for stimulating discussion about the origins of the form, and Jeffrey Robinson for extensive illuminating discussions concerning the effects of the form in particular stanzas.

4

The Singing of Middle English Romance: Stanza Forms and *Contrafacta**

Ad Putter

The recent collection of essays on the Auchinleck manuscript edited by Susanna Fein shows how much progress has been made in our understanding of book production in the fourteenth century, but also how hard it remains for us to imagine the non-literate forms in which some of the romances it contains would have been encountered in the medieval period.[1] We know that Middle English romances were not normally read as we read them today, in private and in silence: they were read aloud – and apparently also sung[2] – in a family or household setting; and, last but not least, they were performed by minstrels to assembled audiences.[3] Such a performance might involve scripted and unscripted recitation and singing (usually to the accompaniment of a musical instrument such as the harp or the fiddle). Mentions of public readings and performances of romance are numerous – an example being the catalogue of festivities at Havelok's coronation: 'Hwan he was king, there mouthe men se … / Romanz-reding on the bok. / Ther mouthe men here the gestes singe'

* This essay draws on my research for the research project 'The Verse Forms of Middle English Romance', funded by the Arts and Humanities Research Council, whose support I gratefully acknowledge. I would also like to thank my colleagues Judith Jefferson and Myra Stokes for suggesting improvements to an earlier version of this essay, and Owen Putter for helping me to edit the two musical examples.

1 *The Auchinleck Manuscript: New Perspectives*, ed. Susanna Fein (York: York Medieval Press, 2016).

2 The French teaching manual *Femina* (c. 1400), ed. William Rothwell, Anglo-Norman On-Line Hub, at http://www.anglo-norman.net/texts/femina.pdf, recommends the singing of stories as a form of relaxation: 'En sale chaunterez les gestez / Pur oblier les grevez molestez.' The Middle English translation reads: 'In halle ye shulle synge thyse gestez / To foryete thyse grevous hurtes' (30.10–11). I have modernised medieval orthography in all quotations taken from primary sources.

3 Karl Reichl, 'Orality and Performance', in *A Companion to Medieval Popular Romance*, ed. Raluca Radulescu and Cory James Rushton (Cambridge: D. S. Brewer, 2009), pp. 132–49; and Ad Putter, 'Middle English Romances and the Oral Tradition', in *Medieval Oral Literature*, ed. Karl Reichl (Berlin: De Gruyter, 2012), pp. 335–52.

(2321–330).[4] However, when a group of literature specialists are commissioned to look at the hard evidence of manuscripts, this aural dimension of medieval romance in performance tends to get lost.

Two essays in Fein's collection illustrate how easy it is for 'bibliocentric' approaches to lose sight of alternative modes of transmission, whether memorial and/or melodic. Derek Pearsall, in an essay that surveys the last forty years of scholarship,[5] initially has minstrels on his radar, but when it comes to the Middle English romances that survive in manuscript he cannot think what minstrels have to do with any of them. The way he deals with the internal evidence of Middle English romances is telling. As is well known, many Middle English romances contain prologues in which the 'I' speaks as a performing minstrel and/or refers to minstrel performance. Examples mentioned by Pearsall himself are the minstrel addresses at the start of *Bevis of Hampton* and of *Emaré*. The latter opens with a prayer and then tells us that that is how minstrels should begin:

> Menstrelles that walken fer and wyde
> Her and ther in every a syde
> In mony a diverse londe,
> Sholde, at her begynnyng,
> Speke of that ryghtwes kyng
> That made both see and sonde. (13–18)[6]

The 'I' of *Emaré* declares that the story circulates in sung form – 'Her name was called Emare / Als I here synge in songe' (23–4). 'Als I here synge' is potentially ambiguous, and Linda Zaerr offers two alternative glosses: 'As I here sing in song' and 'As I hear sung in song'.[7] The latter is probably what the poet intended, for later on in the romance the 'I' again refers to having heard the 'song' of *Emaré*: 'As y have herd menstrelles syng yn sawe' (319). According to Pearsall, and many critics before him,[8] this minstrel-talk is all smoke and mirrors: such devices are 'most likely to be the work of writers trying to create the traditional atmosphere of conviviality associated

4 *Havelok*, ed. G. V. Smithers (Oxford: Clarendon Press, 1987). This and other references to minstrels in medieval romances have recently been collected by Linda Zaerr, *Performance and the Middle English Romance* (Cambridge: D. S. Brewer, 2012), pp. 181–233.

5 Derek Pearsall, 'The Auchinleck Manuscript Forty Years On', in *The Auchinleck Manuscript*, ed. Fein, pp. 11–25.

6 *The Romance of Emaré*, ed. Edith Rickert, EETS e.s. 99 (London: OUP, 1908).

7 Zaerr, *Performance*, p. 187.

8 See, for example, Rosalind Field, 'Romance in England, 1066–1400', in *The Cambridge History of Medieval English Literature*, ed. David Wallace (Cambridge: CUP, 1999), pp. 152–81, at p. 168; and Andrew Taylor, 'Fragmentation, Corruption, and Minstrel Narration', *Yearbook of English Studies* 22 (1992), 39–62, at p. 62.

with minstrels'.[9] 'Minstrels undeniably did exist', Pearsall concedes, but 'the difficulty lies in making the leap from performance to written copies'.[10] And so, when he looks at any romance that has actually survived, he only sees the humdrum work of scribes. *Floris and Blancheflur* and *King Horn* are offered as examples of romances that 'found their way into the manuscript by the usual processes of scribal transmission [...] Karl Brunner proposed that *King Horn* and *Floris*, along with a poem on *The Assumption of Our Lady*, which all appear in a single late-thirteenth-century manuscript (CUL, MS Gg. 4. 27 (2)) were composed by a clerk in a lord's house for the ladies of the household who did not know French' (p. 23).[11]

Ann Higgins, in a very different way, sticks resolutely to the evidence of writing. Focusing on *Sir Tristrem*, she tries to account for the following facts:

1. *Sir Tristrem* is a Northern poem, though it was copied in London, c. 1330.
2. Robert Mannyng refers to *Sir Tristrem* in his *Chronicle*, c. 1335.
3. Some five years later Laurence Minot in one of his political poems makes use of the same stanza form as the one found in *Sir Tristrem*.
4. By the sixteenth century, the Auchinleck manuscript was in Scotland.

To join the dots she turns to the Auchinleck manuscript itself: this book, she argues, was made in London for a Northern book-owner, 'perhaps a Yorkshireman or a native of Lincolnshire' (p. 126), and this Northerner then immediately took the manuscript back to his home region – which would explain how Mannyng (from Lincolnshire) and Minot (from Yorkshire) could have had access to the romance. From there the codex was taken further north, to Scotland (for many Scottish lords had lands in the North of England). To think that the romance of *Sir Tristrem* could have had a life independently of the Auchinleck manuscript, that it was recited and sung by minstrels before and after it was fixed in written form in the Auchinleck manuscript, is to make unnecessary assumptions.

I believe that more should be done to put minstrels and the musical performance of medieval romance back into the frame. In this essay I shall look at some of the evidence that has encouraged me 'make the leap' from written copies to performance, focusing on three romances that have already been mentioned: *Sir Tristrem*, *Horn* and *Bevis of Hampton*. I am particularly interested in the musical performance of romance. This has been explored by a number of scholars, most notably Karl Reichl and Linda Zaerr.[12] I would like to build on their work by taking account of the verse forms of Middle English

9 Pearsall, 'The Auchinleck Manuscript Forty Years On', p. 20.

10 Pearsall, 'The Auchinleck Manuscript Forty Years On', p. 21.

11 The reference is to K. Brunner, 'The Middle English Metrical Romances and Their Audience', in *Studies in Medieval Literature in Honor of Albert Croll Baugh*, ed. M. Leach (Philadelphia: University of Pennsylvania Press, 1961), pp. 219–27.

12 See notes 3 and 4, and further references in these publications.

romances. As I shall argue, verse form suggests a close relationship between medieval song and medieval romance, and attending to these relationships may allow us a possible way back to the lost soundscape of medieval romance.

I would like to begin with *Sir Tristrem*, and, adopting a less bookish perspective on the transmission of this romance, offer an alternative explanation for the interesting facts that Higgins seeks to explain. The first thing that needs correcting in Higgins's account is that the Auchinleck *Sir Tristrem* was written for a 'regional client' from the North (p. 108). *Sir Tristrem* was originally a Northern poem (probably from Yorkshire), and the main reason why many of its rhymes no longer work is that the scribe translated this Northern text into his own London dialect. The evidence for this has been set out elsewhere,[13] and one example must suffice. Below is a single stanza from the poem. Its usual rhyme scheme is abababababcbc (or, less commonly, ababababcdc), but this rhyme scheme has clearly broken down in the stanza below, as the italicised a-rhymes show:

The Quen was wratthed *sore*;
Wroth to chaumber sche yede.
'Who may trowe man *more*,
Than he hath don this dede?'
A palfray asked sche *there*
That wele was loved in lede.
Dight sche was ful *yare*;
Hir pavilouns with hir thai lede
Ful fine.
Bifore was stef on stede
Tristrem and Ganhardine. (3070–80)[14]

Here the scribe first imposed his Southern forms, 'sore', 'more', and 'there', on the Northern forms 'sare', 'mare', and 'thare'; it is only in 'yare' that the scribe retained the original vowel sound of the a-rhymes. If, as Higgins argues, the scribe was writing this for a Northerner, we would not expect him to be translating the original into a Southern dialect. True, scribes were not always conscious of dialectal translation, but there are other changes, such as the replacement of the Northern word *grete* ('cry') by the Southern word *wepe* (as indicated by the faulty rhyme at 350–2),[15] that suggest that the Auchinleck scribe made a conscious attempt to adapt the text for a new London audience.

[13] Ad Putter, Judith Jefferson and Donka Minkova, 'Dialect, Rhyme, and Emendation in *Sir Tristrem*', *JEGP* 113 (2014), 73–92.

[14] I cite the edition by Alan Lupack, in *'Lancelot of the Laik' and 'Sir Tristrem'*, TEAMS (Kalamazoo, MI: Medieval Institute, 1994).

[15] The same substitution lies behind a faulty rhyme in another Auchinleck poem, *Als I lay in winters night*, ed. John W. Conlee, in *Middle English Debate Poetry: A Critical Anthology* (East Lansing, MI: Colleagues Press, 1991), line 377.

Sometime before the compilation of the Auchinleck manuscript, however, *Sir Tristrem* was enjoyed in the North. Although the dialect of *Sir Tristrem* is certainly Northern English rather than Scottish,[16] we should not rule out the possibility that there once existed an older, Scottish, version of the romance. Narratives in very similar stanza forms are found in Scots,[17] and *Sir Tristrem* is attributed in the prologue to the legendary Scottish poet Thomas of Erceldoun:

> I was at Ertheldoun
> With Tomas spak Y thare.
> ...
> Tomas telles in toun
> This aventours as thai ware. (1–2, 10–11)

Higgins supports her hypothesis that Mannyng had read *Sir Tristrem* in the Auchinleck manuscript with reference to a much-cited passage from Robert Mannyng's *Chronicle*. The passage, which is not easy to understand, is worth quoting at length, since it sheds light on the performance of Middle English narrative and on the associations of particular stanza forms.

> I mad noght for no disours,
> Ne for no seggers, no harpours,
> Bot for the luf of simple men
> That strange Inglis can not ken.
> For many it ere that strange Inglis
> in ryme wate never what it is [...]
> If it were made in ryme couwee
> or in strangere or enterlace,
> that rede Englis it ere inowe
> that couth not haf coppled a kowe,
> that outhere in couwee or in baston,
> Som suld have ben fordon,
> so that fele men that it herde
> suld not wite how that it ferde.
> I see in song, in sedgeyng tale
> of Erceldoun & of Kendale;
> Non tham says as thai tham wroght,
> & in ther sayng it semes noght.
> That may thou here in Sir Tristrem,

16 Angus McIntosh, 'Is *Sir Tristrem* an English or a Scottish Poem?', in '*In Other Words': Transcultural Studies in Philology, Translation, and Lexicology Presented to Hans Heinrich Meier on the Occasion of His Sixty-Fifth Birthday*, ed. J. Lachlan Mackenzie and Richard Todd (Dordrecht: Foris, 1989), pp. 85–95.

17 Various poems in the 'Christis Kirk' tradition such as *Peblis to the Play* have bob-and-wheel stanzas beginning *abababab*, though the wheel following the bob in these poems is just a single line. See *The Christes Kirk Tradition: Scots Poems of Folk Festivity*, ed. Allan H. MacLaine (Glasgow: Association for Scottish Literary Studies, 1996).

over alle gestes it has the steem
over alle that is or was,
if men it sayd as made Thomas.
But I here it no man so say,
That of some copple, som is away.
So thare fayre sayng here beforn
is thare trauayle nere forlorn. (75–104)[18]

(I did not write this for storytellers, neither for reciters nor for harpers, but for the love of simple people who do not know unfamiliar English. For there are many people who cannot understand the difficult English used in verse. If I had it made it in tail-rhyme or in a foreign rhyme scheme or in alternate rhyme, there are many who read in English who cannot even match the tail-line; on the other hand, if in tail-rhyme or *baston* it would have got mangled with the result that many people hearing it would not be able to follow the story. I observe this in the song and in the recitation of poems by Erceldoun and Kendal. No reciters tell the story as it was made, and in their telling it seems worthless. You can hear this in *Sir Tristrem*. It is prized above all other stories that are or ever were, if only people told it as Thomas made it. But I cannot hear anyone tell it without something going missing from a stanza. And so the effort of those who told fine narratives before us is almost completely wasted.)

Commenting on this passage, Higgins writes:

> is Mannyng speaking of our romance, and, if he is, is he speaking of the text as it appears in Auchinleck? As Joyce Coleman points out,[19] the Auchinleck *Sir Tristrem*, 'employs every one of the four varieties of strange rhyme mentioned by Mannyng … [I]t is in tail rhyme (*couwee*); its rhymes interlace (*enterlace*); and it is in stanzas (*baston*). It can also be labelled *strangere* … because it qualifies as unusual or recondite.' At lines 100–3, Mannyng speaks of some corruption of the text, as he says 'that of som copple, som is away.' The Auchinleck text of *Sir Tristrem* has five missing lines that were afterwards inserted in the same hand as the original inscription. However, it is also missing two couplets, one each in stanzas 8 and 80, and neither of those omissions is corrected by the copyist. If 'by som copple' Mannyng means couplets, the omissions he speaks of would match the deficiencies found in the Auchinleck inscription.

There are several misunderstandings here, not all of them of Higgins's own making. First of all, since Mannyng conceives of the four varieties of verse

18 *Robert Mannyng of Brunne: The Chronicle*, ed. Idella Sullens (Binghamton: State University of New York at Binghamton, 1996).

19 The reference is to Joyce Coleman, 'Strange Rhyme: Prose and Nationhood in Robert Mannyng's *Story of England*', *Speculum* 78 (2003), 1214–38. The quotation is on p. 1221.

forms he mentions as alternatives (in ryme couwee / *or* in strangere *or* enterlace, / … *or* in baston), the claim that *Sir Tristrem* exemplifies all four of these verse forms seems inherently unlikely. If we look at his terms more closely, some do not really fit the romance at all.

By *ryme couwee*, Mannyng means tail-rhyme. This is clear from other sections of *The Chronicle* which incorporate lyrical insets and proverbs in tail-rhyme. For example, a satirical song mocking the Scots after Edward III's victory at Halidon Hill is in the tail-rhyme stanza. Each couplet (with feminine ending) plus the following tail-line (masculine) is set out in the earliest manuscript (London, Inner Temple Library, MS Petyt 511, vol. 7) as a single long line, but the use of the punctus marks them out as distinct verses:

> He pikes and dikes . in length as him likes . how best it may be
> & thou has for thi piking . mykille ille lykyng . the sothe is to se
> Withoute any lesyng . alle is thi hething . fallen opon the
> For scatred er thi Scottis . & hodred in ther hottes . never thei ne the
> (II, 6600–4)

There are various other examples of inset tail-rhyme lyrics, and in every instance (cf. II, 6683, 6710, 6735, 6764, 6813, 6082), the marginal gloss 'couwe' draws attention to the verse form. *Couwe(e)* here means exactly what we mean by tail-rhyme today. Since *Sir Tristrem* is not in this form, it is doubtful that Mannyng had the Auchinleck *Sir Tristrem* in mind when mentioning poems in *ryme couwee.*

Enterlace is glossed by Mannyng's editor as a noun meaning 'intricate rhymes', but as indicated by the rhyme with *couwee* the word must be a past participle of the verb *enterlacen*, used adjectivally, and with the noun *ryme* understood.[20] *Ryme enterlacé* refers to what the French call *rimes croisées*. A fifteenth-century French handbook of rhetoric explains the term:

> Pour rimer rondealz, balades, nous trouvons *rimes entrelaissiées* comme cy:
>
> N'ai je cause
> De chanter
> Et sans cause
> Bien amer? (my italics)[21]
>
> (To rhyme rondeaux and ballades we find interlaced rhyme, as in the following: 'Have I not got good reason / to sing / and to love well / without cause?')

20 The *Middle English Dictionary* enters it as the only entry under *enterlace* adj., and glosses 'Intricate, elaborate (rimes)'.

21 *Traité de l'art de rhétorique*, in *Recueil d'arts de seconde rhétorique*, ed. E. Langlois (Paris: Imprimerie Nationale, 1902), pp. 199–213, at p. 206.

Ryme enterlacé thus means alternate rhyme (abab). Conceivably, Mannyng might have thought of the first eight lines of the stanza *Sir Tristrem* as *ryme enterlacé*, but I think it more likely that he was actually thinking of narratives in stanzas rhyming abab (or possibly abababab): there are several romances in the abab stanza form (*The Sowdone of Babylone*, the fragmentary version of *Partenope of Blois*, *The Knight of Courtesy*, and *Thomas of Erceldoune*),[22] and there is also one romance in the eight-line stanzas with alternate rhyme, *The Stanzaic Morte Arthur*.

The term *strangere*, parallel with *enterlacé*, must also be an adjective (again with *ryme* understood), rather than a noun. The *Middle English Dictionary* enters it under the noun *straunger(e)*, as the only attestation for sense (h), 'an unusual verse form, but, unless this is the adjective "strange" used in the comparative, the word probably belongs under the adjective *straunger* (from Anglo-Norman *estranger*) meaning "foreign, alien"'. By *ryme straungere*, Mannyng may have meant verse forms imported from abroad.

In the context of Mannyng's complaint that reciters miss out material, Higgins notes that some lines are missing from the Auchinleck copy of *Sir Tristrem*, but it does not follow that Mannyng was thinking of the poem in this manuscript. Mannyng's reason for writing in couplets, he says, is not just to make life easier for his audience but also to avoid lines getting lost in transmission. This is good thinking: in couplets, rhymes are never carried forward for more than one line, and the immediacy of the rhyme guards against accidental omission of verse units. In a more complicated rhyme scheme, such as that of *Tristrem*, where each stanza begins abababab, it is easier for a scribe, let alone a performing minstrel, to miss out lines from a stanza, and this is exactly what happened in the two defective stanzas of *Sir Tristrem* (87–98 and 870–80), where one of the four *ab* sequences has been omitted. Incidentally, when Mannyng writes that 'I here it no man so say, / That of some copple, som is away', he is not saying that some couplets are missing, but that something is missing from some *stanza*. As noted by Coleman,[23] in accordance with medieval French usage, 'copple' means strophe, not couplet. The word is also used in this sense in King James's *Kingis Quair*, which uses exactly one rhyme-royal stanza to relay the content of the bird song overheard by the lover, and announces this in the preceding stanza: 'the text / Ryght of their song' is given in 'the *copill* next' (230–1; italics mine).[24]

The two other phrases that are difficult in the passage from Mannyng are 'that couth not haf coppled a kowe' and 'baston'. The word 'kowe' probably refers to a tail-line; and 'coupling a tail-line' perhaps means completing the

[22] See Judith Jefferson, Ad Putter and Donka Minkova, 'Perfect and Imperfect Rhyme: Romances in the *abab* Tradition', *SP* 111 (2014), 631–51.

[23] Coleman, 'Strange Rhyme', p. 1221.

[24] *Fifteenth-Century Dream Visions: An Anthology*, ed. Julia Boffey (Oxford: OUP, 2003).

tail-rhyme with its corresponding rhyme fellow. *Baston* is glossed as 'stanza' by Coleman and Higgins, but since it stands in contrast to *ryme couwee* this cannot be correct. Possibly it here refers to a poetry written in anisometric stanzas. This appears to be the sense of the word in the Kildare poem 'Hail, Seint Michel with the lange sper!',[25] which is written in this form and which repeatedly refers to itself as a *baston*. For instance:

> Hail be ye bochers, with yur bole-ax!
> Fair beth yur barmhatres, yolow beth yur fax.
> Ye stondith at the schamil, brod ferlich bernes,
> Fleis yow folowith, ye swolowith ynow.
> The best[e] clerk of al this tun
> Craftfullich maked this bastun. (85–90)

> (Hail to you butchers with your large axe. Your aprons are beautiful, and your hair is yellow. You stand at your stall, large, intimidating men. Flies follow you, and you swallow plenty of them. The best clerk of this place artfully made this *baston*.)

In this poem, the first four lines of the stanza seem to be in four-beat strong-stress metre, while the last two lines of the concluding wheel are in iambic tetrameter. In *Somer Soneday*, the word *baston* is also used. The poet is worried about writing 'bastons' (48) about Lady Fortune since this could cause him grief, but nevertheless agrees to give it a go.[26] Significantly, the poem is in the thirteen-line alliterative bob-and-wheel stanza, so again the sense 'verse in stanzas with wheels' is possible, though conceivably the word here simply means 'verse', as Turville-Petre glosses it. This is what the word meant in Middle French – see, for instance, 'Si dois savoir que un chascun rondel atout le moins doit contenir cinq bastons' ('you should know that every roundel must at the very least contain five verse lines'[27]) – and it occurs, in this broader sense, in *Cursor Mundi*, which switches from short couplets to septenaries (grouped in stanzas rhyming *aaaa*) to tell of Christ's passion. The switch is deliberate, as the poet says: 'Es resun that wee vr rime rume / And set fra nu langer bastun' (14922–3).[28]

It is striking that, in his discussion of the kinds of poems that 'disours' corrupt and that confuse uneducated people, Mannyng does not refer to written

[25] The poem is entitled 'Satire' in the recent edition of the poem by Thorlac Turville-Petre, *Poems from BL MS Harley 913: 'The Kildare Manuscript'*, EETS o.s. 345 (Oxford: OUP, 2015), from which my quotation is taken. The emendation 'best[e]' is mine.

[26] *Somer Soneday*, ed. Thorlac Turville-Petre, *Alliterative Poetry of the Later Middle Ages: An Anthology* (London: Routledge, 1989).

[27] Jacques Legrand, *Archiloge Sophie, Livre de bonnes meurs*, ed. Evencio Beltran (Paris, 1986), p. 143.

[28] *Cursor Mundi*, ed. Richard Morris, 7 vols, EETS o.s. 57, 59, 62, 66, 68, 99, 101 (London: OUP, 1874–93), III.

texts.[29] The corrupt versions of the story he refers to are ones he has heard tell: 'Non tham *says* as thai tham wroght', and the original compositions too are conceived of as oral texts: 'So thare fayre *sayng* here beforn / is ... nere forlorn'. As far as the transmission of these 'sayings' is concerned, Mannyng envisages either recitation by 'seggers' or singing by 'harpours'. This also applies to *Sir Tristrem*, which Mannyng assumes his audience know 'in song, in sedgeyng tale' ('sedgeyng tale' being the kind of story that 'seggers' tell). The popularity of *Sir Tristrem* and Mannyng's own knowledge of it are thus to be explained not by the written testimony of the Auchinleck manuscript, but by the oral transmission of storytellers and singers.

The coincidence that the stanza form of *Sir Tristrem* also occurs in one of Laurence Minot's political poems similarly demands another explanation than the one Higgins provides. Angus McIntosh, who first noticed this coincidence, thought that it reflected 'a single locally restricted tradition, in which this verse form was current in the earlier part of the fourteenth century'.[30] Applying Occam's razor, Higgins argues that Minot encountered the form in *Sir Tristrem*, and sees this as further evidence that the manuscript was in the North of England soon after it was made: 'It is interesting – and perhaps significant – that Minot's poem is the only instance we have other than *Sir Tristrem* of this eleven-line form, and that Minot's poem was composed in Yorkshire less than a decade after the only text that now survives of *Sir Tristrem* was copied into the Auchinleck manuscript' (pp. 119–20).

However, the eleven-line stanza with an octave in alternate rhyme and a bob in the ninth line is more widespread than Higgins and McIntosh believed.[31] It occurs also in Mary's Lament in the Towneley Play of the Crucifixion, as becomes clear once we lay out what some editors present as four septenaries (rhyming aaaa) as an octave rhyming abababab, followed by the bob-and-wheel:

> Alas! may euer be my sang
> Whyls I may lyf in leyd;
> Me thynk now that I lyf to lang
> To se my barne thus blede;
> Iue`s wyrke with hym all wrang
> Wherfor do thay this dede?
> Lo, so hy thay haue hym hang

[29] In his other reference to a Middle English romance, the story of *Havelok*, he also refers to oral stories that 'lowed men vpon English tellis' (II, 528), and that 'men redes yit in ryme' (II, 533), meaning 'men still recite in verse'. See Nancy Mason Bradbury, *Writing Aloud: Storytelling in Middle English* (Urbana: University of Illinois Press, 1998), pp. 68–9.

[30] McIntosh, 'Is *Sir Tristrem* an English or a Scottish Poem?', p. 92.

[31] See Ad Putter, 'The Metres and Stanza Forms of Popular Romance', in *A Companion to Medieval Popular Romance*, ed. Radulescu and Rushton, pp. 111–31.

thay let for no drede:
  Whi so?
Hs fomen is he emang?
No freynde he has, bot fo. (406–11)[32]

The same stanza form is found in the *Alphabetical Praise of Women* (also extant in the Auchinleck manuscript), as this stanza demonstrates:

Harpe no fithel no sautri,
Noither with eld no with yong,
Is non so swete to sitten by
Al wiman, ther thai speke with tong.
Her speche resteth a man wel ney
Bitvene his liuer & his long,
That doth his hert rise on hey,
So clot that lith in clay yclong
  So sore:
Who that lacketh wiman in lore,
Y rede, he do no more. (68–78)[33]

By a lucky coincidence the source for the Middle English poem also survives: it is the *ABC a femmes*, preserved in MS Harley 2253. The original is courtlier than the English adaptation,[34] but the stanza form is the same:

Harpe n'autre menestrausie,
Ne oysel que chaunt u boys,
Ne sount si noble melodie
Come de femme oyr la vois.
Mout purrad mener sure vie
Que de femme puet aver choys,
Quar a tous biens femme plye,
Come fet la coudre que porte noys
  E foyl.
Qui bealté plaunta en femme
Molt chosy noble soyl. (100–10)

32 Cited from the edition by G. England and A. W. Pollard, *The Towneley Plays*, EETS e.s. 71 (London: Trübner, 1897), which has the layout in septenaries. The lines are laid out in the eleven-line stanza in the more recent edition by Martin Stevens and A. C. Cawley, EETS s.s. 13–14 (Oxford: OUP, 1994).

33 Quoted from the online edition of the Auchinleck manuscript by David Burnley and Alison Wiggins, at https://auchinleck.nls.uk/. The last three lines normally rhyme cdc, not ccc, as in this example.

34 For discussion see Oliver Pickering, 'Stanzaic Verse in the Auchinleck Manuscript: *The Alphabetical Praise of Women*', in *Studies in Late Medieval and Early Renaissance Texts in Honour of John Scattergood*, ed. Anne Marie D'Arcy and Alan J. Fletcher (Dublin: Four Courts Press, 2005), pp. 287–304.

(Harp nor any other instrument, / Nor bird singing in the woods, / Sounds so noble a melody / As one hears in a woman's voice. / He might lead a very secure life / Whoever can take his choice of women, / For women incline toward all good things, / As does the hazel tree that bears nuts /And leaves. / He who planted beauty in women / Chose a very noble soil.)[35]

Both lyrics, the *Alphabetical Praise of Women* and *ABC a femmes*, are probably from the West Midlands. MS Harley 2253 was copied there, and the alliterative diction of the Middle English version is also characteristic of poetry from this region. Various other imports from the West Midlands also found their way into the Auchinleck manuscript.[36]

There is thus no secure basis for positing a direct connection between Minot's poem and *Sir Tristrem*. The stanza form evidently had a more widespread circulation, in Yorkshire and in the West Midlands, and a more likely connection between the various poems in this stanza form is the possibility that they were meant for singing. Minot's poems are generally assumed to be 'political songs',[37] and Minot himself speaks as a 'disour': 'Minot with mowth had menid to make / suth sawes [...] War mi sorow slaked, sune wald I sing, / when God will sir Edward sal us bute bring' (V, 1–2, 5–6).[38] The manuscript of the *Towneley Cycle* has repeated stage instructions calling for music and singing,[39] and, while Mary's *planctus* is not explicitly marked as requiring music, there may be some hints to this effect in Mary's own words – 'Alas! may euer be my sang' (406), and 'Sore syghyng is my sang' (429) – though the expression may only be figurative. As the above-cited stanzas from the Anglo-Norman *ABC a femmes* and the Middle English version show, music is central to their world of reference, and Ruth Dean and Maureen Boulton describe the form of the *ABC a femmes* as one 'that seems to call for singing to the accompaniment of a stringed instrument'.[40]

In forming this impression, Dean and Boulton were perhaps influenced by the fact that bobs are strongly associated with a genre of poems

35 *The Complete Harley 2253 Manuscript*, ed. and trans. Susanna Fein, TEAMS (Kalamazoo, MI: Medieval Institute, 2014), 2 vols.

36 See Susanna Fein, 'The Fillers of the Auchinleck Manuscript and the Literary Culture of the West Midlands', in *Makers and Users of Medieval Books: Essays in Honour of A. S. G. Edwards*, ed. Carol Meale and Derek Pearsall (Cambridge: D. S. Brewer, 2014), pp. 60–77.

37 Albert Baugh and Kemp Malone, *The Literary History of England*, vol. 1: *The Middle Ages (to 1500)* (London: Routledge, 1967), p. 222.

38 *The Poems of Laurence Minot*, ed. Richard Osberg, TEAMS (Kalamazoo, MI: Medieval Institute, 1996).

39 Richard Rastall, *Minstrels Playing Music in Early English Religious Drama*, vol. II (Cambridge: D. S. Brewer, 2001), pp. 143–85.

40 Ruth Dean and Maureen Boulton, *Anglo-Norman Literature: A Guide to Texts and Manuscripts*, Anglo-Norman Text Society (London: Birkbeck College, 1999), p. 155.

of unquestionable musical pedigree: the medieval carol.[41] To illustrate the characteristic carol form, I cite below the first stanza of the Middle English carol 'Ah man, assay', for which the musical notation survives in Bodl. MS Arch. Selden B.26. Carols begin with a burden (here italicised), which is then repeated at the end of all stanzas:

> *Ah man assay, assay,*
> *and ask mercy while thou may.*
>
> Man have in mind how here before
> For thy misdeed thou were forlore.
> But mercy to give now Christ is bore;
> Assay.
> *Ah man assay, assay,*
> *and ask mercy while thou may.*[42]

The format of the carol, with an initial burden that is to be repeated at the end of every stanza, makes the metrical function of the bob very clear. The bob marks the end of the stanza by introducing a new rhyme sound, and since this rhyme sound is the same as that of the burden, the bob reminds all listeners that it is time to sing the burden. In the manuscript of this carol, as in others,[43] the bob is marked with the word *chorus*, suggesting that in carols the bob also marks the transition between solo singing and group singing. Possibly, as John Stevens suggests, the bob was to be sung twice, first by the solo singer, then by everybody.[44] In the context of Stevens's hypothesis, it is perhaps noteworthy that the word 'bob' is first attested in English (in 1606) in the phrase 'to bear the bob', meaning 'to take up the refrain'.[45]

Returning now to *Sir Tristrem*, there seems to me no good reason to doubt Robert Mannyng's claim that it was heard in 'song'. There is no surviving music, it is true, but the poem is in a form that has musical associations. The romance also makes singing central to the story. Its hero, is, like Sir Orfeo and King Horn, renowned for his harp-playing. In one episode of the romance he competes with and outclasses a professional minstrel (551–72); and he also teaches Ysonde the finer points of storytelling:

[41] E. G. Stanley lists poems with bobs in his appendix to 'The Use of Bob-Lines in *Sir Thopas*', *NM* 73 (1972), 417–26. Although many are carols, it should be said that not all poems with bobs are likely to have been sung, *Sir Gawain and the Green Knight* being an obvious example.

[42] Cited from the edition by John Stevens, *Mediaeval Carols*, Musica Britannica IV (London: Stainer and Bell, 1952), no. 17 (p. 12).

[43] Stevens, *Mediaeval Carols*, no. 18 (pp. 12–13).

[44] Stevens, *Mediaeval Carols*, p. 117.

[45] See *OED* s.v. *bob*, n.1, sense 10.

Ysonde he dede understand
What alle playes were
In lay. (1283–5)

Here 'playes' has the sense of 'stories told for entertainment' (see *MED* s.v. plei(e, 6. (c)), while 'in lay' probably means 'in song'.[46] Tristrem, that is, teaches Ysonde his repertoire of stories with their musical setting.

If we wanted to reconstruct what *Sir Tristrem* may have sounded like 'in song', we would need to look for melodies of texts in a comparable form that do survive with music. The practice of 'borrowing tunes' was quite normal in medieval England, where as we know many medieval secular lyrics were sung to the tune of religious songs (and vice versa).[47] The music of narrative texts could also be adopted for other kinds of texts in the same form, crossing generic boundaries. Although no music survives for any Middle English romance, we do have the tune for 'Greysteil', probably a reference to the Scottish couplet romance *Eger and Grime* ('Greysteel' being the name of the hero's fearsome opponent). The melody, according to the musicologist John Purser who transcribed the tune, 'is not an instrumental one. It [shows] the kind of repetition that represents sung syllables'.[48] There is documentary evidence of *Eger and Grime* being sung to King James IV in 1497 by two fiddlers,[49] and we also know that its tune was adopted for a different kind of text-type: a political song. A seventeenth-century song (also in couplets) mocking the Marquis of Argyle bears the instruction 'to be sung according to Old *Gray Steel*'.[50] Anyone interested in hearing *Eger and Grime* as James IV heard it, in sung form, should listen to the CD recording by Andy Hunter and others.[51]

Notwithstanding their use of bob-lines, Middle English carols offer no suitable models for the stanza form of *Sir Tristrem*. Among texts with surviving music, the closest parallels for the *Tristrem* stanza that I have been able to

46 It is glossed as such by Alan Lupack.

47 For examples and discussion see *The Lyrics of the Red Book of Ossory*, ed. Richard Leighton Green (Oxford: Medium Ævum, 1974).

48 John Purser, 'Greysteil', in *Stewart Style 1513–1542*, ed. Janet Hadley Williams (East Linton: Tuckwell Press, 1996), pp. 142–52, at p. 146.

49 *Eger and Grime*, ed. James Ralston Caldwell (Cambridge, MA: Harvard University Press, 1933), p. 6.

50 Mentioned by Caldwell, in *Eger and Grime*, p. 12, who in turn cites David Laing (*Early Metrical Tales* (Edinburgh, 1826), p. xiv), but neither gives the primary source. This source must be *An Brief Explanation of the Life, or a Prophicy of the Death of the Marquess Argyle* (accessible at Early English Books Online: http://gateway.proquest.com/openurl?ctx_ver=Z39.88-2003&res_id=xri:eebo&rft_id=xri:eebo:image:175780, though the quotation that Caldwell and Laing give from it does not correspond with the actual words of the original, which are as I have given them.

51 *Graysteil: Music from the Middle Ages and Renaissance Scotland*, ed. Andy Hunter et al. (Dorian Discovery, 1997).

find are the lyrics of the trouvère Vidame de Chartres (d. 1204). Vidame also writes stanzas that make use of a short line to segue into the cauda.[52] In the following example, this short line (four syllables) is part of a refrain (here italicised) that returns at the end of all six stanzas:

> Tant ai d'amors qu'en chantant m'estuet plaindre
> Ce m'est avis, en estrange maniere:
> Por ce cuidai a bone amor ataindre
> La ou je n'os faire altre proiere
> Et des paors est ce la more graindre
> Que nel sachent cele gent noveliere
> Qui adès font la bone ore remaindre,
> Et les amans traient toz jors ariere
>   *De joie avoir*
> *Merci, dame, que j'ai el mont plus chiere,*
>   *Sens decevoir.*[53]

> (I am so much in love that I have to complain in song, in a strange manner, as it seems to me. Through this I hope to attain success in love there where I don't dare to make any other kind of request. And this is my greatest worry that the new-fangled people should not know of this, for they invariably set back the moment of opportunity and always impede lovers from getting any joy. Have pity, my lady, whom I love most in this world, without deceiving.)

In *Li plus desconfortez du mont* the short line is not itself part of the refrain but announces its arrival. Below is the first stanza:

> Li plus desconfortez du mont
> Sui, et si chant comme envoisiez.
> Ne ja Deu joie ne me dont
> De la dont je vueil estre liez,
> S'uns autres n'en furst enragiez.
> Mes ma loiauté me confont;
> Or voi bien que li amant sont
>   Mort et traï.
> *Q'a guerredon ai failli*
> *Pour ce que trop ai servi.*[54]

52 See K. A. Noonan, 'Notes on the Structure of Two Old French Courtly Lyrics', *MÆ* 3 (1934), 124–35.

53 *Les chansonniers des troubadours et des trouvères: le chansonnier Cangé*, ed. Jean Beck (vol. 1, facsimile of Paris, Bibliothèque nationale, MS fr. 846; vol. 2, edition with modern transcription of the music) (Paris: Champion, 1927), no. 336 (p. 312).

54 *Les Poésies de Thibaut de Blaison*, ed. Terence Newcombe (Geneva: Droz, 1978), no. XV (pp. 131–5), with modern transcription of the music on p. 152.

(The most disconsolate man in the world I am, and yet I sing as if I were happy. Never does God give me what would make me happy without another person being enraged by it. But my loyalty confounds me. So I see well that lovers are doomed and betrayed. Because I have failed to obtain the reward for which I have served so much.)

Unfortunately, neither of these lyrics provides a close enough match for the *Tristrem* stanza to make them usable as *contrafacta* for the Middle English poem. In terms of rhyme scheme, *Tant ai d'amors* is identical (abababababcbc), but the ten-syllable lines of the octave are longer than the three-beat octave lines of *Sir Tristrem*, and the last line of *Tant ai d'amors* is as short as the ninth. *Li plus desconfortez du mont*, on the other hand, has shorter lines in the frons (eight syllables) and in the last line of the stanza (seven), but is in a ten-line stanza with a different rhyme scheme (ababbaaccc). My search for melodies to which *Sir Tristrem* might be sung has not come up with anything suitable yet.

Can any other Middle English romance help us to make the leap from written text to oral performance? The opening lines of *King Horn* –

Alle beon he blithe
That to my song lythe!
A sang ich schal you singe
Of Murry the Kinge (1–4)[55]

– suggest that the romance was sung to a listening audience, and there is certainly good evidence that the romance was transmitted from memory before the date of the earliest surviving manuscript, CUL MS Gg. 4. 27. We know this from the kinds of errors that occur in this copy of the romance. These are not just the kinds of local variation and errors, such as eye-skip or mistaken anticipation of copy, that is, errors prompted by text in the immediate vicinity of the lines the scribe is copying, but include mistakes resulting from the workings of memory. The clearest examples of memorial errors involve the interference of episodes that are remote from each other in the written text but that are similar in content. When a person recites a poem from memory the similarity of episodes often causes a memory loop whereby lines from one episode are miscued and accidentally transferred to the other.[56] In his study of the oral transmission of Middle English romances, Murray McGillivray

[55] *King Horn, Floris and Blancheflur, The Assumption of Our Lady*, ed. George McKnight, EETS o.s. 14 (London: OUP, 1901).

[56] David C. Rubin, *Memory in Oral Traditions: The Cognitive Psychology of Epic, Ballads, and Counting-Out Rhymes* (New York: OUP, 1995), p. 155. See also Demelza Jayne Curnow, 'Five Case Studies on the Transmission of Popular Middle English Verse Romances' (unpublished PhD dissertation, University of Bristol, 2002), which demonstrates errors of memory in *Eger and Grime* and a number of Percy Folio romances.

calls this phenomenon 'memorial transfer', and he finds various convincing examples in *Floris and Blancheflur* and in *King Horn*.[57]

A good example is the preamble to Horn's announcement of a 'tale' (in which he will reveal his identity). There are three manuscript witnesses. In Bodl. MS Laud Misc. 108 (and with minor variants in BL MS Harley 2253), the episode reads as follows:

> Horn set him in chayere
> & bed hem alle yhere
> he seyde kyng of londe
> mi tale þou vnderstonde
> Ich was ybore in sudenne ... (1271–5)

Gg. 4. 27, however, is radically different:

> Horn sat on chaere
> & bad hem alle ihere
> *'King', he sede, 'þu luste*
> *A tale mid þe beste;*
> I ne seie hit for no blame,
> Horn is mi name ...' (1261–6)

The italicised lines have been repeated from an earlier passage that occurs in all three manuscripts in substantially the same form:

> Aþelbrus also swiþe
> Wente to halle bliue
> *'Kyng', he sede, 'þu leste*
> *A tale mid þe beste;*
> Þu schalt bere crune
> Tomoroȝe in this tune ...' (MS Gg. 4. 27, lines 471–6)

The *tale* at this point refers to Athelbrus's proposition that King Aylmer should knight Horn. It is hard to explain such cross-contamination between episodes that are far removed from each other in the physical exemplar as scribal error. Rather, what seems to have happened is that a similarity between episodes (the protagonist narrates his 'tale' to the king) has accidentally cued lines from one episode for the other: the error is a 'slip of memory'.

Although oral performances of the kind alluded to by Mannyng and by the opening lines of *Horn* are by their nature ephemeral, written texts do sometimes provide traces that they were previously stored in human memories. In the case of *Horn* and *Floris and Blancheflur* such traces are numerous, and tell

[57] Murray McGillivray, *Memorization in the Transmission of the Middle English Romances* (New York: Garland, 1990). This paragraph, including quotations from the manuscript version of *King Horn*, is based on pp. 63–5 of McGillivray's book. On memorial transmission see also Rhiannon Purdie's essay in this collection, especially pp. 15–18, 27–8.

against the view that 'the three manuscripts [go] back to a single original from which all surviving copies can be shown to be derived by the usual processes of scribal corruption'.[58]

The romance of *Bevis of Hampton* similarly describes itself as a 'song', and in so doing hints at a sound-world for narrative poetry that we no longer inhabit:

> Lordingis, lystenyth to me tale!
> That is meriour than the nyghtingale,
> That I wolle yow synge;
> Of a knyght, Sir Beuon,
> That was bore in Southhampton,
> Withouten lesyng. (1–6)[59]

I have seen it argued that 'sing' does not need to mean 'sing' when poets say it,[60] but in this case the comparison of the 'tale' with the song of the nightingale makes no sense at all unless the audience for which these lines were originally written heard music. Such 'minstrel introductions' may have become conventions of the genre, of course, but this is unlikely to apply to the opening lines of *Horn* and *Bevis* for the simple reason that they are the earliest Middle English narratives to be saying this.

It needs to be remembered that both *Horn* and *Bevis* go back to Anglo-Norman *chansons de geste*, composed in *laisses* (lines gathered in strophes based on final assonance).[61] Evidence of the singing of verse in the laisse form is abundant. There are surviving melodies for *chansons de geste* and saints' lives in the laisse form,[62] along with various references to the music of *chansons de geste*. Most relevant to *Bevis* is the remark by the troubadour Guiraut del Luc that his lyric *Ges sitot m'ai ma voluntat fellona* (c. 1190) is set to the tune of Bevis of Hampton (*el son Beves d'Antona*).[63]

Neither the Anglo-Norman *Horn* nor *Boeve,* however, survives with music, nor do they in their prologues announce themselves as songs. In both cases,

58 Pearsall, 'The Auchinleck Manuscript Forty Years On', p. 22.

59 *Sir Bevis of Hampton*, ed. Jennifer Fellows, 2 vols, EETS o.s. 349, 350 (Oxford: OUP, 2017). Citations are from the Naples manuscript (Naples, Bibliotheca Nazionale, MS XIII.B.29).

60 See A. C. Spearing, *Textual Subjectivity* (Cambridge: CUP, 2005), p. 38; and my discussion in 'Metres and Stanza Forms of Popular Romance', p. 116.

61 Marianne Ailes, 'The Anglo-Norman *Boeve de Haumtone* as a Chanson de Geste', in *Sir Beves of Hampton in Literary Tradition*, ed. Jennifer Fellows and Ivana Djordjević (Cambridge: D. S. Brewer, 2008), pp. 9–24.

62 John Stevens, *Words and Music in the Middle Ages* (Cambridge: CUP, 1986), pp. 222–38.

63 Friedrich Gennrich, *Die Musikalische Vortrag der altfranzözischen Chansons de geste* (Halle: Niemeyer, 1923), p. 9.

the 'I' says he will *speak* (*dire*).[64] The Middle English poets thus departed from their sources when using 'sing' instead. In another respect, too, they departed from their sources, and this brings us back to the question of verse form. The *laisse* form (groups of lines with the same syllable count all ending in the same sound) lends itself to the French language, but it is impossible in English. If the Middle English wanted their 'gestes' to be sung, they would have needed to find an appropriate melodic form that could work in English. As Rhiannon Purdie has argued,[65] in the case of *Bevis* the poet appears to have borrowed the form from the Anglo-Norman *Vie de Thomas Becket* (c. 1185) by Beneit, monk of St Albans, who probably wrote his saint's life to be recited or chanted to the monastic community at mealtime.[66] The first stanza reads:

Al Deu loenge e sun servise
Par la grace ke m'ad tramise
  Voil chaunter
De celuy ke sanz feyntise
Se combati pur seinte Eglise
  Avauncier. (1–6)[67]

(In God's praise and service, through the grace which he has given me, I want to sing about him who incessantly fought to advance Holy Church.)

The stanza form of the French poem, *aabaab*, with tail-lines of four syllables and couplet lines of eight, has been transposed in *Bevis* into the English accentual equivalent, couplet lines of four beats and tail-lines of two.[68] In addition to the formal connections, there are many other connections between

[64] The Anglo-Norman *Horn*, ed. Mildred K. Pope, *The Romance of Horn by Thomas*, 2 vols (Oxford: Anglo-Norman Text Society, 1955, 1964), begins 'Seignurs, oi avez le[s] vers del parchemin, / Cum li bers Aaluf est venuz a sa fin. / Mestre Thomas ne volt k'il seit mis a declin / K'il ne die de Horn, le vaillant orphanin' ('Lords, you have heard the verses from the parchment, how the baron Aluf met his end. Master Thomas does not want his own life to draw to an end before he has spoken of Horn, the brave orphan'); and the Anglo-Norman *Boeve*, ed. Albert Stimming (Halle: Niemeyer, 1899), begins 'Seignurs barons, ore entendez a mei / si ws dirrai gestes, que jeo diverses sai, de Boefs de Haumtone, li chevaler curtays ('Lord barons, now listen to me, and I will tell you the deeds, of which I know a great many, of Bevis of Hampton, the courteous knight').

[65] Rhiannon Purdie, *Anglicising Romance: Tail-Rhyme and Genre in Medieval English Literature* (Cambridge: D. S. Brewer, 2008), p. 45.

[66] Ian Short, 'The Patronage of Beneit's *Vie de Thomas Becket*', *MÆ* 56 (1987), 239–56.

[67] *La Vie de Thomas Becket par Beneit*, ed. Börje Schlyter (Lund: Gleerup, 1941).

[68] The tail-rhyme form gives way to plain couplets at line 520, probably in response to a change of form in the original Anglo-Norman, which shifts from short mono-rhymed laisses to longer assonanced laisses at roughly the same point in the narrative. See Ivana Djordjević, 'Versification and Translation in *Sir Beves of Hampton*', *MÆ* 74 (2005), 41–59.

the poems in terms of phrasing and content.[69] However, possibly the most important link between *Bevis* and Beneit's *Vie de Thomas Becket* is one that is now missing: they may once have shared the same melody.

Sadly, we do not have the music of Beneit's *Vie*, but in the case of tail-rhyme narratives it is possible to recover something of the lost soundscape of medieval romances by looking at tail-rhyme texts for which we do have the music. One possible model is the roughly contemporary play of the Raising of Lazarus from Orléans, Bibliothèque municipale, MS 201, better known as the Fleury Playbook (c. 1200).[70] This contains a number of Latin plays that were evidently meant for singing, since they are provided with melodies. Some of the plays are strophic, with a single melody to be repeated with minor variation for each of the stanzas. The Raising of Lazarus play, *Versus de resusciatione Lazari*, is in tail-rhyme. The stanza form is illustrated by the first stanza below:

> Tu dignare per immundiciam
> mee carnis tuam potenciam
>   declarare;
> nobis optatum dones gaudium
> et digneris nostrum hospicium
>   subintrahare. (1–6)

> (May you deign to show forth your power through the impurity of my flesh. May you give us our hoped-for joy, and may you deign to enter our lodging.)

Like *Bevis* and Beneit's *Vie*, the tail-lines are short (four syllables), although the couplets are a little longer (ten rather than eight syllables, as in Beneit's *Vie*). The melody is shown on the next page (musical example 4.1).[71] The play consists of fifty-four tail-rhyme stanzas, confounding the modern idea that hearing the same melody repeated many times over would be monotonous. The prejudice against the sung performance of narrative was not one shared by medieval audiences.[72]

Another possible model, closer to home, is that of the Middle English song *Ar ne kuth ich sorghe non*. This song and its immediate Anglo-Norman source, the Prisoner's Lament (*Eyns ne soy ke pleynte fu*), go back to Mary's *Planctus ante nescia*, attributed to Godfrey of St. Victor. The musical form of *Ar ne kuth* is modelled on that of the Latin sequence, with a different rhyme

[69] Purdie, *Anglicising Romance*, pp. 45–7.

[70] A complete edition of the play with music (in medieval notation) can be found in Edmond de Coussemaker, *Drames liturgiques du Moyen Âge: texte et musique* (Paris: Didron, 1860), pp. 223–34.

[71] Based on the transcription by John Stevens, *Words and Music*, p. 260.

[72] Cf. Stevens, *Words and Music*, pp. 266–7.

4.1 Reconstructed musical phrase from *Versus de resusciatione Lazari.*

scheme and melody for each strophe. The first stanza, however, is quite clearly a tail-rhyme stanza:

> Ar ne kuth ich sorge non,
> nu ich moot imane mi mon;
>   karful, wel sore ich siche.
> Geltles, tholich muchel schame;
> help, God, for thi sweete name,
>   king of hevene riche. (1–6)

> (Once I knew no sorrow, now I must mournfully make my complaint; full of cares, I sigh sorely. Without guilt I endure much shame; help me, God, for your sweet name, king of heaven's realm.)

Since the music survives, this lyric gives us some idea of what an English tail-line stanza may have sounded like:[73]

[73] My edition, based on Helen Deeming's transcription in *Songs in British Sources, c. 1150–1300*, Musica Britannica 95 (London: Stainer and Bell, 2013), no. 92b (pp. 136–7), but with the text as edited by E. J. Dobson and F. Ll. Harrison (eds), *Medieval*

4.2 Reconstructed musical phrase from *Ar ne kuth ich sorghe non.*

Although the tail-lines are longer than those of *Bevis* and Beneit's *Vie*, the melody can easily be fitted to the text of *Bevis*. I have tried and tested it by singing a section of *Bevis* to this melody, accompanied on the rebec by Frances Eustace.[74]

In conclusion, there is strong external evidence for the musical performance of medieval romances by minstrels, and this evidence is consistent with the internal evidence of the romances themselves. A number of these romances show signs of having been transmitted from memory, and some of them, such as *King Horn* and *Bevis*, call themselves songs. Although these 'minstrel tags' are often dismissed as literary conventions, the affinity of medieval romances with medieval song is borne out by the striking fact that they use the same stanza forms. If we want to experience medieval romance as, for example, Mannyng had experienced it, 'in song', the melodies of medieval lyrics and plays that do survive with music may offer us some clues to the vanished sound-world of medieval romance.

English Songs (London: Faber, 1979), no. 4 (ii) (p. 110). I have used slur lines to indicate multiple notes covering a single linguistic syllable.

74 There is a recording on the double CD, *Performing Middle English Romance*, Linda Zaerr et al. (Chaucer Studio, 2015).

5

Deluxe Copies of Middle English Romance: Scribes and Book Artists

Carol M. Meale

I am going to begin with a statistic. Of the ninety plus manuscripts of Middle English romances that survive from the thirteenth century to 1500, only five are illustrated. One dates probably from the early 1330s, one from c. 1400 and three from the fifteenth century. The second of these, containing *Sir Gawain and the Green Knight*, will not be considered in this essay. Its illustrations are so problematic of interpretation that it deserves to have an entire essay devoted to it.[1] This omission leaves, from the fourteenth century, the Auchinleck manuscript, NLS Advocates MS 19.2.1, with its eighteen romances;[2] from the early fifteenth, the portion of Bodl. MS 264, containing the alliterative *Alexander B*;[3] New York, Pierpont Morgan Library MS M 876 with its copy of the couplet *Generides*;[4] and, from the latter part of the century, BL Harley MS 326, containing the prose romance of *The Three Kings' Sons*.[5] There are many questions that these survivals raise, of which the most significant is that of production in relation to patronage and commissioning. That is, there is every sign that these were bespoke productions, specially commissioned for

1 See Kathleen L. Scott, *Later Gothic Manuscripts, 1390–1490*, A Survey of Manuscripts Illuminated in the British Isles, 8, 2 vols (London: Miller, 1996), 2, 66–8, cat. no. 12; also Maidie Hilmo, 'The Power of Images in the Auchinleck, Vernon, *Pearl*, and Two *Piers Plowman* Manuscripts', in *Opening Up Middle English Manuscripts: Literary and Visual Approaches*, ed. Kathryn Kerby-Fulton, Maidie Hilmo and Linda Olsen (Ithaca, NY: Cornell University Press, 2012), pp. 185–9.

2 *The Auchinleck Manuscript*, ed. David Burnley and Alison Wiggins (Edinburgh, 2003), http://auchinleck.nls.uk; and *The Auchinleck Manuscript: National Library of Scotland Advocates' MS. 19.2.1*, ed. Derek Pearsall and I. C. Cunningham (London: Scolar Press, 1977). Both of these reproductions have been used in the writing of this essay.

3 *The Romance of Alexander: A Collotype Facsimile of MS Bodley 264*, intro. M. R. James (Oxford: Clarendon Press, 1933).

4 *A Royal Historie of the Excellent Knight Generides*, ed. Frederick J. Furnivall, Roxburghe Club, 83 (London, 1865; repr. New York, 1971).

5 *The Three Kings' Sons*, ed. F. J. Furnivall, EETS e.s. 67 (London, 1895).

patrons willing to pay the price for one-off, high-end copies of romances. So, the questions which lead on from this are, first: is it possible to tell where the manuscripts were made and for whom? And why are there so few of them that were either made or which survive?

The exceptional nature of Auchinleck in regard to the production of vernacular narrative manuscripts in London in the early decades of the fourteenth century is now accepted, with Laura Hibbard Loomis's theory that it was a product of a London bookshop having been questioned and dismissed.[6] Physically, Auchinleck stands as the battered remains of a once exceptional volume; yet it is still handsome in its comparative ruination, although only five of the original illustrations have survived the ravages of miniature collectors, with thirteen patched leaves and a further eighteen folios, which could have contained miniatures, missing.[7] The paintings in Auchinleck have, not infrequently, been associated with a group of presumed London volumes, identified by association with the group's most famous codex, the Queen Mary Psalter, BL Royal MS 2.B.vii.[8] Yet Lucy Freeman Sandler does not mention Auchinleck

6 See Derek Pearsall, 'The Auchinleck Manuscript Forty Years On', in *The Auchinleck Manuscript: New Perspectives*, ed. Susanna Fein (York: York Medieval Press, 2016), pp. 11–25; L. H. Loomis, 'The Auchinleck Manuscript and a Possible London Bookshop of 1330–1340', *PMLA* 57 (1942), 595–627.

7 Three fragments of Auchinleck survive separately: these are Edinburgh University Library MS 218, two bifolia (from quires 3 and 48); University of London, Senate House Library MS 593, one bifolium (from quire 40); St Andrews University Library MS PR2065.R4 (MS 1034), two bifolia (from quires 48 and 40). In a forensically detailed article Margaret Connolly and A. S. G. Edwards have analysed all portions of the codex which are missing from the volume as it now exists and conclude that it could have remained in smaller units with parchment coverings for some time after it was copied. See their 'Evidence for the History of the Auchinleck Manuscript', *The Library*, 7th series, 18 (2017), 292–304. Some sheets of text are now missing, in addition to leaves containing illustrations. The whole or partial destruction of medieval manuscripts has long been a concern for medievalists. See, for instance, John Ruskin's famous diary entry for 3 January 1854: 'Cut up missal in evening – hard work.' See also, A. N. L. Munby, *Connoisseurs and Medieval Miniatures 1750–1850* (Oxford: Clarendon Press, 1972); M. A. Michael, 'Destruction, Reconstruction and Invention: The Hungerford Hours and English Manuscript Illumination of the Early Fourteenth Century', *English Manuscript Studies* 2, ed. Peter Beal and Jeremy Griffiths, pp. 33–108; Christopher de Hamel, 'Cutting Up Manuscripts for Pleasure and Profit', The 1995 Sol. M. Malkin Lecture in Bibliography, *The Rare Book School 1995 Yearbook* (Charlottesville, 1996), pp. 1–20; and for a wide-ranging study, Roger S. Wieck, 'Folia Fugitiva: The Pursuit of the Illuminated Manuscript Leaf', *The Journal of the Walters Art Gallery* 54, *Essays in Honor of Lilian M. C. Randall* (1996), 233–54.

8 See, most recently, Timothy A. Shonk, 'Paraphs, Piecework, and Presentation: The Production Methods of Auchinleck Revisited', in *The Auchinleck Manuscript*, ed. Fein, pp. 176–94, at p. 179: 'There seems to be general agreement that the miniatures of Auchinleck are in the style of those who produced the Queen Mary Psalter … the identification of this style is based primarily upon similarities in the figures in Auchinleck

in her discussion of a large number of volumes,[9] although both she and Lynda Dennison, significantly, have identified East Anglian, as well as London, associations within the group.[10] Dennison has postulated that an artist affiliated with the Queen Mary Psalter Master, whom she names the 'Subsidiary Queen Mary Artist', worked with other craftsmen in the Fens and East Anglia before travelling to London to work for Andrew Horn, fishmonger and Chamberlain of the City of London from 1320 to 1328. It is with one of Horn's commissioned books – the 'Liber Custumarum' – that she, to my knowledge alone of art historians, connects the Auchinleck illustrations. The association is recorded, however, in a footnote and the purpose of the note, which quotes Laura Hibbard Loomis's now discredited study, is to back up a point she is making in the body of her essay about the London provenance of some of the books she has been discussing,[11] so the argument is somewhat circular.

There is, though, general agreement that the Queen Mary Psalter originated in the metropolis, but the time is long overdue for a detailed art-historical examination of the miniatures in Auchinleck. All I can say in the present context is that I have looked closely at the miniatures in Auchinleck which preface *Reinbrun* and *Richard Coer de Lyon* (fols 167rb and 326ra) and compared them with a battle scene in the Queen Mary Psalter, in which the Philistines attack Jerusalem as punishment for Solomon's lechery (fol. 66v, top) (Figures 5.1, 5.2, 5.3).[12] Allowance has to be made for the different media used – the Queen Mary drawings are tinted, whereas those in Auchinleck are painted – but even once this allowance is made, the differences between the images are striking. Two feature attacks on a walled city from the left of the picture plane, yet the Queen Mary artist shows a finesse in his drawing of horses which is not matched in Auchinleck. In addition, the army in the former is imaginatively composed and gives some impression of the speed and near chaos of a group of mounted soldiers nearing their target. And even on horseback, the anatomy of the right leg of an approaching knight is drawn with delicacy through his chain armour. I would then argue for the images in these books – Auchinleck

miniatures to those in the Queen Mary Psalter.' Ralph Hanna notes in his book *London Literature 1300–1380* (Cambridge: CUP, 2005), p. 80, that J. J. G. Alexander was of the same opinion in a conversation recalled by P. R. Robinson, but he has never published on the matter.

9 Lucy Freeman Sandler, *Gothic Manuscripts 1285–1385*, A Survey of Manuscripts Illuminated in the British Isles 7, 2 vols, cat. no. 56 and discussion, esp. pp. 30–2.

10 Lynda Dennison, 'An Illuminator of the Queen Mary Psalter Group: The Ancient 6 Master', *Antiquaries Journal* 66 (1986), 287–314; and '"Liber Horn", "Liber Custumarum" and Other Manuscripts of the Queen Mary Psalter Workshops', *Medieval Art, Architecture and Archaeology in London*, BAA Conference Transactions 11, 1984 (Leeds, 1990), pp. 118–72.

11 Dennison, '"Liber Horn"', p. 133 n. 70.

12 See the facsimile, *Queen Mary's Psalter*, intro. Sir George Warner (London: British Museum, 1912).

Fig. 5.1 Edinburgh, National Library of Scotland, Advocates MS 19.2.1 ('The Auchinleck Manuscript'), fol. 167rb, *Reinbrun*

and Queen Mary – being the work of at least two hands, although where I am in agreement with other commentators concerns the provenance of the two books.

London, it is widely accepted, is where the Queen Mary Psalter was produced and the same is almost certainly true of Auchinleck. This, however, leads us to the thorny issue of patronage. Derek Pearsall has conjured the image of a wealthy merchant – an 'aspirant middle-class citizen' – enjoying the book,[13] while in contrast, Ann Higgins has argued for a northern patron

13 Pearsall, 'The Auchinleck Manuscript Forty Years On', p. 13.

Fig. 5.2 Edinburgh, National Library of Scotland, Advocates MS 19.2.1 ('The Auchinleck Manuscript'), fol. 326ra, *Richard Coer de Lyon*

who commissioned the volume in London and who then took it back to the north of England, whence it eventually travelled to Scotland, where it certainly was by the early 1600s.[14] She observes that *Sir Tristrem* preserves northern forms of speech that would have been 'linguistically alien to a contemporary London reader',[15] although these are perhaps better explained not as reflecting the language of the intended patron and/or the scribe, but as relicts of a poem composed in the north that was linguistically repurposed by the scribe for a London audience.[16] In terms of material evidence, there are a number of names surviving in late-medieval hands including, on fol. 107r, members of the Browne family: 'Mr Thomas Browne', 'Mrs Isabell Browne' and those

[14] Ann Higgins, '*Sir Tristrem*, a Few Fragments, and the Northern Identity of the Auchinleck Manuscript', in *New Perspectives*, ed. Fein, pp. 108–26.

[15] Higgins, '*Sir Tristrem*', p. 113.

[16] See Ad Putter, Judith Jefferson and Donka Minkova, 'Dialect, Rhyme, and Emendation in *Sir Tristrem*', *JEGP* 113 (2014), 73–92; and also Putter's discussion of Higgins's argument in this collection.

Fig. 5.3 © The British Library Board, Royal MS 2 B vii (Queen Mary's Psalter), fol. 66v, the Philistines attack Jerusalem

of six of their (presumed) children. If Higgins is right, then this family, so far unidentified, would have been Scottish. For those scholars who visualise an audience of children,[17] the presence of these names would seem to be most satisfactory. But to return to the original commissioning, looking at the patrons of other, affiliated manuscripts mentioned here, the range of clientele is broad, including clerics, the mercantile and civic elite of London and royalty, in the shape of Philippa of Hainault, queen of Edward III. She might seem particularly apt as a patron, given that Auchinleck can be dated 1330–40 and the royal marriage took place in 1328, but it may be doubted that a Flemish queen at this period would have ordered, or received as a gift, a book largely in English. This does not, however, rule out the possibility of the volume having a female patron, as Felicity Riddy argued in a paper given at one of

[17] Linda Olsen, 'Romancing the Book: Manuscripts for "Euerich Inglische"', in *Opening Up Middle English Manuscripts*, ed. Kerby-Fulton et al., pp. 95–115, at pp. 99–109; Cathy Hume, 'The Auchinleck *Adam and Eve*: An Exemplary Family Story', in *New Perspectives*, ed. Fein, pp. 36–51.

the early biennial conferences on Middle English Romance, in which she suggested that a wealthy merchant's wife such as Katherine de la Pole could have been instrumental in Auchinleck's inception.[18] This argument has recently been expanded by Siobhain Bly Calkin, though she does not seek to identify the book's actual patron.[19]

Aside from art history and patronage, Auchinleck continues to provide rich pickings for those who are interested in scribal production. The question of whether five or six scribes were involved remains current,[20] and attention is now being directed towards other aspects of the hierarchy of decoration such as paraphs.[21] Another important aspect of the production of this manuscript pertains to the scribes themselves and the kind of work which they carried out for a living. M. A. Michael has demonstrated through examination of documentary evidence the sheer numbers of individuals (including women) who were associated with the book trade in London and other urban centres.[22] Yet the very singularity of Auchinleck should remind us that there was greater fluidity amongst book producers than has generally been acknowledged. There was little distinction drawn between service and devotional books, secular texts (in all languages) and civic treatises in terms of their relative importance to book producers.[23] The Auchinleck scribes, like the book artists, and principally scribe 1, who copied around 70 per cent of the manuscript, may eventually be identified as having contributed to other volumes or to the copying of government documents. It is worth emphasising here Andrew Prescott's general admonition to literary scholars (with some honourable exceptions) to remember that copying literary texts was but a very small part of any scribe's activities. He stresses that at least 90 per cent of scribal activity in

18 As far as I know Riddy has not published this paper, but she has argued elsewhere for a family audience for romance: see 'Middle English Romance: Family, Marriage, Intimacy', in *The Cambridge Companion to Medieval Romance*, ed. Roberta L. Krueger (Cambridge: CUP, 2000), pp. 235–52.

19 See Siobhain Bly Calkin, 'Endings in the Auchinleck Manuscript', in *New Perspectives*, ed. Fein, 156–75, p. 167.

20 Ralph Hanna argues that scribes 1 and 6 are the same; see most recently his essay 'Auchinleck "Scribe 6" and Some Corollary Issues', in *New Perspectives*, ed. Fein, pp. 209–21; other contributors to this volume assume there were six copyists. See also Hanna's other work on the Auchinleck manuscript in *London Literature*, esp. pp. 74–83 and 104–42; and his essay 'Reconsidering the Auchinleck Manuscript', in *New Directions in Later Medieval Manuscript Studies*, ed. Derek Pearsall (York: York Medieval Press, 2000), pp. 91–102.

21 Shonk, 'Paraphs, Piecework, and Presentation'. Shonk's earlier essay, 'A Study of the Auchinleck Manuscript: Bookmen and Bookmaking in the Early Fourteenth Century', *Speculum* 60 (1985), 71–91, remains a fine study.

22 M. A. Michael, 'Urban Production of Manuscript Books and the Role of the University Towns', in *The Cambridge History of the Book in Britain*, vol. 2, *1100–1400*, ed. Nigel Morgan and Rodney M. Thomson (Cambridge: CUP, 2008), pp. 168–94, at pp. 184–8.

23 Cf. Hanna, *London Literature*.

England was generated by the 'great engine' of royal government.[24] The name of Auchinleck's commissioner may never be known, but to look at the manuscript within its putative production context is to see the interconnectedness of the worlds of court and city, united by both wealth and common interests.

With the next volume, Bodley 264, it is to the first of these institutions that we must look.[25] The illustrations to this magnificent volume of the adventures of Alexander, written in the French of Picardy, were completed by a Flemish illuminator in 1344. The date at which it arrived in England is unknown, although there has been much speculation. Attempts have been made to tie it to the Alexander romance listed in the 1397 post-mortem inventories of Richard II's uncle, Thomas of Woodstock, duke of Gloucester, whose wife, Eleanor Bohun, had western connections through her family, which connections may have provided the exemplar of the English Alexander romance (*Alexander and Dindimus* or *Alexander B*) which was added in the early fifteenth century (fols 209r–215v).[26] This conjecture, attractive though it may be, is incapable of proof either way. Albinia de la Mare, however, identified the now-damaged arms on fol. 1 of the volume – gules a chevron argent a lion rampant (?) sable – as those of Humphrey duke of Gloucester, brother of Henry V, who lived from 1399 to 1447.[27] Given that the additions to the volume were made in England probably in the first decade of the fifteenth century, Gloucester is hardly likely to have been the patron. Still, at some point between c. 1400 and 1410, a scribe copied two works into the book, the western Middle English alliterative romance of *Alexander and Dindimus* and the Marco Polo text, *Li Livres du Graunt Caam*. The former is there by a lucky chance: it was copied to make up for what the scribe mistakenly regarded as a lacuna in the French *Alexandre*, as a lengthy note he added on fol. 67rb makes clear.

24 Andrew Prescott, 'Administrative Records and the Scribal Achievement of Medieval England', in *English Manuscripts before 1400, English Manuscript Studies 1100–1700*, 17, ed. A. S. G. Edwards and Orietta Da Rold (London: British Library, 2012), pp. 173–99.

25 M. R. James, *The Romance of Alexander: A Collotype Facsimile of MS. Bodley 264* (Oxford: OUP, 1933); Scott, *Later Gothic Manuscripts*, 2, pp. 68–73, cat. no. 13, and for illustrations, 1, no. 61. The manuscript is the subject of Mark Cruse's book *Illuminating the Roman d'Alexandre: Oxford, Bodleian Library, MS Bodley 264. The Manuscript as Monument* (Cambridge: D. S. Brewer, 2011).

26 A. I. Doyle, 'English Books In and Out of Court from Edward III to Henry VII', in *English Court Culture in the Later Middle Ages*, ed. V. J. Scattergood and J. W. Sherborne (London: Palgrave Macmillan, 1983), pp. 163–81, at p. 167; Viscount Dillon and W. H. St John Hope, 'Inventory of the Goods and Chattels Belonging to Thomas Duke of Gloucester', *Archaeological Review* 54 (1897), 275–308.

27 Albinia C. de la Mare, 'Duke Humphrey's English Palladius (MS Duke Humphrey d. 2)', *Bodleian Library Record* 12 (1985), 48 n. 2. Scott, *Later Gothic Manuscripts*, 2, p. 73, notes that Gloucester's arms were probably added over an earlier set.

> Here fayleth a prossesse of þis rommance of Alixandre, þe which prossesse þat fayleth ȝe schulle fynde at þe ende of þis bok ywrete in Engelyche ryme and whanne ȝe han radde it to þe ende, turneþ hedur aȝen and turneþ ovyr þis lef and bygynneþ at þis reson – Che fu el mois de may que li tans renouele – and so rede forþ þe rommance to þe ende whylis þe Frenche lasteþ.

There were four limners who worked on the later texts, although Hand A contributed only one of the two frontispieces (possibly a representation of Babylon, according to Scott) and nine small miniatures to *Alexander and Dindimus* on fols 209–215v, showing the two figures in conversation (Fig. 5.4 reproduces one of these). Hand A, while not as skilled a craftsman as the renowned 'Johannes', an artist heavily influenced by the International Style, who carried out some of the miniatures illustrating the Marco Polo story, was by no means untalented, as his frontispiece demonstrates.[28] It is vibrant with detail, from the depiction of traps set in trees to catch birds, to a watermill. The figures shown on (?) a balcony are too large to have inhabited the other city buildings painted, but overall the scene is lively and invites the onlooker in by way of the swirling waters in which two boats (?carracks) sail. Clearly this was a commission of some importance and one which, given the dialectal affiliations of the Alexander poem, may have originated in the west country, possibly Glastonbury, although given the often peripatetic lifestyle of book producers at this time, a London/Westminster provenance cannot be completely ruled out.

The next known owner of the volume after Humphrey of Gloucester, if he did indeed own it, was Richard Wydville, 1st Earl Rivers, father to Queen Elizabeth and father-in-law to Edward IV. According to a note on fol. 274r he bought the volume in London on 1 January 1466: 'Cest livre est a monseignour Richart de Widevielle seignour de Rivieres … et ledist seigneur acetast ledist livre l'an de grace mille .cccclxvj, le premier jour de l'an a Londres', etc. This is one of the best documented instances of the second-hand book trade as it operated in London that has survived – though it is much to be regretted that Rivers did not write whence he had obtained the book.[29] He did not, in the event, have long to enjoy it for he was killed in 1469 during the brief readeption of Henry VI. It has recently been suggested, by Omar Khalef, on the basis of another, rather difficult to read, inscription on fol. 274, that Bodley 264 passed to Richard Wydville's eldest son, Anthony. (Anthony was also the recipient of books from his mother, Jaquetta of Luxembourg: the sumptuous collected works of Christine de Pizan, now Harley 4431, contains both their

28 Scott, *Later Gothic Manuscripts*, 1, pl. 61.

29 On the second-hand trade in books see Kate Harris, 'Patrons, Buyers and Owners: The Evidence for Ownership and the Role of Book Owners in Book Production and the Book Trade', in *Book Production and Publishing in Britain 1375–1475*, ed. Jeremy Griffiths and Derek Pearsall (Cambridge: CUP, 1989), pp. 163–99, at pp. 170–8.

Fig. 5.4 The Bodleian Libraries, The University of Oxford, Bodley MS 264, fol. 212r, *Alexander and Dindimus*

signatures.) Given that from 1473 Anthony Wydville was tutor to the young Prince Edward, Khalef postulates that the older man may have used the volume – including the alliterative romance, which centres around the debate on what constitutes good living between the proud and vainglorious Alexander and the monotheistic, moral king of the Brahmans – as a kind of exemplary 'mirror for princes' for Edward to learn from.[30] Once again, this is an attractive hypothesis, but one which is incapable of proof.

The provenance of the third of the illustrated manuscripts I am dealing with here is also unclear. Pierpont Morgan Library M 876 is unfinished both in rubrication and in illumination. Only four of the spaces left throughout for eleven miniatures show preliminary stages of work and even the names of the romance hero and heroine in this unique copy of *Generides* have not been filled in, in red, for over half of the text.[31] The other item in this parchment volume is Lydgate's *Troy Book* and this exists in an equally incomplete state.[32] With regard to the *Troy Book*, A. S. G. Edwards and Derek Pearsall have concluded that 'the Morgan manuscript comes closest to indicating a failure due to economic cause, whether it was the prospective customer or the speculation that failed, since there are no other apparent obstacles to completion'.[33] Considering the size and length of the volume it might be thought to have been a risky speculative venture at the date of c. 1460 which I have assigned to it,[34] though on the other hand the Lydgate text had a proven popularity and might have been deemed worthy of speculative production on the part of an entrepreneurial stationer or bookseller. The first gathering, which may have contained some indication of ownership or patronage, is lost. Martha Driver has, however, looked in depth at the shield lying on the ground as it is portrayed in the miniature showing the hero killing the treacherous steward Amalek, together with its description in the text which runs 'bendes of gold wel besene / The champe of goules red and bright / With riche stones bordred aright'. Though as she points out, in the illustration the 'bendes' are in fact red bendlets on a gold background (Fig. 5.5).[35] On the basis of this shield,

30 Omar Khalef, 'Lord Rivers and Oxford, Bodleian library, MS Bodley 264: A *Speculum* for the Prince of Wales?', *JEBS* 14 (2011), 239–50.

31 For a detailed study of the romance and its manuscript see Carol M. Meale, 'The Morgan Library Copy of *Generides*', in *Romance in Medieval England*, ed. Maldwyn Mills, Jennifer Fellows and Carol M. Meale, pp. 89–104.

32 See Lesley Lawton, 'The Illustration of Late Medieval Secular Texts, with Special Reference to Lydgate's "Troy Book"', in *Manuscripts and Readers in Fifteenth-Century England*, ed. Derek Pearsall (Cambridge: D. S. Brewer, 1983), pp. 41–69.

33 A. S. G. Edwards and Derek Pearsall, 'The Manuscripts of the Major English Poetic Texts', in *Book Production and Publishing*, ed. Griffiths and Pearsall, pp. 257–78, at p. 267.

34 Meale, 'The Morgan Library Copy of *Generides*'.

35 Martha W. Driver, 'Medievalizing the Classical Past in Pierpont Morgan MS M 876', in *Middle English Poetry: Texts and Traditions. Essays in Honour of Derek Pearsall*, ed.

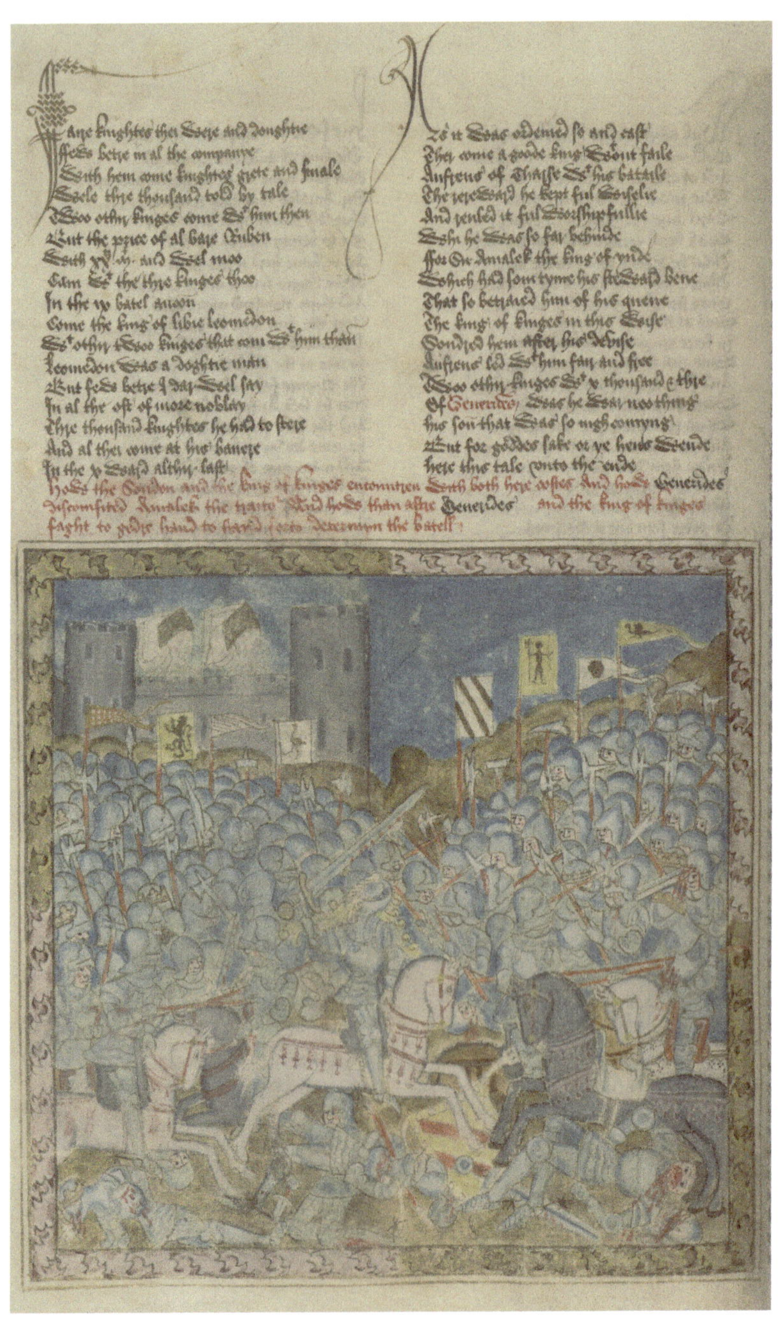

Fig. 5.5 The Pierpont Morgan Library, New York, MS M 876, fol. 121v, *Generides*

Driver raises the possibility that the manuscript was commissioned by Ralph Boteler, Lord Sudeley (who died, deprived of his castle of Sudeley, in 1473), or another member of the Boteler family. Reversal of worldly fortune coming to this loyal servant to Henry VI might therefore explain the unfinished state of the codex. My only objection to this theory is that in the romance the shield belonged to the traitor, Amalek. But it remains an interesting idea.

I have been mildly – and perhaps justifiably – rebuked by Driver for undervaluing the illustrations in Morgan, describing them as 'stiff and mechanical' with 'no attempt at characterization'.[36] Certainly she has a point in indicating, with reference to other codices such as Bodl. Douce MS 271 (including the Statutes of the Order of the Garter) and PML MS M 775, Sir John Astley's book, the extremely detailed and accurate depiction of sailing ships and of armour in M 876 (the latter of which enabled me in part to date the manuscript's production). But I stand by my overall judgement as to the artist's abilities. There is, for example, in the near-completed scene of the battle between Generides and Amalek no use of perspective, and while the drawing of the main protagonists is lively enough, the amassed armies at their backs are just that: groups of soldiers' helmets indistinguishable from each other apart from the different directions in which the soldiers are facing up to one another. Equally, in the scene in Morgan of the wheel of Fortune from the *Troy Book* on fol. 6r of the codex, the individuals who are on a downward cycle, falling from Fortune's favour, hardly look disconcerted at what is happening to them (Fig. 5.6). I would say in this respect that there is a disconnect between the capabilities of the scribe, who writes in an attractive anglicana hand with elaborate calligraphic flourishes, and those of the artist. Perhaps this indicates provincial production, although I doubt that London/Westminster had exclusive rights to only the best artists.

As to who read the manuscript, the earliest signature – and I think that it is a signature – occurs on fol. 102v and is that of one William Hopton. I have suggested that this is the man, son of John Hopton of Blythborough in Suffolk whose life has been recorded by Colin Richmond,[37] who was a member of Henry VI's household in the late 1440s to the early 1450s, was sheriff of Norfolk and Suffolk twice and who was knighted by Richard III at the king's coronation and was made Treasurer of his household a few days later. He died in February 1484.[38] If I am right in this identification then Hopton probably

---

A. J. Minnis (York: York Medieval Press, 2001), pp. 211–39, at p. 226, and pls 1, 6, 8, 10a and 10b.

36 Driver, 'Medievalizing the Classical Past', p. 213; Meale, 'The Morgan Library Copy of *Generides*', p. 91.

37 Colin Richmond, *John Hopton: A Fifteenth Century Suffolk Gentleman* (Cambridge: CUP, 1981).

38 Meale, 'The Morgan Library Copy of *Generides*', p. 102.

Fig. 5.6 The Pierpont Morgan Library, New York, MS M 876, fol. 6r, Lydgate, *Troy Book*

signed the codex prior to his knighting. Certainly another man whose name appears in the manuscript, the sixteenth-century Edward Echingham, who signed fol. 18v with the phrase 'liber meus', had a family connection, through marriage, to the Hoptons. While there is not enough evidence to suggest that the book originated in East Anglia (the scribe's dialect, for instance, is free from East Anglian features) it is virtually certain that it found an early readership there, where it remained part of the Tollemache collection at Helmingham in Suffolk, probably from the seventeenth century.

Confirmation that William Hopton had an interest in books has recently emerged from the work of Tom Johnson.[39] In the Harwich Leet Rolls (i.e. court records) for 10 March 18 Edward IV (1479) in the Essex Record Office, there is a record of a dispute between Richard Curteys, a 'mariner' from Sandwich in Kent, together with Thomas Lytell of Ipswich, a yeoman, and William Hopton esquire concerning two books taken feloniously from Hopton's goods and chattels. These were worth ten pounds and were entitled 'Bertilmew De P*ro*prietatibus Rerum' and 'le sege de Troye'.[40] The translation from the Latin record runs as follows:

> And that Richard Curteys of Sandwich in the county of Kent, mariner, and Thomas Lytell of Ipswich in the county of Suffolk, yeoman, on the 10th March in the 18th year of the reign of King Edward IV, by force and arms feloniously took two books, one called Bartholomew De Proprietatibus Rerum and the other on the siege of Troy, to the value of £10, from the goods and chattels of William Hopton, esquire, at Harwich. And later the same day and year they waived them; the which books had been seized and taken for the use of the lord. And afterwards they came to the hands of the said William by the delivery of the [town] bailiffs.[41]

The first of the stolen volumes was 'On the Properties of Things', the thirteenth-century encyclopaedia by Bartholomeus Anglicus, possibly in the English translation completed by John Trevisa for Thomas, Lord Berkeley in 1398. But it is more difficult to identify the second. The story of Troy was extant in the twelfth-century French *Roman de Troie* of Benôit de Sainte-Maure; the thirteenth-century Latin *Historia Destrucionis Troiae* of Guido della Collonna; and in English poetry, in addition to Lydgate's *Troy Book*, finished for

39 I am most grateful to Dr Johnson for allowing me to use material which he uncovered.

40 D/B 4/38/9, m. 6r. Court and view of frankpledge, Thursday the feast of St Barnabus.

41 Translation courtesy of Dr Johnson. According to Dr Johnson, stolen goods and chattels were forfeit to the king or the local lord if they were abandoned. Harwich was a seigneurial borough and the lords there were the de Veres, earls of Oxford. However, 'it was not unknown for [goods] to be returned to an owner where ownership could be proved. This would suggest, therefore, that the books were somehow identifiable as Hopton's – presumably through his signature or similar.' Personal correspondence, 9 November 2014.

Henry V in 1420, there was the *Seege of Troye*, the so-called Laud *Troy Book* and the alliterative *Destruction of Troy* composed by John Clerk of Whalley in Lancashire. Then there was also the prose *Siege of Troy*, based on Lydgate's work.[42] If the presumption is in favour of an English version of the story, as I think it probably is, then the title given to it in the court minutes is not of much help. But the possibility must at least be raised that it was a copy of Lydgate's text, the most widely circulating in the fifteenth century (nineteen copies survive);[43] and if that can be accepted, then it is at least conceivable that the book was Morgan M 876. We can never know the answer for certain, but it remains a tantalising possibility. Another manuscript containing a romance, this time the prose *Ponthus and the Fair Sidone*, which is preserved in Bodl. Digby MS 185, was also in Hopton ownership, although here there are two candidates for possession: William, or, perhaps more plausibly, his son, George.[44] Digby is not illustrated, but the heraldic scheme contained within its pages is one of a kind and renders the volume highly desirable for its commissioners.[45]

The final manuscript to be discussed, BL Harley MS 326, containing the English translation of a Burgundian romance first copied, but probably not composed, by the scribe and calligrapher David Aubert in 1463, is in many ways the most interesting of the codices looked at here, if only because other work both by its limner and by its scribe is known. No direct source for the English text has been identified and none of the surviving French manuscripts are illustrated, which means that the artist was on his own when devising a scheme of illustration.[46] It is now many years since I first identified the artist of this codex with that of London, Lambeth Palace MS 265, the presentation copy of Anthony Wydville's translation of *The Dictes and Sayings of the Philosophers*, dated to 1477 by the scribe, Haywarde of St James in the Fields, Westminster, and the artist is now known, following Kathleen Scott's catalogue, as the Three Kings Master.[47] There is no certainty as to the date of the

42 For details of these works see MWME 1, ed. J. Burke Severs (New Haven, CT: Connecticut Academy of Arts and Sciences, 1967), pp. 114–18, 274–7; also Thorlac Turville-Petre, 'The Author of *The Destruction of Troy*', *MÆ* 57 (1988), 264–9.

43 Edwards and Pearsall, 'The Manuscripts of the Major English Poetic Texts', p. 270.

44 Carol M. Meale, 'The Politics of Book Ownership: The Hopton Family and Bodleian Library, Digby MS 185', in *Prestige, Authority and Power in Late-Medieval Manuscripts and Texts*, ed. Felicity Riddy (York: York Medieval Press, 2000), pp. 103–31.

45 See Meale, 'The Politics of Book Ownership', pls 15–19, pp. 107–11.

46 Henry Grinberg, 'The *Three Kings' Sons* and *Les Trois Fils de Roi*: Manuscript and Textual Filiation in an Anglo-Burgundian Romance', *Romance Philology* 28 (1975), 521–9. Grinberg lists seven copies of the French text. Coloured reproductions of the English miniatures may be found in the British Library's online *Catalogue of Illuminated Manuscripts*.

47 Carol M. Meale, 'Patrons, Buyers and Owners: Book Production and Social Status', in *Book Production and Publishing*, ed. Griffiths and Pearsall, pp. 201–38, pls 18–20 and p. 212; Scott, *Later Gothic Manuscripts*, 1, pls 467–70; 2, cat. no. 124, pp. 331–2.

Fig. 5.7 © The British Library Board, Harley MS 326, fol. 29v, *The Three Kings' Sons*.

Lambeth miniature – it is found on a separate folio from the text and so was added in – but it must be dated before 1483 since it depicts Edward IV and the king died on 10 April in that year. Harley 326 contains four half-page miniatures and eighteen smaller ones: all include gold in the palette. The limner's skill is evident in his choice (if it was his choice and not the commissioner's) of subjects to illustrate. There is a splendid seascape, depicting the Christian fleet approaching Graeta in their clinker-built ships, in which the details of the fleet in full sail are observed minutely (Fig. 5.7). The concluding tournament of the romance is full of movement and again alive with significant detail. And then there are scenes of travel, of domestic interiors and of weddings. It is very much to the point that none of the extant French manuscripts are illustrated and although the Master is in one sense deploying 'stock' images that would be of relevance to any number of Middle English romances, he must be credited with both imagination and professionalism. The date at which Harley 326 was produced is ultimately determined by the artist's association with the Lambeth book, probably in the region of the 1470s to the early 1480s, and there is nothing in the Flemish/Burgundian lettre bâtarde-influenced scribal hand to contradict this. The place of origin for the volume's production, again by analogy with Lambeth 265, is likely to have been London.

In terms of the scribe's *oeuvre* – and here I must thank Dr Ian Doyle for his customary knowledge and generosity of spirit in pointing me in the right direction[48] – I should like to look first at New York, Columbia University Library Plimpton MS 256. This manuscript contains an acephalous copy of the accomplished verse *Court of Sapience* of c. 1460, sometimes misattributed to John Lydgate; devotional texts in English entitled *The Twelve Profits of Tribulation* and *A Treatise of Love*, both translated from French sources; the *Treatise of the Seven Points of True Love* translated from the *Orologium Sapientiae* of Henry of Suso (Fig. 5.8); and a seven-stanza rhyme royal poem copied in on the last page.[49] One of the points which should be made is that the decorator who was responsible for the coloured initials in *The Three Kings' Sons* sometimes worked alongside the scribe on other texts, Plimpton 256 being a good example. The initials in the romance are quite plain: although painted in gold they have no foliage emerging from them and this plainness distinguishes them from Plimpton where foliage is added by (?) another hand. The only clue as to early ownership of Plimpton, aside from the fact that some of the devotional texts were apparently intended for a female audience, is the inscription 'Sum William Hodges' of c. 1500 which occurs on what is now the opening folio of *The Court of Sapience* (fol. 2r). I have not been able to trace this man. The last of the English codices which the Harley scribe copied was the section from fol. 41r onwards of BL Cotton Vespasian MS B ix, the English version of the Latin Book of the Foundation of St Bartholomew's Hospital in Smithfield, London, complete with its inscription of provenance (Fig. 5.9).[50] From Smithfield, presumably after the Reformation, the book passed into the ownership of one Thomas Otwell (the inscription 'Iste liber pertinet ad Thomam Otwell de London' appears at the end of the volume) and below his note of possession is the name of 'Tomas Powell of London, stacioner'. Powell is well known from sixteenth-century records (he died in

[48] Personal correspondence, 22 February 2014.

[49] Images from the manuscript may be found through the online Digital Scriptorium: www.digital-scriptorium.org. The text describing the Plimpton manuscript should be treated with caution: for example, virtually the entire contents of the book are attributed to Lydgate.

[50] *The Book of the Foundation of St Bartholomew's Church in London*, ed. Sir Norman Moore, EETS o.s. 163 (London, 1923). The opening initial of the introduction also resembles those I have discussed in Harley 326 and Plimpton 256, although a different book artist was responsible for the elaborate initial marking the beginning of the text proper.

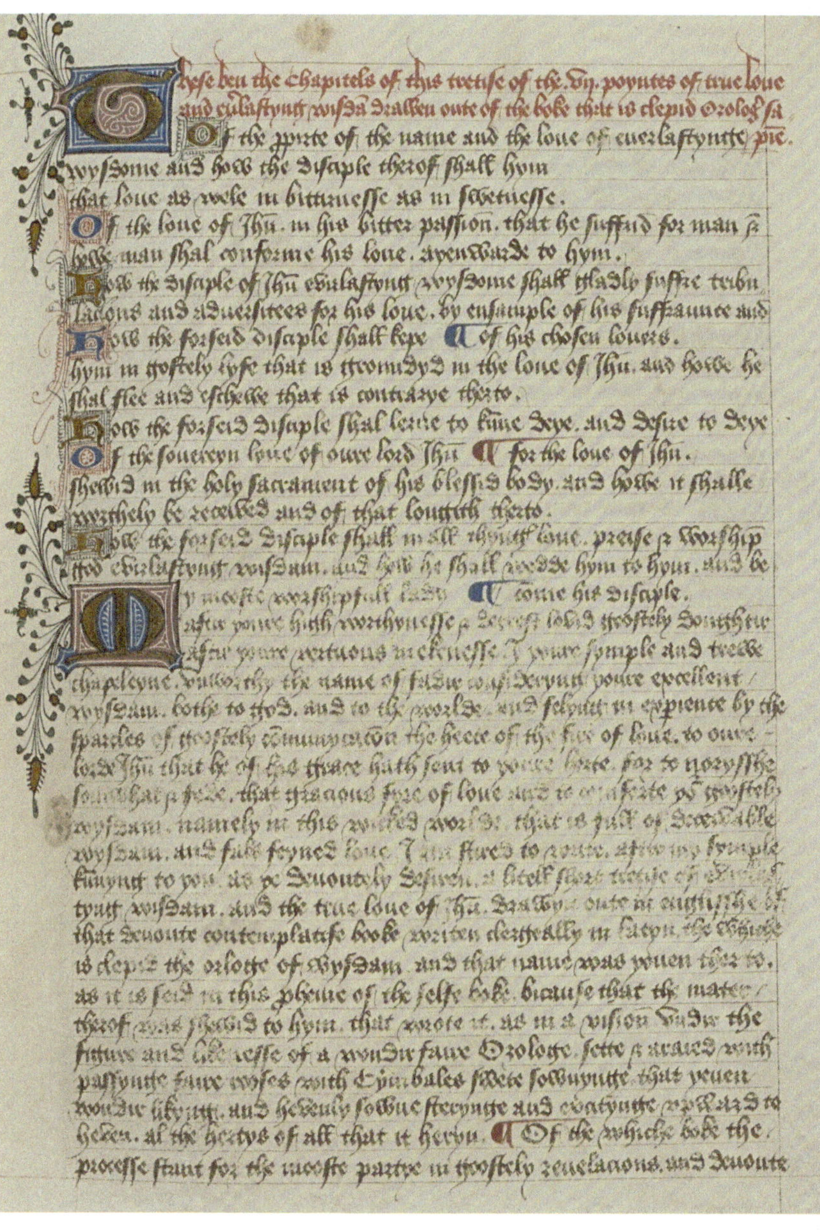

Fig. 5.8 Columbia University Library, New York, Plimpton MS 256, fol. 93r, translation of Henry Suso, *Treatise of the Seven Points of True Love*

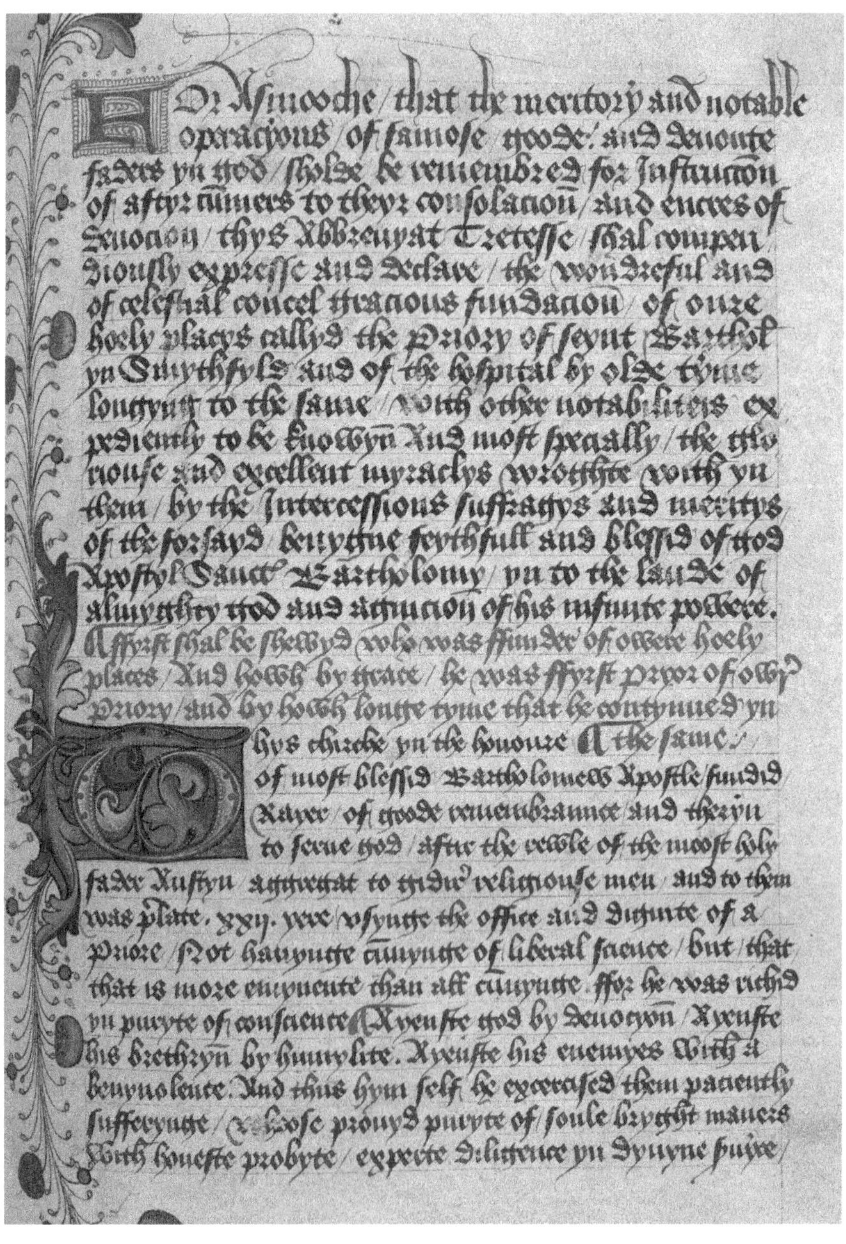

Fig. 5.9 © The British Library Board, Cotton Vespasian MS B ix, fol. 41r, account in English of the Foundation of St Bartholomew's Hospital, Smithfield, London.

1563) and he seems to have a connection of some sort, though one not easy to fathom, with the one-time royal printer, Thomas Berthelet.[51]

The Harley scribe was also proficient in copying Latin. One of the books he produced was Bodl. Fairfax MS 4, the *Compendium Morale* of the fourteenth-century royal administrator Roger Waltham, who died between 1332 and 1341.[52] This text has an elaborate and highly competent opening border and initial.[53] This manuscript cannot have been copied before 1474 because the text contains a table of contents compiled by one Master Thomas Graunt in that year. In the sixteenth century the volume was still in the hands of an Oxford University man. This scribe also appears to have been commissioned to copy four manuscripts in Latin for Roger Marchall, who died in 1477.[54] Royal physician to Edward IV, Marchall was a Peterhouse, Cambridge graduate from Bedfordshire. Having been admitted to the college as a foundation fellow in 1437/8, he had gained the MD degree by 1453. He had strong ties to the City of London as well as to the court through his brother, Nicholas, who was an alderman of the City from 1463 to 1465 and a warden of the Ironmongers in 1463. Marchall was a bibliophile – and, presumably, rich. Linda Voigts has worked out that forty-four codices survive which bear either his ownership mark or traces of use by him. Another six, in Voigts's phrase, 'may have passed through his hands'[55] and records exist which list another twelve volumes that can no longer be found. He donated his books freely – principally to Peterhouse.

The four codices copied for Marchall by the scribe of Harley 326 were all in Latin. They were: Cambridge Peterhouse MSS 161 and 162, commentaries by Albertus Magnus; Harley MS 637, a series of early fifteenth-century astronomical, astrological and geographical texts; and lastly a copy of Roger Bacon's *Opus Maius* written around a fourteenth-century section comprising Bacon's *De perspectiva*, now Bodl. Digby MS 235.[56] The latter manuscript is of especial interest in the context of this essay because it contains border decoration on the first page by the London artist identified by Kathleen Scott,

[51] Peter W. M. Blayney, *The Stationers' Company and the Printers of London 1501–1557*, 2 vols (Cambridge: CUP, 2013), II, 789–93.

[52] M. C. Buck, 'Roger Waltham', *ODNB* online.

[53] Otto Pächt and J. J. G. Alexander, *Illuminated Manuscripts in the Bodleian Library Oxford*, 3 (Oxford: Clarendon Press, 1973), cat. no. 1098 and pl. CIV.

[54] Linda Ehrsam Voigts, 'Roger Marchall', *ODNB*; Linda Ehrsam Voigts, 'A Doctor and His Books: The Manuscripts of Roger Marchall, d. 1477', in *New Science out of Old Books: Studies in Manuscripts and Early Printed Books in Honour of A. I. Doyle*, ed. Richard Beadle and A. J. Piper (Aldershot: Scolar Press, 1995), pp. 249–314; C. H. Talbot and E. A. Hammond, *The Medical Practitioners in Medieval England: A Biographical Register* (1965), p. 168.

[55] Voigts, 'A Doctor and His Books', p. 249.

[56] Pl. 35 in Linda Ehrsam Voigts, 'Scientific and Medical Books', in *Book Production and Publishing*, ed. Griffiths and Pearsall, pp. 345–402.

whose work appears in approximately twenty-seven codices during the 1460s and 1470s.[57] Possibly the most famous of the books to which he contributed his skills was the sumptuous copy of *The Mirroure of the Worlde*, Bodley 283, commissioned by the wealthy London draper, Thomas Kippyng.[58]

All this evidence suggests that the scribe, as well as the artist, of Harley 326 had a client-base composed of the upper echelons of London society: as was probably the case with the Auchinleck scribes and book artists, there was an intermingling of court and city among these patrons. As to the commissioner of this unique copy of *The Three Kings' Sons*, there is no visible indication left. The volume has been heavily cropped, there are no coats of arms and even under ultraviolet light no signatures become visible. A court audience might well be presumed, given the connections with Lambeth 265, but this can only be speculation. It should be added here that the material prefatory to the romance – a paper copy of the descent of Edward IV from Rollo – a piece of royal propaganda, written, I believe, to aid the king in raising taxes for his projected war with France, is not integral to the romance manuscript: it is codicologically quite distinct. It does not, therefore, suggest a royal connection either of itself or of the book now known as Harley 326. The pedigree was in circulation in a number of copies in the late fifteenth and early sixteenth centuries, most of which are either known or have been conjectured to have been in the possession of a middle-class readership.[59]

Having looked at the four illustrated romance manuscripts in some detail and dealt as thoroughly as possible with the question of commissioning, it is time to consider the other issues raised in the introduction to this essay. To begin with, why were so few romance manuscripts illustrated – approximately 5 per cent of the total number which survive? There is no immediate answer to this. Both Kathleen Scott and Lesley Lawton discovered through exhaustive examination of medieval secular narratives in Middle English that few had a tradition of illustration.[60] There is, for instance, no customary practice of illustrating Chaucer or Hoccleve and the illustrative programme linked to Gower's *Confessio Amantis* is a modest one. Indeed, Lydgate's *Troy Book*

57 Scott, *Later Gothic Manuscripts*, 2, p. 354.

58 Scott, *Later Gothic Manuscripts*, 2, cat. no. 136, pp. 352–5; 1, pls 487–9, 494.

59 Carol M. Meale, 'London, British Library, Harley MS 2252, John Colyns' "Boke": Structure and Content', in *Tudor Manuscripts 1485–1603, English Manuscript Studies 1100–1700*, 15, ed. A. S. G. Edwards (London: British Library, 2009), pp. 65–122, cat. no. 41, pp. 100–1; Michael A. Hicks, 'Edward IV's *Brief Treatise* and the Treaty of Picquigny of 1475', *Historical Research* 83 (2010), 253–65; Raluca Radulescu, 'Yorkist Propaganda and *The Chronicle from Rollo to Edward IV*', *SP* 100 (2003), 401–24. Radulescu identifies only two of the five known manuscripts, while Hicks does not recognise the presence of a full text in Harley 2252.

60 Scott, *Later Gothic Manuscripts*; Lawton, 'Illustration of Late Medieval Secular Texts'.

was one of the few secular texts which did have an established pictorial cycle. Hence it may have been considered appropriate that in Morgan M 876 where it was planned that the *Troy Book* should be illustrated it was decided that the romance of *Generides* should be also. Equally, there is no tradition of illustration associated with alliterative poetry (aside, once more, from the *Gawain* manuscript) and it may be considered purely accidental that the scribe of *Alexander and Dindimus* in Bodley 264 worked with a limner: the rest of the manuscript was of so high a standard of production that to have a section left without pictures may have appeared an odd choice to either or both producers (in this case a stationer, or overseer of the project) and patron. Although there are some individual copies of works which have programmes of illustration[61] – the Advocates' manuscript of Nicholas Love's *Myrrour of the Blessed Lyf of Jesu Christ* (NLS Advocates MS 18.1.7) is one such[62] – it is somewhat ironic that the only series of texts which are regularly illustrated by pictorial cycles are not narratives at all: they are psalters, books of hours and missals.[63] So secular narrative illustration, it may be concluded, was simply not part of an English manuscript production system, though whether this was due to the demands, or lack of them, on the part of the buying public (or an inherent insular stinginess, as Ian Doyle has suggested)[64] or to the lack of a sufficiently well-established tradition in the book trade, is difficult to resolve. Perhaps all these factors played their part.

Given this situation, it is perhaps not so strange after all that not many romances were given a fully deluxe treatment in their production. But having acknowledged this, it is not the case that all the remaining copies of romance were workaday, although a good number were. There were prestige copies made, such as Bodl. Digby MS 185 containing *Ponthus and the Fair Sidone* and Cambridge Trinity College MS 0.5.2, with its copies of the stanzaic *Generydes* and, once more, Lydgate's *Troy Book*; both of these codices are decoratively embellished with coats of arms of the families to which they belonged. Digby, as noted above, is a Hopton book, while Derek Pearsall has associated Trinity with the Norfolk gentry families of Thwaites and Knyvetts.[65] Then there is CUL Ff.3.11, the fullest extant copy of the mid-fifteenth-century prose *Merlin*, and Longleat MS 257, containing the prose *Ipomydon C*. The first

61 See Kathleen L. Scott, 'Design, Decoration and Illustration', in *Book Production and Publishing*, ed. Griffiths and Pearsall, pp. 31–64, at p. 46.

62 Kathleen L. Scott, 'The Illustration and Decoration of Manuscripts of Nicholas Love's *Mirror of the Blessed Life of Jesus Christ*', in *Nicholas Love at Waseda*, ed. Shoichi Oguro, Richard Beadle and Michael G. Sargent (Cambridge: D. S. Brewer, 1997), pp. 61–86.

63 Scott, 'Design, Decoration and Illustration', pp. 46–7, gives details.

64 Doyle, 'English Books In and Out of Court from Edward III to Henry VII', p. 180.

65 Meale, 'The Politics of Book Ownership'; Derek Pearsall, 'Notes on the Manuscript of *Generydes*', *The Library*, 5th series, 16 (1961), 205–10.

of these is associated with a female member of the Tudor courtier family of Guildford, the latter has Richard III's name and motto while he was duke of Gloucester, which has been taken as proof of ownership. Each of these codices has champ initials.[66]

I would suggest, then, that romance as a genre was not especially different from any other genre or author's *oeuvre* in the Middle Ages in terms of the production values brought to bear upon individual copies. But certain conclusions do arise from looking at the deluxe copies that survive. Most significantly, perhaps, is the apparent prominence of London as a centre for the manufacture of luxury books, which is in line with its flourishing in the promulgation of literary texts from the early fifteenth century onwards. That this should be so comes down to the city's unique position as a place in which prosperity, whether deriving from court circles or from the upper ranks of mercantile or civic elite, determined aspects of the trade in books.[67] In addition, the information to be gleaned from the evidence provided by these manuscripts as to the activities of their scribes and book artists gives us an insight into the workings of a profession which was not exclusively devoted – at least at the beginning of the period considered here – to the manufacture of books containing literary texts. Over the time-span I have covered – approximately 140 years – there are differences to be observed. The organising scribe of Auchinleck and his fellows and the book artists(s) who worked alongside him did not, it would seem fairly certain, derive their living from producing secular books. The situation may well have been different for the scribe of Harley 326 and the eight (and probably counting) manuscripts which he copied.

It was not to be long after the making of Harley 326 that pictorial images in copies of romances became commonplace – not extensively so for Caxton, but routinely for Wynkyn de Worde and his contemporaries.[68] Printed woodcut blocks could be generic images of knights on horseback, used time and time again;[69] or they could, as with de Worde's edition of *Helyas, Knyght of the Swanne*, dated 6 February 1512, be specially commissioned from foreign sources. Here, the illustrations have been copied and cut from Jean Petit's

66 Carol M. Meale, 'The Manuscripts and Early Audience of the Middle English *Prose Merlin*', in *The Changing Face of Arthurian Romance: Essays on Arthurian Prose Romances in Memory of Cedric E. Pickford*, ed. Alison Adams, Armel H. Diverres, Karen Stern and Kenneth Varty (Cambridge: D. S. Brewer, 1986), pp. 92–111; and Carol M. Meale, 'The Middle English Romance of *Ipomedon*: A Late Medieval "Mirror" for Princes and Merchants', *Reading Medieval Studies* 10 (1984), 136–91; Anne E. Sutton and Livia Visser Fuchs, *Richard III's Books* (Stroud: Sutton, 1997), passim.

67 This is not to say that other towns and cities did not have a flourishing trade, but they did not share London's potential market in the court. See Michael, 'Urban Production of Manuscript Books'.

68 Edward Hodnett, *English Woodcuts 1480–1535* (Oxford: OUP, 1973).

69 E.g. Hodnett, *English Woodcuts*, cat. no. 1122, p. 292 and fig. 103.

La Genealogie auecques les gestes & nobles faitz darmes du trespreux et renomee prince Godeffroy de Boulion (Paris, 1504), a process which is evident from the reversal and slight coarsening of the images.[70] Whichever route these woodcuts travelled, be it the short distance within de Worde's printing premises or across the Channel, a process of democratisation had begun in the world of the illustrated romance.[71]

70 Hodnett, *English Woodcuts*, p. 23 and cat. nos. 1245–54; Carol M. Meale, 'Caxton, de Worde, and the Publication of Romance in Late Medieval England', *The Library*, 6th series, 14 (1992), 283–98, at p. 292 and n. 32.

71 Jordi Sánchez-Marti, 'Illustrating the Printed Middle English Verse Romances, c.1500–c.1535', *Word & Image: A Journal of Verbal/Visual Enquiry* 27 (2011), 90–102.

6

Is *Cheuelere Assigne* an Alliterative Poem?

Thorlac Turville-Petre

The only text of *Cheuelere Assigne* is in the mid-fifteenth-century romance anthology, BL MS Cotton Caligula A ii. In 370 lines the poem retells the story of Godfrey de Bouillon's legendary ancestor, the Knight of the Swan, as set out at nearly ten times the length in the *Beatrix* version of the *Naissance du Chevalier au Cigne*, the opening section of the French Crusade Cycle.[1] The poem narrates how Queen Beatrice gave birth to seven babies, each wearing a silver necklace. Her wicked mother-in-law Matabryne presents seven puppies to King Oriens, alleging the queen had slept with animals, and orders that Beatrice should be imprisoned and the babies drowned; instead her servant leaves them alive in the forest where they are found by a hermit, who takes care of them for twelve years. But the wicked Matabryne learns that they are still living and sends the forester to kill them. He cuts off their silver necklaces and the children are transformed into swans, all except for Cheuelere Assigne who is elsewhere in the forest with the hermit. An angel instructs him to save his mother who is about to be burnt to death. Cheuelere Assigne kills his opponent in single combat, the queen is released, and Matabryne is burnt in her stead. One silver chain has been melted down, but the others are returned, and five of the swans become human again. Here is the opening eight-line verse-paragraph:

> ¶ All weldynge God · whenne it is his wylle,
> Wele he wereth his · werke with his owne honde;
> For ofte harmes were hente · þat helpe we ne myȝte
> Nere þe hyȝnes of hym · þat lengeth in heuene.
> For this I saye by a lorde · was lente in an yle
> That was kalled Lyor · a londe by hymselfe.

[1] *The Old French Crusade Cycle*: vol. I, *La Naissance du Chevalier au Cygne: Beatrix*, ed. Jan A. Nelson (Tuscaloosa, AL: University of Alabama Press, 1977). See W. R. J. Barron, '*Chevalere Assigne* and the *Naissance du Chevalier au Cygne*', *MÆ* 36 (1967), 25–37.

The kynge hette Oryens · as þe book telleth,
And his qwene Bewtrys · þat bryȝt was & shene. (1–8)[2]

The syntax runs over pairs of lines, and each pair is linked by alliteration. Most lines follow the classic pattern, with both lifts in the first half-line alliterating with the first lift in the second (aa/ax). Possibly the scribe has reversed the b-verse of l. 4, which could be corrected to read 'in heuene þat lengeth'. As it stands l. 5 is xa/ax, but substituting *lerne* for *saye* would make it regular. The mid-line punctus in l. 2 should obviously follow *werke* rather than preceding it; the scribe has overlooked the 'mute stave' *with* in the b-verse, a feature very common in *Piers Plowman*, with a close parallel in B.3.74, 'Wite what þow werchest · wiþ þi riȝt syde'.[3] Similarly the b-verse of l. 7 alliterates on the conjunction *as*; exactly the same b-verse alliterating on the vowel is formulaic in the *Wars of Alexander* (ll. 17, 35, 2360, etc.);[4] while the noun *book* provides the link to the next line alliterating on /b/. This introductory paragraph is a display of the poet's craft, matching in a less elaborate fashion the introduction to the *Wars*, which was composed as a twenty-four-line paragraph structured as four-line units alliterating together.[5]

However, the opening of *Cheuelere Assigne* gives a misleading impression of the metrics of the poem as a whole. According to the statistics computed by J. P. Oakden, only 14 per cent of lines are the traditional aa/ax, in 10 per cent the alliteration doesn't span the line, and the same percentage have no alliteration at all.[6] How do we account for this irregularity? I have shown that a couple of easy emendations would regularise the opening lines, and this might indicate that the text is massively corrupt. Immediately preceding *Cheuelere Assigne* in the manuscript is another alliterative poem, *The Siege of Jerusalem*. Here are some lines from the poem as it appears in Caligula A ii:

¶ And after þat euery manne · to þe soper wente
Thogh þe woundes were sore · þer was none þat of woo menede
But daunsynge & no sorow · with noyse of pypes
And with nakeres nysely · all þe nyȝte tyme

2 *The Romance of the Cheuelere Assigne*, ed. Henry H. Gibbs, EETS e.s. 6 (London: OUP, 1868). Also in *Medieval English Romances*, ed. Diane Speed, 2 vols (3rd edn, Durham: Durham Medieval Texts, 1993), I, 149–70 (text), II, 289–300 (notes). The Caligula scribe marked off the preceding text, the alliterative *Siege of Jerusalem*, in quatrains, and *Cheualere Assigne* mechanically in eight-line 'paragraphs'.

3 *Piers Plowman: The B Version: Will's Visions of Piers Plowman, Do-Well, Do-Better and Do-Best*, ed. George Kane and E. Talbot Donaldson (London: Athlone Press, 1975).

4 *The Wars of Alexander*, ed. Hoyt N. Duggan and Thorlac Turville-Petre, EETS s.s. 10 (Oxford: OUP, 1989).

5 *The Wars of Alexander*, ed. Duggan and Turville-Petre, pp. xxiii–iv, and note to ll. 1–22.

6 J. P. Oakden, *Alliterative Poetry in Middle English: The Dialectal and Metrical Survey* (Manchester: Manchester University Press, 1930), p. 187.

> ¶ Whenne þe nyght was doone · & þe day spronge
> Soone aftur þe sonne · were gedered þe grete

The Caligula text of *The Siege of Jerusalem* belongs to a family in which the text has been systematically revised to appeal to a more southerly audience than its Yorkshire original, and in the process the strictly regular alliteration of the poem has been ignored. The vocabulary has been modified to get rid of words unusual outside alliterative verse, often substituting 'man' and other common words for those alliterative synonyms *freke*, *gome*, *segge* and the like, and avoiding words such as *blonk* for 'horse'. Only one line in this passage alliterates according to the regular aa/ax pattern. Yet a bold editor familiar with the alliterative style could suggest emendations to put the metre right. In the first line *manne* is a classic scribal substitution for an alliterating synonym such as *segge*, and if that is right then *sithen* suggests itself in place of *after þat*. In the second line *wide* in place of *sore* might commend itself. The third line is tricky, since an editor might easily assume alliteration on /n/, but on further consideration reflect that *dole* is a synonym for *sorow*, and, having made that imaginative leap, hit upon *din* for *noyse*, prompted by the line 'For dauncesynge of Duchemen· and dynnyng of pypez' in the alliterative *Morte Arthure* (l. 2030). Luckily, such half-right conjectural emendations are unnecessary, since the better text in Bodleian Library, MS Laud Misc. 656 (followed by modern editors) reads:

> suþ eu*er*eche a segge · to þe soper ȝede
> þoȝ þey wou*n*ded wer*e* · was no wo nempned
> bot daunsyng & no deil · w*ith* dy*n*nyng of pipis
> & þe nakerer noyse · alle þe nyȝt tyme
> whan þe derk was dou*n* · & þe day spryngen
> sone aft*er* þe so*n*ne · se*m*bled þe grete (853–8)[7]

If *Cheuelere Assigne* is the product of a similar rewriting, then the revision was incomparably more thorough-going than the Caligula copy of *The Siege of Jerusalem*. One feature of the metre of *Cheuelere Assigne* is that, where there is alliteration, it often falls on the last stave of the line, commonly with the patterns ax/aa (e.g. l. 4), ax/xa ('Sythen he toke hit by þe lokkes · & in þe helm leyde', l. 338), and aa/xa (e.g. l. 17). If this was revision, it apparently involved not only substitution of synonyms but also frequent reordering of the line, and there seems no motive for that. In any case, extensive editorial 'correction' of the text would be impossible. Occasionally an emendation seems particularly attractive: at the end of the poem the swan children are baptised: 'Thenne þey formed a fonte · & cristene þe children' (365). Substituting *folwe*,

7 Compare *The Siege of Jerusalem*, ed. Ralph Hanna and David Lawton, EETS o.s. 320 (Oxford: OUP, 2003). The editors emend *spryngen* to *sprongen*.

'baptise', for *cristene* would give a regular line, and furthermore the word is part of the poet's vocabulary. Indeed it is used four lines later in a non-alliterating line 'The sixte was fulwedde · Cheuelere Assygne'(369), which might, of course, have provided a motive for the poet to avoid it here. Certainly a few lines need to be emended on grounds of sense. When the hero engages in combat with Malkedras, his steed Feraunce makes a very unchivalric assault by kicking out the eyes of the opposing horse: 'Whenne þat þe chylde þat hym bare · blent hadde his fere' (323–5). Clearly *chylde* is an error, picked up from the previous line, and must be emended to a word for 'horse'. Editors make the obvious emendation to *blonk* for the alliteration. There is one problem with this: the word is not elsewhere in the poem; and this points to a remarkable feature: the complete absence of the characteristic alliterative vocabulary. None of the classic synonyms for 'man', *freke*, *lede*, *schalk* and the like, occur in the text, none of the range of verbs meaning 'go', or the adverbs meaning 'quickly', all those words restricted to alliterative verse, are found in the poem. It seems most unlikely that behind the present text of *Cheuelere Assigne* lies a traditional alliterative composition.

Another poem with very irregular alliteration is *Joseph of Arimathie*.[8] Again this work is an abbreviated version of an episode in a long French cycle romance, the *Estoire del Saint Graal*.[9] The text was copied before the end of the fourteenth century into the huge Vernon manuscript by a west Midland scribe, and it may be that it is an early product of the Alliterative Revival, composed before the standard patterns of the alliterative lines had become established. Oakden calculated that just 64 of its 709 lines have the standard aa/ax pattern, while 113 lines have no alliteration at all.[10] It differs from *Cheuelere Assigne* in that it makes considerable use of the characteristic vocabulary of alliterative verse, with words such as *burne*, *leod* and *schalk* for 'man', *bent*, 'battlefield', *carpe*, 'speak', and *þroly*, 'eagerly', though the poem by no means approaches the lexical range of major poems of the Revival such as *Sir Gawain and the Green Knight*, *Morte Arthure*, *The Wars of Alexander* and *The Siege of Jerusalem*. The character of *Joseph of Arimathie* at its best is illustrated by this battle description, a favourite topos of alliterative verse:

> In þe þikkeste pres · he preuede his wepne,
> Breek braynes abrod · brusede burnes,
> Beer bale in his hond · bed hit aboute.
> He hedde an hache vppon heiȝ · wiþ a gret halue,

8 *Joseph of Arimathie*, ed. Walter W. Skeat, EETS o.s. 44 (London: Trübner, 1871). *Joseph of Arimathea: A Critical Edition*, ed. David A. Lawton (New York: Garland, 1983).

9 See W. R. J. Barron, '*Joseph of Arimathie* and the *Estoire del Saint Graal*', *MÆ* 33 (1964), 184–94.

10 Oakden, *Alliterative Poetry*, pp. 185–6.

Huld hit harde wiþ teis · in his two hondes;
So he frusschede hem with · and fondede his strengþe,
þat luyte miȝte faren him fro · and to fluiȝt founden.
¶ þere weore stedes to struien · stoures to medlen,
Meeten miȝtful men · mallen þorw scheldes,
¶ Harde hauberkes toborsten · and þe brest þurleden,
Schon schene vppon schaft · schalkene blode.
¶ þo þat houen vppon hors · heowen on helme;
¶ þo þat hulden hem on fote · hakken þorw scholdres.
mony swouȝninge lay · þorw schindringe of scharpe,
And starf aftur þe deþ · in a schort while. (500–14)

The passage with its wide range of vocabulary is in the high alliterative style and would not be out of place in *Morte Arthure*. Particularly characteristic of the style are the combination of individual combat with a general mêlée, and the detailing of armour, weapons and body-parts. One may compare *Morte Arthure* 2979–94, where Gawain 'ruysches one helmys, / Riche hawberkes he rente · and rasede schyldes', and the Britons 'Hittes full hertely' so that 'Ketell-hattes they cleue · euen to þe scholdirs'.[11] In the penultimate line the use of *scharpe* as a noun, 'sharp weapon', as in *Morte Arthure* 3842, is noteworthy; the collocation with 'shinder' is repeated in *Gawain* 424, 'þe scharp ... schyndered þe bones'.[12] As in *Morte Arthure*, consecutive lines are linked by alliteration, in *Joseph of Arimathie* in pairs; a-verses have increased alliteration (lines 503, 508, 510) or all four lifts of the line alliterate (501, 506, 511). There is, indeed, a scene of combat in *Cheuelere Assigne*, but it has none of these characteristics:

Thenne thei styrte vp on hy · with staloworth shankes,
Pulledde out her swerdes · & smoten togedur.
'Kepe þy swerde fro my croyse' · quod Cheuelrye Assygne.
'I charge not þy croyse', quod Malkedras · 'þe valwe of a cherye,
For I shalle choppe it fulle smalle · ere þenne þis werke ende'.
An edder spronge out of his shelde · & in his body spynnethe,
A fyre fruscheth out of his croyse · & rapte out his yen;
Thenne he stryketh a stroke · Cheualere Assygne,
Euen his sholder in twoo · & down into þe herte,
And he bowethe hym down · & ȝeldethe vp þe lyfe. (326–35)

The passage begins with an uncharacteristically traditional alliterative line (cf. *Gawain* 846: 'Sturne, stif on þe stryþþe · on stalworth schonkez', and 431: 'styþly he start forth · vpon styf schonkes'), but there the comparison

[11] *Morte Arthure*, ed. Mary Hamel (New York: Garland, 1984).

[12] *Sir Gawain and the Green Knight*, ed. J. R. R. Tolkien and E. V. Gordon, rev. Norman Davis, 2nd edn (Oxford: OUP, 1967).

with alliterative description ends, and we should look more to the metrical romances for parallels.

It has been proposed – unconvincingly, in my view – that *Joseph of Arimathie* in its extant state represents the author's first draft, which he would subsequently have improved by adding alliteration to regularise the metre,[13] and so we need to ask whether *Cheuelere Assigne* could similarly be a draft. The whole notion of the survival of draft copies of medieval texts seems to me fraught with improbabilities; would an unscrupulous scribe snatch a draft from the author's desk, or might it have been circulated after his death by his literary executor? But more importantly, such a notion surely falsifies the process of literary composition. A colleague who will remain nameless joined me in composing a long alliterative romance, the episodic adventures of the questing knight, Sir Erkenwald. We began composing with the formal features – the alliteration and rhythm – in our minds, and tried to fit the content into those structures, rather than thinking in prose and then adding the verse features. Surely that is how real alliterative poets would have composed? Can we suppose that Chaucer would have added rhyme to *Troilus* at a subsequent stage? There is just one passage of alliterative verse which has plausibly been put forward as a poet's unrevised draft, and that is the Ophni and Phinees story that Langland added in the C-Text of *Piers Plowman*, Prologue 106–24.[14] Many of the lines in this passage lack alliteration and one scribe made a ham-fisted attempt to 'improve' some of them.[15] Furthermore, the episode has been slotted into the B-Text Prologue in a way that does not quite fit. Possibly, therefore, this is a passage not fully revised and added at the last moment, but this is a difficult argument to maintain with a poet whose approach to the metre is flexible, perhaps particularly so in the C-Text revisions.[16] I prefer to think that this is late Langland, more relaxed in matters of alliteration and rhythm, and concentrating on the message rather than the form.

Instead of entertaining the possibilities of draft composition or pervasive corruption, we might instead read the text of *Cheuelere Assigne* as it is and

13 *Joseph of Arimathea*, ed. Lawton, pp. xxviii–xxix.

14 *Piers Plowman: The C Version: Will's Visions of Piers Plowman, Do-Well, Do-Better and Do-Best*, ed. George Russell and George Kane (London: Athlone Press, 1997).

15 *Piers Plowman*, ed. Russell and Kane, Appendix II, pp. 191–2. For demonstration of the scribal character of this passage see Ralph Hanna, *Pursuing History: Middle English Manuscripts and Their Texts* (Stanford, CA: Stanford University Press, 1996), pp. 204–14.

16 For older views of Langland's practice, see E. Talbot Donaldson, *The C-Text and Its Poet* (New Haven, CT: Yale University Press, 1949), pp. 37–49; for a reassessment see Hoyt N. Duggan, 'Notes on the Metre of *Piers Plowman*: Twenty Years On', in *Approaches to the Metres of Alliterative Verse*, ed. Judith Jefferson and Ad Putter, Leeds Texts and Monographs, new series 17 (Leeds: School of English, University of Leeds, 2009), pp. 159–86.

see how well it stands up to scrutiny. In fact the author seems to me to be quite skilled in several respects. To condense the account in a French romance of over 3,000 lines to just 370 lines is an achievement in itself.[17] The narrative is clear, the expression lively. Particularly amusingly handled is what might be described as the knightly education of the young hero, who has been brought up in isolation from civilisation. His hermit-protector tells him he must fight for his mother, but has first to explain to him what a mother is. To explain what a horse is is even more difficult for the hermit, since he himself has never seen one, so on his arrival in court our hero is singularly ill-prepared for mounted combat. Here is a comic version of a standard romance topos, the arming of the hero, as the king equips the young man with the horse Feraunt, with armour and with shield. All of this is mystifying to Cheuelere Assigne, so he asks a friendly knight:

> 'What beeste is þis,' quod þe childe · 'þat I shalle on houe?'
> ¶ 'Hit is called an hors,' quod þe kny3te · 'a good & an abull.'
> 'Why eteth he yren?' quod þe chylde · 'Wyll he ete no3th elles?
> And what is þat on his bakke · of byrthe or on bounden?'[18]
> 'Nay, þat in his mowth · men kallen a brydell,
> And that a sadell on his bakke · þat þou shalt in sytte.'
> 'And what heuy kyrtell is þis · with holes so thykke?
> And þis holowe on on my hede? · I may no3t wele here!'
> 'An helme men kallen þat on · & an hawberke þat other.'
> ¶ 'But what broode on is þis on my breste? · Hit bereth adown my nekke.'
> 'A bry3te shelde & a sheene · to shylde þe fro strokes.'
> 'And what longe on is þis · that I shall vp lyfte?'
> 'Take þat launce vp in þyn honde · and loke þou hym hytte!' (288–300)

The diction is entirely suited to express the comic ignorance of the hero and the conversational tone of the exchange: the nicely descriptive metonomies *holowe on* for helmet, *broode on* for shield, and *longe on* for lance, are striking examples, equivalent to informal 'long thing' in modern English. There are no words drawn from the alliterative stock. In the last line it would be tempting, but wrong, to emend *honde* to the northern *loue*,[19] and metrically just two lines (297, 298) can be analysed as regular aa/ax, another two (290, 296) perhaps as aa/aa. All the other lines have irregular alliterative patterns, yet the last seven lines are grouped by alliteration as a triplet and two couplets.

[17] See Tony Davenport, 'Abbreviation and the Education of the Hero in the *Chevalere Assigne*', in *The Matter of Identity in Medieval Romance*, ed. Phillipa Hardman (Cambridge: D. S. Brewer, 2002), pp. 9–20.

[18] That is, 'was he born with it, or is it tied onto him'.

[19] See *Wars* 2193 'Held þe lettir in his loue'. In *Wars* 923 the editors emend *hand* to *looue* for the alliteration.

The alliteration of the poem is quite irregular, there is a complete absence of alliterative vocabulary, and the set-piece descriptions of alliterative poetry, the arming of the hero and the battle, are treated quite differently from the way a traditional alliterative poet would handle them. So does this mean that *Cheuelere Assigne* is not an alliterative poem? I argue that it is. We naturally assume that the defining feature of alliterative verse is its alliteration. I see it instead as a characteristic feature, its function being to reinforce the metrical shape of the long line. From this perspective *Pearl* is not written in the alliterative line but in stanzas of iambic tetrameter with heavy but irregular alliteration.[20] Another characteristic feature of classic alliterative verse is its specialised vocabulary, but this is not an essential component. After all, large stretches of *Piers Plowman* make no use of it, and there is almost no alliterative vocabulary in *Pierce the Plowman's Crede*, though it alliterates fairly regularly and is properly classed as an alliterative poem. What defines alliterative verse is the accentual rhythm in a line consisting of balanced half-lines (in Caligula punctuated by the scribe). The lines may or may not be rhymed. The essential feature is that the rhythm is heteromorphic, that is, it avoids the regular alternation of stress and unstress that is the essence of syllabic verse.[21]

The b-verse rhythms have been closely studied because they are tightly patterned. To put it simply, a b-verse must have one but only one long dip, that is to say an unstressed element of two or more syllables.[22] So if we look at the passage just quoted, we see that the structure of a short (one-syllable) dip followed by a long, as in the first line, 'þat **I** shalle on **hou**e', is the commonest. A long followed by a short is in the third line: 'Wyll he **ete** noȝth **ell**es' (taking *ete* as a monosyllable). The only unmetrical b-verse is 296, '& an **haw**berke þat **oth**er', and this could easily be corrected by dropping *&*. The long line regularly ends on one and only one unstressed syllable; some analysts argue that it must do so.[23] All the lines here fulfil that requirement, with plural *strokes*, final *-e* invoked for infinitives *houe, sytte, here, lyfte* and *hytte*; the adjective *thykke* comes from OE *þicce* and is in any case plural (cf.

[20] See Hoyt N. Duggan, 'Meter, Stanza, Vocabulary, Dialect', in *A Companion to the Gawain-Poet*, ed. Derek Brewer and Jonathan Gibson (Cambridge: D. S. Brewer, 1997), pp. 221–42, at pp. 232–7.

[21] See *Joseph of Arimathea*, ed. Lawton, p. xxiii; Ralph Hanna, 'Defining Middle English Alliterative Poetry', in *The Endless Knot*, ed. M. Teresa Tavormina and R. F. Yeager (Cambridge: D. S. Brewer, 1995), pp. 43–64.

[22] For detailed analysis see Hoyt N. Duggan, 'The Shape of the B-Verse in Middle English Alliterative Poetry', *Speculum* 61 (1986), 564–92.

[23] See Ad Putter, Judith Jefferson and Myra Stokes, *Studies in the Metre of Alliterative Verse*, Medium Ævum Monographs, new series 25 (Oxford: Medium Ævum, 2007), pp. 19–71.

Gawain 138, 'so sware and so þik', for which read *þikke*),[24] and *nekke* from OE *hnecca* (cf. *Gawain* 2310, 'bi þe bare nek', but read *nekke*).

These b-verses are representative of those throughout the poem. The great majority follow the b-verse rules, with a few problematic exceptions. Early in the poem are a couple of lines:

> The kynge was witty · whenne he wysste her with chylde
> And þankede lowely our Lorde · of his loue & his sonde. (35–6)

The first line might perhaps be regularised by shifting the caesura to follow *whenne*, and the second by dropping the repeated *his*. More interesting is the line: 'And noyse was in þe cyte · felly lowde' (225). The b-verse is a syllable too short, lacking a long dip. In other respects it fits a well-recorded pattern. For example *The Siege of Jerusalem* has 'Tymbris and tabourris · tonelande loude' (530), and *Gawain* has 'Þenne he carped to þe knyȝt · criande loude' (1088). These are regular because the disyllabic ending *-ande* provides the long dip. But *felly* will not do as it stands. It is an adverb formed on *fell*, 'cruel', used as an intensive. A device used by the *Gawain* poet to provide the required syllable is to add an adverbial *-ly* to an adjectival *-ly* ending, as shown in the following from *Gawain*: 'and ferlyly long' (796), 'and luflyly sayde' (2389), 'semlyly fayre' (266), 'sellyly ofte' (1083). But there is no adjective *felly* so we must look for a different explanation. The adverbial ending *–ly* derives from the OE *-līce*, so here we may read *felliche*. The question is extensively discussed by Putter, Jefferson and Stokes, who offer examples from *Gawain* such as 'semlych ryche' (882) where we must read *semlyche*, and 'fersly brenned' (832) where we should read *fersliche*.[25]

I conclude that *Cheuelere Assigne* is composed by a poet who understood and for the most part followed the rhythmic rules of alliterative verse. Topics such as the arming of the hero and the description of battle are handled with ironic humour. Why did the poet choose not to adopt the alliterative vocabulary and not to conform more rigorously to the standard alliterative patterns? The answer lies, I believe, in the nature of his audience.

The consensus is that the author came from the traditional home of alliterative poetry, the north-west Midlands, and his language was altered by the scribe who was from the south east, perhaps based in London. This placing of *Cheuelere Assigne* derives from too ready acceptance of Oakden's rather confused analysis of the language.[26] He identified a handful of what he judged to be western forms, and concluded that 'here was obviously an eastern scribe

24 Marie Borroff, in her classic study, *Sir Gawain and the Green Knight: A Stylistic and Metrical Study* (New Haven, CT: Yale University Press, 1962), p. 188, is wrong to cite this as a 'clearly masculine ending'.

25 Putter et al., *Studies*, pp. 101–17.

26 Oakden, *Alliterative Poetry*, pp. 61–3.

who forgot to alter these forms in a N. Midl. poem', on the grounds that 'no other alliterative romances are found in the east'. This, of course, is a circular argument, and untrue in any case: the major alliterative romance *Morte Arthure* was composed in Lincolnshire.[27] The scatter of forms that Oakden identified as north-west Midland are as follows:

(a) Pres. 3 sg. -<es> (6x). *LALME* only maps the feature for the northern half of the country (dot map 645). It is generally northern and north Midland, but certainly present in London at this date. Chaucer used it occasionally in rhyme as early as c. 1368 (*Book of the Duchess* 73, 257, *House of Fame* 426). By the later fifteenth century it was well established among the mobile population of London by a process that has been called 'dialect hopping'.[28]

(b) l. 310 *falleth* for 'felled'. Oakden's phonological explanation for this feature (pp. 15–16) is faulty. This represents contamination between intransitive *fall* and transitive *fell*; see *OED fall v.* IX. ME examples from east Midland texts recorded by *MED* are *Sowdone of Babylone* 3009, *Laud Troy Book* 6999.

(c) Occasional *ony*, *mony* for 'any', 'many'. The former is not western but predominantly East Anglian: *LALME* dot map 99. The latter is generally regarded as west Midland (dot map 91), but the Caligula scribe has it also in non-western texts, e.g. 6x in *Emaré* (15, 468, 599 etc.)

(d) l. 82 pr. pl. *ar* for *arn*: *LALME* dot map 118 has many eastern examples, especially around London.

Unlike *Joseph of Arimathie*, copied by a west Midland scribe, there is nothing to place *Cheuelere Assigne* in the north-west Midlands, though the six examples of -<es> for pr. 3 sg. may suggest a text originating somewhere to the north of London. The language of the scribe is mixed, but generally south-eastern,[29] and the texts that he copied suggest a Londoner with access to a wide range of material to appeal to a London readership, including tail-rhyme romances from the north-east Midlands, such as *Sir Eglamour*, from

27 First proposed by A. McIntosh, 'The Textual Transmission of the Alliterative *Morte Arthure*', in *English and Medieval Studies Presented to J. R. R. Tolkien*, ed. N. Davis and C. L. Wrenn (London: George Allen and Unwin, 1962), pp. 231–40. See now Ralph Hanna and Thorlac Turville-Petre, 'The Text of the Alliterative *Morte Arthure*: A Prolegomenon for a Future Edition', in *Robert Thornton and His Books: Essays on the Lincoln and London Thornton Manuscripts*, ed. Susanna Fein and Michael Johnston (York: York Medieval Press, 2014), pp. 131–55.

28 See Roger Lass, 'Phonology and Morphology', in *The Cambridge History of the English Language*, ed. Richard M. Hogg, vol. 2 (Cambridge: CUP, 1992), pp. 23–155, at pp. 138–9; Terttu Nevalainen and Ingrid Tieken-Boon van Ostade, 'Standardisation', in *A History of the English Language*, ed. Richard Hogg and David Denison (Cambridge: CUP, 2006), pp. 293–4.

29 Hanna and Lawton provide a summary analysis of the scribal language in their edition of *Siege*, p. xxvi. They date the manuscript s. xv$^{3/4}$.

the central Midlands, such as *Emaré*, and from the London area itself, such as *Sir Launfal* and *Lybeaus Desconus*.[30] I suppose the author of *Cheuelere Assigne* modified the alliterative line because he was writing for a London and east Midland audience brought up on such romances, as well as *Octavian Imperator*, and *Sir Isumbras* which follows *Cheuelere Assigne* in Cotton Caligula A II. The question, then, is not why did he modify the style but why did he choose the alliterative line in the first place? But that is another story.

30 For the placing of these texts see Rhiannon Purdie, *Anglicising Romance: Tail-Rhyme and Genre in Medieval English Literature* (Cambridge: D. S. Brewer, 2008), pp. 178–82, 209–14.

7

Language Tests for the Identification of Middle English Genre[1]

Donka Minkova

1. Preliminaries

The linguistic 'identity' of a text comprises properties such as codicological setting, dialect features, vocabulary, metre, rhyme and alliteration, in the case of poetic compositions; such properties are essential to the characterization of any surviving document. That philological foundation is the gateway to literary interpretations and evaluations of the poet's narrative skills, artistry, and originality. A good grasp of the bidirectional interaction of the linguistic and the literary facets of the material has the potential of being mutually informative. The selection of specific language forms for specific literary forms can be used both for charting and testing linguistic change, and for charting and testing literary history. This project explores some possible links between the prosodic, semantic, and pragmatic characteristics of Middle English romance texts and our assumptions about the genre's intended audience. The goal of the study is to formulate some new research questions and to outline a research methodology to address these questions; it seeks to identify new ways of quantifying and interpreting the accommodation of linguistic features in verse and thereby to enrich the repertoire of tests that help us uncover and contextualize historical language use.

The choice of verse texts for this study should be no surprise: this volume is focused on the history of medieval romance, and verse was the natural vehicle

[1] The approach to *genre* in this study is strictly traditional. I follow Amy J. Devitt's broad definition: 'Genres exist [...] in the sense that they are patternings from repeated actions according to which (or in reaction against which) readers and writers use language', in 'Integrating Rhetorical and Literary Theories of Genre', *College English* 62 (2000), 696–718, at p. 702. For a pilot study of how different genres are affected differently by linguistic change, see Devitt, 'Genre as Textual Variable: Some Historical Evidence from Scots and American English', *American Speech* 64 (1989), 291–303.

of romance composition and transmission until practically the end of what we think of as 'Middle' English. Moreover, verse texts are always a fertile testing ground for linguistic reconstruction. In verse, we count syllables, their relative prominence, their prosodic weight, and their arrangement in units or metrical feet. All of these elements are recursive and quantifiable; their *controlled* recursiveness distinguishes verse metre from the natural rhythm of speech.

The linguistic competence of the poet is the raw material for verse; linguistic competence implies also awareness of ubiquitous variation and different levels of formality associated with different discourse modes. The ways in which that awareness is manifested in the metre of a particular verse form are therefore a useful heuristic for the poet's, or the copyist's, intuitions and responses to the nature and the destination of a composition. With this premise in mind, we can ask whether the composers and copyists of Middle English romances make metrical and stylistic choices that can be considered genre-specific.

This study draws its new data from two well-known romances, both copied by Scribe 1 of the Auchinleck manuscript: *The King of Tars* and *Sir Orfeo*. The first linguistic feature investigated in Section 2 is the status of phrasal prominence within the noun phrase. Section 3 turns to a related topic: the possible link between semantic weight, frequency, and the prosodic prominence of attributive adjectives in these romances. Section 4 adumbrates an additional line of diachronic investigation: the attributive vs. predicative use of adjectives as possibly promising tests for genre. The results are summarized in Section 5.

2. Phrasal stress in Middle English: continuity or innovation?

2.1. The Nuclear Stress Rule in Present-Day English

The first linguistic property tested as a potential diagnostic for genre-specific usage is the placement of adjective-noun phrases in the verse line. Rising prominence within syntactic phrases is a common, though not invariant pattern across languages. In Present-Day English (PDE) this pattern is known as the Nuclear Stress Rule (NSR):

(1) *Nuclear Stress Rule* (NSR): The rightmost member of a phrase is strongest.[2]
NSR: *stay cóol, get sét, three-tén, call hóme, nice dréss*

[2] The wording is from Bruce Hayes, *Metrical Stress Theory: Principles and Case Studies* (Chicago: University of Chicago Press, 1995), p. 368. The term originates with Noam Chomsky and Morris Halle, *The Sound Pattern of English* (New York: Harper and Row, 1968), p. 16. See also Liberman and Prince, 'On Stress and Linguistic Rhythm', *Linguistic Inquiry* 8 (1977), 249–336, at p. 257, who note: 'In any pair of sister nodes [AB]

Establishing phrasal prominence relations in living languages is hard because the basic principle of rightward prominence can be overridden by independent syntactic, semantic, and pragmatic considerations, but the general definition in (1) serves well as a starting point. In what follows, the NSR manifestations will be examined for a very narrowly defined subset: adjective-noun phrases of the type *nice dréss*. If the *default* prosodic pattern of such phrases is rising, the expectation is that poets would tend to place the head of the phrase, the noun, in a strong/ictic metrical position, while the subordinate adjective will be placed in a weak or non-ictic position. Even though prominence reversal can be quite common in poetic texts, Joseph C. Beaver found that 'in a random sampling from some dozen poets (nine of them British) in seven or eight different periods, occurrences of adj-noun with back-to-back stress are well over twice as frequent in the weak-strong configuration, a fact which would tend to support operation of nuclear stress assignment'.[3] Similarly, Marina Tarlinskaja found that throughout the history of English verse the expected correspondences between phrasal prosodic prominence (NSR) and ictus do not fall below 60 per cent, and they exceed that figure most of the time.[4] The examples in (2) illustrate the expected distribution:

(2) Monosyllabic adjectives in Shakespeare's *Sonnets*[5]

And with **old** wóes **new** wáil my dear time's waste	30
If the **dull** súbstance of my flesh were thought	44
To leap **large** léngths of miles when thou art gone	44
I think **good** thóughts, whilst others write **good** wórds	85
Take heed, **dear hart**, of this **large** prívilege	95
And beautie making beautifull **old** ríme	106
In the **old** áge black was not counted faire	127

X, where X is a phrasal category, B is strong.' For the greater stability of phrasal stress compared to compound stress, see Liberman and Sproat, 'The Stress and Structure of Modified Noun Phrases in English', in *Lexical Matters*, ed. I. A. Sag and A. Scabolcsi (Stanford, CA: Stanford University Press, 1992), pp. 131–81; and Heinz Giegerich, 'Compound or Phrase? English Noun-Plus-Noun Constructions and the Stress Criterion', *ELL* 8 (2004), 1–24. Early discussion of the interplay of speech prosody and metrical placement of adjective-noun phrases in English poetry appears in Joseph C. Beaver, 'The Rules of Stress in English Verse', *Language* 47 (1971), 586–614; and Paul Kiparsky, 'Stress, Syntax, and Meter', *Language* 51 (1975), 576–616.

3 Beaver, 'The Rules of Stress in English Verse', p. 592.

4 Marina Tarlinskaja, *Shakespeare's Verse: Iambic Pentameter and the Poet's Idiosyncrasies* (New York: Peter Lang, 1987); and Marina Tarlinskaja, 'General and Particular Aspects of Meter', in *Phonetics and Phonology*, ed. Paul Kiparsky and Gilbert Youmans (San Diego, CA: Academic Press, 1989), I: *Rhythm and Meter*, pp. 121–54.

5 See also Tarlinskaja, *Shakespeare's Verse*, pp. 32–9; Tarlinskaja, 'General and Particular Aspects of Meter'; Marina Tarlinskaja, *Shakespeare and the Versification of English Drama, 1561–1642* (Burlington, VT: Ashgate, 2014), pp. 19–22.

Such findings support a hypothesis that in poetry composed in regular stress-alternating metre the poets tend to respect speech rhythm and match the peaks of stress to the beats of the verse line.

2.2. Adjective-noun prosodic contour in Old English

The historical depth of the adjective-noun phrase prosodic contour in English is a vexed issue, so before getting into the Middle English attestations, we need to clarify the diachronic input. In the absence of synchronic commentary, the placement of the components in verse is our only source of potentially useful data, yet the interpretation of these data is far from straightforward. The 'usual' pattern of alliteration in adjective-noun phrases in Old English verse is linear: in a string of adjectives, nouns, and non-finite verbs, it is the first element that has to alliterate, but not to the exclusion of the second element. Thus: ***l****ange hwile* 'a long time'[6] alliterates on [l-], and *ond seo* ***d****eorce niht* 'and the dark night'[7] and *ofer* ***d****eop wæter* 'over deep water'[8] alliterate on [d-]. C. B. McCully and R. M. Hogg interpreted the occurrence of alliteration on the adjective as evidence that Old English lacked right-prominent phrasal contour, specifically in noun phrases; therefore the Nuclear Stress Rule could not be projected back to Old English.[9] The implication of that position is that phrasal right prominence was a post-Old English innovation. D. Minkova and R. Stockwell tested the claim in the matching of adjective-noun phrases to metrical positions in Old English verse and argued that the obligatory alliteration on the first/left-hand item in such phrases is a *metrical* artifice, which overrides and obscures the 'natural' rhythm of speech.[10] This can be shown in lines where the syntactic order is inverted to give prominence to the noun:

(3)	Inversion NP + adj. as a stylistic choice in OE:	
	þæt wæs **w**ræc *micel* / **w**ine Scyldinga	*Beo* 170
	þa wæs **w**undor *micel* / þæt se **w**insele	*Beo* 771
	oþþæt **h**refn *blaca* / **h**eofones wynne	*Beo* 1801
	se þe him **w**ines *glæd* / **w**ilna bruceð	*JDay* 78
	þrea wæron **þ**earle, / **þ**egnas *grimme*	*Guthlac* AB 547
	on þam **c**ampstede / **c**yningas *giunge*	*Brun* 29

There are some additional details not previously considered in this context. First, in a structure of single attributive adjective + noun, the default

6 *Beowulf,* 16a. Further references are given after quotations in the text.

7 *Phoenix*, 98b.

8 *Genesis A*, 2876b.

9 Christopher B. McCully and Richard M. Hogg, 'Dialect Variation and Historical Metrics', *Diachronica* 11 (1994), 13–34.

10 Donka Minkova and Robert Stockwell, 'Against the Emergence of the Nuclear Stress Rule in Middle English', in *Studies in Middle English Linguistics*, ed. Jacek Fisiak (Berlin: Mouton de Gruyter, 1997), pp. 301–34.

arrangement in Old English prose is the same as in Present-Day English, e.g. the adjective precedes the head noun;[11] inversions are found almost exclusively in the verse.[12] This substantiates the argument that the remarkably high rate of noun-adjective inversion in verse is driven by the requirements of alliteration. If the parametrical rules of alliteration trump the norms of syntax, that those rules also trump the norms of phrasal prosody becomes more plausible.

A second consideration comes from within the poetic corpus. B. Rand Hutcheson gathered statistical information on the distribution of alliteration in adjective-noun phrases which is quite revealing.[13] He separated verse subtypes depending on the syntactic composition of the string in the relevant verse type. Type A is by far the most frequent verse type in the corpus (47 per cent of the on-verses and 39 per cent of the off-verses are Type A).[14] Within that group, the most common pattern is the basic pattern S w S w, as in ***l**ange hwile* (*Beo* 16a), no resolution, no secondary stress. One very robustly represented group is A1b: adjective + noun – there are 719 verses of this subtype.[15] Fifty-seven per cent of these are in the b-verse, which is the one part of the long line in Old English that disallows double alliteration, e.g. ***s**incfāge **s**el / **s**weartum nihtum* 'jewelled hall / in black nights' (*Beo* 167); on ***b**earm nacan / **b**eorhte frætwe* 'into bosom of ship / bright trappings' (*Beo* 214). Given the metrical linear precedence rule for alliteration, we cannot construe this distribution as proof of the prosodic relations within the noun phrase in the spoken language. Moreover, the rest of the data for the adjective-noun attestations of A1b-type on-verses shows that there is a significant body of on-verses with double alliteration: 117, or 16.4 per cent, of this subset are of the type ***s**īdra **s**orga* 'spacious sorrows' (*Beo* 149a), ***g**rimre **g**ūðe* 'grim warfare' (*Beo* 527a), ***n**eowle **n**æssas* 'towering crags' (*Beo* 1411). Double alliteration is uninformative as to the prosodic relations in the phrase; it would be unreasonable to use these attestations as evidence *against* the reconstruction of rising phrasal prominence in speech. This leaves 191, or 26.5 per cent of the total A1b data,

[11] Bruce Mitchell, *Old English Syntax* (Oxford: OUP, 1985), I: *Concord, the Parts of Speech and the Sentence*, pp. 75–80.

[12] In *Old English Syntax*, p. 75, Mitchell comments on the frequency of inversions (noun-adjective) in poetry, but does not give specifics. It is notable that David L. Shores found no single post-positioned adjectival modifier in the *Peterborough Chronicle* 1122–54 in *A Descriptive Syntax of the Peterborough Chronicle from 1122–1154* (The Hague and Paris: Mouton, 1971), pp. 159–61; this excludes genitives, prepositional phrases, etc. Moreover, in OE verse, *mycel* is placed after the noun in the great majority of cases, unlike other adjectives such as *leoht*, *beorht*, *grim*, and *wis*, which resist the inversion. This point is relevant to the discussion of semantic weight in Section 3.

[13] Bellenden Rand Hutcheson, *Old English Poetic Metre* (Cambridge: D. S. Brewer, 1995).

[14] Hutcheson, *Old English Poetic Metre*, p. 297.

[15] The total and the percentages are calculated from the basic numbers in Hutcheson, *Old English Poetic Metre*, p. 287.

where there is single alliteration in on-verse adjective-noun phrases. In view of the conservative nature of OE verse we can hardly claim that the evidence of alliteration in the verse makes a good case against the NSR in Old English.[16]

2.3 Testing adjective-noun prosody in Middle English

Turning to Middle English, if we start with the assumption that the preference for rising prominence within a simple noun phrase was a feature of the spoken language, we can inquire whether that prosodic contour influences the placement of the phrase elements in the verse line. Further, we can ask whether the degree to which the prosodic contour of basic NP phrases carries over to 'popular' verse could be associated with the secular nature of romances, their narrative tone, and presumably broader audience. The examples in (4) illustrate the pattern one would expect if we project the rule back to Middle English:

(4) Projecting the NSR back to Middle English:[17]

Gret iόie þai hadde, wiþouten les	*King of Tars* 310
Þe sóudan, wíþ **gode wílle** anón	*King of Tars* 922
Þan was king Memaroc in **gret péyn**	*King of Tars* 1189
In sómer he líveth bí **wild** frút	*Sir Orfeo* 257
To hére his glé he háth **gode wílle**	*Sir Orfeo* 444
That hím was só **hard gráce** y-yarked	*Sir Orfeo* 347

Compare:

For wíth **good hópe** he gán fully asséntе	*Tr* I 391
Gret hónour did hem Deiphebus, certeyn	*Tr* II 1569

[16] It is also of interest that even in the iambic verse of much later vintage when poets resort to alliteration in monosyllabic adjective-noun phrases, it is the adjective that is marked by alliteration. Moreover, the rate of alliteration on the adjectives in Shakespeare's poem *The Rape of Lucrece* is 'almost three times higher' than in his history play *Richard II*, as noted by Tarlinskaja, *Shakespeare's Verse*, p. 289.

[17] I have used Judith Perryman's 1980 edition of *The King of Tars*, in *Advocates 19.2.1*, Middle English Texts 12 (Heidelberg: Carl Winter), checked against the 1988 online edition based on F. Krause, 'Kleine Publikationen aus der Auchinleck-hs: IX, *The King of Tars*', *Englische Studien* 11 (1888), 33–62, Vernon and Auchinleck MSS in parallel with variants from Simeon. The date of the Auchinleck version is c. 1310–30 and its provenance is London or the South Midlands; see Rhiannon Purdie, *Anglicising Romance: Tail-Rhyme and Genre in Medieval English Literature* (Cambridge: D. S. Brewer, 2008), p. 208. (Online: *Manual I, 130; 289. Index 1108*; http://gateway.proquest.com/openurl?ctx_ver=Z39.88-2003&xri:pqil:res_ver=0.2&res_id=xri:lion&rft_id=xri:lion:ft:po:Z200435624:2). The citations from *Sir Orfeo* are from Anne Laskaya and Eve Salisbury, *The Middle English Breton Lays* (Kalamazoo, MI: Medieval Institute Publications, 1995), http://d.lib.rochester.edu/teams/publication/laskaya-and-salisbury-middle-english-breton-lays, checked against A. J. Bliss, *Sir Orfeo*, 2nd edn (Oxford: OUP, 1966). The Chaucer citations are from Larry D. Benson, *The Riverside Chaucer*, 3rd edn (Oxford: OUP, 1986).

The first text for which data were gathered was *The King of Tars*.[18] Although traditionally characterized as a romance, the centrality of the religious theme in *The King of Tars* has prompted classification in the sub-category of 'homiletic romances',[19] or 'popular didactic romance'. Pious edification notwithstanding, it fits other characteristics of romances; see Pearsall, Reichl, and Purdie,[20] who point out the formal affiliations of the text, with a large group of romances exhibiting 'an unmistakable stylistic uniformity, which reveals their roots in popular story-telling'.[21] The poem is written in 'close adherence to classical tail-rhyme techniques'.[22] The stanzas follow a demanding $aa^4b^3aa^4b^3cc^4b^3dd^4b^3$ rhyming formula:

(5) The metre of *The King of Tars*:

	Rhyme	Beats
Herkneþ to me boþe eld & ȝing,	a	4
For Maries loue þat swete þing,	a	4
Al hou a wer bigan	b	3
Bitvene a trewe Cristen king	a	4
& an heþen heye lording,	a	4
Of Dames þe soudan.	b	3
Þe king of Tars hadde a wiue,	c	4
Feirer miȝt non ben oliue	c	4
Þat ani wiȝt telle can.	b	3
A douhter þai hadde hem bitven,	d	4
Non feirer woman miȝt ben,	d	4
As white as feþer of swan.	b	3

The rhythm of the lines is predominantly iambic. The syllabic count ranges between seven and nine syllables per line for the four-beat lines and between five and seven for the three-beat lines.[23] The scansion follows the normal practice of controlling for pre-vocalic elision, where 'pre-vocalic' includes

[18] *The King of Tars* was one of the texts analysed for the use of infinitival forms in Donka Minkova and Emily Runde, 'Genre, Audience, and Scribal Adaptation to Language Change: The Case of Infinitival Marking', in *Essays and Studies in Middle English*, ed. Jacek Fisiak, Magdalena Bator and Marta Sylwanowicz (Bern: Peter Lang, 2016), pp. 95–120, where we offer more extensive text descriptions and scansion details.

[19] Dieter Mehl, *The Middle English Romances of the 13th and 14th Centuries* (London: Routledge & Kegan Paul, 1969).

[20] Derek Pearsall, 'The Development of Middle English Romance', in *Studies in Medieval English Romances: Some New Approaches*, ed. Derek Brewer (Cambridge: D. S. Brewer, 1988), pp. 11–37; Karl Reichl, '*The King of Tars*: Language and Textual Tradition', in *Studies in the Vernon Manuscript*, ed. Derek Pearsall (Cambridge: D. S. Brewer, 1990), pp. 171–86; Purdie, *Anglicising Romance*, p. 95.

[21] Reichl, '*The King of Tars*', p. 172.

[22] Pearsall, 'The Development of Middle English Romance', p. 29.

[23] Nine syllables for the four-beat lines and seven syllables for the three-beat lines involve counting the line-final <-e>'s as extrametrical unstressed syllables. Seven syllables for

pronominal initial <h->. Combing through the text, I analysed the placement of all relevant adjectives. The overall numbers of relevant attestations are quite low, because of numerous exclusions, recorded in (6):

(6) Data-base exclusions:

(a) Determiners: *this, sum, each, min, his*[24]

For ín him ís *mine* hópe, apliȝt 757

He schúld forlés(s)e þát *ich* dáy 1223

Ín *al* máner wíse (3-stress, l. 915) rhymes with ... *arise*[25]

(b) Disyllabic adjectives: *heþen, gentil, wicked, miri, hali, Cristen, fairer, better*

Sche lerd þe *heþen* lawe 501

& *duhti* men on hors to ride 517

(c) Grammatical (weak declension and/or plural/feminine) final –e

Bot sche wil wiþ hir *gode* wille 46

A *riche* bed þer was ydiȝt 401

Bifor þe *heyȝe* lordinges alle 389

Þe soudan made a riche fest 143

---

the four-beat lines and five syllables for the three-beat lines are headless, e.g. l. 32: *Hé wald hír win ín batáyl*; l. 117: *Bóþe lést & mast*; 771: *As y ȝou tel may.*

[24] The exclusion here applies to demonstratives, quantifiers, possessives, though what should be included under the cover term 'determiner' can be debated, and not all items under this rubric are equally weak. Rodney Huddleston and Geoffrey K. Pullum, in *The Cambridge Grammar of the English Language* (Cambridge: CUP, 2002), pp. 354ff, 538ff, define determiners in terms of function within the NP, which could potentially include 'regular' adjectives. Their terminology distinguishes between adjectives and *determinatives*, and it is acknowledged that the criteria for determinatives are not absolute, so that, for example, *many, few, much, little* 'bear a considerable resemblance to adjectives' (p. 539). 'Commentary on the LAEME Grammels in *LAEME: A Linguistic Atlas of Early Middle English, 1150–1325*, Version 3.2', compiled by Margaret Laing (Edinburgh: The University of Edinburgh), http://www.lel.ed.ac.uk/ihd/laeme2/laeme2.html, treats the following as either adjectives or pronouns: *any, both, each, eachone, either, evereach, fela, few, geon, geond, hwo:n, n+any, neither, other, self, some, such, what, whether, which*; I have used this list as a basic guideline for exclusions, adding *all* to the list; see also Ad Putter, 'A Prototype Theory of Metrical Stress: Lexical Categories and Ictus in Langland, the Gawain-Poet and Other Alliterative Poets', in *The Use and Development of Middle English*, ed. Richard Dance and Laura Wright (Frankfurt: Peter Lang, 2012), pp. 281–98, at p. 281. The function and status of these words is subject to diachronic change; see the discussion of, for example, *other* in Tine Breban, 'Structural Persistence: A Case Based on the Grammaticalization of English Adjectives of Difference', *ELL* 13 (2009), 77–96.

[25] Line 915 is the only relevant example with *all* and it is predictably placed in a weak metrical position. In *Sir Orfeo* all six relevant attestations of *all* are in weak positions. On the special status of quantifiers see Putter, 'A Prototype Theory of Metrical Stress', pp. 285–7. Putter shows convincingly that in the alliterative verse the nature of the adjective, its ranking in a scale of 'lexicality', is a major factor in determining whether it should be assigned higher prominence than the adjacent noun – they should be evaluated with respect to each other; see also the discussion at the end of Section 3.

(d) Predicative uses:
Wel *stout & strong* þai were 1077

(e) Post-positioned adjective
Wiþ kniȝtes *fele* & stedes *stiþe* 350
Wiþ browes *brod & hore* 438
(*Þe leuedi þonked God þat day*,)
For ioie sche wepe wiþ eyȝen *gray* 941

All examples are from *The King of Tars*. (6a) excludes various sub-categories of determiners. Their predictable prosodic 'weakness' has been reflected in the verse from the earliest times.[26] Disyllabic adjectives, whether etymologically disyllabic, such as *heathen*, *gentle*, or morphologically complex items such as *Christian*, *fairer*, are also kept out of the picture: their placement in stress-alternating metre is not revealing.[27] (6c) covers adjectives in the grammatical frame of determiner + adj. + noun (an extension of the earlier 'weak declension' frame) and potential plurals that require disyllabic scansion. By common consent they are inflection-preserving, which goes hand-in-hand with rhythmic optimization.[28] I have also been careful to isolate cases where the final *e*- may signal gender, preceding a feminine noun like *feast*. All predicative uses, as in (6d), are also excluded. Finally, post-positioned adjectives are separated because they may have additional stylistic value: they foreground the noun, or, as in line 941, the word order is inverted to satisfy the rhyme scheme.

The findings: all monosyllabic adjectives can be positioned in strong metrical positions, as in (7a), but *not* all adjectives are found in weak positions, as in (7b). The results are shown in Graph 7.1.

26 'Proclitics also are the adjectives of indefinite quantity: *fela, fēa, ǣnig, nǣnig, manig, sum, nān*, as may be seen by the manner in which they often stand before their noun in a metrical dip, or bearing a non-alliterating life: *ealles* m*oncynnes* (Beow 1955a); *þær him nænig* w*æter* (id 1514a). The numerals, on the contrary, are fully stressed adjectives', as noted by Alastair Campbell, *Old English Grammar* (Oxford: OUP, 1959), §96. The significance of the different semantic weight of the items in the NP will be addressed in Section 3.

27 The flexibility of metrical placement of monosyllables allows a meaningful testing of the placement of monosyllables in the line, while disyllabic words are much more restricted in their position; see Kiparsky, 'Stress, Syntax, and Meter'; and Paul Kiparsky, 'The Rhythmic Structure of English Verse', *Linguistic Inquiry* 8 (1977), 189–247. Except for *gentil*, an early loan (c. 1225), stressed initially in Chaucer and in alliterative verse, the disyllabic adjectives are native, and they are consistently positioned in ictus in this poem.

28 Donka Minkova, *The History of Final Vowels in English* (Berlin: De Gruyter, 1991), pp. 171–85.

(7) Monosyllabic adjectives in *The King of Tars*[29]

(a)	Wiþ **bríȝt** armour & **bród** banér	158–9 (rhyme on *fer*, *ner*)
	& þat was **grét** pité	213 (rhymes with *fre*, *þre*)
	Alle þurch þi **fáls** biléue	591 (rhymes with *preue*, *aneue*)[30]
(b)	**Gret** ióie þai hadde, wiþouten les	310
	Þai sett him on a fúl **gode** stéde	190

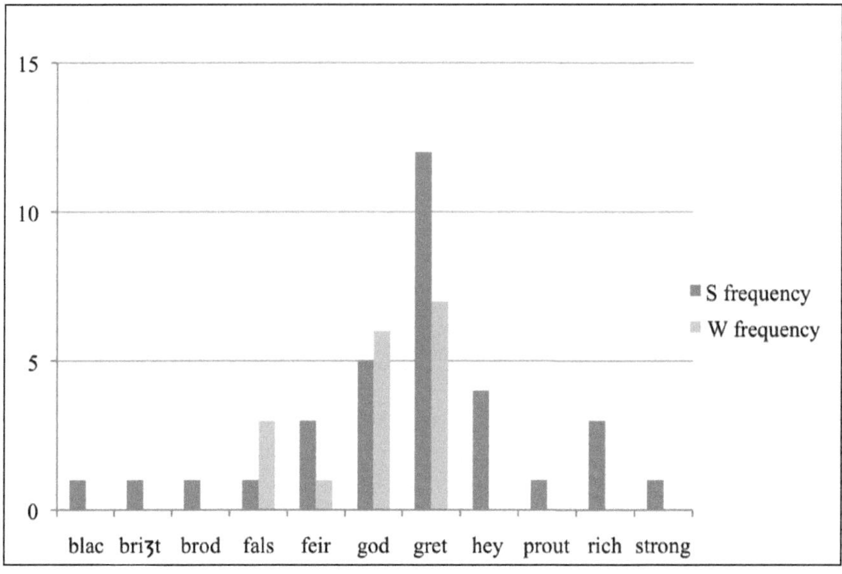

Graph 7.1 Monosyllabic adjectives in S(trong) and W(eak) metrical positions in *The King of Tars*

The placement of monosyllabic adjectives in strong positions can be attributed to two factors. First, if the adjective follows a prosodically weak/function word, and the head noun is disyllabic of the shape W S, as *unskille* in l. 735: *With wróng and grét unskílle*, or l. 1081: *Þo fif kinges of prout parayle*, the principle of stress alternation, both in speech, and in the metre, allows the monosyllabic adjective to occupy a strong position without incurring any violation. Another factor in the placement of the adjective in strong metrical position is the constraint operation at the end of the line, where the prominence on

[29] The one example of weak *fair* is: 766–7: *Þe prest no leng nold abide, A feir vessel he tok þat tide* (*vessel* is AN, stressed initially in Chaucer).

[30] The weak uses of *fals* are only *fals law*, *fals lay*; compare (c. 1400) *Sowdone of Babylone* l. 764: *If he will Baptised be And lefe his fals laye.*

the rhyme position is inviolable, e.g. l. 5: *& an hé*þ*en héye lordíng* (rhyming with *king*).

Again, the exclusions in (6) lower the number of relevant attestations. It is nevertheless noticeable that instances such as l. 58, *Þe máiden ánswerd wí*þ *mild mód*, which conform to the NSR, are very rare outside the two most frequent adjectives *good* and *great.*

Sir Orfeo, another popular romance in the Auchinleck manuscript, is also attributed to Scribe 1. It is composed in short couplets. The predominant rhythm in the 604 lines is iambic.[31] The lines are mostly octosyllabic four-beat lines, but occasional three-beat lines occur too, e.g. l. 193: *Wi*þ *fairi for*þ *ynome.* In this text too the numbers are low, and not all of the items found in *The King of Tars* are used in *Sir Orfeo*. The adjective showing the most stable placement in weak position is *good*, an overlap with the data in Graph 7.1. In the instances where adjectives are placed in S the metrical constraints are the same as the ones noted for *The King of Tars*: l. 240: *Bot euer he liue*þ *in grét maláis*; l. 299: *In quéynt atíre gisely*.

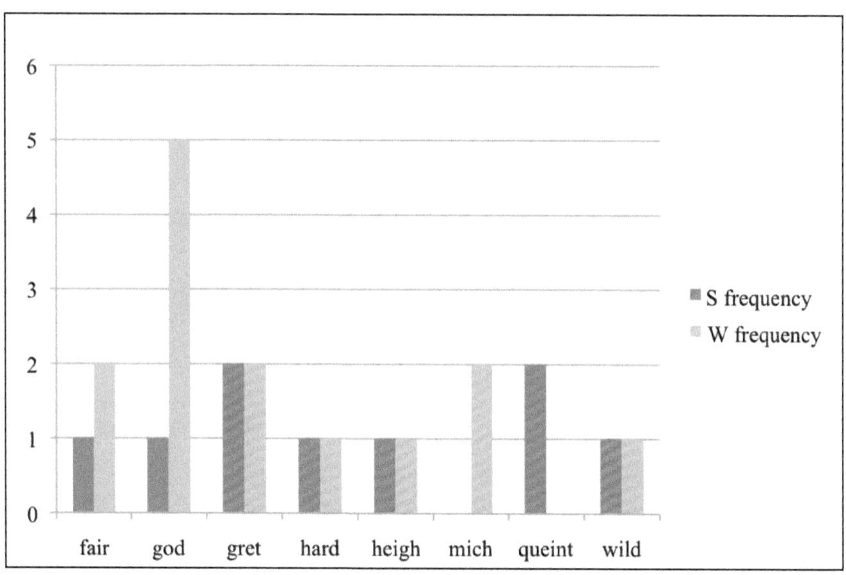

Graph 7.2 Monosyllabic adjectives in S and W metrical positions in *Sir Orfeo*

So the poet, and his Auchinleck Scribe 1, one of the 'carpenters of Romance',[32] had a good ear for distinctions based both on the prosodic input

[31] Bliss edition.

[32] The phrase is cited in Reichl, '*The King of Tars*'.

from speech and on the requirements of metre. Stepping outside the Auchinleck and looking for attestations of the same attributive monosyllabic adjectives in other tail-rhyme romances confirms that the pattern identified for the romances copied by Scribe 1 is unexceptional. The results for all six romances concorded by Karl Reichl and Walter Sauer are shown in Graph 7.3.[33] It is obvious that there is no significant difference between the distributions of the relevant adjectives in these texts.

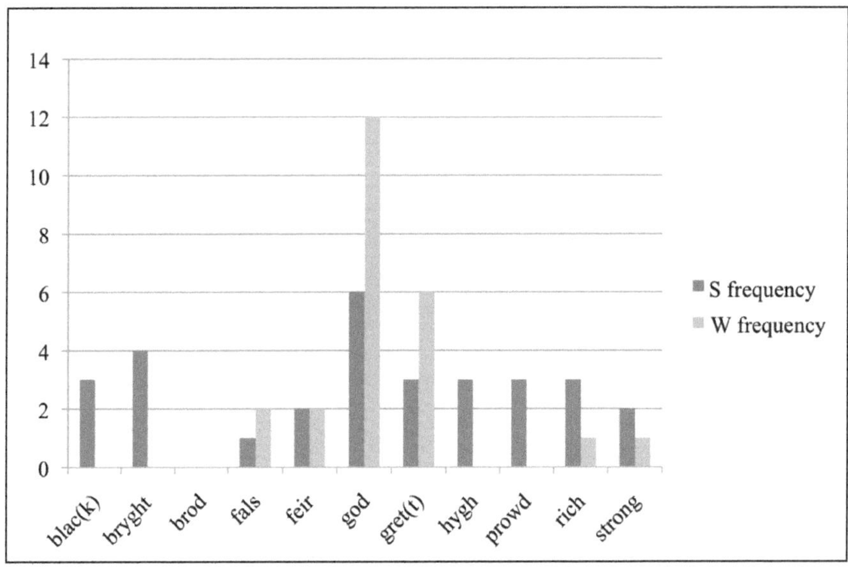

Graph 7.3 Monosyllabic adjectives in S and W positions in other tail-rhyme romances[34]

The highly compatible distributions in texts associated with the romance genre are suggestive, but the statistics are insufficiently robust to be taken as a strongly positive linguistic correlate of 'popular' style. A comparison of the placements of the same adjectives in *Sir Gawain and the Great Knight* is shown in Graph 7.4.[35]

33 *A Concordance to Six Middle English Tail-Rhyme Romances*, ed. Karl Reichl and Walter Sauer, 2 vols (Bern: Peter Lang, 1993).

34 The texts included in Reichl and Sauer's *Concordance* are *Sir Eglamour of Artois*, *Le Bone Florence of Rome*, *Sir Isumbras*, *Octavian* (Northern version), *The King of Tars*, and *Sir Tryamowr.*

35 Data from Barnet Kottler and Alan Markman, *Concordance to Five Middle English Poems* (Pittsburgh: University of Pittsburgh Press, 1966).

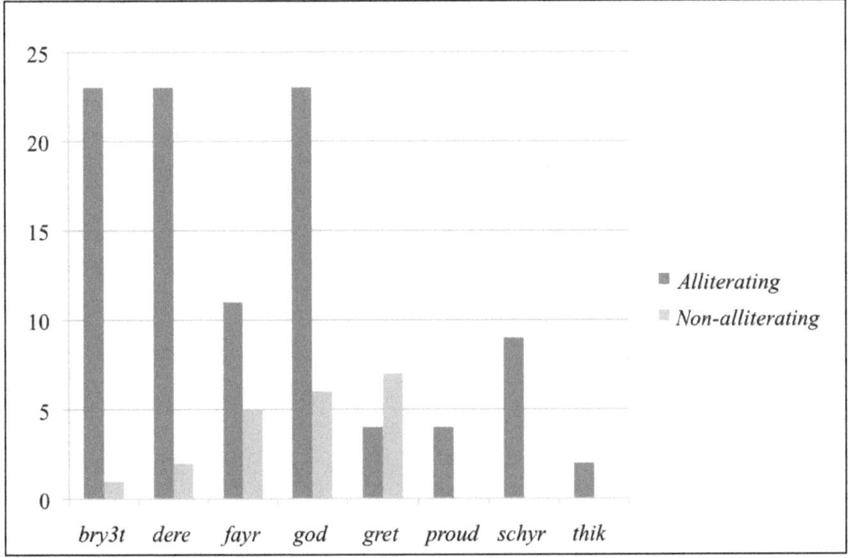

Graph 7.4 Adjectives in Adj. + N phrases in *SGGK*

Predictably, pre-nominal adjectives alliterate freely, but note also that the probability of non-alliterating use increases in accord with the frequency with which adjectives are placed in weak position in Graphs 7.1–7.3. Once again *good* and *great* are the most likely items to appear unstressed.

Finally, using the raw data in Appendix 3 in Minkova and Stockwell,[36] Graph 7.5 charts the distribution of a set of adjectives in the same syntactic frame in Chaucer.

[36] Minkova and Stockwell, 'Against the Emergence of the Nuclear Stress Rule in Middle English', pp. 329–34.

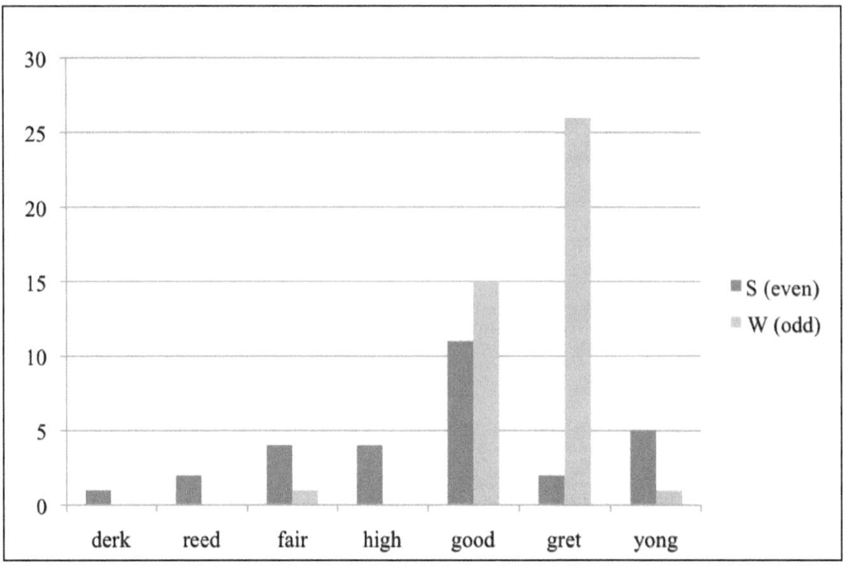

Graph 7.5 Adjectives in Adj. + N phrases in *The Romaunt of the Rose*

The distributions in all five graphs are equiprobable, with differences in attested tokens, but the types are less varied: the preponderance of *good* and *great* in weak positions is a common denominator. However, the question posed at the beginning of Section 2.3, whether conformity to the Nuclear Stress Rule is a good linguistic bridge to 'orality' of the composition and the 'popularity' of its consumption, remains open. The continuing presence of a final <-e> limits the number of types and tokens of testable monosyllabic items in the frame adjective + noun. It is likely that a more comprehensive search replicating the outlined methodology could yield robust results on which the NSR can be tested, but this work lies in the future.

3. Semantic content and lexical frequency

In speech, and even more in art verse, the novelty and expressivity of an adjective can obscure and override the unmarked rising prosodic contour within the noun phrase. Minkova and Stockwell argued that one of the statistically testable factors influencing the relative prominence of the modifier and the head in the noun phrase was the different degree of semantic expressivity of the modifier, as in (8), where adjectives of the type *great* are much more likely to fill a weak position in the line, while the adjectives as in (8b) appear regularly in ictus. A check of all relevant attestations of *blind, blue, deep, dark, fresh, high* in Chaucer yields no instances comparable to (8a).

(8) Semantic load as a factor in Adj. N placement in ictus:[37]

(a) That is the man of so gret sápience *Tr* I 515
But well I woot þat in this wórld greet pýne ys *KnT* 1324
Hym to grèt sháme and to grèt víleynýe *MancT* 260

(b) And Nysus doughter song with fréssh entente *Tr* V 1110
A whít còte and a bléw hòod wered he *GP* 564
And for to drynken stróng wỳn, reed as blood *GP* 635

The discussion of adjective-noun groups in Putter, Jefferson and Stokes shows the importance of the relative semantic weight of the two members of the phrase for alliterative verse.[38] The examples in (9) illustrate their observations:

(9) Stress and beat in alliterative metre[39]

(a) With rỳch réuel orýȝt and réchles mérþes *SGGK* 40
Rỳche róbes ful rád rénkkez hym bróȝten *SGGK* 862

(b) I schal gíf hym of my gýft þys gíserne rýche
(Þis ax, þat is heue innogh, to hondele as hym lykes) *SGGK* 288–9

(c) And al watz ráyled on réd rýche golde náylez *SGGK* 603

In (9a) the adjective *rich* is metrically subordinate to *revel*, *robes*, as one would expect from the application of the Nuclear Stress Rule; under this scansion the relevant 'extended' a-verses become regular two-beat verses. In (9b) the inversion of *ryche* highlights the novelty of the noun, the 'heavy axe' apparently needed as a gloss in the next line. The adjective is prosodically subordinate and does not alliterate, but attracts the beat as the last word of the line. In (9c) the rhythm rule (the tendency for the second of a series of three adjacent content words to receive weaker stress, as in a 'héavy round stóne') subordinates the adjective 'golde'. Putter and Jefferson calculate that about 65 percent of their adjective-noun data alliterate on the noun.[40] They find that 'the needs of alliteration will not normally coerce adjectives into unaccented position unless semantic factors ... or rhythmical tendencies (such as the rhythm rule) cooperate'.[41]

Similarly, Tarlinskaja has argued in favour of attending to semantic factors in matching prominences in verse.[42] Although, as noted in (2), the NSR

[37] The examples in (8a) are *not* from Minkova and Stockwell, 'Against the Emergence of the Nuclear Stress Rule in Middle English'.

[38] Ad Putter, Judith Jefferson and Myra Stokes, *Studies in the Metre of Alliterative Verse* (Oxford: Medium Aevum, 2007), pp. 196–216.

[39] For a full coverage see Putter et al., *Studies in the Metre of Alliterative Verse*, chapter 4. Chapter 4 is cited here as Jefferson and Putter, following the statement in Putter et al., p. vii.

[40] Putter and Jefferson, p. 211.

[41] Putter and Jefferson, p. 168.

[42] See Tarlinskaja, *Shakespeare's Verse*; Tarlinskaja, 'General and Particular Aspects of Meter'; Tarlinskaja, *Shakespeare and the Versification of English Drama*, pp. 19–22.

is generally observed, semantic factors are likely to interfere. In (10) *good thóughts* and *good wórds* are rising cadences, iambs, the adjective is in weak metrical position, while *sád slave* is left-prominent:

(10) Monosyllabic adjectives in Shakespeare
I think good thóughts, whilst others write good wórds *Sonnet* 85
But, like a sád slàve, stay and think of nought *Sonnet* 57

Such studies bring new evidence to bear on the organization and the strictness of the metrical template. The additional semantic considerations are compatible with a reconstruction of continuous NSR in English. Likewise, the overview of the adjectival placement in Graphs 7.1–7.5 reveals one steady correlation: adjectives placed in weak positions are also semantically weak, reaffirming the conclusions based on alliterative verse and iambic pentameter. The results for the romances in Section 2 cannot yield definitive conclusions about the stress-alternating patterns in these compositions, but they do suggest another angle of inquiry that helps us uncover usage-related patterns that characterize the texts' proximity to the spoken language. This angle is lexical frequency in relation to the findings on metrical placement. It is known that lexical frequency interacts bidirectionally with the semantic force of an item: 'Frequency of use leads to weakening of semantic force by habituation.'[43] Frequent lexical items undergo semantic bleaching and are less likely to convey new and important information that would attract prosodic prominence. Conversely, rare words command more attention, and they are unlikely to undergo reduction and prosodic subordination.

As the correlation between the semantic and pragmatic weight of an item in verse and its lexical frequency could be of relevance in identifying textual properties, Table 7.1 shows the frequency and ranking of the adjectives found and charted in Graphs 7.1–7.5 from Old English to Present-Day English.[44]

[43] Joan Bybee, *Frequency of Use and the Organization of Language* (New York: OUP, 2007), p. 338.

[44] Two items found in Graphs 7.1–7.5 are not included: *proud* and *rich*, because of the etymological connection with Old French. Headword entries in the online *DOE* are currently (as of June 2018) only available from A to G: https://tapor.library.utoronto.ca/doe/. For *hard, high, strong, wild*, I used the Old English Corpus Variant Word/Phrase Search: http://tapor.library.utoronto.ca/doe/dict/help/aboutdoeonlineindex.html. The ME counts are from *LAEME* Version 3.2. For PDE the rankings are from *COCA*, the *Corpus of Contemporary American English*: http://www.wordandphrase.info/frequencyList.asp.

Table 7.1 Frequency ranking for some common monosyllabic adjectives

OE adjective	*OE freq.*	*OE rank*	*LAEME counts*	*PDE gloss*	*COCA freq.*
gōd	2,500	14	1,578 (1)	good	386,236 (1)
geong	900		240 (7)	young	173,683 (4)
fæger	450		584 (3)	fair	30,013 (11)
beorht	450	208	243 (6)	bright	32,290 (9)
heah	300	174	516 (4)	high	277,214 (2)
brād	275		63 (12)	broad	29,419 (12)
strang	230		433 (5)	strong	90,550 (7)
blæc	150		77 (11)	black	161,425 (5)
grēat	150	61	619 (2)	great	244,358 (3)
dȳre	140		209 (9)	dear	9,877 (13)
heard	140		212 (8)	hard	94,488 (6)
wilde	120		136 (10)	wild	31,900 (10)
deorc	80		13 (*13*)	dark	51,653 (8)

The adjectives examined and included in the graphs in Section 2 are arranged in descending order of frequency in the *Dictionary of Old English* (DOE). The first column shows the Old English (OE) base forms as headword entries; the numbers to the left of the OE headwords are the OE frequency ranking. The second column shows the full counts of all adjectival forms in the DOE corpus. The third compares the DOE data to the few available relevant rankings in Barney,[45] based on 2,000 words of all classes found in the poetry. The *LAEME* frequency counts are based on lexel and grammel (aj) tokens.[46] The rightmost column shows the token count for the same subset of adjectives in the *Corpus of Contemporary American English* (*COCA*). The parentheses in the ME and the PDE columns indicate the set-internal ranking derived respectively from the *LAEME* data-base and from the *COCA* data-base. Items that have the same ranking in two out of the three periods are italicized.

[45] Stephen A. Barney, *Word Hoard. An Introduction to Old English Vocabulary*, 2nd edn (New Haven, CT and London: Yale University Press, 1985).

[46] See http://www.lel.ed.ac.uk/ihd/laeme2/laeme2_manual.html, for an explanation of these terms.

As expected, the frequency of individual words varies through time, and reflects the subject matter of the text, but such base-line statistics are still informative. It is reassuring to see that *good* is the top adjective in this subset, consistently ranking as the most frequent one for all three periods. For that item, the overlap between prosodic weakness and frequency of occurrence is perfect. The frequency ranking of *great* has climbed to second place in ME, which also tallies with our findings on its placement. The high frequency of *fair* in OE and ME matches the results; its stability is reflected in Graphs 7.2–7.5, which show *fair* appearing in weak metrical positions, unlike less frequent *dark, broad, black, wild.*

These are only first steps in a new area of research – I am not aware of attempts to quantify the behaviour of adjectives in ME verse that relate frequency in the ambient language to metrical placement and possibly text type. The claim is not that there is an absolute match between semantic content and frequency ranking – this is necessarily context-dependent – but that adjectives, other than the quantifiers, are hierarchized in the spoken language, and that their selection and placement in the text mirrors that hierarchy. For PDE the frequencies can be tested in different kinds of English – spoken, fiction, magazines, newspapers, academic writing – these are the *COCA* basic categories. Not surprisingly, more than 30 per cent of the attestations of *good* in PDE are from spoken records, and less than 10 per cent come from academic writing. The ratios are reversed for *broad,* for which the academic prose attestations exceed the spoken language data by 3:1. The increasing availability of digitized texts and tagged corpora opens up this line of inquiry into a broader spectrum of ME verse data.

A fine-grained comparison of item frequency and metrical placement is desirable in another way. In PDE 90 per cent of the word types are never spoken in isolation and the situation in medieval England cannot have been very different.[47] The statistics on the adjectives alone can and must be enriched with comparable statistics on the individual frequencies of the head nouns and the frequency of the adjective-noun collocations, controlling for formulaic stock phrases. Therefore a methodology allowing differential semantic weighting of the phrasal components, as in Putter and Jefferson or Putter, is the right direction for future inquiry. It is only after a much wider search and data analysis that we can address the question of whether the placement of adjectives and

[47] While it is not surprising that normal communication does not imply using single words, it is still striking that over 90 per cent of the word types are never spoken in isolation. Even in the nursery, 'On average, 9.0% of the maternal utterances consist[ed] of isolated words'; see Michael R. Brent and Jeffrey Mark Siskind, 'The Role of Exposure to Isolated Words in Early Vocabulary Development', *Cognition* 81 (2001), B33–B44, at p. B36.

their head nouns can be one of the criteria for defining 'Romance' texts as 'popular' compositions, replicating patterns in the spoken language.

4. Attributive vs. predicative adjectival use

The spectrum of linguistic properties correlating textual form with textual function can be enriched further; this final short section outlines yet another potential direction for new research. In his sociolinguistic and discourse pragmatic study of adjective use in PDE, Robert Englebretson shows that formality level and social intimacy influence the grammatical choice of using an adjective attributively or predicatively: 'a greater number of attributive adjectives corresponds to increased formality level and social distance, while a greater number of predicative adjectives correlates with informal interaction among intimates'.[48] Englebretson argues that 'genre' (his word!) is a primary determinant in the selection of attributive vs. predicative use, i.e. predicative adjectives are more frequent when interlocutors are discussing referents that are shared knowledge among themselves, either based on social intimacy or situational context.

This stylistic dimension of grammatical adjectival choice has never been explored in the context of English medieval romance. Further, given the predicative/rhematic nature of post-posed adjectives (adj. + noun *and* adj., e.g. *A stalworth man and hardi bo* (*Sir Orfeo* 41); Malory's *a passing true man and a faithful*), and the unsettled state of word order,[49] the semantic properties of the adjectives are also of consequence. The stylistic characterization of adjectival placement can be extended to the use of intensifiers. Intensifying adverbs such as *full*, *very*, and *right* go through a process of semantic bleaching which develops parallel to their more frequent predicative use in Middle English.[50] In this connection it is of interest that the use of adjectival intensifiers in PDE has been identified as a signal of 'ingroup membership' in current sociolinguistic research. Rika Ito and Sali Tagliamonte's detailed study of the two most frequent intensifiers in PDE, *very* and *really*, shows that 'intensifiers

48 Robert Englebretson, 'Genre and Grammar: Predicative and Attributive Adjectives in Spoken English', in *Proceedings of the Twenty-Third Annual Meeting of the Berkeley Linguistics Society: General Session and Parasession on Pragmatics and Grammatical Structure* (1997), pp. 411–21, at p. 418. https://www.linguisticsociety.org/lsa-publications/elanguage.

49 Olga Fischer, 'On the Position of Adjectives in Middle English', *ELL* 10 (2006), 253–88.

50 Tauno F. Mustanoja, *A Middle English Syntax* (Helsinki: Société Néophilologique, 1960), p. 330.

occur far more frequently with predicate adjectives than with attributive adjectives. Moreover, this is consistent for all age groups.'[51]

Whether the findings and the stylistic inferences for PDE can be replicated in the older texts is an open question that can only be addressed by gathering more data. A tally of the placement choices of some adjectives in *The King of Tars* backs up the idea of associating predicative use with informality: the ratio of predicative to attributive use of *black* (x1/Ø), *white* (x4/x2), *proud* (x2/x1), *strong* (x4/x2), *wise* (x1/Ø) is in favour of predicative use. In *Sir Orfeo*, however, the ratios are less illuminating: *bright* is the only adjective in that text for which the preferred placement is predicative (x4) vs. attributive (x2).[52] These are very preliminary figures, and further metrical, semantic and syntactic information is needed, but since the link between grammatical properties and style is beyond doubt, the search for clues along these lines can be productive.

5. Summary

> Stories are the property of everyone, but a formal tradition is the property only of its practitioners, and it is *through its formal and stylistic aspects* – in combination with the others – that the history of romance can be most objectively analysed.[53]

In the spirit of Pearsall's call for analytical objectivity, this essay is a pilot attempt to establish and start documenting formal properties of some verse romances in the hope that they will illuminate the oral and popular nature of these compositions. After considering the historical roots and presenting arguments in favour of the continuity of rising, right-hand phrasal prominence in English, specifically the Nuclear Stress Rule, Section 2 details the metrical positioning of monosyllabic adjectives in attributive noun phrases. The results are in line with a reconstruction of continuous presence of the rising prominence in the spoken language, but the metrical distribution did not show anything in the romances that would be outside the 'generic' norms in medieval verse. On the other hand, a better understanding of the salience and lexical ranking of the adjectives does show a more complex and fine-grained

51 Rika Ito and Sali Tagliamonte, 'Well Weird, Right Dodgy, Very Strange, Really Cool: Layering and Recycling in English Intensifiers', *Language in Society* 32 (2003), 257–79, at p. 272. I cannot address the extent to which the heaviness of the group *adverb + adjective + noun*, i.e. 'stacked modification' (see Huddleston and Pullum, *The Cambridge Grammar of the English Language*, pp. 547–8), plays into that distribution, but since the default predicative use is (linking) verb followed by complement, it is to be expected that the weight of the complement will be significant.

52 In the entire *Sir Orfeo*, 123 adjectives are used attributively versus 53 used predicatively.

53 Pearsall, 'The Development of Middle English Romance', p. 16.

interplay between a metrical template and the subtle ways in which poets and/or scribes respond to its constraints. The metrical use of adjectives is in accord with the oral and popular character of the metrical romances, but it is not unique to them. As for the 'uniqueness' of metrical romances in this respect, therefore, the question of whether conformity with the NSR is a good linguistic test for this type of text must be answered in the negative – it does not appear that adjectival placement is a reliable test of genre specificity.

However, the data collection was productive in a different direction. Putter makes a compelling case for reconsidering the correspondence between lexical categories and ictus in light of prototype theory. Drawing on the idea of categorial fuzziness, he shows that in alliterative verse metrical stress on adjectives and nouns can be sensitive to the 'centrality' or 'peripherality' of a lexical item. Items at the core of a lexical category behave predictably in the metre; such nouns and adjectives align with strong metrical positions, while non-prototypical items, for example quantifiers and common nouns such as *man*, can be non-ictic. Putter writes that it would be fruitful to see whether prototype effects apply more generally to categories not included in his data-base. His observations are confirmed by the examined set of adjectives.[54] As in other Middle English verse, in the romances 'the beats will fall on the words that do most of the semantic work in the context'.[55]

Building on the same idea, Section 3 turns to lexical frequency as another way of calibrating semantic weight. While the statistical match between prosodic weakness, low semantic weight, and frequency of occurrence is theoretically unsurprising, it is also a good base for evaluating the rather evasive properties of the romance genre. The correspondences plotted in Graphs 7.1–7.5 show discourse-based gradience. When the ambivalence of the evidence is evaluated against the variability of semantic weight, the continuity of the NSR gains in credibility. Taken singly, the tests in Sections 2 and 3 are not clearly determinate, but in the aggregate the examination of the romances has yielded a positive clue, both in terms of theory, and in terms of identifying features of the ambient language.

Finally, Section 4 is more programmatic than evidential: it turns briefly to the distribution of predicative vs. attributive adjectives. The idea that preponderance of attributive use in formal discourse presupposes social distance in PDE prompts an interesting direction of investigation, bearing in mind, of course, that 'formality' is a very different notion for us and for texts in a largely oral culture, commissioned by patrons, composed and copied by the literary elite, and intended for a very select audience. These factors have to be taken into consideration when analysing the transfer and preservation of the linguistic features of speech in the verse.

54 Putter, 'A Prototype Theory of Metrical Stress'.

55 Jefferson and Putter, p. 212.

In his introduction to *Understanding Genre and Medieval Romance*, Kevin Whetter defends the usefulness of the term *genre* for the identification of properties of the narrative poems known as romances.[56] The replicable formal tests isolated here add to the multiple ways of characterizing the distinctness of the much debated genre or species of insular romance. In an attempt to harness philology to provide clues to literary history, I have spotlighted some prosodic, syntactic, semantic and pragmatic properties of adjective-noun phrases which are suggestive enough to render further investigation desirable and promising. To end on an optimistic note: I believe that the research model is applicable to a wide range of sources, allowing for comparisons between texts traditionally considered as belonging to the romance genre and other types of texts.

56 Kevin Whetter, *Understanding Genre and Medieval Romance* (Burlington, VT: Ashgate, 2008), p. 5.

8

The Problem of John Metham's Prosody

Nicholas Myklebust

For 567 years, John Metham's *Amoryus and Cleopes* has quietly eluded scholarly inquiry. Composed in 1449 by an unremarkable member of the Stapleton retinue in Norfolk, its genre, style, and metre conspire to keep its stature diminutive – a mere footnote in the register of forgotten mid-century romances.[1] Few studies of the poem exist, and those that do exist seem content either to censure the work for its apparent formal defects or tactfully to suspend judgement on aesthetic matters altogether.[2] Indeed, the past half-century has seen much industry applied to the project of not discussing Metham or his poem.

This essay aims to contextualise this reluctance to engage seriously with Metham's romance in light of the poem's failure to fit convincingly into either

1 Little information concerning Metham's life, education, or employment has survived. On Metham's ancestry, see Philip Saltmarshe, 'Some Howdenshire Villages', *Transactions of the East Riding Antiquarian Society* 16 (1909), 1–49. On Metham's patrons and the East Anglian manuscript network they cultivated, see James Lee-Warner, 'The Stapletons of Ingham', *Norfolk Archaeology* 8 (1882), 183–233; Walter Rye, *Norfolk Families* (Norwich: Goose and Son, 1913), pp. 844–6; and Joseph Foster, *Pedigrees of the County Families of Yorkshire* (London: W. Wilfred Head, 1874). For Norfolk patronage networks, see Gail McMurray Gibson, *The Theater of Devotion: East Anglian Society in the Late Middle Ages* (Chicago: University of Chicago Press, 1989), pp. 1–18, 67–106; Richard Beadle, 'Prolegomena to a Literary Geography of Later Medieval Norfolk', in *Regionalism in Late Medieval Manuscripts and Texts*, ed. Felicity Riddy (Cambridge: D. S. Brewer, 1991), pp. 89–108; G. A. Lester, 'The Books of a Fifteenth-Century Gentleman, Sir John Paston', *NM* 88 (1987), 200–17; Samuel Moore, 'Patrons of Letters in Norfolk and Suffolk, c. 1450', *PMLA* 27 and 28 (1912 and 1913), 188–207, 79–105; and H. S. Bennett, *The Pastons and Their England: Studies in an Age of Transition*, 2nd edn (Cambridge: CUP, 1932), p. 111.

2 See, for instance, Jamie Fumo, 'John Metham's "Straunge Style": *Amoryus and Cleopes* as Chaucerian Fragment', *CR* 43 (2008), 215–37; Roger Dalrymple, '*Amoryus and Cleopes*: John Metham's Metamorphosis of Chaucer and Ovid', in *The Matter of Identity in Medieval England*, ed. Phillipa Hardman (Cambridge: D. S. Brewer, 2002), pp. 149–62; and Stephen F. Page, 'John Metham's "Amoryus and Cleopes": Intertextuality and Innovation in a Chaucerian Poem', *CR* 31 (1996), 201–8.

of the competing critical narratives concerning fifteenth-century metrics: one a chronicle of prosodic decline and collapse, the other a chronicle of prosodic cunning and sophistication. Despite their divergent conclusions, both accounts take Chaucer's decasyllable as their starting point, framing it either as an object unpersuasively imitated by later poets or as the raw material refined by them. In the story of post-Chaucerian prosody, miscarriage and mastery depend equally on the transmission of Chaucer's metrical line. *Amoryus and Cleopes*, by contrast, offers a model of late medieval English metre that does not descend from, and does not participate in, the transmission or reception of Chaucer's Anglicised hendecasyllable. A historical and aesthetic outlier, it thwarts existing scholarly accounts of fifteenth-century form. Neither narrative can accommodate the *Amoryus* metre within its representation of Lancastrian literary culture, and this limitation may not only illuminate Metham's unique contribution to late medieval metre; it may also offer an alternative to the factional and binary aesthetic ideologies that command and orient textual histories and formal reconstructions of the fifteenth century, as well as critical models for the transmission of metrical form.

Amoryus and Cleopes survives in a single witness, Princeton University Library's Garrett 141, a modest manuscript of eighty-seven vellum leaves copied in a single hand in Anglicana Formata.[3] Although it presents *Amoryus* as its centrepiece, the manuscript also contains a miscellany of minor scientific works by Metham, including treatises on palmistry, lunation, physiognomy, and prognostication. Internal evidence fixes the date of the poem's composition in the year 1449, when Metham was twenty-five, although paleographical evidence suggests that two or more decades separate the poem's composition from its copying.[4] An adaptation of Ovid's tale of Pyramus and Thisbe from Book 4 of the *Metamorphoses*, the poem draws heavily on conventions of

3 In 1903, Frederick Furnivall produced the first description of Garrett 141. According to Furnivall's notes, each manuscript leaf is ruled for twenty-eight lines, with a decorative *T* containing the armorial shields of the Stapleton and de La Pole families to mark the incipit. The top margin, which has been trimmed, contains a floriated border of acanthus leaves that also adorns the left and bottom margins. Two-line high initial capitals occur at lines 1, 71, 232, 248, 325, 724, 1024, 1779, and 1807, with a human head in profile drawn to face the left margin at lines 71 and 248. One-line high initials varying in colour mark the beginning of all other stanzas, which run as a single block text not delineated by blank spaces between stanzas. The remaining, non-initial lines begin with a minor capital with a yellow wash running down the page. See *Political, Religious, and Love Poems*, ed. Furnivall, EETS o.s. 15 (London: K. Paul, Trench, Trübner, 1903), p. xxvii.

4 In lines 2176–7 of *Amoryus*, Metham declares, 'Thys lady was, qwan I endytyd this story, / Flouryschyng the seuyn and twenty. xxvij. yere of the sext Kyng.' And in his palmistry the author writes that he is in the twenty-fifth 'wyntyr of hys age'. As Derek Pearsall observes, in the lines referencing Metham's patron, Lady Katherine Stapleton, 'Metham is probably using the regnal dates, as was common, to refer to the calendar year 1449'. See his *John Lydgate* (London: Routledge & Kegan Paul, 1970), p. 299, n. 7.

chivalric romance and Christian miracle appearing in such texts as the anonymous twelfth-century *Piramus et Tisbé*, *Ovide Moralisé* and Bersuire's *Ovidius Moralizatus*; but it also blends stock motifs from popular romance with the rarefied discourse of *roman antique*, and of *Troilus* in particular. The result is something of a ludic revision of the structural codes on which allegorical readings of romance depend, in which folk *topoi* burlesque the genre and swap ironic self-commentary for moral knowledge, reducing gods to an abusive annoyance and philosophical envoys to giddy non sequiturs. In fact, much of the poem's 'mitigated catastrophe' (as Hardin Craig memorably described its conclusion) seems singularly designed to reform the high seriousness of *Troilus* into mock epic.[5]

Metham's comedic re-scripting of Chaucerian romance, however, is more experimental than mere imitation or homage. It is also the most expedient reason for dismissing the poem as kitsch, as Craig does by labelling the poem's *mélange* of genres a 'degenerated form' emblematic of mid-century decadence – a standard Lancastrian production offering 'no peculiarities of special interest' to scholars of fifteenth-century literature.[6]

Whether the form is 'degenerated' must remain an open question. Its signature instability of genre distinguishes it as a work indebted to, but ungoverned by, conventional aesthetic codes. And so, in a sense, the liminality that marks *Amoryus and Cleopes* as potentially unreadable also insists on its paradoxical importance to the tradition it defies and exceeds. By invoking, and then deforming, both popular romance and *roman antique*, the text situates itself perpetually on the margin of accessibility. This formal hesitation – a sort of canonical hedged bet – not only accounts for the poem's perennial status as an object of historical curiosity rather than literary value; it also explains the paucity of scholarly criticism on *Amoryus and Cleopes*. Metham's romance serves no formal master and fits neatly into no formal category. Indeed, the poem's difficulty lies in its form, and, specifically, in its prosody, which is neither fixed nor formless but, like its composite genre, constitutes a singularly strange set of statistical inferences and probabilistic patterns. Its metre works, but it does not work well enough in relation to any known prosody operating in the fifteenth century to offer critics a foothold for thick description or reconstruction.

5 *The Works of John Metham, Including the Romance of Amoryus and Cleopes*, ed. Hardin Craig, EETS o.s. 132 (1916), p. xiii. See also Barbara Nolan, *Chaucer and the Tradition of the Roman Antique* (Cambridge: CUP, 1992). On the circulation of Chaucer's manuscripts in East Anglia, for which the Stapletons' estate served as a hub, giving Metham access to romance exemplars, see Ralph Hanna III and A. S. G. Edwards, 'Rotheley, the De Vere Circle, and the Ellesmere Chaucer', *HLQ* 58 (1996), 11–35.

6 *The Works of John Metham*, ed. Craig, pp. xiii, xliii.

Indeed, no description of its metre exists precisely because the metre cannot be reconciled with prevailing critical narratives of medieval metrical transmission. At present, two contrary narratives tell the story of post-Chaucerian prosody, but neither succeeds at describing Metham's metre. One narrative, passed from Ritson to Skeat, and from Saintsbury to Bennett, holds that 'the further we go from Chaucer the feebler the general sense of rhythm'.[7] According to this perspective, Chaucer's death stirred in his successors a sort of 'poetic imbecility' that precipitated a 'history of decay' in which Chaucer's rhythms suffered a series of degradations. This commonplace has kept control of the critical conversation for more than a century.

Recent years, however, have seen a sea-change in prosodic scholarship, with the metres of such poets as John Lydgate and Thomas Hoccleve rehabilitated. Long disparaged as unruly, their verses now can be read not as botched imitations of Chaucer's line but as creative alternatives to it. This reappraisal of post-Chaucerian prosody as fastidious and strategic rather than wayward aligns gainfully with a more general shift in critical perspective on fifteenth-century aesthetics that seeks to reframe Lancastrian literary culture as novel and daring rather than derivative and dull.[8]

As the two poets most celebrated as disciples of Chaucer, Lydgate and Hoccleve have gained most from this critical reappraisal, and as their works have garnered scholarly attention, that attention has eroded the notion that they wrote artless metres in imitation of Chaucer. Statistical analysis of their corpora reveals a professional rivalry between the poets, with each luring the other into an escalating confidence game designed to bait one's rival into sabotaging his own poems by crafting rhythms too complicated to be read.[9] Through this process, Hoccleve coaxed Lydgate out of the cloister and rechristened him a servant of the bureaucratic muse, even as Lydgate baptised Hoccleve an inadvertent brother of Bury St Edmunds. This livelier lens through which to view Lancastrian metrical competition illuminates prosodic gamesmanship as a flourishing practice of early fifteenth-century poets. Hoccleve in particular

7 George Saintsbury, *A History of English Prosody from the Twelfth Century to the Present Day*, vol. 1 (New York: Russell and Russell, 1966), p. 264. See also, for example, H. S. Bennett, *Chaucer and the Fifteenth Century* (Oxford: Clarendon Press, 1947), pp. 129–30; and *English Verse between Chaucer and Surrey*, ed. Eleanor Prescott Hammond (Durham, NC: Duke University Press, 1927), Introduction, pp. 21–4.

8 On metrical reconsiderations, see Judith Jefferson, 'The Hoccleve Holographs and Hoccleve's Metrical Practice: More than Counting Syllables?', *Parergon* 18 (2000), 203–26; Martin Duffell, 'Lydgate's Metrical Inventiveness and His Debt to Chaucer', *Parergon* 18 (2000), 227–49; Thomas Cable, 'Fifteenth-Century Rhythmical Changes', in *Essays on Medieval English Presented to Professor Matsuji Tajima on his Sixtieth Birthday*, ed. M. Connolly and Y. Iyeri (Tokyo: Kaibunsha, 2002), pp. 109–25; and Nicholas Myklebust, 'Misreading English Meter' (unpublished PhD dissertation, University of Texas at Austin, 2012).

9 See Myklebust, 'Misreading', pp. 734–41.

no longer appears as a dour figure, less the bureaucrat-beggar lodged in complaint at the bottom of Fortune's wheel than a nimble prosodic opportunist. And Lydgate, pilfering the repertoire of privy rhythms in order to produce a more extreme style of writing, seems less a prolix, self-posturing puppet than an aesthete or *symboliste* – a Lancastrian Mallarmé. Eleanor Johnson's study of Hoccleve's prosimetra, for instance, and David Watt's analysis of Hoccleve's *Series* as self-referencing commentary on the circumstances of book production – a sort of gloss on the making of the *Series* itself – show convincingly that the narrative of decline neglects not only the prosodic complexities of Lancastrian verse but also the material culture that contained and articulated the codes of metrical and generic competition and transmission.[10]

However, even as scholarship turns to a model of fifteenth-century culture rooted in formal innovation and meta-textual mythmaking, only a handful of studies, such as those of Johnson and Watt, have located and made explicit the complex network of aesthetic ideologies competing for dominance in the literary market following Chaucer's death – a network no longer parasitic on Chaucer as an authorising interest but, instead, self-authorising. One consequence of this relative lack of description has been a widespread neglect of later Lancastrian poets, such as Osbern Bokenham, George Ashby, and John Metham, whose metrical codes remain unexamined, or, when they do attract scholarly attention, seem to confirm the status of their authors as minor poets with tin ears who, when writing well, which was seldom, failed unremarkably in their art and, when writing poorly, which was often, precipitously ruined English poetry.

And yet even Bokenham and Ashby may profitably be contextualised within the narrative of prosodic sophistication. Statistical analysis of their verse suggests that between 1447 and 1476 Bokenham and Ashby produced the first dipodic English metre,[11] in which weaker and stronger syllables alternate as offbeats and beats, but in which lighter and heavier *beats* also alternate to form an intermediate prosodic structure above the level of the syllable but below the level of the line, as in John Masefield's *Ballad of John Silver*:

/ x / x / x / x / x / x / x /
She was **boar**ded, she was **loo**ted, she was **scut**tled till she **sank**

In Masefield's line, the dipodic template may be scanned programmatically to assign maximum prominence to every fourth syllable:

(w) s w **S** w s w **S** w s w **S**

10 For Johnson, see *Practicing Literary Theory in the Middle Ages: Ethics and Mixed Form in Chaucer, Gower, Usk, and Hoccleve* (Chicago: University of Chicago Press, 2013), pp. 19–43, 202–8; and for Watt, see *The Making of Thomas Hoccleve's* Series (Liverpool: Liverpool University Press, 2013).

11 See Myklebust, 'Misreading', pp. 750–63.

Simple dipodic rhythms strictly alternate in this fashion, but, as George Stewart observes, in dipody 'use of the metrical pause is so common as to be characteristic',[12] leading to complex rhythms marked by deleted beats and offbeats as well as double offbeats and variable syllable and beat counts. Such complexity is a hallmark of late Victorian metrical experiments in dipody, such as one finds in George Meredith's 'Love in the Valley'; and it is also a hallmark of late Lancastrian metrics. Reading Hoccleve, one can be reasonably certain that, wherever the beats fall, the number of syllables is assured:

x / x / x / x / x /
Seekynge reste, but certeynly shee (*Regiment* 72)[13]

x / x / x x / x x /
Six marc. That sit to **myn herte** so colde (*Regiment* 935)

In line 72 final *–e* acts as a guide to scanning the line: in order to obtain the required ten syllables (a precept from which Hoccleve did not deviate often, if at all), final *–e* must be scanned on both *Seekynge* and *reste*; and the phonological salience of *–e* on the participle requires that stress be shifted from the root morpheme to the inflection. Even in line 935, which appears to lack a beat, the number of syllables is not in question: despite the prosodic boundary between the clitic *myn* and its host *herte*, any attempt to recover a fifth beat by placing that beat on *myn*, pausing, and treating *herte* as a trochaic inversion will seem artificial and aesthetically unconvincing.[14]

Conversely, when reading Lydgate, one can rely on the steady alternation of beats in all positions except at the colon boundary of the fifth metrical position, and so ambiguities of phrasal or lexical stress rarely arise:

↓——— left edge of the second colon
x / x / (x) / x / x /
Ageynes **deth** vayleth lit or noght (*Siege of Thebes* 592)[15]

Organisation of the line into distinct phonological phrases blocks the possibility of subordinating the first syllable of *vayleth* to *lit*, or *deth* to *vayleth*, and demoting it to an offbeat. As a consequence of this prosodic diligence, in Lydgate's metre, as in Hoccleve's, a certain minimum legibility can be assumed:

x / x / / x / x /
Ageynes **deth vay**leth lit or noght

[12] *The Technique of English Verse* (Port Washington, NY: Kennikat, 1958), p. 82.

[13] *The Regiment of Princes*, ed. Charles Blyth, TEAMS (Kalamazoo, MI: Medieval Institute, 1999).

[14] Cf. Jefferson, 'The Hoccleve Holographs', p. 217.

[15] *Lydgate's Siege of Thebes*, ed. Axel Erdmann and Eilert Ekwall, EETS 125, vol. 2 (1930).

This is not true for the metres of Ashby and Bokenham, which inherited from Hoccleve a powerful licence to fix the beat by retracting it from a host to a clitic, and from Lydgate an equally powerful licence to delete an offbeat aligned with a colon boundary:

x / x / x / (x) / x /
George Ashby is my **name**, that ys greued (*Active Policy* 29)[16]

x / x / x / x / x /
Wych þat she louyd **& had** in vsage (*Lyf of Saint Elyzabeth* 9650)[17]

Bokenham and Ashby combined and expanded licences inherited from Hoccleve and Lydgate in order to sculpt a subtle, strenuous metre that deploys metrical pauses, deletes both beats and offbeats from the metrical line, and varies its syllable count to stir elusive rhythms in which an appearance of disorder masks an order so intricate it can barely be detected. Ashby's offbeat deletion in *Active Policy* relocates the missing syllable from the fifth to the seventh metrical position; and Bokenham's beat retraction in his prologue to *Lyf of Saint Elyzabeth* obscures the line's prosodic order by shifting the beat not merely from a host to a clitic but from a finite verb (*had*) to a conjunction (*and*) coordinating two verb phrases. Such order soon proved difficult to perceive, and their dipodic innovation was consigned to obscurity and written out of histories of English prosody.[18] The outstanding features of their dipody – a creative accounting of syllables and a penchant for deleting weaker beats in a scaffold of alternating weak and strong beats – encoded a complex series of prosodic negotiations going back to Chaucer, whose decasyllable provided poets with a foundation on which to build new metres. When, in the first decades of the sixteenth century, Stephen Hawes and Alexander Barclay rejected such lavish inventions, seeking both to reclaim simplicity as a prosodic rationale and to restore Lydgate and Chaucer as models of reasonable metre-making, they naturally swept Ashby and Bokenham out of the line of Chaucerian reception and transmission.

Because of this retrospective bias against Lancastrian experimentation, and because, unlike the verse designs of Ashby and Bokenham, John Metham's metre does not derive from prosodic reformulations of Chaucer's decasyllable,

16 *George Ashby's Poems*, ed. Mary Bateson, EETS e.s. 76 (1899). Final *–e* in *name*, historically justified, is probably not pronounced by Ashby.

17 *Bokenham's Legendys of Hooly Wummen*, ed. Mary Serjeantson, EETS o.s. 206 (1938).

18 In part, loss of access to late Lancastrian dipodic codes might be seen as a logical endgame of any prosodic system in which beat and offbeat deletion become an operative principle of verse practice. Because both Ashby and Bokenham constrain beat deletion so that it occurs only within and not between phonological phrases, readers familiar with the metrical code will know which beats are candidates for deletion and which are not: the greater the number of weak nodes dominating a designated terminal element, the likelier the syllable is for deletion.

Amoryus and Cleopes has attracted censure but no sustained formal analysis. Derek Pearsall pronounced its metre 'unspeakable';[19] and George Saintsbury wrote that Metham 'evidently *meant* decasyllables; but his actual syllables meander cheerfully from 8 to 17'.[20] Even those critics who would defend Metham's poem against its detractors concede that its metre is no good or else proffer generalised apologies that lack corroborating data. Stephen Page excuses the metre as 'fluid and nuanced rhymed prose' whose author 'was simply not interested in prosody';[21] and Jamie Fumo rejects the 'sporadic dismissals of its inconsistent prosody' but fails to explain in what way the metre *is* consistent.[22] Resistance to the poem's metre, of course, is understandable, as the line it draws between complexity and chaos seems perilously thin. In fact, Page notes an irony in the apparent 'metrical ineptitude' of the poem's sonnet – twice referred to as a 'songe' by the narrator – with 'such obvious inattention to prosody' and 'lack of metrical sense' exposing the poet's 'real concern': not versification but rather 'an effective narrative' delivered as an oral performance in mimicry of the illumination in the Corpus Christi frontispiece to *Troilus*.

The poem's prosodic eccentricity cannot be ascribed either to the time separating the poem's composition from its copying – approximately twenty-six years, from 1449, the poem's *terminus post quem*, to 1475, the probable scribal *terminus ante quem* – or to its dialect, which, although East Anglian, differs from Chaucer's only in phonological and lexical forms that have no bearing on such prosodic matters as final *–e* or stress doublets.[23] On the contrary, the poem's difficulty stems primarily from its unpredictable and often extreme variations in syllable count and its comparably unpredictable variation in the number of beats per line, with any given verse instance containing between eight and nineteen syllables and between four and eight beats. Even the poem's first stanza spares no extravagance:

> The chauns of love and eke the peyn of Amoryus, the knygt,
> For Cleopes sake, and eke how bothe in fere together

[19] Derek Pearsall, 'The English Romance in the Fifteenth Century', *Essays and Studies* 29 (1976), 56–83, at p. 69.

[20] Saintsbury, *English Prosody*, vol. 1, p. 264, n. 5.

[21] *Amoryus and Cleopes*, ed. Stephen F. Page, TEAMS (Kalamazoo, MI: Medieval Institute), Introduction, p. 16.

[22] Jamie Fumo, 'John Metham's "Straunge Style": *Amoryus and Cleopes* as Chaucerian Fragment', *CR* 43 (2008), 215–37, at p. 215.

[23] Plural and possessive nouns inflect with *–ys*, and East Anglian secondary features include free variation among nouns ending in *–ght*, *–t*, *–th*, and *–ht*, an idiosyncrasy extending to the third person singular in verbs. Still more conclusive are the lowering of high front vowels, as in *kend* for *kind* and the loss of lateral sonorant approximant before voiced stops, as in *wordly* (line 379). Retention of obsolete regional lexemes, such as *sqweme*, also mark the text as East Anglian. But none of these affects the poem's metre.

Lovyd and aftyr deyd, my purpos ys to endyght.
And now, O goddes, I thee beseche of kunnyng, that Lanyfyca hyght:
Help me to adornne ther chauns in sqwyche manere
So that qwere this matere dotht yt reqwyre,
Bothe ther lovys I may compleyne to loverys dysyre. (1–7)[24]

Here the number of beats veers wildly from seven, to six, to eight, to five, and, finally, back to six in a modified rhyme royal stanza accommodating lines of ten to seventeen syllables. Some, like line 6, seem curiously unproblematic:

x / x / x / x / x /
So that qwere this matere dotht yt reqwyre

But other lines are not so generous, and their indifference to standard decasyllabic cues suggests that although the metre may occasionally echo Chaucer's, its rationale is unlikely to be found among those of Chaucer's metrical stewards. The combination of an elastic syllable count and a flexible beat count frustrates any attempt to construct a stable metrical hypothesis on which to make predictions. Furthermore, this failure to form reliable, feed-forward metrical expectations inhibits rhythmic entrainment, so that, at any given verse instance, readers must reason their way through the poem's artifice rather than assigning values intuitively on the basis of anticipatory schemata imposed on the line's prosodic shape. Readers are likely to interpret such interference as an absence of design and conclude that if the poem contains any controlling form, that form must be underconstrained and therefore massively overgenerate a set of rhythms.

However, as Page notes, Metham's poem also varies unpredictably in its rhyme scheme, generally following the template of a rhyme royal stanza – a calculated demonstration of received authority in the *Troilus* tradition of *roman antique* – but also prone to eccentric re-scripting of that stanza, with twenty-eight stanzas adopting a scheme of *ababacc* and eighteen a scheme of *abaabcc*. Thirteen stanzas forgo the final *c* rhyme for a six-line scheme and nine stanzas opt for an extra *c* rhyme in an eighth-line burden. However, in nearly every departure from rhyme royal, as in nearly every departure from conventions of popular romance or *roman antique*, the poem plays the formal convention against itself for some ironic gain and drives the poem to further levels of hybridity and sophistication.[25] The poem's opening stanza,

[24] All quotations are from *Amoryus and Cleopes*, ed. Page.

[25] On Metham's ironic appropriation of Chaucer's *roman antique*, see Roger Dalrymple, '*Amoryus and Cleopes*: John Metham's Metamorphosis of Chaucer and Ovid', in *The Matter of Identity in Medieval England*, ed. Phillipa Hardman (Cambridge: D. S. Brewer, 2002), pp. 149–62; and Stephen F. Page, 'John Metham's "Amoryus and Cleopes": Intertextuality and Innovation in a Chaucerian Poem', *CR* 31 (1996), 201–8. On the rhyme royal stanza as a space for intellectual and rhetorical performance, see Elizabeth Robertson, 'Rhyme Royal and Romance', in this volume, pp. 50–68.

for example, which rhymes *abaabcc*, is an ironic *tour de force*. In its first attempt at a Chaucerian stanza, the text gently repositions *hyght* as a partner to *endyght* and *knygt* in the *a* series rather than *together* and *manere* in the *b* series. Just as *endyght* announces the poet and *knygt* his subject, so *hyght* declares his craft or mode: with his gift he will endeavour to sing of the same subject as Chaucer, but with a new measure, a new genre, and a new form – a form that binds singer and song to his subject with a novelty, élan, and vigour that the *romans antique* lack. Pruning the *b* series of *hyght* undermines the poet's place within the tradition of *romans antique*, and yet it does so to his advantage. His *manere* will not be that of his models, and certainly not that of Chaucer, whose stanza he scavenges only to rebrand it as his own. To read the stanza as a failed attempt to write in rhyme royal reduces its florid recasting of conventional form to an impoverished complaint that it does not favourably conform to expectations – just as to read its handling of romance motifs as an undisciplined or naïve transgression against decorum grievously misreads its lightness of touch as the absence of a shaping hand. Of course, failure to conform may be precisely the poet's point.

In light of the poet's playfulness with stanza and genre and his habit of complicating rather than simplifying form, it may be prudent not to infer either the absence or presence of design in the poem's organisation of beats and syllables but, instead, to ask how, given correlate expansions of genre and stanza, one may determine whether the metre does have any design. That is, what assumptions must a reader *not* make in order to navigate successfully the poem's metrical landscape?

To begin, it cannot be assumed that ten-syllable, five-beat lines signify a Chaucerian decasyllable:

> In May, that modyr ys of monthys glade
> Qwan flourys sprede, the qwyche wythin the rote (8–9)
>
> And thus I ende this rude descrypcion (626)
>
> The qwyche thei drynk for ther salvacion (1285)
>
> Thei gan them fast aray qwan thei gan se (1595)

Each of these lines could have been written by Chaucer. All produce a marked contrast between weaker and stronger syllables alternating to a count of ten:

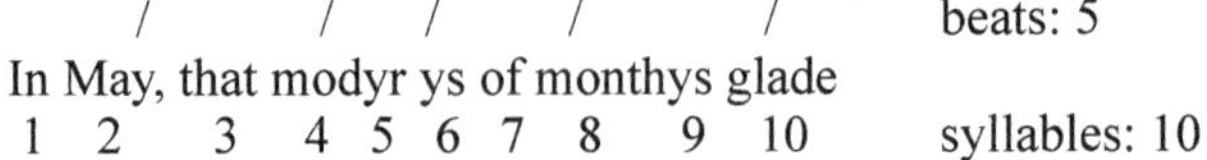

/ / / / / beats: 5
In May, that modyr ys of monthys glade
1 2 3 4 5 6 7 8 9 10 syllables: 10

However, such lines comprise only a subset of attested verse instances, and many of the conflicting instances occur in the same stanza as an apparent decasyllable:

For Phebus exaltyng, wyth sundry hwys smellyd sote (11)
To Norwyche a Greke, to home I schewyd in specyal (67)
In her hertys thus thei ment, at hos partyng was a privy peyn (848)

If one approaches these lines expecting a Chaucerian decasyllable, or even the knotty dipody of Bokenham, they will sound like nonsense. Indeed, if one approaches the poem expecting *anything*, its metre will not scan, because despite the poem's insistent narrative, generic, and stanzaic echoes, it has no metrical precedent and therefore no fixed reference within the tradition of late medieval versification with which to be reconciled.

How, then, to proceed? Metham's metre poses a unique problem. In non-alliterative verse the syllable count typically acts as a framework for matching beats to syllables. That framework, in turn, promotes a metrical hypothesis that can be applied to all verse instances as a logical constraint for determining, in ambiguous cases, how best to reconcile local rhythmic disturbances to the schematic template. (It is a parsing function for organising the line's syllables into well-defined rhythmic figures.) Setting a limit on how many beats can occur in a line, the count specifies an outermost boundary for the reader's metrical expectations, so that, as one reads, one uses the count to maintain one's working hypothesis and remain synchronised to the optimal number and placement of beats in the line. Because the right-edge domain of a colon performs a privileged cognitive and prosodic function in the line (each confirms the closure of a hierarchical unit dominated only by the line and therefore shapes a reader's perception of the line's rhythmic architecture),[26] the second and fifth beats in a decasyllable receive maximal contrasts in prominence with their adjacent offbeats in order to boost the salience of the fourth and tenth positions. (Occasionally the third rather than the second beat may receive this maximal contrast if the first colon extends not to the fourth but to the sixth position, a structure that is more marked than its alternative but is nevertheless attested in the literature.) In a Chaucerian decasyllable, the ten-count parses alternating pairs of weaker and stronger syllables into a stable, recurring pattern of attentional energy that targets the second stimulus event as more marked and, therefore, an ideal candidate to carry the beat:

[26] Cf. Kristin Hanson, 'Nonlexical Word Stress in the English Iambic Pentameter: A Study of John Donne', in *The Nature of the Word: Studies in Honor of Paul Kiparsky*, ed. Kristin Hanson and Sharon Inkelas (Cambridge, MA: MIT, 2008), pp. 21–60; and Bernhard E. K ten Brink, *Chaucers Sprache und Verkunst* (Leipzig, 1884), trans. M. B. Smith, *The Language and Metre of Chaucer*, 2nd rev. edn (London: Macmillan, 1901), pp. 218–19.

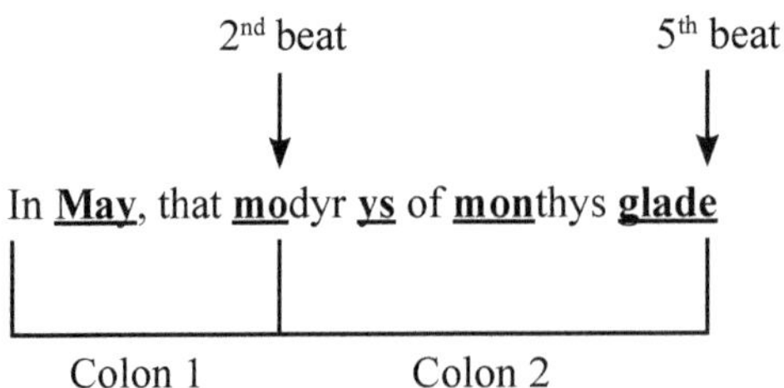

In the context of a Chaucerian decasyllable, Metham's line would acquire this style of hierarchical structure, with the reader's metrical hypothesis confirmed at each closure of the cola. Metham's elastic count, by contrast, prevents the reader even from constructing a template for selecting candidate beat-bearing syllables, so that, in this case, one may assign beats to the second, fourth, sixth, eighth, and tenth syllables, but those beats will not group to form a hierarchical infrastructure that can be applied consistently to every line. In fact, the line seems engineered specifically to defeat the body's reflexive synchronisation to a beat – that stable, recurring pattern of attentional energy that allows readers to predict which syllables and positions will be prominent and target them for salience; in which case, one must democratise the line so that any syllable, in principle, may carry a beat. One cannot preferentially target positions in advance but must, instead, work out in real time which syllables to select as candidate beats. And although an oral performance of the text may simulate a sort of prose, as Page maintains, when read as verse, the poem requires deliberate metrical reflection, a hermeneutical thinking through of the text rather than a passive audition of it.

Any description of the *Amoryus* metre, then, must begin with this problem of *thinking*. And if the function of a metre is to entrain the reader to a beat, and if that beat is, in part, a product of constraints on syllable count, with *Amoryus* one must first consider variations in the syllable and beat counts independently and *then* compare the two distributions in order to determine how often the lines strictly alternate weaker and stronger syllables. The strength of this method lies in its lack of assumptions: it does not try to reconcile the poem's data with decasyllabic expectations, which, in any case, will be defeated by fluctuations in the counts. Instead, it correlates those counts to determine where the mean number of beats per line matches the mean number of syllables, a figure that tells the reader what the *average* rhythm is like. Having established a norm, one can then work outward to find its periphery. Once the boundaries of the metre are defined, one can generalise about its design and make predictions about what, if any, rhythms it excludes.

As a first approximation, one might take a 10 per cent sample of the total count beginning at line one and running through line 203. For each line, one would count the number of syllables and the number of beats, noting that final *–e* is unlikely to be sounded and that the metre does not license metrical pauses by deleting a midline offbeat, as in Lydgate's line. Finally, one would exclude feminine rhyme from the syllable count, as a line-final extra syllable does not affect the alternation between weak and strong syllables or the matching of syllables to beats.

/ x x / x / x / x /
Yevying hym omage and possession
x / x / x / x / x /
Of alle this forsayd regyon of Perse. (24–5)

Here again the line may mislead readers into thinking the metre is a decasyllable, especially when the following line seems to repeat its counts, placing the beats on every other syllable:

/ / / / /
The regyon of Perse and of Medys[27]

Such notions, though, are quickly dispelled by conflicting rhythms through the rest of the stanza, including lines of seven beats rather than five and fifteen syllables rather than ten:

27 I assume synaeresis in *regyon*, as *Perse* appears in rhyme position in lines 25, 71, 566, and 1022, where its rhyme complements are, respectively, *cyté*, *equité*, *sle*, and *prosperyté*. *Medys* here rhymes with *Pansopherys*, with stress on the final syllable of the proper noun. One may argue that *Perse* does not undergo stress shift line-internally (as may be the case in line 993). However, as Ten Brink and E. Talbot Donaldson observe, lexical disyllables ending in a tense vowel remain candidates for shift. See Ten Brink, *The Language and Metre of Chaucer*, p. 194; and E. Talbot Donaldson, 'Chaucer's Final *–e*', *PMLA* 63 (1948), 1101–24. It is true, as Donka Minkova and Michael Redford object, that critics have extended stress shift to words that do not, on etymological grounds, qualify as stress doublets. See Michael Redford, 'Middle English Stress Doubles: New Evidence from Chaucer's Meter', in *Development in Prosodic Systems*, ed. Haike Jacobs and Paula Fikkert (Berlin: Mouton de Gruyter, 2003), pp. 159–95; and Donka Minkova, 'Nonprimary Stress in Early Middle English Accentual-Syllabic Verse', in *English Historical Metrics*, ed. C. B. McCully and J. J. Anderson (Cambridge: CUP, 1999), pp. 95–119. And yet, as Elizabeth Solopova and Marina Tarlinskaja have shown, word class accounts only for one part of variable stress; the other part is word position in the line, with words occurring before a colon boundary likelier to shift stress than words not occurring before a colon boundary. See Elizabeth Solopova, 'Computer-Assisted Study of Chaucer's Metre', *Parergon* 18 (2000), 157–79; and Marina Tarlinskaja, *English Verse: Theory and History* (The Hague: Mouton, 1976), p. 103. In general, we may observe of variable stress in *Amoryus* that a word of Old English origin is unlikely to shift stress from its root morpheme unless the affix retains a degree of stress or a non-reduced vowel, as in *–ness*, *–yng*, or *–ly*; a word is likelier to shift stress prior to a colon boundary; and proper nouns and recent loans, particularly from Romance donors, are more variable in their placement of stress. We may further note that inflectional affixes with reduced vowels (such as *–yd*) regularly undergo syncope.

/ x x / x x / x / x / x / x /
Yeldyn the keys to the emperour of this forsayd cite (23)

The variations – which are representative of the sample generally – suggest that the metre tolerates double offbeats but not missing offbeats, and that double offbeats can occur anywhere in the line. Considering the entire sample, one finds seventy-nine lines with six beats (38.9 per cent); seventy-two with five (35.5 per cent); twenty-eight with seven (13.8 per cent); thirteen with four (6.4 per cent); and eleven with eight (5.4 per cent).

Table 8.1 Lines by number of beats

No. of beats	% of total
4	6.4
5	35.5
6	38.9
7	13.8
8	5.4

More lines contain six beats than contain five and 74.4 per cent of all lines contain either five or six beats. The norm, therefore, is a five- *or* six-beat line:

x / x / x / x / x / x /
But for that this contré was gret and populus (29)

x / x / x / x / x /
And brevely this proces for to trase (155)

The upper limit of syllables per line is nineteen and the lower limit is eight. Eight syllables occur only when a four-beat line is strictly alternating, a verse instance present in 1.9 per cent of lines:

x / x / x / x /
And theruppon ther othe thei toke (27)

Nine-syllable lines, which occur only through the presence of a double offbeat in a four-beat line (as no five-beat line loses a syllable either through beat deletion or through acephaly), occur in 1.47 per cent of lines:

x / x / x x / x /
Thyse princys dwellyng in pes and rest (41)

Ten-syllable lines occur in 13.3 per cent of lines and represent five beats strictly alternating or four beats with two double offbeats:

x / x / x / x / x /
Be longe contynwauns, never founde in blame (74)

x x / x / x x / x /
For the rude endytyng of this story (187)

Eleven-syllable lines occur in 12.3 per cent of lines and indicate a five-beat line with a double offbeat:

x / x / x x / x / x /
The nwe was made and complet be twenty day (178)

Twelve-syllable lines occur in 17.24 per cent of lines – the most of any count – and represent either a six-beat line in duple metre or a five-beat line with two double offbeats:

x x / x / x x / x / x /
That betwene ther placys ther was no more dystauns (80)

x / x / x / x / x / x /
The fame of hys manhod and of hys lovlynes (102)

Lines of thirteen and fourteen syllables are also common, occurring in 14.78 per cent of lines and 16.75 per cent of lines, respectively, and represent six-beat lines with one double offbeat and six-beat lines with two double offbeats or a strictly alternating line of seven beats:

x / x / x / x / x x / x /
The fame of her beute was spred, and of here stature (151)

x x / x / x / x x / x / x /
For so womanly was sche, so benygne to yche creature (152)

x / x / x / x / x / x / x /
Precellyd in fayrenes; that yn the reme so specyal (150)

Fifteen-syllable lines are rarer, occurring in only 9.35 per cent of lines, and from there the counts decline precipitously. Challenges to the metre typically manifest as double offbeats and, more rarely, as ambiguities in the promotion to beat-bearing status of a function word or a syllable in a lexical word that does not carry primary stress but is nevertheless eligible to carry the beat (as in line 150 above).

Table 8.2 Lines by number of syllables

No. of syllables	% of total
8	1.9
9	1.47
10	13.3
11	12.3

No. of syllables	% of total
12	17.24
13	14.78
14	16.75
15	9.35
16	4.43
17	5.4
18	0.98
19	1.47

The data show that the number of beats in a line is half the number of syllables (that is, a strictly alternating duple rhythm) in 25.6 per cent of lines, with 2.4 per cent containing four beats, 10.8 per cent containing five beats, 6.9 per cent containing six beats, 4.4 per cent containing seven beats, and 1 per cent containing eight beats. Most duple lines, therefore, by a considerable margin, are five-beat lines, despite the prevalence of six-beat lines in the poem – a curious figure indicating that although Metham wrote more lines with six beats in them, he wrote more *strictly alternating five-beat lines*. That is, the line least likely to contain a double offbeat is a five-beat line. It would be difficult not to read this metrical sleight-of-hand as subtle commentary on Chaucer's decasyllable – a nod to the reader to compare the two metres and ask which is the more athletic, intelligent, and arduous; to confuse the two metres, if only for a moment, in order to reflect on the clockwork stiffness of one and the organic agility of the other. Did Metham intend his verse to whisper Chaucerian rhythms now and then, so that they haunt the poem like a metrical *déjà vu*? In light of the distribution of five-beat duple rhythms, it would be hard to deny that he did, especially when one considers, first, that the poem prefers an apparent alexandrine, with its six beats and twelve syllables, to an apparent decasyllable, and, second, that the poem's optimal count of twelve syllables can be met either by the competing model to Chaucer's hendecasyllable (the alexandrine) or by a facsimile of Chaucer's own rhythm inflated by two double offbeats.

More compelling is the distribution of count differentials. In seventy-nine instances a line exceeds its count by one syllable, indicating that the line has one double offbeat. In forty-three instances a line exceeds its count by two syllables, indicating that the line has two double offbeats. In one instance a line exceeds its count by three syllables, indicating that the line has three double offbeats. What is the significance of this distribution? In 78.3 per cent of lines the metre remains within one double offbeat of a duple count, and in 99.5 per cent of lines it remains within two double offbeats, suggesting that the metrical norm is not strictly alternating, as if Chaucer had written the line, but neither is it ad hoc or haphazard. Statistically, any line is likeliest to remain within one syllable of its optimal count, with a restricted licence for a run of weak syllables not to exceed two. Further, the metrical threshold beyond which the line's coherence is in jeopardy is two double offbeats in one line, so that one excluded set of possible rhythms concerns lines with three or more runs of weak syllables:

x x / x / x x / x / x x /
*For the rude endytyng of this story of a kyng

Lines of thirteen syllables occur in *Amoryus*, as do lines of five beats, but no lines of five beats occur with three double offbeats or thirteen syllables.

Comparing the syllable counts and beat counts, one can say, then, that a line may contain between four and eight beats and up to but not more than two double offbeats. This statement will generate all attested verse instances and exclude all but one verse instance:

Or to speke of the hythe, or the brede, or of the facion (171)

It is unclear whether scribal error produced this line; it would be reasonable to infer an article was inserted before *brede* for parallel phrasal structure – but in any case such an instance comprises 0.5 per cent of all lines. One may further note that 9.8 per cent of double offbeats occur across a midline caesura, as in an epic caesura:

x / x / x x / x x /
Was clepyd Dydas, hos wurchyp and fame (107)

And another 19.7 per cent occur under conditions resembling an anacrusis:

x x / x / x x / x x / x / x /
And the sempyl wryter besechyth of supportacion (50)

It is possible that the metre may license an extra syllable following a midline pause or at the beginning of the line, and that these syllables do not count metrically.

What, then, of the unpredictability of beats from line to line? As Graphs 8.1 and 8.2 indicate, the *Amoryus* metre neutralises its unpredictability in both beat and syllable counts by conditioning its reader not to expect that each line will adhere to an invariant templatic percept but, instead, to expect that the distribution of syllable and beat counts *throughout* the poem will not be random.

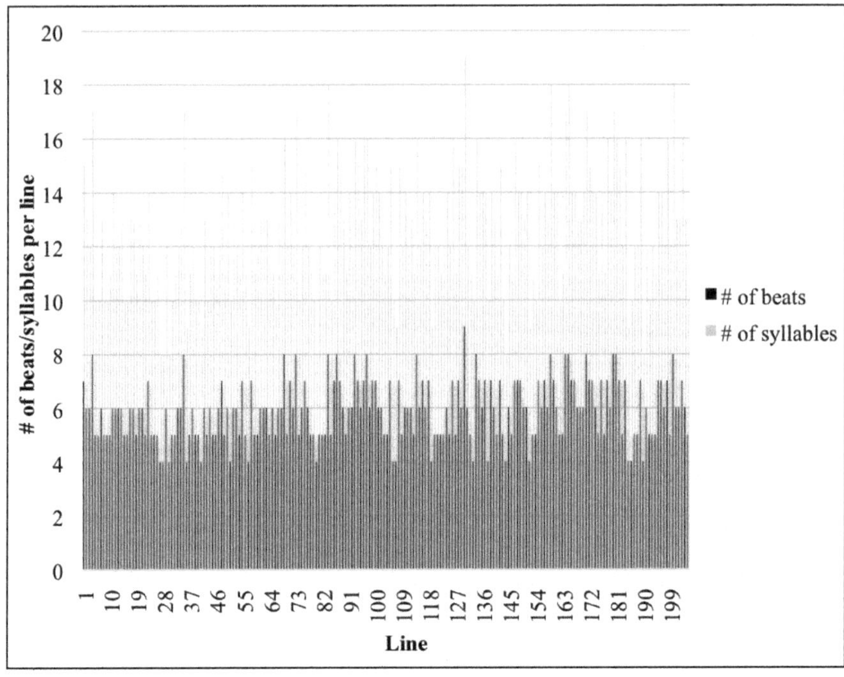

Graph 8.1 Beat and syllable count compared: *Amoryus and Cleopes*

Lines of five beats and ten syllables (with an optional double offbeat) will form concentrated clusters, offering cues *above* the level of the line and inscribing into the text a 'metre' that runs both in and among lines so that the entire poem, like an individual line, functions as a single metrical unit, with recurrences or 'beats' sometimes occurring at intervals of several dozen lines. The second stanza of the poem, in fact, is composed entirely of a three-line sequence of five-beat lines and a four-line sequence of six-beat lines. And the eighteenth stanza is composed entirely of lines with two double offbeats. Such groupings of lines offer an alternative to conventional styles of rhythmic entrainment. This tactic keeps the incidence of prototypical lines, in which the beat-to-syllable ratio is 1:2 (a duple rhythm), high enough to cycle continuously in the reader's working memory. These clusters, in which six-beat lines occur in tightly grouped bursts with other six-beat lines, and five with five, and four or seven with four or seven, comprise a non-random distribution that calibrates those rhythms to mould the reader's memory:

x / x / x / x /
And theruppon ther othe thei toke,

/ x x / x / x /
Sqweryng upon the tempyl boke (27–8) 4 beats

/ x x / x / x / x /
Help me to adornne ther chauns in sqwyche manere
x / x / x / x / x /
So that qwere this matere dotht yt reqwyre (5–6) 5 beats

x / x / x / x / x / x / (x)
For Cleopes sake, and eke how bothe in fere together
/ x x / x / x / x / x /
Lovyd and aftyr deyd, my purpose ys to endyght. (2–3) 6 beats

The specific types of syllable and beat counts are not strewn randomly but concentrated in chunks. Each variant has a distinctive distributional fingerprint determined by the shape of its clusters – how often each occurs and how widely spaced its lines are – so that the variant counts access contrary but complementary parts of the reader's working memory. Because the rhythms do not compete for the same mental 'space', working memory is not overburdened by them and the reader can efficiently store and access them as variants of the metrical prototype: a 1:2 duple metre with an optional double offbeat.

What is the advantage of clustering the variant counts? When one variant occurs in close proximity to other members of its variant class, the reader learns to associate like rhythm with like rhythm and to form an exemplar of that rhythm: an ideal form of the variant count that can be stored for easy access and used to retrieve a simpler, more economical version of the specific line. If a variant count were to occur randomly, the reader would have no way to predict its recurrence, and so the difficulty of processing the rhythm and, by extension, categorising it as a member of the prototypical set, would increase:

x / x / x / x x / x / x /
That causyd me to mervel that yt so gloryusly
x x / x / x / x / x / x /
Was adornyd, and oftyn I enqwyryd of lettyryd clerkys
x / x / x / x / x x / x /
Qwat yt myght be that poyntyd was wyth so merwulus werkys. (61–3)

Here three consecutive six-beat lines with a double offbeat close the poem's eighth stanza – a typical grouping for this rhythm. Were these occurrences accidental, the reader would be unlikely to anticipate the event successfully, and the rhythm would be less intelligible. However, because irregularities occur in close proximity to one another, as they do here, the processing burden drops sharply.

Curiously, the metre adopts different strategies for reducing this burden depending on how proximate the line is to the metrical prototype. Five- and six-beat lines, which lie considerably closer to the metrical prototype, cluster in groups separated by no more than three or four lines, with gaps between clusters minor and frequent, so that, as in pointillism, the lines form a smooth, transitional texture in which rhythms recycle through working memory in a 'rehearsal loop'. Gaps between clusters of four-, seven-, and eight-beat counts, by contrast, are infrequent but robust, with more prominent intervals separating the clusters. The texture of clusters for these less prototypical lines is rougher than the five- and six-beat counts because, as lines more likely to contain a second offbeat and a less predictable syllable-to-beat ratio, they are more complex rhythmically and require a more conspicuous formal cue. Although both sets of counts entrain the reader to a beat *among* rather than *within* lines, counts prone to two double offbeats resemble a light switch turned on and off, whereas counts prone to a single offbeat resemble a dimmer switch. The result, in both cases, is enhanced clarity and a reduction in metrical noise. Eight-beat and four-beat lines show the most prominent gaps, with mean intervals of 12.25 lines and 9.5 lines, respectively. Seven-beat lines exploit a more modest mean interval of 5 lines between clusters. Five- and six-beat lines yield mean intervals of 3.1 and 3.3, respectively, confirming that the poem's prototypical rhythm is a five- or six-beat line with an optional double offbeat. And by distributing these counts in controlled bursts, the metre accomplishes two things at once. First, it entrains readers to synchronise to the mean interval characteristic of each line type, which acts as signature cue for clusters of four-, five-, six-, seven-, or eight-beat lines. Faster recognition frees up conscious awareness to attend to new information and reduces the burden of processing each line.

Second, stretches between double-offbeat counts provide a 'zone' of normalcy within which readers decrease their metrical vigilance. In *Amoryus*, although the beat and syllable counts are constantly in flux, the metre organises the incidence of strictly alternating (duple) lines so that they tend to occur in bursts, as do lines of the same number of beats, whether four, five, six, seven, or eight. Fluctuations occur *predictably*: as one reads the poem, one learns to anticipate that although lines vary in number of beats and syllables, groups of lines with five beats will occur more often together than apart, as will lines with four, six, seven, or eight beats. The technique effectively mitigates the variations in count, making the metre more readable and accessible than Saintsbury and Craig imply. And with final *–e* not relevant metrically, and with stress clash rarely a concern, once a reader entrains to the count clusters that comprise the poem's global beat – its style of thinking – local variations in syllable and beat count no longer prove distracting.

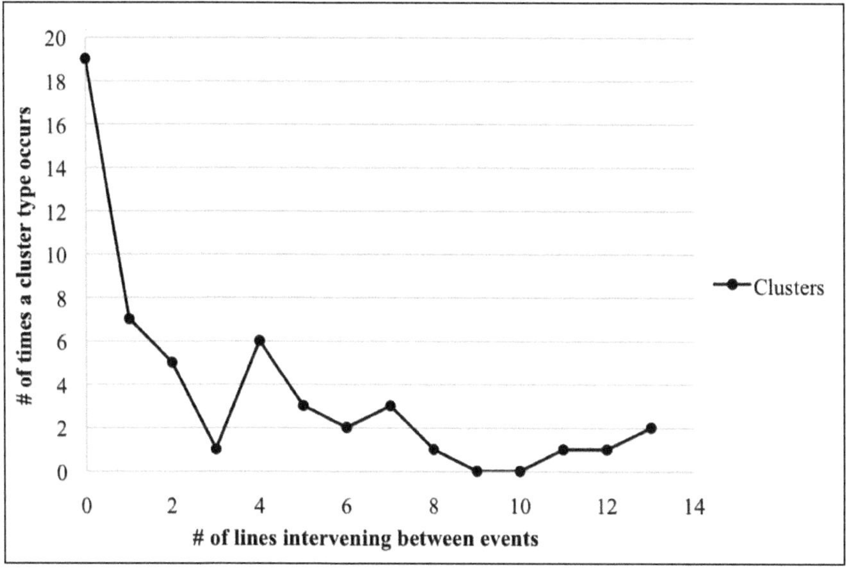

Graph 8.2 Beat/syllable count correspondences: *Amoryus and Cleopes*

And yet, for all its ingenuity in ironising Chaucer's line by refusing even to adapt it, the *Amoryus* metre nevertheless offers its readers only a model of what other poets decidedly did not do: decline to participate in the transmission of Chaucer's line through one hundred years of elaboration that moulded five beats and ten syllables into a miscellany of rhythms. Its refusal to do so, though, poses a question to scholars of late medieval literature: can one *not* read Lancastrian metre in the context of Chaucer? Perhaps that question is Metham's most significant contribution to criticism. For whether one tells the story of fifteenth-century metre as a cautionary tale of poetasters and formal tedium or as a celebration of wit and competition, one must weigh the narrative against Metham's example, and that example is likely, if not to break our mythmaking, then to strain it, and some truth, at least, may come from the pressure it places not only on literary traditions of romance and metre but also on critical traditions of contextualisation and reconstruction.

9

The Printed Transmission of Medieval Romance from William Caxton to Wynkyn de Worde, 1473–1535

Jordi Sánchez-Martí

The first book printed in English is a romance, namely the *Recuyell of the histories of Troy* (see below, Table 9.1), which significantly was published not in England but in Flanders by William Caxton (d. 1492), an Englishman who, as he himself reveals, 'contynued by the space of xxx yere for the most parte in the contres of Braband, Flandres, Holand and Zeland'.[1] Originally composed in French by Raoul Lefèvre in 1464–65 at the request of Philip the Good, Duke of Burgundy, the *Recuyell* was soon translated by Caxton: he started his translation in Bruges on 1 March 1468/9 at the command of Margaret of York, Duchess of Burgundy and sister to Edward IV, and finished it in Cologne on 19 September 1471. While in Cologne, Caxton became acquainted with the business opportunities the printing press offered and even decided to publish three Latin books, all of them with clear English associations.[2] Early in 1473, when he returned to Flanders, probably to Ghent,[3] Caxton was determined to try his luck with the printing press. For this new enterprise he relied on his hands-on experience in Cologne, as a result of which he devised a publishing strategy with lasting influence in his career, and with consequences for the printing culture of late medieval England in general, and the printed dissemination of romances in particular.

1 This information he reveals in the prologue to the *Recuyell* as given in *Caxton's Own Prose*, ed. N. F. Blake (London: Deutsch, 1973), p. 98.27–9; subsequent quotations from Caxton's prologues are cited from this edition with reference to page and line number. George D. Painter, *William Caxton: A Quincentenary Biography of England's First Printer* (London: Chatto & Windus, 1976), pp. 14–15, dates Caxton's initial move to Bruges to 1444.

2 For Caxton's stint in Cologne, see Lotte Hellinga, *William Caxton and Early Printing in England* (London: British Library, 2010), pp. 26–32. See also Severin Corsten, 'Caxton in Cologne', *Journal of the Printing Historical Society* 11 (1976–77), 1–18.

3 For locating Caxton in Ghent instead of Bruges, see Lotte Hellinga, 'William Caxton, Colard Mansion, and the Printer in Type 1', *Bulletin du bibliophile* 1 (2011), 86–114.

During his time in Cologne, Caxton learnt that the trade in Latin books was highly specialised and competitive and realised that it would be difficult to carve a niche for himself in this line of business.[4] Thus, instead of imitating the dominant publication trends on the Continent, Caxton had the foresight to see the market potential for books printed in English, and the acumen to devise a business plan to exploit such potential. In order to bring his plan to fruition Caxton chose to focus and capitalise on the strengths he derived from his personal circumstances. First, he was the first Englishman to master the art of printing which, as he explains in the epilogue to the *Recuyell*, 'I have practysed and lerned at my grete charge and dispense' (Caxton, p. 100.10–11). Second, owing to his prolonged and privileged stay on the Continent, Caxton had access to the fashionable literature consumed by the elite and was therefore confident that he could supply the English market with texts that would be appealing, though unfamiliar, to the majority of his potential customers. In his prologue to the *Recuyell* Caxton adduces this sense of novelty to justify its publication: 'this booke was newe and late maad and drawen into Frenshe and never had seen hit in oure Englissh tonge' (Caxton, p. 97.12–13). Third, in translating Lefèvre's work Caxton realised not only that he was a competent translator – Margaret of York even commended him – but also that his translating competence could be instrumental in developing his business plan: 'I thought in myself hit shold be a good besynes to translate hyt [i.e. the *Recueil*] into oure Englissh to th'ende that hyt myght be had … in the royame of Englond' (Caxton, p. 97.13–16). While the primary sense of *besynes* is 'activity' (*OED*, s.v. *business*, n. 2), the term also carries professional and economic connotations in view of the weight translations had in his printing enterprise.[5] And fourth, as someone who had been an active and successful merchant for the better part of his life, Caxton was well aware of the commercial side of printing and of its financial risks too. Thus, he cultivated the patronage of the nobility, as in the case of Margaret Beaufort, although he also tried to

4 Caxton's decision not to compete in the Latin book trade was followed by the other early English printers, who, for the most part, also focused on printing vernacular texts. England was therefore dependent on the Continent for its consumption of Latin books. For further discussion, see Alan Coates, 'The Latin Trade in England and Abroad', in *A Companion to the Early Printed Book in Britain, 1476–1558*, ed. Vincent Gillespie and Susan Powell (Cambridge: D. S. Brewer, 2014), pp. 45–58.

5 Cf. *OED*, s.v. *business*, n. 12. Sixty of the eighty different works printed by Caxton can be described as translations, most of which were produced by Caxton himself, as notes A. E. B. Coldiron, 'William Caxton', in *The Oxford History of Literary Translation in English*, vol. I: *To 1550*, ed. Roger Ellis (Oxford: OUP, 2008), pp. 160–9, at p. 160; translations represent 47 per cent of all his publications (BMC, XI, p. 48). For a discussion of the importance of translation for the early English printers, see Julia Boffey, 'Banking on Translation: English Printers and Continental Texts', in *The Medieval Translator*, vol. 15: *In Principio Fuit Interpres*, ed. Alessandra Petrina and Monica Santini (Turnhout: Brepols, 2013), pp. 317–29.

establish a select circle of clients as stated in the epilogue to the *Recuyell*: 'I have promysid to dyverce gentilmen and to my frendes to adresse to hem as hastely as I myght this sayd book' (Caxton, p. 100.8–10).[6] It became apparent to him, however, that unlike the production of manuscript books, which was mainly bespoke, the publication of printed books had to be fully speculative and hence made available to a wider public.[7] In sum, the combination of these four strengths represents the hallmark of Caxton's printing venture and results in an individualist business model centred on him, since he acted as printer, publisher, translator and book-dealer.

Year	Title	Format	BMC	Duff	STC
1473	*Recuyell of the histories of Troy*	Fol.	IX: 129	242	15375
1474	*Recueil des histoires de Troie*	Fol.	IX: 131	243	–
1477?	*Histoire de Jason*	Fol.	–	244	–
1477	*History of Jason*	Fol.	XI: 107–8	245	15383
1481	*Godfrey of Boloyne*	Fol.	XI: 124	164	13175
1485	Malory, *Morte Darthur*	Fol.	–	283	801
1485	*Charles the Great*	Fol.	XI: 160–1	83	5013
1485	*Paris and Vienne*	Fol.	XI: 161	337	19206
1490	*Four sons of Aymon*	Fol.	–	152	1007
1490	*Eneydos*	Fol.	XI: 174–5	404	24796
1490	*Blanchardyn and Eglantine*	Fol.	XI: 176–7	45	3124

Table 9.1 Romances printed by W. Caxton, 1473–90[8]

6 There is evidence that the *Recuyell* was purchased by customers connected to the English court; see BMC, XI, p. 56. Although Caxton devoted effort to seeking patronage, the involvement of a patron seldom implied a significant financial subvention; see A. S. G. Edwards and Carol M. Meale, 'The Marketing of Printed Books in Late Medieval England', *The Library*, 6th ser., 15 (1993), 95–124, at pp. 96–7. See also Russell Rutter, 'William Caxton and Literary Patronage', *SP* 84 (1987), 440–70.

7 See BMC, XI, p. 58.

8 For the corpus of medieval romances, I take as reference the list compiled by Helaine Newstead, 'Romances. General', in MWME, I, pp. 13–16. I also follow Carol M. Meale, 'Caxton, de Worde, and the Publication of Romance in Late Medieval England', *The Library*, 6th ser., 14 (1992), 283–98, at p. 285, in excluding from Newstead's list 'texts originating in Scotland … and examples of the genre written by Chaucer, Gower and Lydgate'. The dates and publication details of Caxton's editions printed on the Continent are taken from Hellinga, *William Caxton*, p. 51, table 1. For editions printed

In what ways did Caxton's publication policy affect the romance genre? One direct consequence was a departure from the romance tradition found in England in the manuscript period. Except for Malory's *Morte Darthur*, Caxton did not publish any of the English romances that were composed before 1475, either in prose or in verse, and are now preserved in manuscript form.[9] The failure to provide printed continuity to the English romance tradition cannot be attributed to Caxton's prolonged stay abroad, since these texts were still attracting readerly interest when Caxton relocated back to England in 1476, as suggested by the production after 1450 of around fifty extant manuscripts containing medieval romances.[10] It seems rather that Caxton strategically chose to neglect this textual corpus, which he certainly considered to belong among the 'olde bookes whyche at thys day ought not to have place ne be compared emong ne to hys [i.e. Chaucer's] beauteuous volumes and aournate writynges'.[11] His decision was based on a personal prejudice against a group of texts that he associated with the past, both aesthetically and ideologically, whereas he was interested in being perceived as promoting the latest literary fashions representing the supposedly more sophisticated preferences of the elite. In contrast to the outmoded English medieval romances, Caxton's romances, in his own view, stand out owing to their novelty and unavailability in English, as he remarks in his prologues.[12] His literary taste was

in England, I follow dates as given in BMC, XI. For a brief but useful literary discussion of these romances, see Douglas Gray, *Later Medieval English Literature* (Oxford: OUP, 2008), pp. 205–9; and Helen Cooper, 'Prose Romances', in *A Companion to Middle English Prose*, ed. A. S. G. Edwards (Cambridge: D. S. Brewer, 2004), pp. 215–29.

9 Approximately seventy-three metrical romances composed before 1475 are now extant, including those surviving in sixteenth-century manuscripts. In addition, the following prose romances contained in manuscripts, probably produced before 1475, should also be considered: *Ipomedon*, Longleat House, MS 257, fols 90–105; *King Ponthus and the Faire Sidone*, Bodl., MS Digby 185, fols 166–203, and Bodl., MS Douce 384; *The Prose Life of Alexander*, Lincoln Cathedral, MS 91, fols 1–49; *Prose Merlin*, CUL, MS Ff.3.11; *The Siege of Jerusalem*, NLW, MS Brogyntyn II.i, fols 157v–84, and another prose version in Cleveland Public Library, MS Wq091.92-C468, fols 77–99; *The Siege of Thebes*, Bodl., Rawlinson MS D. 82, fols 1–10; *The Siege of Troy*, Bodl., Rawlinson MS D. 82, fols 11–24.

10 See Gisela Guddat-Figge, *Catalogue of Manuscripts Containing Middle English Romances* (Munich: Fink, 1976).

11 Caxton, p. 61.15–18. These *olde bookes* should be distinguished from *hystories of olde tyme* (cf. n. 12) or 'auncyent hystoryes of noble fayttes and valyaunt actes of armes and warre' (Caxton, p. 57.16–17), since the latter have didactic value.

12 In his prologue to *Jason*, Caxton explains that he prints it 'for the novelte of the histories whiche as I suppose hath not be had bifore the translacion herof' (Caxton, pp. 104.63–105.65); about *Godfrey* he states that it is 'not knowen emonge us here' (Caxton, p. 139.88–9); of *Morte* he emphasises that the stories therein contained 'have late ben drawen oute bryefly into Englysshe' (Caxton, 108.91–2); he printed *Charles* 'to th'ende that th'ystoryes, actes and lyves may be had in our maternal tongue' (Caxton, p. 67.54–8); he printed *Aymon* 'to have … hystories of olde tyme passed of vertues

no doubt influenced by the time he spent in Burgundy, as his prologues to the *Recuyell* and *Jason* perfectly attest, although it would be inaccurate to pretend that Caxton's intention was to transplant Burgundian literary culture into England. Instead, as Megan Leitch argues, Caxton's choice of romance texts 'capitalized upon a keen awareness of English tastes in order to provide "Burgundian" texts whose genres and values paralleled those already popular with their intended readership'.[13] Moreover, if we take Caxton's assertions at face value, it seems that he was responding to and taking advantage of market demands existing in England prior to his return, since, excluding *Recuyell* and *Jason*, the publication of four out of the seven remaining romances was carried out at the suggestion or command of English customers.[14] Whether we think his paratexts are truthful or not, Caxton's publishing policy was not subordinate to the desires of his readers and patrons, but instead he showed interest in publishing texts that could be marketed as suitable reading matter for the nobility.[15]

---

chyvalry reduced ... into our Englishe tongue' (Caxton, p. 84.24–6); he describes *Blanchardyn* as a 'boke I late receyved in Frenshe ... to reduce and translate it into our maternal and Englysh tonge' (Caxton, p. 57.8–11); *Eneydos* is 'a lytyl booke in Frenshe whiche late was translated oute of Latyn by some noble clerke of Fraunce' (Caxton, p. 78.4–5). There is no prologue to *Paris*.

13 *Romancing Treason: The Literature of the Wars of the Roses* (Oxford: OUP, 2015), p. 142; see pp. 140–5 for a critical overview of scholarly positions concerning the Burgundian and English nature of Caxton's romances.

14 *Charles* was printed 'to satysfye the desyre and requeste of my good synguler lordes and specyal maysters and frendes' (Caxton, p. 67.59–60), among whom Caxton singles out a 'Maister Wylliam Daubeney, one of the Tresorers of the Jewellys of ... Kyng Edward the Fourth' (Caxton, p. 68.2–5); see Painter, *Caxton*, p. 149. *Morte* was printed because 'noble jentylmen instantly requyred me t'emprynte th'ystorye of ... Kyng Arthur', of whom 'one in specyal' (Caxton, p. 107.35–7, 49) has been tentatively identified as Anthony Woodville, 2nd Earl Rivers, c. 1440–83, also considered as purveyor of the manuscript used by Caxton for his edition; see Lotte Hellinga, *Caxton in Focus* (London: British Library, 1982), pp. 89–94; and S. Carole Weinberg, 'Caxton, Anthony Woodville, and the Prologue to the *Morte Darthur*', *SP* 102 (2005), 45–65. *Aymon* was printed at the request of 'the ryght noble and vertus erle, John Erle of Oxeforde' (Caxton, p. 83, 16–17), i.e. John de Vere, 13th Earl of Oxford. *Blanchardyn* was produced at the command of Margaret Beaufort (1443–1509); cf. Caxton, p. 57.1–5. For the view that there was pre-existing demand for his romances, see Meale, 'Romance in Late Medieval England', pp. 294–5. For a sceptical consideration of Caxton's paratexts, see N. F. Blake, 'William Caxton: The Man and His Work' (1976–77), repr. in his *William Caxton and English Literary Culture* (London: Hambledon Press, 1991), pp. 19–35, at pp. 28–33; for the opposite view, see William Matthews, 'The Besieged Printer', in *The Malory Debate: Essays on the Texts of 'Le Morte Darthur'*, ed. Bonnie Wheeler, Robert L. Kindrick and Michael N. Salda (Cambridge: D. S. Brewer, 2000), pp. 35–64.

15 It is possible that Caxton was offered the opportunity to publish some of the Middle English verse romances but declined, and that exemplars of verse romances were among the 'many dyverse paunflettis and bookys' (Caxton, p. 78. 2–3) that lay scattered in his studio; for this interpretation I follow Julia Boffey, 'From Manuscript to Print:

Edwards and Meale state, 'it seems to have been the choice of books to print which constituted his [i.e. Caxton's] most significant marketing decision'.[16] In the case of his romances, scholars have explored their origin and attached great significance to the printer's time in Burgundy. Yet there has been no comparable effort to place his publication of romances within a wider European context.[17] Table 9.2 shows that for almost all of Caxton's romances there existed a printed version either in French or in Dutch, or both. It is certainly no coincidence that so many correspondences exist between Tables 9.1 and 9.2; these correspondences show that a common European literary culture was emerging, aided by the spread of the new technology of printing. Readers and customers in different countries could find in bookstalls the same titles for sale, including romances, much like happens nowadays with international bestsellers. Caxton partook in this publishing development, first by printing romances in French and English during his time in Flanders, and later by exploiting the same genre from his Westminster premises. But it would be misleading to assign the English printer a subservient or derivative role and to regard him as a minor figure in this Europe-wide phenomenon. In fact Caxton was in the vanguard of publishing trends on the Continent, since he committed himself to printing vernacular books, as was beginning to happen independently in France, Italy and Iberia. Even more significant is that he pioneered the publication of romances, since his editions of Lefèvre's *Recueil*, both in English and in French, are the first to appear in the region encompassing France, the Low Countries and Britain.[18] Caxton's romance

Continuity and Change', in *A Companion to the Early Printed Book*, ed. Gillespie and Powell, pp. 13–26, at p. 14.

16 'The Marketing of Printed Books', p. 95.

17 Comparison with the printed production in French is partially presented in Jennifer R. Goodman, 'Caxton's Continent', in *Caxton's Trace: Studies in the History of English Printing*, ed. William Kuskin (Notre Dame, IN: University of Notre Dame Press, 2006), pp. 101–23. Useful for ascertaining the French influence in Caxton's romances is Jeanne Veyrin-Forrer, 'Caxton and France', *Journal of the Printing Historical Society* 11 (1976–77), 33–47. A European context, although without focus on the romance genre, is discussed by A. S. G. Edwards, 'Continental Influences on London Printing and Reading in the Fifteenth and Early Sixteenth Centuries', in *London and Europe in the Late Middle Ages*, ed. Julia Boffey and Pamela King (London: Westfield Publications in Medieval Studies, 1995), pp. 229–58. See also Meale, 'Romance in Late Medieval England', p. 287.

18 The first romance printed in French, other than Caxton's *Recueil*, was probably *Le livre et l'istoire de Pierre filz du conte de Provence et de la belle Maguelone* (Lyons: Guillaume Le Roy pour Barthélemy Buyer), dated to c. 1477 (GW 12703). The text was translated into English and it is not unlikely that it could have been printed here early in the sixteenth century; see Arne Zettersten, 'Pierre of Provence and the Faire Maguelonne: A Prose Romance Edited from Bodleian MS. Lat. misc. b. 17 and Bibliothèque nationale ms. fr. 1501', *ES* 46 (1965), 187–201. For bibliographical information on romances printed in French, see Richard Cooper, '"Nostre histoire renouvelée":

publication in Ghent, therefore, marks the starting point for the printing of chivalric literature, which was a genre well suited to the medium of print, as soon became apparent to other European printers, particularly in Antwerp, Geneva and Lyons.

When he transferred to England, Caxton did not interrupt this programme of romance publication, but in sacrificing the geographical centrality of Flanders and the linguistic prestige of French, his leading position was undermined. New, original texts were no longer immediately available to him, so instead of printing the *editio princeps* of a romance for the European market, Caxton found himself translating printed French romances for English customers. This new state of affairs is confirmed by his editions of *Charles*, *Paris*, *Aymon* and *Eneydos*, all of them preceded by French versions printed in Lyons.[19] Although Caxton was no longer spearheading the continental publication of romances, he still exercised independent judgement and printed romances he translated directly from French manuscripts, as in the case of *Godfrey* and *Blanchardyn*.[20] More significantly, his publication of Malory's *Morte* in 1485 anticipated the printed circulation of the long Arthurian prose romances in French. The first of these texts, *Lancelot du Lac*, did not appear in print until 1488 (GW 12621), followed by *Tristan* in 1489 (GW 12815) and *Merlin* in 1498 (GW 12668), all of which achieved remarkable

The Reception of the Romances of Chivalry in Renaissance France', in *Chivalry in the Renaissance*, ed. Sydney Anglo (Woodbridge: Boydell Press, 1990), pp. 175–238. For romances in Dutch, see Luc Debaene, *De Nederlandse volksboeken. Ontstaan en geschiedenis van de Nederlandse prozaromans gedrukt tussen 1475 en 1540* (Antwerp: De Vlijt, 1951); and Emile H. van Heurck, *Les livres populaires flamands* (Antwerp: J. E. Buschmann, 1931). I have focused on these two linguistic areas because they are the ones with which Caxton and his successors maintained direct personal and literary engagement. The earliest romance printed in German was probably *Apollonius von Tyrus* (1471; GW 2273).

19 Veyrin-Forrer, 'Caxton and France', p. 43, remarks that from 1483 Caxton became increasingly dependent on editions printed mainly in Geneva and Lyons. For *Charles* he possibly used the edition printed by Guillaume Le Roy in 1484 (BMC, XI, p. 21 n. 1 and p. 160); for *Aymon* it is likely that he used Le Roy's edition of 1480 (see H. M. Smyser, 'Charlemagne Legends', in MWME, vol. 1, p. 98); for his *Paris*, he probably used Le Roy's edition of c. 1480; see Veyrin-Forrer, 'Caxton and France', p. 44; and Hellinga, *William Caxton*, p. 74. Although the French *Éneides* was published much earlier than the English *Eneydos* was translated, it seems that Caxton used a manuscript instead of the printed edition; see Caxton, p. 78.4–6; and BMC, XI, p. 175. For the use of printed editions for Caxton's translations, see Lotte Hellinga, *Texts in Transit: Manuscript to Proof and Print in the Fifteenth Century* (Leiden: Brill, 2014), pp. 257–60.

20 For his translation of *Godfrey* Caxton used a manuscript of the French translation of William of Tyre's *Historia rerum in partibus transmarinis gestarum* close to Paris, BnF, MS fr. 68 (BMC, XI, p. 124); *Blanchardyn* is translated from a manuscript Caxton himself had previously sold to Lady Margaret Beaufort, as he states in the prologue (Caxton, p. 57.8–12), close to BnF, MS fr. 24.371; see Robert H. Wilson, 'Malory and Caxton', in MWME, vol. 3, p. 798.

commercial success.[21] The fact that Caxton's edition of *Morte* predates the transmission of the French Arthurian romances in print is further indication that the English printer had contrived to interpret the literary preferences of the European reading classes. Caxton, thus, seems to have favoured romance texts that could be perceived and presented as modern and refined, while he neglected the traditional English romances because they were old-fashioned, popular and trite. If Caxton's general publication policy is considered to be conservative, as Edwards and Meale argue,[22] he seemingly made an exception with romances and chose to revivify the genre rather than simply reproducing the existing, outdated models.

The corpus of romances published by Caxton in England, however, failed to attain a degree of success comparable to the French and Dutch editions of the same texts (see Table 9.2), let alone the printed French Arthurian romances. Taking into consideration that Caxton did not reprint any of his romances for the English market, and the printers of the following generation showed limited interest in these same works (see Table 9.3), it seems safe to argue that the demand for this type of text in England was limited. Edwards contends 'that Caxton failed to gauge the market for that interest [i.e. in French prose romances] accurately', while Felicity Riddy considers Caxton's publication of romances an ineffectual and misguided experiment in cultural transplantation of a foreign literary mode into England.[23] In spite of the interest this literary corpus did excite among certain readers and its potential relevance to contemporary historical events in England,[24] Caxton was unable to stimulate a strong demand.

[21] Cf. Goodman, 'Caxton's Continent', pp. 110–11; see Jane H. M. Taylor, *Rewriting Arthurian Romance in Renaissance France: From Manuscript to Printed Book* (Cambridge: D. S. Brewer, 2014). In the prologue to *Morte*, Caxton reveals he had read these texts, obviously in manuscript form: 'I have seen and redde [them] beyonde the see' (Caxton, p. 108.88–9). Significantly and similar to Caxton's *Morte*, the 1488 *Lancelot du Lac* is also organised in sections and chapters, with rubrics and a table of contents, and contains a prologue with some verbal resemblance to Caxton's; see Matthews, 'Besieged Printer', pp. 48–9.

[22] 'The Marketing of Printed Books', p. 95.

[23] See Edwards, 'Continental Influences', p. 244 n. 43; and Felicity Riddy, *Sir Thomas Malory* (Leiden: Brill, 1987), pp. 11–12. For a more favourable opinion, Arundell Esdaile, *A List of English Tales and Prose Romances Printed before 1740* (London: Bibliographical Society, 1912), considers that in his choice of romances Caxton 'showed good judgment of the public favour' (p. xiv). For a complete list of Caxton's publications with indication of reprint editions, see Duff, pp. 205–7. Note that the Dutch printers Bellaert and Leeu both printed multiple editions of romance texts using respectively French and Dutch.

[24] See Leitch, *Romancing Treason*.

Title	Lang.	Year	City	Publisher	Format	BMC	ILC	GW
Fierabras (Charles the Great)	Fr.	1478	Geneva	A. Steinschaber	Fol.		—	12542
	Fr.	c. 1480	Geneva	S. du Jardin	Fol.	VIII: 368	—	12543
	Fr.	1483	Geneva	L. Cruse	Fol.	VIII: 365	—	12544
	Fr.	1484?	Lyons	G. Le Roy	Fol.		—	12545
	Fr.	1485?	Lyons	G. Le Roy	Fol.	VIII: 237	—	12546
	Fr.	1486/7	Lyons	G. Le Roy	Fol.			12547
	Fr.	1489	Lyons	J. Maillet	Fol.		—	12548
Enéides	Fr.	1483	Lyons	G. Le Roy	Fol.	VIII: 236	—	M50125
Historie Hertoge Godevaerts van Boloen	Dutch	c. 1488	Gouda	n.p.	Fol.	IX: 38	1110	12573
Histoire de Jason / Historie van den vromen ridder Jason	Fr.	1478–80	Lyons	N. Philippi, M. Reinhard	Fol.	VIII: 244	—	M17460
	Dutch	1484–85	Haarlem	J. Bellaert	Fol.	—	1417	M17467
	Fr.	1485–86	Haarlem	J. Bellaert	Fol.	—	1416	M17455
	Fr.	1487?	Lyons	G. Le Roy	Fol.	VIII: 240	—	M17458

Paris et Vienne / Parijs ende Vienna	Fr.	c. 1480	Lyons	G. Le Roy	Fol.		—	12684
	Fr.	1485–87	Lyons	M. Huss	4°		—	12685
	Fr.	1487	Antwerp	G. Leeu	Fol.	—	1691	12686
	Dutch	1487	Antwerp	G. Leeu	Fol.	—	1692	12700
	Fr.	c. 1491	Paris	D. Meslier	4°	—	—	12687
	Fr.	c. 1491	Paris	D. Meslier	4°	—	—	12688
	Dutch	1491–92	Antwerp	G. Leeu	Fol.	—	1693	12701
Quatre fils Aymon / Historie van de vier Heemskinderen	Fr.	1482–85	Lyons	G. Le Roy	Fol.	VIII: liii	—	3133
	Fr.	c. 1485	Lyons	n.p.	Fol.	VIII: 274	—	3134
	Dutch	c. 1489	Gouda	n.p.	4°	—	319	12486
Recueil des histoires de Troie / Vergaderinge der historien van Troyen	Fr.	1485–86	Haarlem	J. Bellaert	Fol.	—	1420	M17434
	Dutch	1485	Haarlem	J. Bellaert	Fol.	—	1421	M17453
	Fr.	1490	Lyons	M. Topié, J. Heremberck	Fol.		—	M17441

Table 9.2 Caxton romances printed in Dutch and French, 1478–92[25]

25 This table contains only editions printed contemporaneously with Caxton's career. The information is limited to editions printed in Dutch and French, since these are two literary cultures Caxton seems to have been more in contact with. In establishing the publication date, the order of priority has been BMC, ILC and GW.

It is also probable that he was unconcerned about expanding his client base, but was primarily focused on serving the reading needs of 'noble prynces, lordes and ladyes, gentylmen or gentylwymmen' (Caxton, pp. 109.125–6; 3.12–13), the exclusive and socially-cohesive clientele to whom he targeted his edition of Malory's *Morte*. This possibility is actually reinforced by all the extant ownership evidence, which suggests that Caxton's chivalric narratives found a new home among customers that could roughly be described as belonging to the gentry.[26] It is significant, however, that most owners of manuscript books containing romance texts belonged to this same social class,[27] thus indicating that Caxton failed to capitalise both on the multiplying effect of the technology of print and on his own modernisation of the genre in order to diversify the social profile of the consumers of chivalric romances in England. Instead, Caxton ensured the continuity of the socio-literary dynamic he inherited from manuscript culture by catering to a reading public belonging to the same social segment and with similar literary aspirations.

Caxton's death in the early months of 1492 left England bereft of the country's only purveyor of literary texts in English.[28] Since he had such a dominant position in the book market, his demise opened up unique business opportunities. By an Act of 1484 it was decreed that there should be no 'impediment to any Artificer or merchaunt straungier of what Nacion or Contrey he be or shalbe of, for bryngyng into this Realme, or sellyng by retaill or otherwise, of any maner bokes wrytten or imprynted'.[29] It is therefore not surprising that the Antwerp-based, Dutch printer Gheraert Leeu (fl. 1477–92) grasped this opportunity for penetrating the English book trade and competing for Caxton's market share. Leeu, who had previously expanded his market operations beyond the Dutch-language area,[30] wasted no time in trying to fill the gap left by Caxton, and in June 1492 he published two books for the English market, significantly two romances, namely *Jason* and *Paris* (see Table 9.3). He moved fast: an indication that Leeu prepared his edition of *Jason* in haste is that it reproduces unrevised Caxton's original prologue mentioning the Prince of Wales, the future Edward V, who had died in 1483. Although he was merely

26 See Yu-Chiao Wang, 'Caxton's Romances and Their Early Tudor Readers', *HLQ* 67 (2004), 173–88.

27 See Michael Johnston, *Romance and the Gentry in Late Medieval England* (Oxford: OUP, 2014).

28 For tentatively dating Caxton's death sometime in February or March, 1492, see Howard M. Nixon, 'Caxton, His Contemporaries and Successors in the Book Trade from Westminster Documents', *The Library*, 5th ser., 31 (1976), 305–26, at pp. 312–14.

29 A facsimile of the Act is included in Peter W. M. Blayney, *The Stationers' Company and the Printers of London, 1501–1557* (Cambridge: CUP, 2013), vol. 1, fig. 4, p. 42, whose interpretation (pp. 38–45) I follow. The Act is edited in *CHBB III*, p. 608, with spelling mistakes corrected by Blayney, p. 41, n. A.

30 See Hellinga, *Texts in Transit*, pp. 333–4.

reprinting some of Caxton's books, Leeu developed an effective commercial strategy designed to enhance the saleability of his wares by experimenting with the marketing possibilities of textual presentation. Leeu's *Jason*, printed in two columns with illustrations, opens with a title page combining the use of an inviting xylographic title in display gothic letters and a woodcut illustration (see Fig. 9.1), thus making his edition much more attractive than Caxton's and visually superior to the productions of other contemporary English printers.[31] Leeu's plans for commercial expansion into England, however, came to an abrupt halt in December 1492, when he was killed by the type-cutter Henric van Symmen.[32]

31 The illustrations used by Leeu for his *Jason* are all derived from the series prepared by the so-called Bellaert Master for Jacob Bellaert's edition of his Dutch *Jason* (ILC 1417) and ultimately inspired by the drawings produced by the Jason Master for the manuscript copy of *L'Histoire de Jason* in BL Additional MS 10290. For the correspondence between the drawings made by the Jason Master and the woodcuts in Leeu's *Jason* of 1492, see Hellinga, *Texts in Transit*, pp. 362–3, and see p. 316 (fig. 12.2A) for the original drawing on which the woodcut in Fig. 9.1 in this chapter is based; for a description of this series of woodcuts, see Kok, vol. 1, pp. 369–73, with facsimiles reproduced in vol. 4, nos. 160.1–21; for the illustration of his *Paris and Vienne*, see Kok, vol. 1: pp. 230–5 and facsimiles nos. 168.1–11, 168.13–25. For the evolution of the title page in early printed books, see Margaret M. Smith, *The Title-page: Its Early Development, 1460–1510* (London: British Library, 2000), esp. pp. 79–80 for Leeu's important role in developing the format of the kind of title page we see in *Jason*.

32 For a brief biography of Leeu, see Anne Rouzet, *Dictionnaire des imprimeurs, libraires et éditeurs des XVe et XVIe siècles dans les limites géographiques de la Belgique actuelle* (Nieuwkoop: De Graaf, 1975), pp. 121–3. Further indication that Leeu was seriously considering expanding into the English market is that he had a special fount made imitating English types that he used for his English books; see E. Gordon Duff, *The Printers, Stationers and Bookbinders of Westminster and London from 1476 to 1535* (Cambridge: CUP, 1906), p. 91. For Leeu's *Jason*, see Duff, 246, ILC 1418 and BMC, IX, p. 214; for his *Paris*, see ILC 1695. Note that Leeu also prepared an edition of the *Chronicles of England* (Duff, 100; ILC 559; BMC, IX, p. 197; STC 9994), published posthumously before 21 July 1493, based on the first edition printed by Caxton in 1480 (see BMC, XI, p. 117), and sometime between 1489 and 1492 published *The Dialogue of Solomon and Marcolphus* (Duff, 115; ILC 1926; STC 22905; IPMEP 796), probably a translation of the version in Dutch he had published after 14 May 1488 (ILC 1920). For Leeu's English printing of 1492, see Lotte Hellinga, 'The Bookshop of the World: Books and Their Makers as Agents of Cultural Exchange', in *The Bookshop of the World: The Role of the Low Countries in the Book-Trade, 1473–1941*, ed. Lotte Hellinga et al. ('t Goy-Houten: Hes & De Graaf, 2001), pp. 11–29, esp. pp. 20–2; see also BMC, IX, p. xlii n. 2; and Painter, *William Caxton*, pp. 150, 189–90. N. F. Blake, 'Wynkyn de Worde: The Early Years', *GJ* (1971), 62–9, has argued that Leeu's reprint of Caxton's romances is an indication that 'clearly there was still a market for chivalric books' (p. 64): since Leeu's was the last edition of *Jason* to be published within the chronological scope of this essay, it is likely that he chose these texts not to satisfy an existing customer demand, but to position himself rapidly into the English market.

The veray trew
history of the val
iãut knight Jasõ

How he conquerydy or wan the golden fles. by the Counsel of Medea. and
of many othre victoryouse and wondrefull actis and dedys that he dyde by
his prowesse and chevalrye in his tyme . : .

Fig. 9.1 © The British Library Board, London, British Library, IB. 49847, title page, *History of Jason* (Antwerp: G. Leeu, 1492).

Before the end of 1492 Wynkyn de Worde (d. 1534/5) managed to put Caxton's printing house back in operation, despite the legal disputes over settling Caxton's estate. Of Dutch origin, De Worde had joined Caxton before 1479 and worked for him until his master's death.[33] Therefore, he was perfectly placed to look after his late master's business interests. Initially De Worde sought to be perceived as giving continuity to his predecessor's firm by referring in his imprint to Caxton's house, using Caxton's devices and reprinting Caxton's editions, which made up a significant amount of his output until 1496. De Worde was indeed the natural heir to Caxton's business, but inherited neither his strengths nor his privileged position. His greatest strength was the experience gained while working alongside Caxton for well over a decade, although De Worde was no longer in a position to have a virtual monopoly on printing, as Caxton enjoyed in 1476. In addition, he lacked his master's familiarity with fashionable literature and his linguistic competence to make his own translations. As a foreign speaker of English whose command of French may have been limited, De Worde decided to hire the services of translators, such as Robert Copland (d. 1547) and Henry Watson (fl. 1500–18), and to pay more attention to literary texts in English. In sum, whereas Caxton developed a business plan centred on his own personal capabilities, De Worde had to engage the collaboration of other agents to compensate for his own personal shortcomings.[34]

Under the print house's new ownership, Caxton's publishing policy was critically reassessed to adapt it to changes in the market conditions. This policy revision directly affected romances. Better acquainted with the book trade in England than his fellow countryman Leeu, De Worde significantly chose not to print any romance during the initial years at the head of the print house. Hellinga has argued that De Worde 'did not share Caxton's love of prose romances, for not one of his [i.e. Caxton's] translations of such texts was reprinted by him [i.e. De Worde] until the early years of the sixteenth century'.[35] But this statement needs some clarification, since all the evidence suggests that De Worde was just as enthusiastic about prose romances as Caxton, if not more (see Table 9.3). What Hellinga seems to imply is that De Worde had misgivings about publishing *Caxton*'s romances, since until 1502

33 See Blayney, *The Stationers' Company and the Printers of London*, vol. 1, pp. 60–3. It seems likely that he was originally from Woerden in Holland; see Lotte Hellinga, 'Wynkyn de Worde's Native Land', in *New Science out of Old Books: Studies in Manuscripts and Early Printed Books in Honour of A. I. Doyle*, ed. Richard Beadle and A. J. Piper (Aldershot: Scolar Press, 1995), pp. 342–59.

34 See Edwards and Meale, 'The Marketing of Printed Books', pp. 120–2. For a brief overview of the evolution of the book trade in England from 1476 to 1534, see Tamara Atkin and A. S. G. Edwards, 'Printers, Publishers and Promoters to 1558', in *A Companion to the Early Printed Book*, ed. Gillespie and Powell, pp. 27–44, at pp. 27–36.

35 *William Caxton*, p. 140.

he did not reprint any of those his master translated and he abandoned this line of work in 1505 after having reprinted only three such romances.[36] The first edition of a romance printed by De Worde was a reprint of Caxton's *Morte* published in 1498 in which an evolution in textual presentation becomes visible.[37] Unlike Caxton's edition of 1485, De Worde's adds book titles for the first ten books, headings at the beginning of each chapter and running page headers, and imposes an illustrations programme consisting of twenty-one woodcuts tailor-made for this edition.[38] This enhanced visual presentation not only made the book more attractive but also more accessible and, ultimately, more desirable to more socially diverse potential customers.

In fact, one of De Worde's primary concerns was to attract a broader clientele than Caxton. To do so he changed his target market from the upper classes to a more socially diverse one, a strategic change that gets verbalised in the preface to his 1498 edition of *Morte*. While this edition reproduces Caxton's prologue, De Worde introduces a textual variant in order to appeal not just to the nobility, as his predecessor did (see above), but also to a more popular social group he describes as 'comynaltee'.[39] To engage the interest of the *comynaltee*, De Worde adjusted his publishing policy as to the form and nature of the printed romances. Apart from the use of woodcuts and other techniques of textual presentation applied to his *Morte*, De Worde favoured the adoption of the quarto format, especially after 1505, thus bringing down the price of his romances. In fairness, however, we should say that De Worde was probably just imitating the Parisian printers, who preferred to print the romances in

[36] In view of the amount of religious texts De Worde printed, Blake, 'De Worde: The Early Years', p. 69, argued that 'the most probable explanation [for the change in his publishing policy] is that Wynkyn was a man of religious convictions who preferred to print books for a religious clientele'. This explanation might be acceptable had De Worde abandoned the publication of courtly and chivalric texts, but that is not the case.

[37] Note that De Worde's is not actually an exact reprint; see Tsuyoshi Mukai, 'De Worde's 1498 *Morte Darthur* and Caxton's Copy-Text', *RES*, n.s., 51 (2000), 24–40. It seems that De Worde had access to the copy-text used by Caxton and used it to make textual emendations. See also P. J. C. Field, 'De Worde and Malory', in *The Medieval Book and a Modern Collector: Essays in Honour of Toshiyuki Takamiya*, ed. T. Matsuda, R. A. Linenthal and J. Scahill (Cambridge: D. S. Brewer and Yushodo Press, 2004), pp. 285–94.

[38] See Kevin T. Grimm, 'Wynkyn de Worde and the Creation of Malory's *Morte Darthur*', in *The Social and Literary Contexts of Malory's 'Morte Darthur'*, ed. D. Thomas Hanks, Jr (Cambridge: D. S. Brewer, 2000), pp. 134–53.

[39] I.e. 'the common people as distinguished … from those of rank and title', *OED*, s.v. *commonalty*, n. 3. See *Caxton's Malory: A New Edition of Sir Thomas Malory's 'Le Morte Darthur'*, ed. James W. Spisak (Berkeley: University of California Press, 1983), p. 632 n. to p. 2 line 40. This kind of editorial intervention is attributable to De Worde himself; see Field, 'De Worde and Malory', p. 291.

quarto.[40] With regard to the nature of the romances he printed, De Worde challenged Caxton's prejudice against the English metrical romances and exploited their commercial potential, printing at least twelve separate verse romances after 1497–98.[41] He took the same approach with the prose romances and selected texts that had already circulated in England and could be expected to be familiar to his customers. Although *Robert the Devil* was translated from French, its plot parallels that of the Middle English *Sir Gowther*, extant in two fifteenth-century manuscripts. What is more, it seems that 'the translator may ... have seen a copy of *Sir Gowther*'.[42] *King Ponthus* revives and adapts the story of *Horn et Rimenild*, first composed in Anglo-Norman in the twelfth century and with various Middle English versions, most notably *King Horn*. The French *Ponthus* was composed c. 1390 and translated into English prose in the first half of the fifteenth century. De Worde's translator, possibly Henry Watson, may have consulted 'the earlier English version ... keeping it open before him as he translated from the French'.[43] It is likely that *Mélusine* circulated in England in French, and a translation independent from the printed edition was made c. 1500.[44] The plot of *Helyas* was in part familiar to English readers because of its similarity to the alliterative romance *Cheuelere Assigne*, preserved in a fifteenth-century manuscript.

40 The following Paris editions were printed in quarto: *Destruction de Jerusalem* (1491; GW 12499–500), Pierre Desrey's *Godeffroy de Bouillon*, of which *Helyas* is a free translation (1504; FB 15930), *Melusine* (1517; FB 30843), *Olivier de Castille* (1505; FB 39810), *Ponthus et la Belle Sidoine* (1520; FB 44513), *Valentin et Orson* (1515; FB 50250); *Appollin roy de Thir* was printed in octavo (1530; FB 1492). Joseph A. Dane and Alexandra Gillespie, 'The Myth of the Cheap Quarto', in *Tudor Books and Readers: Materiality and the Construction of Meaning*, ed. John N. King (Cambridge: CUP, 2010), pp. 25–45, have warned against assuming that quarto books were necessarily cheaper, although the evidence they provide tends to suggest they were generally cheaper to produce.

41 See Jordi Sánchez-Martí, 'The Printed History of the Middle English Verse Romances', *MP* 107 (2009), 1–31, at pp. 8–12.

42 Kari Sajavaara, 'The Sixteenth-Century Versions of *Robert the Devil*', *NM* 80 (1979) 335–47, at p. 338.

43 F. J. Mather, Jr, '*King Ponthus and the Fair Sidone*', *PMLA* 12 (1897), xxxix. For the manuscripts of the English *Ponthus*, see n. 9 above. For the manuscript circulation of the French *Ponthus* in England, see Meale, 'Romance in Late Medieval England', pp. 296–7. Brenda M. Hosington, 'Henry Watson, "Apprentyse of London" and "Translatoure" of Romance and Satire', in *The Medieval Translator: Traduire au Moyen Âge*, ed. Jacqueline Jenkins and Olivier Bertrand, The Medieval Translator, 10 (Turnhout: Brepols, 2007), pp. 1–25, explores the possibility that it was Watson who translated *Ponthus* for De Worde.

44 This translation is preserved in BL, MS Royal 18.b.II. For an analysis of the printed edition and its relation to the manuscript version, see Tania M. Colwell, 'The Middle English *Melusine*: Evidence for an Early Edition of the Prose Romance in the Bodleian Library', *JEBS* 17 (2014), 254–82.

Year	Title	Printer	Format	Duff	STC	IPMEP
1492	*The history of Jason*	G. Leeu	Fol.	246	15384	226
1492	*Paris and Vienne*	G. Leeu	Fol.	338	19207	377
1498	Malory, *Morte Darthur*	W. de Worde	Fol.	284	802	394
1501–04?	*Paris and Vienne*	W. de Worde	4°	–	19207a–8	377
c. 1502	*Robert the Devil*	W. de Worde	4°	Suppl. 36	21070	396
1503	*Recuyell of the histories of Troy*	W. de Worde	Fol.	–	15376–7	825
c. 1505	*Four sons of Aymon*	W. de Worde	Fol.	–	1008	80
1506?	*King Ponthus*	W. de Worde	4°	–	20107	609
1509?	*Valentyne and Orson*	W. de Worde	4°	–	24571.3	52
1510	*Kynge Appolyn of Thyre*	W. de Worde	4°	–	708.5	361
c. 1510	*King Ponthus*	R. Pynson?	4°	–	20107.5	609
c. 1510	*Four sons of Aymon*	J. Notary	Fol.	–	1009.5	–
1510?	*Dystruccyon of Jherusalem*	W. de Worde	4°	–	14518	241
1510	*Melusine*	W. de Worde	Fol.	–	14648	–
1511	*King Ponthus*	W. de Worde	4°	–	20108	609
1512	*Helyas Knyght of the Swan*	W. de Worde	4°	–	7571	809
1513?	*Dystruccyon of Jherusalem*	R. Pynson	4°	–	14517	241
c. 1515	*William of Palermo*	W. de Worde	4°	–	25707.5	534
c. 1515	*Huon of Burdeux*	J. Notary	Fol.	–	13998.5	–

Year	Title	Printer	Format	Duff	STC	IPMEP
1517?	*Robert the Devil*	W. de Worde	4°	–	21071	396
1518	*Olyver of Castylle*	W. de Worde	4°	–	18808	107
1518?	*Lyfe of Virgilius*	J. Doesborch	4°	–	24828	739
c. 1522	*Helyas Knyght of the Swan*	W. de Worde	4°	–	7571.5	–
c. 1525	*Faits merveilleux de Virgile*	W. de Worde	8°	–	24827.5	–
1528	*Dystruccyon of Jherusalem*	W. de Worde	4°	–	14519	241
1529	Malory, *Morte Darthur*	W. de Worde	Fol.	–	803	394
1532–34	*Kynge Appolyn of Thyre*	W. de Worde	4°	–	708.5	361

Table 9.3 English prose romances printed 1492–1535[45]

45 This list is based on Newstead's (see n. 8), excluding accounts of the life of *Joseph of Arimathia* owing to their hagiographic nature (cf. Meale, 'Romance in Late Medieval England', p. 285 n. 8) and adding the *Life of Virgilius* following George R. Keiser, 'The Romances', in *Middle English Prose: A Critical Guide to Major Authors and Genres*, ed. A. S. G. Edwards (New Brunswick, NJ: Rutgers University Press, 1984), pp. 271–89, at pp. 285–6; note that 'Virgyls lyfe' is listed among the romance titles contained in the library of Captain Cox, for which see Robert Langham, *A Letter*, ed. R. J. P. Kuin (Leiden: Brill, 1983), p. 53. The dates in Table 9.3 follow STC with some exceptions. For *Paris and Vienne* (STC 19207a and 19208) I follow Joseph J. Gwara, 'Dating Wynkyn de Worde's Devotional, Homiletic, and Other Texts, 1501–11', in *Preaching the Word in Manuscript and Print in Late Medieval England: Essays in Honour of Susan Powell*, ed. Martha W. Driver and Veronica O'Mara (Turnhout: Brepols, 2013), pp. 193–234, at p. 203. For *Robert the Devil* (STC 21070) I take Hellinga's view that it should be dated 'not before 1502' (Duff, p. 141); see also Sajavaara, 'The Sixteenth-Century *Robert the Devil*', pp. 339–40. For *Recuyell* (STC 15376), I follow Blayney, *The Stationers' Company and the Printers of London*, vol. 2, p. 1048. For *Valentyne and Orson* (STC 24571.3) I follow Gwara, 'Dating De Worde's Texts', pp. 212, 232. For *King Ponthus* (STC 20107) I follow Gwara, 'Dating De Worde's Texts', p. 204. In the case of De Worde's *Paris and Vienne* I follow STC in considering that, 'from similarity of type and makeup, this [i.e. 19207a] and the following [i.e. 19208] may be the same edition'. For De Worde's edition of *Recuyell*, I give the two entries in STC as one edition, since STC 15377 is a variant of 15376. Furthermore, there is evidence indicating that the unique copy of *Kynge Appolyn of Thyre*

This circumstance probably explains why the English translator, Robert Copland, mentions in his prologue that the purpose of his translation was 'to haue ye sayde history *more amply* and vniuersally knowen' in England (my emphasis),[46] perhaps implying that the story was already known but not in its entirety. *King Appolyn*, also translated by Copland, had a centuries-old tradition in England.[47] *William of Palermo* is a prose adaptation of the alliterative *William of Palerne*, composed in the mid-fourteenth century.[48] The *Dystruccyon of Jherusalem*, though translated from a French prose version, was familiar to English audiences from multiple versions, including the couplet *Titus and Vespasian*. The only prose romances newly printed by De Worde without known previous English circulation are *Oliver of Castille* and *Valentine and Orson*, both translated by Watson. In sum, whereas Caxton preferred to print romances with a continental appeal, De Worde prioritised mainly texts with English antecedents. Yet he adhered to his master's policy and published romances that were fashionable on the Continent, since all De Worde's English prose romances, except *William of Palermo*, had already been published in French and most of them also attained printed distribution in Dutch.[49]

(STC 708.5) was printed in 1532–34 and contains gatherings from an earlier edition printed in 1510; see Joseph J. Gwara, 'Robert Copland and *The Judgement of Love*', *SB* 59 (2015), 85–113, at p. 101 n. 40; and Gwara, 'Dating De Worde's Texts', pp. 214–15 n. 24. One could add a further title to this list, namely Lord Berners's *Arthur of Lytell Brytayne*, a translation of the French *Artus de Bretagne* (1493; GW 2676), since a reference in the prologue to his translation has led scholars to surmise that a now missing edition would have been printed during Berners's lifetime (d. 1533); see Joyce Boro, 'Lord Berners and His Books: A New Survey', *HLQ* 67 (2004), 236–49, at pp. 238–9. For a brief literary commentary on some of the romances newly printed by De Worde and those translated by Lord Berners, see Gray, *Later Medieval Literature*, pp. 209–15.

46 The quotation is taken from the 'Prologue of the Translatour' of William Copland's edition of 1560 (STC 7572), sig. A2r.

47 For Copland, see *Robert Copland: Poems*, ed. Mary C. Erler (Toronto: University of Toronto Press, 1993). For the tradition of *Apollonius* in England, see Elizabeth Archibald, *Apollonius of Tyre: Medieval and Renaissance Themes and Variations* (Cambridge: D. S. Brewer, 1991).

48 See *William of Palerne: An Alliterative Romance*, ed. G. H. V. Bunt (Groningen: Bouma's Boekhuis, 1985), pp. 23–6.

49 Here I list the first French edition of De Worde's prose romances: *Robert le diable* (1496; GW 12736), *Ponthus et Sidoine* (c. 1480; GW 12716), *Appollin roy de Thir* (c. 1482; GW 2279), *Valentin et Orson* (1489; GW 12840), *Destruction de Jerusalem* (c. 1479; GW 12493), *Melusine* (1478; GW 12649), Pierre Desrey's *Godefroy de Bouillon* (1500; GW 12570), *Olivier de Castille* (1482; GW 2770); cf. Meale, 'Romance in Late Medieval England', pp. 295, 298. Here follow the editions in Dutch of De Worde's romances: *Robrecht de Duyvel* (1516; not in NK), *Apollonius van Thyro* (1493; ILC 263), *Meluzine* (1491; ILC 1322), *Helias* (c. 1515–20?; NK 3172), *Olyvier van Castillen* (c. 1510; NK 3170), *Destructie van Jherusalem* (c. 1505; NK 4430). I retain reference to Dutch editions, first, because Hellinga, in 'De Worde's Native Land', has shown that De Worde maintained professional contact with his homeland, probably

From c. 1498 until 1535 De Worde printed at least eighteen editions of verse romances and twenty of prose ones, a not inconsiderable amount, particularly when compared to the eleven editions of romances Caxton was involved with between 1473 and 1490. This intensification in the publication of medieval romances suggests that De Worde was intent on obtaining a stranglehold on the genre, a goal he certainly achieved in the case of the prose romances with twenty of the twenty-four editions published between 1498 and 1535, and only one title not issued from his press, namely *Huon*.[50] With the metrical romances, however, he faced fiercer competition and managed to produce just half of the thirty-six editions published before his death. These figures indicate that the market in verse romances was more dynamic and attractive to readers, and also less risky for printers, whereas that in prose romances was rather sluggish. Of the nine prose romances newly issued by De Worde, five were reprinted, namely *Robert the Devil, King Ponthus, Helyas, Dystruccyon of Jherusalem* and *Kynge Appolyn of Thyre*. It seems that the prose romances were less lucrative and eventually De Worde chose to stop printing this literary corpus. No new prose romance was printed after the publication of *Olyver of Castylle* in 1518, with the exception of the anomalous *Virgilius*. Conversely, new verse romances continued appearing in the following years, a clear indication that they were more profitable. The new titles of verse romances published after 1518 include *Squyr of Low Degre* (1520?), *Ipomydon* (c. 1523–24),[51] *Kyng Alisaunder* (1525?), *Jeste of Sir Gawaine* (1528?), *Sir Isumbras* (c. 1530) and *Sir Lamwell* (c. 1530–32?).

---

with Gouda and Leiden, not too far from Woerden; secondly, because Dutch printers remained relevant for the English book trade during the early sixteenth century; see M. E. Kronenberg, 'Notes on English Printing in the Low Countries (Early Sixteenth Century)', *The Library*, 4th ser., 9 (1928), 139–63.

[50] For Notary's *Huon*, see Joyce Boro, 'The Textual History of *Huon of Burdeux*: A Reassessment of the Facts', *N&Q*, n.s., 48 (2001), 233–7. Note that *Huon* also enjoyed printed circulation in both French and Dutch: *Huon de Bordeaux* (FB 30228–9; Paris, 1513) and *Hughe van Bourdeus* (NK 3163; Antwerp, c. 1540). In the case of *Virgilius*, De Worde published a French version of the romance since Doesborch had previously printed the English *Lyfe of Virgilius* (NK 4052). See further in Robert Proctor, *Jan van Doesborgh, Printer at Antwerp: An Essay in Bibliography* (London: Bibliographical Society, 1894), with a description of his edition of *Virgilius* on pp. 27–9; Debaene, *De Nederlandse volksboeken*, pp. 191–7; and P. J. A. Franssen, 'Jan van Doesborch (?–1536), Printer of English Texts', *Quarendo* 16 (1986), 259–80. Boffey argues that De Worde's *Virgille* is 'an interesting scrap of evidence that he expected English book-buyers to read in French as well as in English', in 'Banking on Translation', p. 322; the Dutch *Virgilius* (NK 2145) was printed in Antwerp c. 1525(?), although an earlier edition seems not unlikely; cf. Franssen, 'Doesborch', pp. 269–70.

[51] For this date I follow Joseph J. Gwara, 'Three Forms of w and Four English Printers: Robert Copland, Henry Pepwell, Henry Watson, and Wynkyn de Worde', *PBSA* 106 (2012), 141–230, at p. 185 n. 35.

Despite having pioneered the publication of chivalric romances and despite having persevered with this choice of genre throughout his printing career, Caxton seems to have failed to elicit the public response he would have hoped to. Acquainted with this lukewarm reception given to the printed romances, De Worde revised some of the publishing decisions of his predecessor, hoping to enhance the genre's market penetration. In order to appeal to a larger clientele De Worde resolved to choose texts that could be appealing to more kinds of readers, including the *comynaltee*, to present them in a more attractive way and to offer them at affordable prices. As a result he adopted the cheaper quarto format for his romances and illustrated them with woodcuts. Like Caxton, De Worde printed prose romances that were fashionable on the Continent, but unlike Caxton, he also focused on romances that had previous dissemination in England, in particular the popular metrical romances. The commercial success he achieved with the latter contrasts with the limited demand for the prose romances, to the extent that after 1518 the printing of new prose romances was discontinued in England. Considering that the list of prose romances printed in English between 1473 and 1518 is made up primarily of continental bestsellers, it seems reasonable to surmise that both Caxton and De Worde were ahead of their time in trying to sell these texts to English readers, whose taste remained mostly anchored in insular traditions and removed from mainstream continental literary culture.[52]

[52] Research for this chapter was funded in part by the Spanish Ministry of Science and Innovation (ref. FFI2011–22811), whose support is herewith gratefully acknowledged. I would also like to thank Bart Besamusca, Elisabeth de Bruijn, Rita Schlusemann and Frank Willaert for introducing me to the printing of romances in the Low Countries.

10

Compiling Sacred and Secular: *Sir Orfeo* and the Otherworlds of Medieval Miscellanies

Michelle De Groot

Miscellany and its discontents

In the three manuscripts in which it survives, *Sir Orfeo* sits in company not only with other romances but also with religious verse. In the Auchinleck manuscript (NLS Advocates' MS 19.2.1, c. 1330–40), *Sir Tristrem*, *Sir Orfeo*, and the 'The Four Foes of Mankind' compose the entirety of Auchinleck's ninth booklet, that final religious lyric stressing precisely the truth that one nobleman tells Orfeo's steward: 'It nis no bot of ma*n*nes deþ' (Auchinleck l. 552).[1] In Bodl. MS Ashmole 61 (c. 1490–1500), our hero enters the compilation near its end, after a lyric dedicated to the Five Wounds of Christ and before a poem called 'Vanity', which is filled with a world-weary detachment similar to the 'Four Foes', this time drawn from the Book of Ecclesiastes. In its least assuming incarnation, BL MS Harley 3810 (c. 1400–50), *Sir Orfeo* appears as the first entry in what has been theorized as an abortive compilation, thirty-four early fifteenth-century folios of a similar blend to Ashmole 61, to which were later added medical and scientific texts in a less systematic way.[2] There, *Orfeo* is followed by the exemplum of a woman who sacrilegiously buries a consecrated host, only to find a pear-tree with a bleeding child sprouting from the plot. With the exception of one love letter, the rest of the initial

1 *Sir Orfeo*, ed. A. J. Bliss (Oxford: OUP, 1966), p. 46. Future citations appearing parenthetically refer to this edition, which usefully provides parallel texts of each manuscript. For practical purposes, I will follow Bliss's lead in favouring Auchinleck's text over Ashmole's and Harley's, since she regards the latter as descended either from Auchinleck or from a parallel but 'inferior' ancestor (pp. xiii–xv), but I will of course note when textual divergences are significant enough to affect interpretation of *Sir Orfeo*'s place within its respective manuscripts.

2 Julia Boffey, *The Manuscripts of English Courtly Love Lyrics in the Later Middle Ages* (Cambridge: D. S. Brewer, 1985), p. 20.

entries are devoted to explicitly religious material, enjoining devotional observances on Fridays and penitential reading of Maidstone's translated Psalms.[3]

These manuscripts were produced across nearly two centuries and represent a range of financial backing, from the extravagance of Auchinleck to the cramped modesty of Harley. They nevertheless share the material form and, in consequence, aesthetic impact of the 'compilation' or 'miscellany'. Derek Pearsall and I. C. Cunningham have described Auchinleck as

> the first, and much the earliest, of those libraries of miscellaneous reading matter, indiscriminately religious and secular, but dominated by the metrical romances which bulk large in the popular book production of the late Middle Ages in England [...] The exceptional nature and significance of the Auchinleck, for its period, whether it is exceptional in fact or only in the accident of its survival, is demonstrated [in part] by comparison with earlier and contemporary manuscript miscellanies [...] which are dominated by clerkly and educated interests, both religious and secular, and which accommodate Latin and Anglo-Norman texts equally with English. Auchinleck contains English alone, apart from the Anglo-Norman macaronics of item 20 and the Latin insertions of items 8, 10, and 36, and this, together with the dominantly secular provenance and unsophisticated tone of the contents, already marks the first significant emergence of a new class of readers.

They go on to theorize Auchinleck's patron as an 'aspirant middle-class citizen, perhaps a wealthy merchant'.[4] Assuming this theory is right,[5] the miscellaneous Auchinleck catered to the growing urban middle class, setting the precedent for later volumes like Bodl. Ashmole 61 and BL Harley 3810.[6] These families and households desired books of mixed materials as entire libraries, 'contain[ing] many books between two covers [...] compilations for the whole family'.[7]

Such manuscripts are assigned a shifting set of classifications: anthology; compilation; assemblage; miscellany. Despite the fact that these words are far from synonyms, they are frequently used interchangeably to describe books of eclectic genres, forms, and themes. This shifting lexicon also brings other

3 Transcription of the four less-known texts from the initial 'core' of Harley 3810 can be found in Richard Jordan, 'Kleinere Dichtungen der Handschrift Harley 3810', *Englische Studien* 41 (1910), 253–66.

4 *The Auchinleck Manuscript: National Library of Scotland Advocates' MS. 19.2.1*, ed. Derek Pearsall and I. C. Cunningham (London: Scolar, 1977), pp. vii–viii.

5 Carol Meale's discussion highlights other possibilities. See above, p. 96.

6 For a discussion of the ways in which Auchinleck was 'ahead of its time', see Julia Boffey and A. S. G. Edwards, 'Middle English Literary Writings, 1150–1400', in *CHBB II*, 380–90.

7 Malcolm Parkes, 'The Literacy of the Laity', in *Literature and Western Civilization*, 6 vols, ed. David Daiches and Anthony Thorlby (London: Aldus Books, 1972–76), II: The Medieval World (1973), pp. 555–77, at p. 569.

ideas with it, as Pearsall and Cunningham's remarks show: in these textual kaleidoscopes, we see 'indiscrimination', 'unsophistication', and nascent secularity, and by extension, we assign these traits to lay middle-class readers of the late Middle Ages. Seeking to clarify terminology, Theo Stemmler, discussing Harley 2253, has argued for a distinction between miscellanies, anthologies, and 'well-wrought books', suggesting that while miscellanies are 'somewhat arbitrary, casual collection[s] of texts', anthologies are 'careful collection[s] of texts selected as representative specimens of various genres'.[8] Any particular volume can be situated along this spectrum between 'well-wrought book' and 'miscellany', but at least in books intended as a single unit of production the criteria for diagnosing true randomness, the 'indiscriminate' quality we see in the juxtaposition of *Sir Orfeo* with the Five Wounds of Christ, remain elusive.[9]

It would seem that Auchinleck, Ashmole 61, and Harley 3810 were all planned with at least some level of intentionality, although opinions vary widely in each case regarding the content of such intentions or the focus with which they were applied. It is usually argued that Auchinleck was commissioned by a wealthy London merchant with an interest in aristocratic culture; he most likely ordered the volume from the manuscript's Scribe 1, who copied roughly 70 per cent of the manuscript and outsourced the rest to other scribes.[10] Thematically, the volume seems to be grouped in three sections: religious material primarily at the beginning, followed by romance, followed by history

8 Theo Stemmler, 'Miscellany or Anthology? The Structure of Medieval Manuscripts: MS Harley 2253, for Example', *Zeitschrift für Anglistik und Amerikanistik: A Quarterly of Language, Literature, and Culture* 39.3–4 (1991), 231–7 (repr. and rev. in *Studies in the Harley Manuscript: The Scribes, Contents, and Social Contexts of British Library MS Harley 2253*, ed. Susanna Fein (Kalamazoo: Medieval Institute, Western Michigan University, 2000), pp. 111–21).

9 For up-to-date reflections on the interpretive questions raised by miscellanies and their modes of production, see *Insular Books: Vernacular Manuscript Miscellanies in Late Medieval Britain*, ed. Margaret Connolly and Raluca Radulescu, Proceedings of the British Academy (Oxford: OUP, 2015); and *The Dynamics of the Medieval Codex: Text Collections from a European Perspective*, ed. Karen Pratt et al. (Göttingen: V&R, 2017), openly accessible at http://www.v-r.de/_uploads_media/files/9783847107545_meyer_etal_dynamics_wz_083454.pdf.

10 Timothy A. Shonk, 'A Study of the Auchinleck Manuscript: Bookmen and Bookmaking in the Early Fourteenth Century', *Speculum* 60 (1985), 71–91. See also Ralph Hanna, *London Literature, 1300–1380* (Cambridge: CUP, 2005), pp. 74–9; and Susanna Fein, 'The Auchinleck Manuscript: New Perspectives', in *The Auchinleck Manuscript: New Perspectives*, ed. Susanna Fein (York: York Medieval Press, 2016), pp. 1–10, at pp. 5–6. Arthur Bahr has intriguingly suggested 'some sort of collective confraternal or civic ownership of the manuscript' on the model of the London *puy.* See Arthur Bahr, *Fragments and Assemblages: Forming Compilations of Medieval London* (Chicago: University of Chicago Press, 2013), pp. 32–3.

and political writing.[11] These sections are not explicitly delineated, and there is a great deal of overlap among them.[12] Ashmole 61, meanwhile, was most likely the product of an amateur scribe called Rate in north-east Leicestershire, who felt remarkably free, even by medieval standards, to edit his texts.[13] Although some thematic groupings are discernible in the manuscript – for instance, in the grouping of courtesy texts at the beginning of the volume and the series of devotional narratives toward the end – these series are often interrupted by apparently unrelated materials, like *Sir Orfeo*'s appearance between two religious lyrics. All we can confidently say about its audience comes from analysis of its texts – details in Rate's versions of *How the Wise Man Taught His Son* and *How the Good Wife Taught Her Daughter*, for instance, suggest a bourgeois rather than an aristocratic audience. About Harley 3810 we know even less, beyond a tentative Warwickshire provenance,[14] but its composition of texts shares a similar set of interests to Ashmole 61: lay devotion, appropriate social behaviour, and entertainment. Given these facts, does *Sir Orfeo* hail from miscellany or anthology?

One of the problems for modern scholars in the naming of these books is that any one of them is the result of a variety of factors, some artistic, intentional, or intellectual, and others practical, financial, or simply subject to fortune. Many of these books were created for specific people or circumstances, whether deliberately ordered from professionals, as Auchinleck was, or copied by an idiosyncratic amateur like Ashmole's Rate. As such, these manuscripts 'testify to highly individualistic canon-creating efforts by individuals variously inserted into discrete and fragmented social positions'.[15] How are we to evaluate the interplay of these factors in manuscript production? If Auchinleck's Scribe 1 had chosen texts and arranged them in a particular order, would that qualify the manuscript as an 'anthology', whereas if a class-conscious patron had requested a few of his favourite romances and some psalms, and the scribe performed his request by rote, we would have mere miscellany? What elevates the scribe's organizational intentions above the patron's tastes in understanding what kind of volume Auchinleck might be? Similarly, regardless of whose mind (or minds) lay behind its production, are there thematic or literary impulses behind the decision to follow *Sir Orfeo*

[11] Thorlac Turville-Petre, *England the Nation: Language, Literature, and National Identity, 1290–1340* (Oxford: OUP, 1996), pp. 112–14.

[12] Hanna, *London Literature*, p. 105.

[13] *Codex Ashmole 61: A Compilation of Popular Middle English Verse*, ed. George Shuffelton (Kalamazoo: Medieval Institute, Western Michigan University, 2008), pp. 3–6.

[14] Bliss, p. xi.

[15] Ralph Hanna, 'Miscellaneity and Vernacularity: Conditions of Literary Production in Late Medieval England', in *The Whole Book: Cultural Perspectives on the Medieval Miscellany*, ed. Stephen G. Nicholas and Siegfried Wenzel (Ann Arbor: University of Michigan Press, 1996), pp. 37–51, at p. 47.

with 'The Woman Who Buried the Host' in Harley 3810, or might it simply be that the exemplars of those two texts were available to the scribe at that moment and happened to fit the general requests of the person who ordered the manuscript?[16] Even if there were a way to know for certain, the answer would likely fall somewhere between those two poles, as scribes and patrons might communicate about both the desired content and the practical or financial limitations of a volume.[17] The balance of interpretive or thematic factors with more mundane exigencies does not preclude substantive connection among the texts in a volume.[18]

There are ways to approach this problem when thinking about the production of a manuscript. Theo Stemmler systematically analyses Harley 2253, seeking concordances among a number of categories and subcategories to show thematic, generic, and, most interestingly, linguistically associative premeditation on the part of the manuscript's scribe.[19] Ralph Hanna meanwhile argues that miscellaneity must be evaluated with reference to 'the scribe's source materials and their prior configurations'.[20] I would like to suggest that we might think profitably about miscellaneity and compilation not only through the lens of book production but also of book consumption – that is, from the reader's side of the equation.

What constitutes valid evidence is more difficult to define when looking down this end of the telescope. As we have seen, we know precious little about the ownership histories of any of *Sir Orfeo*'s manuscripts. Nevertheless, Arthur Bahr has recently suggested that manuscript compilations might be interpreted in ways similar to those we apply to individual literary texts:

> Selection and arrangement of texts in manuscripts, like that of words in poetry, can produce those 'metaphorical potentialities' [a phrase of Derek Pearsall's to describe poetic language], discontinuities and excesses, multiple and shifting meanings, resistance to paraphrase, and openness to rereading that have deservedly become resurgent objects of critical value.[21]

16 Hanna, 'Miscellaneity and Vernacularity', p. 47.

17 Shonk imagines ongoing conversation between client and scribe about the content of Auchinleck. See Shonk, 'A Study of the Auchinleck Manuscript', pp. 90–1; and Hanna, *London Literature*, p. 76.

18 It is difficult, at least for me, to imagine what 'randomness' would really look like in an object created by human beings. I have a notebook into which I copy poems that I like. The poems are not organized by any principle other than the order in which I found them, so the book is limited and structured only according to (1) my taste and (2) the access I had to poems in order to copy them. While neither of these could be said to be 'planned', the notebook is still 'united' in that it says quite a lot about my own taste and about the kinds of books and websites I have visited at various times in my life.

19 Stemmler, 'Miscellany or Anthology?', pp. 231–7.

20 Hanna, 'Miscellaneity and Vernacularity', p. 40.

21 Bahr, *Fragments and Assemblages*, p. 10.

The 'resurgence' Bahr invokes is the recent renewed interest in formalism and the category of 'the literary' over social and cultural history. We do not need to banish history – as indeed Bahr emphatically does not – to benefit from what formalism has always done best: free us from the need to prove a creator's intention when discussing the meanings, and shades of meaning, available in a text. By virtue of their miscellaneity, by the formal and material arrangement of their contents, by the relationship of the part to the whole, Auchinleck, Ashmole 61, and Harley 3810 all invite particular modes of reading and interpretation, modes which tell us about the aesthetic sensibilities of the manuscripts' readers. Bahr discusses this phenomenon using Walter Benjamin's idea of history as expressed in *The Arcades Project.* He argues that critics can think 'compilationally' without 'mak[ing] claims about the essential nature' of an object.[22] Here I diverge from him, as I am making the claim that historically grounded interpretations are made available by formal readings of the books themselves. These interpretations cannot be proven in the same way that textual provenance or aspects of manuscript production can be proven, and they are thus arguable in the way that most literary interpretations in our discipline are. Nevertheless, I contend that at our historical distance, formal evidence is sometimes the best available to us in theorizing possible reader responses to medieval manuscripts.

The owners of miscellanies expected to return to them many times throughout their lives. As their books catered to a variety of moods and domestic requirements over time, multiple interpretations and responses would have arisen both to each poem and to the book as a whole. Each miscellany contains numerous possible interpretive 'stories'. Here, I will tell one of them, the story of *Sir Orfeo* and its devotional companions. By connecting *Sir Orfeo*'s interior formal features to the themes of the texts which surround it in its manuscript compilations, I hope to show that those companion texts which have overtly doctrinal or spiritual interests suggest interpretations and valences of meaning in *Sir Orfeo* that help define what 'secular romance' might mean in a bourgeois medieval context. In particular, the relationship between *Sir Orfeo* and texts like the *Stimulus Consciencie Minor* or *Saint Patrick's Purgatory* helps to define the terms of any opposition between sacred and secular we might propose. This method suggests particular interpretations of *Sir Orfeo* and, by extension, its more overtly religious companions, showing how their meanings become dependent upon one another within their manuscript contexts. The physical presentation of the late medieval miscellany invites a mode of recursive reading which places texts in constant conversation with one another.

22 Bahr, *Fragments and Assemblages*, pp. 11–18.

A way to hell from the gates of heaven

However moralistic or even dull some of the religious poems in Auchinleck, Ashmole 61, or Harley 3810 might seem, they all treat something very dramatic: how the natural can interact with the supernatural; how the divine discloses itself to the human. Take up holy practices on Friday, a poem in Harley 3810 urges, because every significant event from the creation of man through the Annunciation to the Passion took place on a Friday; you can participate in this way in something eternal. Meditate on the wounds of Christ, says Ashmole, and avoid the Seven Deadly Sins which caused them. Perform an act of sacrilege by burying the host in your backyard, and expect natural laws to be broken in proof and reproof of it; something outside the order of nature is at work.

What we call secular romances share this interest in the fracture of the natural order through marvellous events. Auchinleck's *Lay le Freine* begins with a description of the many lays 'of ferli þing' that have been written. The thirst for wonder, for the unusual and even spectacular, is surely as sated by a bloody child appearing in a pear-tree as it is by faerie abduction. The kinship of miracle story, wonder tale, and secular romance becomes particularly clear in a romance like *Sir Isumbras*, which appears in Ashmole 61 and promises 'a wonder case' (l. 4).[23] At the beginning of the romance, a bird singing in a tree warns Isumbras to repent. He immediately takes its advice and embarks on a long life of suffering, ill fortune, and privation. Thus far, the story resembles another of the Ashmole's narrative poems, *Saint Eustace*, but unlike *Saint Eustace*, *Isumbras* ends with a family reunion and reassertion of lay social bonds rather than heroic martyrdom. Similarly, Ashmole's *Sir Cleges* seems to begin as a story about a knight who is holy through his generous hospitality and thus experiences a miracle – a cherry tree that gives fruit at Christmas – but after the initial miracle it becomes a comedic tale about tricking Uther Pendragon's greedy servants. The status of the singing bird or miraculous cherries becomes oddly ambiguous – they are wonders, marvels, 'ferlys', but the agency and meaning behind them are underdeveloped and thus mysterious, defined only by wondrousness and not by any single religious or literary frame of reference. These marvels suggest a world in which nature is ready to be fractured at every moment, and explanation is not always required. This is a world in which God is constantly active, but it is also the world of romance, in which, as Auchinleck's *Sir Degaré* tells us, knights can go out expecting to find 'ferli fele' (l. 4).[24]

[23] Shuffelton, *Ashmole 61*, p. 39. All future citations of texts from MS Ashmole 61 are from this edition.

[24] *Sir Degaré*, quoted from the online edition of the Auchinleck manuscript, by David Burnley and Alison Wiggins, at https://auchinleck.nls.uk/. The overlap between 'ferly', 'wonder', and 'marvel' is attested well beyond the manuscript context of *Sir Orfeo*. *Piers Plowman* famously begins by invoking all these categories. Langland asserts that

Both *Sir Cleges* and *Sir Isumbras*, of course, invite devotional or loosely theological interpretations. As stories of holy knights, they fall into the category of 'pious romance' or 'secular hagiography'.[25] *Sir Orfeo* has however been most often considered in terms of secular romance or the adaptation of pagan (whether Roman or Celtic) myth.[26] Alternatively, it has been read wholly exegetically, as a symbolic rendering of Christian, scriptural, or Boethian principles.[27] We do not have to read *Sir Orfeo* symbolically, however, to discern the interests it shares with the other texts in its manuscripts. Like *Sir Degaré* and like 'The Woman Who Buried the Host', *Sir Orfeo* is invested in the interaction between the supernatural and the natural, certainly most clearly through the uncanniness of Faerie. *Sir Orfeo* however also invokes religious discourse on several occasions, most clearly in its allusions to the Heavenly Jerusalem of Revelation 21. This is not symbol but quotation; not, initially, interpretation but rather linguistic association of the kind used by Theo Stemmler to connect the items of Harley 2253.

At the end of the Book of Revelation, after the old heaven and earth have been wiped away, John sees a new Jerusalem descending from heaven. He describes it thus:

> And [the angel] shewed me the holy city Jerusalem coming down out of heaven from God, having the glory of God, and the light thereof was like to a precious stone, as to jasper-stone, even as crystal. And it had a wall great and high having twelve gates, and in the gates twelve angels and names written thereon, which are the names of the twelve tribes of the children of Israel [...] And the building of the wall thereof was of jasper-stone, but the city itself pure gold, like to clear glass. And the foundations of the wall of the city were adorned with all manner of precious stones. The first foundation was

---

he 'wente wide in this world wondres to here', and he first describes his indubitably religious vision as 'a ferly, of Fairye me thoghte', given to him in 'a merveillous swevene' (B.Prol., ll. 1–10). See William Langland, *The Vision of Piers Plowman: A Critical Edition of the B-Text Based on Trinity College Cambridge MS B.15.17*, ed. A. V. C. Schmidt, 2nd edn (London: Everyman, 1995).

25 For 'pious romance', see Susan Crane, *Insular Romance: Politics, Faith, and Culture in Anglo-Norman and Middle English Literature* (Berkeley and Los Angeles: University of California Press, 1986), pp. 92–133; and for 'secular hagiography', see Ojars Kratins, 'Middle English *Amis and Amiloun*: Chivalric Romance or Secular Hagiography', *PMLA* 81 (1966), 347–54.

26 See, for example, Kenneth R. R. Gros Luis, 'Robert Henryson's *Orpheus and Eurydice* and the Orpheus Tradition of the Middle Ages', *Speculum* 41 (1966), 643–55; Curtis R. H. Jirsa, 'In the Shadow of the Ympe-Tree: Arboreal Folklore in *Sir Orfeo*', *ES* 89 (2008), 141–51; Paul Beekman Taylor, 'Sir Orfeo and the Minstrel King', *ANQ* 13 (2000), 12–16.

27 See, for example, Patrizia Grimaldi, '*Sir Orfeo* as Celtic Folk-Hero, Christian Pilgrim, and Medieval King', in *Allegory, Myth, and Symbol*, ed. Morton Bloomfield (Cambridge, MA: Harvard University Press, 1981), pp. 147–61; John Block Friedman, 'Eurydice, Heurodis, and the Noon-Day Demon', *Speculum* 41 (1966), 22–9.

> jasper, the second sapphire, the third a chalcedony, the fourth an emerald, the fifth sardonix, the sixth sardius, the seventh chrysolite, the eighth beryl, the ninth a topaz, the tenth a chrysoprasus, the eleventh a jacinth, the twelfth an amethyst. And the twelve gates are twelve pearls, one to each, and every several gate was of one several pearl. And the street of the city was pure gold, as it were transparent glass. And I saw no temple therein, for the Lord God almighty is the temple thereof and the Lamb. And the city hath no need of sun nor of the moon to shine in it, for the glory of God hath enlightened it, and the Lamb is the lamp thereof (Apocalypse 21.10–11, 18–23).[28]

Here, now, is Orfeo's first sight of Faerie. The differences among the three manuscripts are significant enough to be worth quoting in full.

Auchinleck:

He com in-to a fair cuntray
As bryȝt so sonne on somers day,
Smoþe & plain & al grene,
– Hille no dale nas þ*er* non y-sene.
Amidde þe lond a castel he siȝe,
Rich & real & wonder heiȝe.
Al þe ut-mast wal
Was clere and schine as cristal;
An hundred tours þ*er* were about,
Degiselich and bataild stout;
Þe butras com out of þe diche
Of rede gold y-arched riche;
Þe vousour was auowed al
Of ich maner divers aumal.
Wiþ-in þer wer wide wones
Al of precious stones;
þe werst piler on to bihold
Was al of burnist gold.
Al þat lond was ever liȝt,
For when it schuld be þerk and niȝt,
þe riche stones liȝt gonne
As briȝt as doþ at none þe sonne.
No man may telle no þenke in þouȝt
þe riche werk þat þer was wrouȝt;
Bi al þing hi*m* þink þat it is
þe proude court of Paradis. (ll. 351–73)

[28] *The Vulgate Bible, Douay-Rheims Translation*, 6 vols (Cambridge, MA: Dumbarton Oaks Medieval Library, Harvard University Press, 2013), VI: The New Testament, ed. Angela M. Kinney. All future citations refer to this edition.

Ashmole 61:

He com into a fair cu*ntr*ey
Als bryȝt as son in som*er*ys dey;
Hyll ne dale was þ*er* non sen
– Jt was a welle feyre gren.
Orfeo full wele it seye,
A feyr castell, ryall and hyȝe.
He be-held þe werke full wele:
The ou*er*yst werke a-boue the walle
Gan schyne as doth þe crystalle;
An hu*n*dreth tyret*ys* he saw, full stout,
So godly þei w*er* bateyled a-boute;
The pylers þ*at* com oute off þe dyche
All þei w*er* of gold full ryce;
The frontys, þei w*er* amelyd all
W*yth* all man*er* dyu*er*se amell.
Ther-in he saw wyde wonys,
And all w*er* full of p*re*syos stonys. (ll. 353–69)

Harley 3810:

He cam to fayr contray
Was bryȝt as ony day,
Feyr palys, & alle grene
– Hille ne dale was nouȝt sene.
Amyd þe lau*n*de a castel he sye,
Noble & ryche, ryȝt wo*n*der hie,
& al þe oueryst walle
Schone as doþ þe crystal;
Fayr touris þ*er* wer aboute,
Gayly set w*ith* p*er*les stoute;
Þe utmest, þ*at* stode on þe dyche,
Was of golde & selu*er* ryche;
Þe fronte, þ*at* was amyd all,
Was of dyu*er*s metalle.
W*ith*in were wyde wonys
Of golde, selu*er* & p*re*cious stones;
Feyr pilers þ*er*on wer dyȝt
Of p*re*cious stones & safyre bryȝt.
Hit schone so fayre by nyȝt
Þ*at* al þe towne þ*er*of was lyȝt,
Þe ryche stones schone so cu*n*
Also bryȝt as ony su*n*.
No man myȝt telle, ne þink in þouȝt,
Þe ryches þ*at* þerin was wrouȝt. (ll. 337–60)

Like John in Revelation, then, Orfeo encounters a structure that is at once singular and plural, an architectural structure of unified design in which there are many 'wones', or, as the Vulgate calls them when speaking of heaven, 'mansions'.[29] That structure is made of gold, encrusted with gems, almost blindingly bright as 'cristal'. Moreover, that blinding light emanates not from the sun, but within the structure itself. John tells us that sun and moon are no more in the New Heaven and New Earth, and Orfeo here is, technically, inside a rock where there can be no light. In the New Jerusalem, the light comes from the Lamb, from God himself. In this castle, on the other hand, the light seems to emanate from the reflective stones themselves, a common topos in accounts of faerie otherworlds that becomes particularly eerie when juxtaposed with the New Jerusalem.[30] When he finally enters the castle, in both Auchinleck and Ashmole he finds the Faerie King sitting in a 'tabernacle', the same word used to describe the New Jerusalem in the Book of Revelation.[31] Even the smooth green field surrounding the castle, although it does not appear in Revelation, had become commonplace iconography in discussions of heaven, as the Earthly Paradise, the threshold to heaven where not-quite-perfect souls await their final fulfilment. We see it most famously in Dante, but it also appears closer to home in *Pearl*, *The Prick of Conscience*, *The Vision of Tundale*, and indeed, right in Auchinleck in *Saint Patrick's Purgatory.*

In fact, these heavenly topoi – the jewelled city and the Christianized Elysian fields – appear at length in other texts in both Auchinleck and Ashmole 61, although not in Harley 3810. In *Saint Patrick's Purgatory*, Sir Owain crosses the bridge and immediately sees jewelled gates. Certain key words that we saw in *Orfeo* and Revelation – like 'red gold' (l. 772), 'crystal' (l. 790), and 'tabernacle' (l. 785) – appear again, sometimes indeed appearing slightly forced as though the poet knew they belonged in heavenly discussions but could not always find a good place to deploy them. Thus we find jewels that 'in tabernacles [...] wer ywrouȝt' (l. 785).[32] Despite seeing this jewelled city, Owain cannot enter because he is not completely purified, so he learns about heaven from the bucolic heavenly fields where it is eternally summer (ll. 863–98). In Ashmole 61, the sweet melodies and bounteous fields of heaven, though not the city, appear in the *Stimulus Consciencie Minor* (ll. 201–88), crystalline heavens are referenced in *Ypotis* (ll. 43–72), and the Earthly

[29] 'In my Father's house there are many mansions [*mansiones*]' (John 14.2).

[30] For a discussion of this topos, see Aisling Byrne, *Otherworlds: Fantasy and History in Medieval Literature* (Oxford: OUP, 2016), pp. 32–3 and 91.

[31] 'And I, John, saw the holy city, the new Jerusalem, coming down out of heaven from God, prepared as a bride adorned for her husband. And I heard a great voice from the throne saying, "Behold: the tabernacle [*tabernaculum*] of God with men, and he will dwell with them"' (Revelation 21.2–3).

[32] *Saint Patrick's Purgatory*, quoted from the online edition of the Auchinleck manuscript by David Burnley and Alison Wiggins, at https://auchinleck.nls.uk/.

Paradise makes an appearance in *The Adulterous Falmouth Squire* as the visionary's uncle camps in a golden tent under the Tree of Knowledge to help instruct his nephew on the afterlife (ll. 140–87). The scriptural allusions in *Sir Orfeo*, then, would not only be available to readers or listeners who knew their Bible well but also to those who had read other texts in their volumes.

Auchinleck in particular makes sure that the parallel is noticed, saying that Orfeo thought it was indeed the proud court of Paradise, perhaps in part because of a recognized inability to describe what he has seen, master bard though he is. As all three versions of the poem note, 'No man may telle no þenke in þouȝt | þe riche werk þat þer was wrouȝt', echoing St Paul's reflection after his own vision of heaven: 'The eye hath not seen, nor ear heard, neither hath it entered into the heart of man what things God hath prepared for them that love him' (I Corinthians 2.9).

These parallels have been noted before. Ad Putter has commented that the New Jerusalem often underlies descriptions of castles in medieval romance, acting as a means of creating what he calls 'superlative worlds', which the faerie kingdom of *Sir Orfeo* certainly is.[33] Neil Cartlidge has also suggested that the paradisiacal allusions in the poem emphasize how uncanny and possibly diabolical the faerie kingdom really is – a perverted paradise where light has no true source.[34] Most recently, Aisling Byrne has argued that *Sir Orfeo* uses a pastiche of 'imagery associated with the afterlife', including the heavenly city, to pursue the 'game of subterfuge that the text plays with the audience's interpretive faculties' from which the poem's aesthetic impact derives.[35]

The New Jerusalem certainly does function as an aesthetic tool for what modern writers of speculative fiction call 'world building'; the world built with it, I think, also expresses very specific anxieties about the afterlife itself. The poem shows a preoccupation with death apart from its description of the Heavenly Jerusalem. Right away, Orfeo is identified as the grandson of Pluto, god of the Underworld. When Heurodis falls into madness after her first encounter with the faeries, Orfeo laments that she is 'al wan as þou were ded' (l. 108). She in turn laments that although she has loved her husband 'as my liif', 'now we mot delen ato; / – Do þi best, for y mot go' (124–5).[36] She equates Orfeo with life, and now relinquishes both of them. When he then

33 Ad Putter, 'The Influence of Visions of the Otherworld on Some Medieval Romances', in *Envisaging Heaven in the Middle Ages*, ed. Carolyn Muessig and Ad Putter (London and New York: Routledge, 2007), pp. 237–51, at pp. 238–9.

34 Neil Cartlidge, 'Sir Orfeo in the Otherworld: Courting Chaos?', *SAC* 26 (2004), 195–226, at pp. 208–9. For further discussion of the uses of cultural allusion to undermine interpretive order, see also Alan J. Fletcher, '*Sir Orfeo* and the Flight from the Enchanters', *SAC* 22 (2000), 141–77.

35 Byrne, *Otherworlds*, pp. 91–6.

36 In MS Harley 3810, 'as my liif' appears as 'w*ith* alle my hert' (l. 122), and in Ashmole 61, it becomes 'j haue louyd þe all my lyfe' (l. 109). These divergences, in my view, still

takes on the garb of a pilgrim and leads a life of privation in the wilderness, he walks in well-trod penitential footsteps; penitence itself being associated with recognition of death and, in the context of the season of Lent, leading through death to Resurrection. Indeed, Orfeo's penitential season follows precisely that trajectory: after a long period in the wilderness, he enters into a rock, for all the world like a tomb, goes into a kingdom with a great deal in common with the afterlife, and, like Christ, harrows it, bringing both himself and someone else back to the ordinary world. These structures of penitence and reflection on death would be familiar from other poems in the manuscripts. To take just a few examples, they appear in Auchinleck in *Saint Patrick's Purgatory*, *The Harrowing of Hell*, and the *Seven Deadly Sins*; in Ashmole in Maidstone's *Seven Penitential Psalms*, the *Stimulus Consciencie Minor*, and any number of shorter devotional poems that enjoin detachment from the world; and in Harley in the poem 'Friday' and the same *Penitential Psalms* that appear in Ashmole.

I am not trying to build a strictly exegetical interpretation of *Sir Orfeo*, turning its tantalizing narrative set-pieces into a code in which Heurodis should be read as dead and the Faerie King is not actually the Faerie King but the devil. Such a project would not only be reductive, but it would also ignore the fact that many of these parallels or references to death and the afterlife are distorted versions of accepted doctrine or else cannot coexist without being dangerously subversive. Most strikingly, if we accept that Orfeo has undergone some kind of journey through suffering and death to resurrection, then we have to admit that the realm of suffering and death includes a twin of the New Jerusalem. Based only on appearances, by bringing Heurodis back to the world, Orfeo has harrowed not hell but heaven. The passage in which he tricks the Faerie King into giving up Heurodis by disguising his identity and gaining admittance to the court even bears some resemblance to, for example, the York Harrowing of Hell, in which Christ tricks Satan by concealing his identity as the Son of God in order to free the righteous souls trapped there. If Orfeo is our hero, however, the harrowing Christ figure in this scenario, then the one sitting on the throne, in the tabernacle, is at best an extremely uncanny vacuity, like the gems that reflect a light with no source.

The liminal figures at the gates of the faerie castle also make visible a nightmarish version of heaven. They are people who were taken from the world, '& þouȝt dede, & nare nouȝt' (l. 390). They line the walls of the castle, reminiscent of images of the New Jerusalem in which the walls are composed of people. Illuminators of thirteenth-century apocalypses had taken to replacing the 'names' of tribes above the gates of the New Jerusalem with the actual sons of Israel or the apostles themselves, as in the fourteenth-century

preserve the sense of the original phrase, in linking Orfeo with life, although I admit the full force of Auchinleck is lost.

English illuminated Apocalypse manuscript (Bodl. MS 401, fol. 66r) shown in Fig. 10.1.

In *Sir Orfeo*, instead of standing tall, however, these figures are supine and miserable. Despite the assertion that they are not dead, a few lines later, there are women in labour, 'sum ded & sum awedde' (l. 400). Appropriately, even the poet will not make a definitive judgement of their ontological state. What he does show, however, is that they are all caught in stasis, a kind of eternity which is neither desirable nor completely conceivable. Even the tortured souls in visions like *Saint Patrick's Purgatory* or *The Vision of Tundale* experience a hellish dynamism: they are torn apart and then put back together again so they can be dismembered once more. Here, eternity means a total lack of dynamism, stasis rather than eternal life.

All of this could be in the service of sheer diabolism, a way to render the fairies all the more frightening. Certainly, the perversion of heaven has that effect. However, the New Jerusalem – or jewelled cities that certainly seem to have it in the background – often appears in Middle English poetry with the same kind of ambivalence that is writ particularly large in *Sir Orfeo.* Consider another poem about losing something precious under a tree: *Pearl.* There, the Dreamer's ambivalence about the Otherworld, and the ambivalence created in readers by the unfamiliarity and ineffability of paradise, renders the vision of the New Jerusalem anti-climactic and unsatisfying. In interpreting the poem, we always have to make sense of the fact that heaven seems abstract, unkind, and cold – quite problematic for a place that is meant to be the ultimate object of desire. It seems to have very little to do with what humans experience, desire, and love in life, and therefore it corresponds to very few fundamental human questions. It is also a poem about the failure of human understanding and human tools of communication like language and metaphor, containing images that would be oxymorons in the Dreamer's world: uncompetitive queens, harmonious courts, and thousands of brides for one groom, who is an animal. *Pearl* ends with an emphatic statement of the alterity of heaven; indeed, in some ways it agrees with some of its more critical modern readers, insisting that living people do not belong there, not only because they are alive but because they do not know how to want what it offers. The Dreamer's resolution is to take up a life that will result in his becoming a pearl as well. Having approached heaven once, he is thrust back and must approach again.

Closer to *Sir Orfeo*, *Saint Patrick's Purgatory*, although ostensibly full of celestial desire, actually avoids the question of heaven almost completely. The New Jerusalem is glimpsed only distantly, as a wall beyond which beautiful singing can be heard and over which sweet aromas waft. The city itself is an asymptote which Sir Owain is always approaching but can never reach. After his journey through the afterlife, as well, Sir Owain takes up pilgrimage. Like *Pearl*'s dreamer, having made his journey, he must make it again to a constantly receding object of desire. There is a fundamental recursiveness

Fig. 10.1 Oxford, Bodleian Library MS 401, fol. 66r. Illuminated Apocalypse. Printed with permission of The Bodleian Libraries, University of Oxford.

to these narratives which suggests that humans and heaven have a troubled relationship, even if Christ has apparently opened the way. These poems hold up heaven as the object of ultimate desire and fulfilment in Christian life, but they also dramatize the problem of heaven's incompatibility with an earthly life that is undeniably beloved and beautiful, or at the very least important, in itself. When the Heavenly Jerusalem appears in these contexts, its effect is often not to advocate detachment from life but to emphasize how significant it is.

Thus, in *Sir Orfeo*, our hero and his wife return to the court, to civilization and earthly responsibilities. Their encounter with the strange and beautiful Otherworld is not a positive good. In some ways *Orfeo* reaches a similar conclusion to *Pearl* – the living do not belong here. St Augustine called the world of sin a 'region of dissimilitude',[37] but here, the jewelled paradise itself deserves the title. The loss of dynamism is not only frightening but also inappropriate to a human being, and the image of the Heavenly Jerusalem, far from exciting desire for eternal life, becomes indistinguishable from an uncanny hellscape.

It does not follow from this, however, that *Sir Orfeo* is actually a cunningly disguised epicurean manifesto, purveying a deeply subversive materialism under the veil of romance. Rather, what we find in *Sir Orfeo* is a particularly drastic instantiation of the same anxieties about the tension between immanence and transcendence that lie behind *Pearl* and *Saint Patrick's Purgatory*. It can afford to be drastic since it is not dealing with religion and orthodoxy directly. That task is left to other poems in the manuscript.

'The Four Foes of Mankind', the lyric which immediately follows *Sir Orfeo* in Auchinleck, ends with a call to action and responsibility for one's spiritual life. 'Now haue y founden þi fas', it proclaims, having identified Death as perhaps the worst. Now, it is up to the reader to '[f]inde tow þi frendes' (ll. 111–12). It is a particularly appropriate injunction to follow *Sir Orfeo*, so replete with foes and concerned with death. If we are to seek the friends of mankind in the poem, we find the faithful steward, who has taken care to preserve worldly order against his master's return. The truly effective friend to Orfeo, however, is his harp. The sweetness of his music gives him back his wife, and in fact it is a heaven of its own, for anyone that 'miȝt of his harping here [...] schuld þenche þat he were / In on of þe joies of Paradis, / Swiche melody in his harping is' (ll. 35–9). Semblances of heaven, then, are not confined to the faeries' world or to the realm of lapidary perfection. They are present in ordered courts, in human love, and in human skill. In *Sir Orfeo*, the purity and sweetness of the hero's music provides a thread that is constant

[37] *'Inveni longe me esse a te in regione dissimilitudinis, tanquam audirem vocem tuam de excelso: Cibus sum grandium; cresce, et manducabis me.'* Augustine of Hippo, 'S. Aurelii Augustini Hipponensis Episcopi Confessionum Libri Tredecim', *Patrologia Latina* 32, col. 657–868 (col. 742, VII.10.16).

between the Otherworld and this one. Both within and without the region of dissimilitude, it can be relied on.

It is also worthwhile to note that the courtier's assertion that 'It nis no bot of mannes deþ' proves incorrect in the context of the poem. The conventions of storytelling – of the kind of romance that Orfeo sings – bring about the resurrection, mythically speaking, of Heurodis. These stories are told, too, in the context of a community – that 'new class of readers' who wanted to hold entire libraries in their hands. Despite the ostentatious heavenly city in the Otherworld, then, there are intimations of heaven everywhere. The castle of *Sir Orfeo* serves as a surrogate Otherworld onto which anxiety about heaven and the resurrection of the body is displaced. The object of desire becomes not a jewelled, immortal city but the ordinary world of civilization, court, and family. The narrative is simultaneously subversive and typical of Middle English constructions of heaven, which frequently resist utopianism and demand that if heaven is to fulfil human desire, it must be reflected in and reached through the communities and bonds of this world.

Conclusion

In so many of the poems which late medieval readers consumed, heaven appears as a horizon which, when approached, thrusts its supplicants back to the beginning of their journey. Every encounter with what appears to be the renewed Jerusalem ends in dissatisfaction, anxiety, or exile, demanding a new, deeper, more purified approach to the ultimate desired reality. These frustrated expectations never reject the New Jerusalem proper but, as we see in *Sir Orfeo*, they do emphasize how easy it is to mistake something diabolical for something heavenly. The locus in the poem that appears to be most like heaven is a faerie palace, but the actual intimations of divine eternity available to Orfeo come through the human effort of music and the human bonds of loyalty and matrimony. In *Sir Orfeo*, as in so many of its Revelation-quoting cousins, to speak of heaven is to speak of interpretation and misinterpretation.

As a result, for modern critics, to speak of heaven in Middle English literature is in part to speak of Middle English reading, of the process by which readers might learn to interpret and prioritize the materials in multivocal books which contained a host of values and interests, from the social and sensationalistic to the devotional and doctrinal. These manuscripts were consumed by readers very much engaged in the secular world – in medieval terms, the world outside of the monastery – through trade, business, family life, government, or even, for secular clerics, Church politics. The pursuit of salvation for the non-ascetic, non-mystical believer would demand constant judgement and discernment, at least in theory if not always in practice. As in the mixed life, so also in the mixed manuscript: *Sir Orfeo*'s readers would have to learn to distinguish friend from foe, both spiritually and materially, in a multivocal world.

Sir Orfeo invites its readers to weigh its own jewelled city against the heaven encountered in *Saint Patrick's Purgatory* or the *Stimulus Consciencie Minor.* It places the wonder of roving faerie bands against the wonder of miraculous Eucharistic visions, depicting a world full of supernatural incursions that are salvific, dangerous, or both. These juxtapositions do not separate 'secular romance' from 'devotional narrative'; instead they blur the boundary between these categories, giving voice to an implicit assumption that these spheres of discourse are deeply intertwined, casting doubt on and enriching one another. The texts of Auchinleck, Ashmole 61, and Harley 3810 offer their readers numerous possibilities for considering the relationship between the natural world and the supernatural one which might at any time rupture it, bringing both terror and joy. This is instantiated very clearly in the juxtaposition of Ashmole 61's *Saint Eustace* and *Sir Isumbras*, two very similar stories that end very differently: one in martyrdom; the other in the reassertion of family life and prosperity.

Sir Orfeo enacts such multivocalism within itself, travelling through both death and life, just as its manuscripts do, allowing readers to traverse the blurred boundaries between sacred and secular in the pursuit of a happy ending. Far from unsophisticated, the contents of the late medieval miscellany facilitate fluid, ongoing interpretation by readers and re-readers. The relationships that can develop among the texts in these volumes create an implicit aesthetic of secular and spiritual life, an aesthetic native to professional book production rather than high theological discourse. In miscellanies, romance and religious verse need each other.

11

The Woodville Women, Eleanor Haute, and British Library Royal MS 14 E III*

Rebecca E. Lyons

This chapter is concerned with the fifteenth-century ownership and readership of the manuscript now identified by shelf mark BL Royal MS 14 E III.[1] Consisting of three of the five Arthurian prose romances of the full *Lancelot-Grail Cycle* (the *Estoire del Saint Graal*, *Queste del Saint Graal* and *Mort Artu*),[2] this codex also contains inscriptions and *ex libris* in six hands – all from the fifteenth century. Four appear to have been written by women from the Woodville family: Elizabeth Woodville's eldest daughters Elizabeth of York (later Henry VII's queen) and Cecily; Elizabeth Woodville's sister Joan (or Jane) Grey; and possibly also Edward VI's queen, Elizabeth Woodville herself.[3] Another was written by Eleanor Haute – a lady of the court

* This essay is based on research in my PhD dissertation 'Women and Their Books: The Ownership and Readership of Arthurian Literature in Fifteenth- and Sixteenth-Century England' (University of Bristol, 2017). I am very grateful for useful conversations with Roger Middleton, Linda Gowans and Ceridwen Lloyd-Morgan whilst researching this essay.

1 Hereafter BL Royal MS 14 E III. This manuscript is fully digitised and available to view online. See http://www.bl.uk/manuscripts/FullDisplay.aspx?ref=Royal_MS_14_e_iii (accessed 22 February 2017).

2 The cycle is also known as the *Prose Lancelot*, the *Vulgate Cycle*, or the *Pseudo-Map Cycle*. The cycle comprises the *Lancelot propre* (*Lancelot Proper*), the longest section at half of the entire cycle; the *Queste del Saint Graal* (*Quest for the Holy Grail*); and finally the *Mort Artu* (*Death of Arthur*). These were supplemented by the *Estoire del Saint Graal* (*The History of the Holy Grail*) and the *Estoire de Merlin* (*The History of Merlin* – also called the Vulgate or Prose *Merlin*), to which was added the Vulgate *Suite du Merlin*, or Vulgate *Merlin Continuation*, detailing more of Arthur's early adventures. For more on the manuscript contexts of these literary works, see Roger Middleton, 'Manuscripts of the Lancelot-Grail Cycle in England and Wales: Some Books and Their Owners', in *A Companion to the Lancelot-Grail Cycle*, ed. Carol Dover (Cambridge: D. S. Brewer, 2003), pp. 219–35.

3 Some uncertainty surrounds one of the inscriptions, 'E Wydevyll', which has been argued by some scholars to have been written by Edward Woodville. I discuss this later in

connected to the Woodvilles by marriage – and another by Eleanor's uncle, Sir Richard Roos. The women's inscriptions form the main focus of this essay – each is analysed in order to gauge something of its author (for instance marital or social status), and each is situated against a backdrop of relevant events and contemporary contexts – both political and personal.

This evidence suggests a specific window of time in which some of these inscriptions are likely to have been written: sometime during the year 1483–84. The Woodvilles were in sanctuary at Westminster for much of this period, from 1 May 1483 until 22 January 1484 – just under eight months in total during the period of Richard III's accession to the throne.[4] Locating the inscriptions at this specific juncture in the lives of their writers, within particular political contexts (the Ricardian usurpation) and geopolitical spaces (Westminster), has an important bearing on our analysis and understanding of the ways in which the book may have been used. The combined presence of the inscriptions raises some intriguing possibilities regarding the use, transmission, and sharing of secular literary objects within royal and courtly family circles. Manuscript owning, sharing, and reading emerge as a significant mechanism of community: a nexus around which familial activity can take place, even providing consolation and support in and between social networks of friends and family during a period of *extremis*. The book's literary content also matters in these analyses. What was it about these Arthurian prose romances that might have influenced the Woodvilles' decision to take the book into sanctuary with them, and how might they have influenced the ways in which the book was used whilst there, including the act of inscription? The three texts in this manuscript are more religious and sober in theme than the two *Lancelot-Grail Cycle* texts that have been omitted (the *Estoire de Merlin* and the *Lancelot propre*), and may therefore have made this book a particularly suitable choice to accompany and console a family in what was undoubtedly a challenging time of personal and political adversity – including the death of a husband and father (Edward IV), their betrayal by his brother Richard as he claimed the throne for himself, and the declaration of Edward's children – including Elizabeth and Cecily – as illegitimate. These Arthurian texts also repeatedly place emphasis on reading, writing, and other activities associated with the written word, in both textual and illustrative content.[5] The possible bearing of this on the annotations in the book is considered.

---

the essay.

4 Dates given in *The Croyland Chronicle: Part VII – The Third Continuation of the History of Croyland Abbey: January, 1477 – June, 1483*, trans. Henry T. Riley (London: Bohn, 1855). Online edition: http://newr3.dreamhosters.com/?page_id=518 (accessed 28 August 2015).

5 For an example, see the miniature on folio 140r of this manuscript (catalogued by the British Library as King Arthur dictating to a scribe).

Summary of inscriptions in BL Royal MS 14 E III

To contextualise subsequent analyses, each of the manuscript's five inscriptions are now listed. Almost certainly the earliest to be written – also the longest (and the only inscription by a man in the book) – is that of Sir Richard Roos of Gedney (d. 1482) (see Fig. 11.1).[6] At the manuscript's outset on the facing page of the ornately-decorated opening page of the first Arthurian text, the *Estoire del Saint Graal* (History of the Holy Grail), he pens a partially-erased list of contents:

> The begynnyng of þe first boke of Sankgrealle endureth to þende of þe iiii xx viii[7] lefe w*ith* þis sig<ne> <*there follows half a line of erased and illegible contents*> & endureth to þe com*myng* in of <L>auncelot
>
> And aft*er* þ*at* þe boke of Tristram and launcelot <*erasure*> bene þe boke of paper & þe olde boke of parchment and aft*er* þ*at* þe mort darthur wher*e* of þe begynnynge ys yn this same boke and <begynneth> at <*half a line of erased and illegible content*>[8]

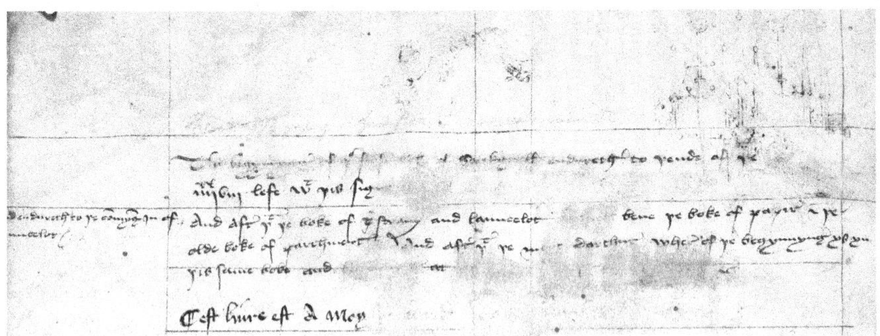

Fig. 11.1 © The British Library Board, Sir Richard Roos's inscription in BL Royal MS 14 E III, fol. 2v.

There follows a line space, and then, on a new line: 'Cest livre est a moy'. The name of the owner is now very faint but according to the British Library

6 For more on Sir Richard Roos's life and writing, see Douglas Gray, 'Roos, Sir Richard (c.1410–1482)', rev., in *Oxford Dictionary of National Biography* (Oxford: OUP, 2004). Online edition: http://www.oxforddnb.com/view/article/37912 (accessed 22 February 2017); and Ethel Seaton, *Sir Richard Roos* (London: Rupert Hart-Davis, 1961).

7 I.e. quatre vingt huit, or 88.

8 This transcription is my own, with abbreviations expanded in italics, and erasures indicated in angle brackets. I am grateful for discussions with Roger Middleton regarding this inscription.

catalogue reads 'Richard Roos chivaler'.[9] This list of contents and his *ex libris* raise some interesting questions: there is no 'boke of Tristram and launcelot' in Royal MS 14 E III, so what exactly is Roos referring to here? Royal MS 14 E III is made from parchment, so what is the 'boke of paper' that he mentions? These are interesting questions, which unfortunately cannot be pursued in this essay.[10]

Upon his death in 1482 Sir Richard bequeathed the book in his will to his niece, Eleanor Haute née Roos (c. 1430–86).[11] Perhaps imitating the earlier example of her uncle, creating a mark of ownership on a book that now belonged to her, Eleanor also inscribed an *ex libris*: 'Thys boke ys myne dame Alyanor Haute' (see Fig. 11.2). However, unlike her uncle's, her inscription is in English and comes at the very end of the manuscript, opposite the final page of text (fol. 62r).[12]

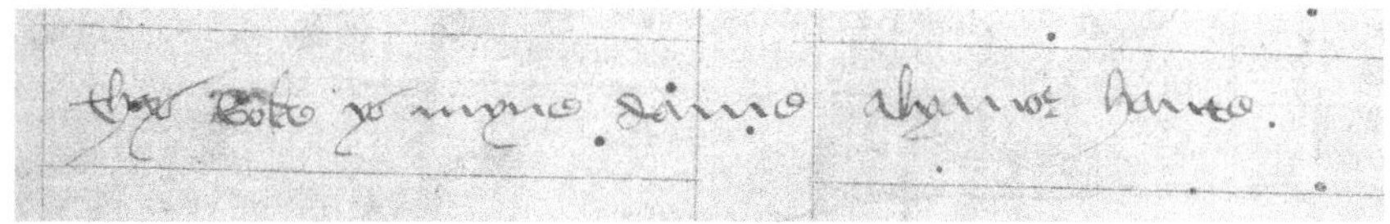

Fig. 11.2 © The British Library Board. Alyanor Haute's inscription in BL Royal MS 14 E III, fol. 162r.

Eleanor Haute's fluent writing runs horizontally across the centre of the page. On the same page there is a much smaller, somewhat scrawled signature in the top left-hand corner. It is a name only: 'E. Wydevyll' (see Fig. 12.3).

9 See the detailed record for BL Royal MS 14 E III for a transcription of this inscription: http://www.bl.uk/catalogues/illuminatedmanuscripts/record.asp?MSID=7793 (accessed 1 June 2017).

10 There is no space to discuss either question in this essay; however, they certainly merit further attention.

11 Sir Richard Roos's will is available at The National Archives: PROB 11/7/61. For a full transcription of the will, see Seaton, 'Appendix A: Sir Richard Roos's Will: March 8, 1481/2', in *Sir Richard Roos*, pp. 547–50. Variant spellings of Eleanor's first name and surname include Alyanor, Eleanor, Elyanor, Hawte, Haut, Haulte, etc., but Eleanor Haute is preferred throughout this essay.

12 Anthony Woodville's ownership note in MS Bodley 264 is also in French (discussed further below). Again, there is scope here for further study beyond the remit of this chapter. For Anthony Woodville's note, see Omar Khalaf, 'An Unedited Fragmentary Poem by Anthony Woodville, Earl Rivers in Oxford, Bodl., MS Bodley 264', *N&Q* 58 (2011), 487–90. Online version: doi: 10.1093/notesj/gjr163.

Fig. 11.3 © The British Library Board. E. Wydevyll's inscription in BL Royal MS 14 E III, fol. 162r.

The identity of the person behind this scrawl is not entirely certain. It is possible that this person was Edward Woodville,[13] but the most recent discussion, by Sarah Peverley, suggests that the signatory is Elizabeth Woodville:[14] since the signature is in Elizabeth's maiden name, it may have been 'from a time before she was queen'. Other examples of her signature during her time as queen, and during the reign of Henry VII (see Peverley), are more fluent than this inscription, which looks like a child's hand. David Baldwin points out that Elizabeth is 'unlikely to have signed herself as anything but Elizabeth after 1465', but also notes that 'the book was clearly a favourite within the family, and that Eleanor Haute could have presented it to her before Edward IV died in April 1483'.[15] Before it was owned by Roos, the book was owned by John, Duke of Bedford (1389–1435), who was the first husband of Elizabeth's mother. Elizabeth was born two years after his death, but the volume may have remained in the family for a time after this date, which may provide an explanation for the signature, if a juvenile Woodville – Edward or Elizabeth – signed the manuscript.

Returning our attention to the beginning of the manuscript, two signatures, also in an unpractised hand, are positioned beside one other on folio 1r (see Fig. 11.4). They provide the name and political/familial status of two of Elizabeth Woodville and Edward IV's daughters: 'Elysabeth, the kyngys dowther' and 'Cecyl the kyngys dowther' (later Elizabeth of York, queen of England, and Cecily, Viscountess Welles, respectively). Directly beneath the inscription of 'Cecyl' (Cecily) on the right-hand side of the page is that of Jane

[13] As suggested by the British Library catalogue entry for this manuscript, followed by Anne F. Sutton and Livia Visser-Fuchs, *Richard III's Books: Ideals and Reality in the Life and Library of a Medieval Prince* (Stroud: Sutton, 1997), p. 35.

[14] See Peverley, https://sarahpeverley.com/2013/06/23/smale-stufe-and-goodes-elizabeth-woodvilles-signature-and-will/ (accessed 22 February 2017).

[15] David Baldwin, *Elizabeth Woodville: Mother of the Princes in the Tower* (Stroud: History Press, 2002), p. 75.

(sometimes Joan or Eleanor) Grey (d. c. 1491),[16] one of Elizabeth Woodville's eleven siblings to have survived childhood, and wife of Anthony Grey de Ruthin, heir of the Earl of Kent. Her inscription merely states her name, 'Jane Grey'.

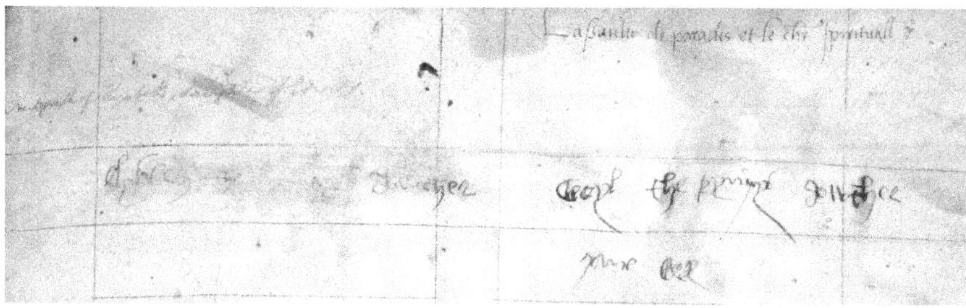

Fig. 11.4 © The British Library Board. Inscriptions by Elizabeth (left), Cecily (top right), and Jane Grey (bottom right), in British Library Royal MS 14 E III, fol. 1r.

BL Royal MS 14 E III's ownership history

Before analysing these inscriptions it will be useful to examine the book's known movements between owners before reaching Roos, Haute, and the Woodvilles, in order to identify the resonances and affiliations already associated with this object when it came into their possession. We will also consider the transition of the book between these inscribers, in order to situate them, the book, and their inscriptions within the context of a book-transmitting and sharing network. I will then suggest the likely timeframe within which some of these inscriptions occurred, and consider the implications that the timing of each inscription has on our understanding of the ways in which the book was used by its readers. Finally, the overarching question I will consider is why four women from the same family – a mother, assuming Elizabeth Woodville was the signatory, two daughters, and their maternal aunt (as well as their cousin by marriage) – signed the book whilst leaving no other markers (such as glosses or annotations), and what this might suggest about the place that this specimen of Arthuriana had at this dramatic moment in their lives.

Compiled in northern France sometime between 1315 and 1325, BL Royal MS 14 E III enjoyed a prestigious existence in the late Middle Ages, being owned by royalty and nobility.[17] The movement of this codex echoes the drama of the later Middle Ages: the Hundred Years War, the Wars of the Roses

[16] For the identification of this hand as Jane Grey's see Sutton and Visser-Fuchs, *Richard III's Books*, p. 35.

[17] Dates provided by the British Library catalogue.

between the Houses of Lancaster and York, and the changing fortunes of each side and its various players. It is not known who commissioned the manuscript, nor to whom it originally belonged. The book's composition has been dated to the first quarter of the fourteenth century, but the first owner that can be confidently asserted is Charles V of France (d. 1380), who was not born until 1338.[18] After Charles V the book passed to his son, Charles VI (d. 1422),[19] after which it was acquired by John, Duke of Bedford: 'probably purchased by him with the entire library of Charles V after Charles VI's death'.[20] This movement is symptomatic of 'the wider issue of the cross-Channel circulation' of literary objects and materials in the early part of the fifteenth century, as nobles and the individuals in their service travelled back and forth across the Channel.[21] From Bedford, the manuscript probably passed to his brother, Humphrey, Duke of Gloucester – a known bibliophile, literary patron, and book collector.[22] Between 1430 and 1442 Gloucester was the literary patron of one of the book's subsequent owners, Sir Richard Roos – a court poet and courtier. It is likely that he gave the book to Roos.[23] The exact conditions and date of this transaction are unclear – perhaps it was gifted to the poet for his service, whether in war or literature. Before this point the book had enjoyed the highest status of owner – French royalty and two brothers to an English king, brothers who were arguably the most important powers in France and

[18] It was listed in the catalogue of his library at Louvre. See Léopold Delisle, *Recherches sur la Librairie de Charles V*, 2 vols (Paris: Champion, 1907). See also the bibliographical information in the British Library catalogue entry for this manuscript.

[19] It was inherited by him with the Louvre Library (listed in the inventories of 1411, no. 186, 1413, no. 228, and 1424, no. 219). See Delisle, *Recherches sur la Librairie de Charles V*, vol. II, no. 1113.

[20] See also the British Library catalogue entry for this manuscript.

[21] For more on this, see Margaret Connolly and Yolanda Plumley, 'Crossing the Channel: John Shirley and the Circulation of French Lyric Poetry in England in the Early Fifteenth Century', in *Patrons, Authors and Workshops: Books and Book Production in Paris around 1400*, ed. G. Croenen and P. Ainsworth (Louvain, Paris, Dudley, MA: Peeters Publishers, 2006), pp. 311–32, at p. 312.

[22] For more on Gloucester and his books see: B. L. Ullman, 'Manuscripts of Duke Humphrey of Gloucester', *English Historical Review* 52 (1937), 670–2: http://www.jstor.org/stable/553709 (accessed 23 February 2015); Susanne Saygin, *Humphrey, Duke of Gloucester (1390–1447) and the Italian Humanists* (Leiden: Brill, 2001); Alessandra Petrina, *Cultural Politics in Fifteenth-Century England: The Case of Humphrey, Duke of Gloucester* (Leiden: Brill, 2004).

[23] Roos is often cited as the English translator and redactor of Alain Chartier's *La Belle Dame Sans Merci*. Gloucester's connection with the Roos family (even before his acquaintance with Richard) was significant. When Richard's eldest brothers were killed in military action in France, the next brother, Thomas, succeeded as the eighth Lord Roos. As he was only fifteen, Gloucester was appointed his guardian, taking an annuity from the Roos lands and approving a marriage for the young heir. See Seaton, *Sir Richard Roos*, p. 28.

England following the death of Henry V and the minority of his young son, Henry VI.[24] Therefore before it reached our inscribers the manuscript's impressive journey through the royal families of France and Britain had arguably imbued it with prestige, historical interest, and fiscal value – a network of intangible associations that arguably would have influenced the use and reception of the book by the Woodvilles.

Tracing the book's progress from owner to owner, we find that Sir Richard Roos bequeathed the manuscript in his will to his niece Eleanor, the daughter of his brother, Sir Robert Roos. Roos's will was drawn up on 8 March 1482 and proved on 1 April 1482.[25] It has been suggested that at the time of his death he had a post at the court of Edward IV, and 'sufficient moveable property but with hardly any land'.[26] He was evidently aware that the manuscript was a valuable item as he goes into some descriptive detail about his 'grete booke' in his will:

> ALSO I BIQUETH to Alianore Haute my Nece suster of the saide sir henry Roos my little Roos of golde sett and garnysshed with a Ruby and viij perles and my little potte of siluer and parcel gilte withoute foote and coueryng and my grete booke called saint Grall bounde in boordes couerde with rede leder an plated with plates of laten.[27]

The 'grete' book stands in contrast to the 'little' items listed as the first two effects, and though it is the only book to be mentioned it is nevertheless given a title – 'called saint Grall'. In physical stature the book is indeed great – large but sleek – a parchment codex measuring 485 x 335 mm and consisting of 162 folios. In terms of sumptuousness of design and decoration it is fairly ornate, containing 116 illuminated miniatures, as well as borders with creatures and human figures at the beginning of each text – certainly suitable for royal and aristocratic usage.[28] The exact date that Eleanor received the will is uncertain, as are the circumstances in which the book physically passed into her ownership. Eleanor took absolute ownership with an unequivocal *ex libris*: 'Thys boke is myne dame Alyanor Haute'.[29]

[24] For more on Gloucester and Bedford's powers following the death of Henry V, see R. A. Griffiths, 'Chapter Two: The King's Councillors', in *The Reign of King Henry VI*, 2nd edn (Stroud: Sutton, 1998), pp. 28–50.

[25] Dates given by Gray in 'Roos, Sir Richard (*c.*1410–1482)'.

[26] Gray, 'Roos, Sir Richard (*c.*1410–1482)'.

[27] Seaton, 'Appendix A', pp. 547–8.

[28] As a comparison, the Shrewsbury Book contains two full-page illuminated miniatures, thirteen two-column illuminated miniatures and four one-column illuminated miniatures, as well as 126 smaller illuminated miniatures within text columns.

[29] Seaton, *Sir Richard Roos*, p. 81, describes Eleanor's inscription as an 'almost childish scrawl' compared to the 'careful' and 'conventional elegance' of her uncle's inscription in the same book. However, Eleanor's inscription is far more confident than the halting

What does this inscription suggest about Eleanor, her use of the book, and the situation surrounding her transmission of this manuscript to the Woodvilles?

Eleanor Haute, BL Royal MS 14 E III, and the Woodville connection

Eleanor's inscription appears at the very end of the manuscript, occupying the blank recto page facing the final page of text of the *Mort Artu* on the verso page opposite. Eleanor at least opened the book. This is not saying very much, but there are very few things we can say with certainty about medieval women readers (there are no book reviews, blog posts, or book club notes to tell us how women received literature in this period). The manuscript has certainly been read – the stunning opening page of the *Estoire* (the first text in the book, on folio 3r) bears signs of use, particularly on the bottom margin, and towards the middle of the right-hand side of the page; places where the leafing of fingers and thumbs has worn away the ink of the beautiful border illustrations. But with anywhere between 100 and 150 years of owners before her, this wear was not necessarily caused by Eleanor. Aside from the wearing at the bottom and right-hand of the opening page, it is harder to trace reader activity throughout the rest of the book – not only is it made of hard-wearing parchment, but the rest of the manuscript has generous blank margins surrounding the text, meaning that there is no ink to supply tell-tale smudging by readers' fingers. Some page corners seem more dirtied and thumbed than others – folio 7r is the first page after the colourful title page to show similar signs of use. This is also the first page to contain illuminations (on both folios). It is easy to imagine medieval readers flicking through to the pages with illustrations, just as a modern reader might.

Unlike her uncle's, Eleanor's *ex libris* is in English. We might surmise that this indicates English as the language she felt most comfortable using. However, given our knowledge of Eleanor it is more than likely that she would have been able to read the French Arthurian texts contained in the manuscript. Much of the detail of Eleanor's life is unknown, but the picture that emerges is of a noblewoman born into a staunch Lancastrian family, with a degree of prominence at the court. The eldest child of Sir Robert Roos of Northamptonshire and Anne de Bohun, Eleanor had two younger siblings, Henry (b. 1439), and John. Her father Robert assumed responsibility for Château Gaillard from the earl of Shrewsbury on 5 December 1435. Like her uncle Richard, her father was also connected to Humphrey, Duke of Gloucester, who was Robert's guardian as a minor.[30] Even before Eleanor's inscription there is a tangible tradition of

and awkward hands of Elysabeth, or Cecyl the 'kyngys dowter' on f. 1r of Royal MS 14 E III.

30 Seaton, *Sir Richard Roos*, p. 44.

book-sharing and annotating between the Roos and the royal family, as one of Gloucester's books bears the inscription: 'Cest livre est A moy Homfrey duc de Gloucestre, du don mess. Robert Roos, chevalier, mon cousin.'[31] It appears that Robert gave this book to Gloucester. Another book, BL Royal MS 19 A XX, appears to have been owned by Gloucester first, before passing to Robert, and contains the signatures of both men (again in French): 'Mon bien mondain Gloucestre Au duc' – now erased – on the second folio, and 'Ce liure de linformacion des princes est a moy Robert Roos chivaler', on folio 152v. Seaton suggests that these manuscripts provide evidence of Robert and Gloucester remaining 'on terms of some intimacy',[32] even into Robert's adulthood.

Eleanor's father died on 30 December 1448, when she was eighteen. He had contributed to the ambassadorial arrangements for King Henry VI's wedding to Margaret of Anjou, and her uncle Richard had also escorted Margaret to England from France in 1445, which may explain why we later see Eleanor as one of Margaret's ladies.[33] In 1452–53 the household account of Margaret of Anjou lists 'Alienore Roos' receiving New Year's gifts with ten other ladies as '*damicellis prefate Regine*' (ladies of the aforesaid queen).[34] Eleanor also features with Margaret of Anjou over twenty years later in a 1475 entry in London, Guildhall Library MS 31692: The London Skinners' Company's *Book of the Fraternity of the Assumption of Our Lady*.[35] Folio 34v commemorates Margaret of Anjou's induction into the fraternity, depicting her kneeling at a *prie-dieu* with a lady behind her (possibly Katherine Vaux, her lady-in-waiting).[36] Below this illustration two women are said to be 'with the Qween': 'My lady Vawys dam Kat[r]ine' and 'Mastresse Elyanor Hawte'.[37]

31 The book is a French translation of Aegidius Romanus, *De Regimine Principum*, and Vegetius, *De Re Militari*, now CUL MS Ee 2 17. Inscription taken from Seaton, *Sir Richard Roos*, p. 43.

32 Seaton, *Sir Richard Roos*.

33 For Richard Roos's activities, see Gray, 'Roos, Sir Richard (*c.*1410–1482)'.

34 '... et Alienore Roos damicellis prefate Regine, pro feodis.' A. R. Myers, 'The Household of Queen Margaret of Anjou, 1452–3: II', *Bulletin of the John Rylands Library* 40 (1957), 391–431, at p. 405. Also referenced in C. Meale, '"... alle the bokes that I haue of latyn, englisch, and frensch": Laywomen and Their Books in Late Medieval England', in *Women and Literature in Britain, 1150–1500*, ed. Carol M. Meale (Cambridge: CUP, 1996), pp. 128–58, at p. 140.

35 This manuscript contains ordinances and annual lists of wardens and members from 21 Richard II to 1549.

36 See London, Guildhall Library MS 31692 (The London Skinners' Company's *Book of the Fraternity of the Assumption of Our Lady*), folio 34v. Diana Dunn has suggested that the lady behind Margaret is Katherine Vaux. See Dunn, 'Margaret of Anjou, Queen Consort of Henry VI: A Reassessment of Her Role, 1445–53', in *Crown, Government, and People in the Fifteenth Century*, ed. Rowena E. Archer, Fifteenth Century Series, 2 (New York: St Martin's Press, 1995), p. 112, n. 15.

37 This folio is reproduced in Kathleen L. Scott, *Later Gothic Manuscripts, 1390–1490*, 2 vols (London: H. Miller, 1996), II, 342–4; and in Mary Erler, 'The Book of Hours as

Eleanor's aristocratic upbringing and lengthy close connection to this French queen of England are convincing reasons to assume she had at least a working knowledge of French, written and spoken, and would therefore have been able to read the Arthurian contents of Royal MS 14 E III. It also suggests why Sir Richard Roos would have felt this rich manuscript to be an appropriate gift for his niece, moving as she did in such illustrious circles.

Indeed, Eleanor successfully 'continued her affiliation with the court' during both the Lancastrian and the succeeding Yorkist rule.[38] Eleanor entered the Haute family via marriage (her third) to Sir Richard Haute in 1474 (one year before her appearance with Margaret of Anjou in the Skinners' manuscript), making her a first cousin by marriage to Elizabeth Woodville, Edward IV's queen.[39] Elizabeth also appears in the manuscript mentioned above (London, Guildhall Library MS 31692), in a striking portrait commemorating her membership of the fraternity in around 1472 – three years before Margaret of Anjou's entry into the same company.[40] This tangibly and symbolically reinforces the network of association between Margaret of Anjou, Elizabeth Woodville, and Eleanor. Eleanor seems to have successfully traversed the potentially perilous political situation that the change of dynasty during the Wars of the Roses prompted, shifting her affiliations successfully from one ruling queen to another – her success indicated by her continued presence at the court from the reign of Henry VI to Edward IV. She is also recorded as being present at the court of Henry VII.[41] In her study of books of hours, Mary Erler suggests that the 'inclusion of royal names along with those of family and friends confirms the personal element in late medieval and early modern service, which was often characterized by ties of emotion as well as obligation'.[42] It would be fair to assume similarly blurred lines in Eleanor's case.

The literary predilections of Eleanor's Roos kin (with their manuscript owning and sharing, and the writing of courtly poetry as discussed above) may have had some bearing on her engagement with the Arthurian book. There are also indications that Eleanor already had literary interests that spanned secular works, as well as a propensity to sign her name in such books, before

---

Album Amicorum: Jane Guildford's Book', in *The Social Life of Illumination: Manuscripts, Images, and Communities in the Late Middle Ages* (Turnhout: Brepols, 2013), pp. 505–36, at p. 513.

38 Meale, '"… alle the bokes that I haue of latyn, englisch, and frensch"', p. 140.

39 Peter Fleming, 'Haute family (per. c.1350–1530)', in *Oxford Dictionary of National Biography* (Oxford: OUP, 2004). Online edition January 2008: http://www.oxforddnb.com/view/article/52786 (accessed 9 March 2017).

40 J. L. Laynesmith provides a facsimile of this image and gives this date as an estimate. See J. L. Laynesmith, *The Last Medieval Queens: English Queenship 1445–1503* (Oxford: OUP, 2004), pp. 33, 142–3.

41 See Meale, '"… alle the bokes that I haue of latyn, englisch, and frensch"', p. 140.

42 Erler, 'The Book of Hours as *Album Amicorum*', p. 512.

receiving BL Royal MS 14 E III in 1482. A manuscript dating from the second quarter of the fifteenth century also bears an inscription by Eleanor: BL Royal MS 17 D VI contains Thomas Hoccleve's *The Regiment of Princes*, with other poems. On f. 1r, amid a sea of prior inscriptions and signed names from the upper echelons of fifteenth-century English society (including Courtenay, Arundel, and Berkeley), she has inscribed 'Alyanor Roos' (see the bottom right-hand corner of Fig. 11.5).[43]

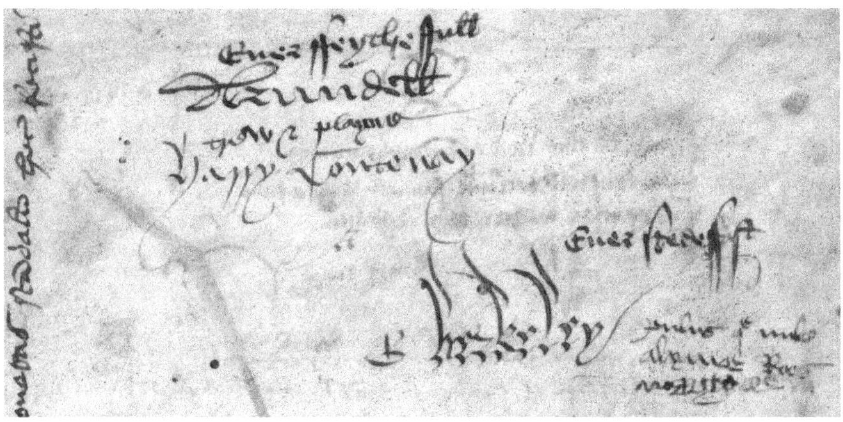

Fig. 11.5 © The British Library Board. Detail from BL Royal MS 17 D VI, fol. 1r, showing various inscriptions, including 'Alyanor Roos' (bottom right).

The hand is identical to Eleanor's in BL Royal MS 14 E III, confirming that it is indeed our Eleanor. It is unclear who the 'Margeree' is, signed in a different hand just beneath Eleanor's, or what the script above Eleanor's name represents. The presence of her signature in this manuscript offers a tantalising precursor to her *ex libris* in the Arthurian BL Royal 14 E III, and echoes that manuscript as a hub of high-status ownership activity. Her inscription in both manuscripts also suggests a continuity of practice in terms of Eleanor's book-owning and reading, and furthermore, if she read and inscribed this book with her siblings, it also suggests a delightful continuity in terms of family practices of reading and sharing non-devotional literature in fifteenth-century England.

[43] This manuscript has been fully digitised and is available online at British Library Digitised Manuscripts: http://www.bl.uk/manuscripts/FullDisplay.aspx?ref=Royal_MS_17_D_VI (accessed 11 March 2017).

Inscription as political and personal

This section attempts to establish, on the basis of the available evidence, a window of time for some of the inscriptions in BL Royal MS 14 E III. Establishing this timeframe will allow us to draw certain conclusions regarding the manner of usage of this book, including as a symbol of connection between female family members, and a medium in which to express political protest. Eleanor probably died in 1486, and so must have penned her *ex libris* sometime in the four intervening years between the bequest of the manuscript in 1482 by Sir Richard Roos and her death.[44] It is impossible to know whether she passed the book to the Woodvilles during her lifetime, or bequeathed it to them in her will. No will has yet been discovered for Eleanor, but she and Elizabeth were certainly connected in this period until the end of Eleanor's life: both had both served as ladies to the former queen, Margaret of Anjou, and as already stated, they were also cousins by marriage through the Hautes. Added to this, Eleanor's last recorded court appearance was at the christening of Prince Arthur – Elizabeth of York's son and Elizabeth Woodville's grandson – in 1486.[45] This is compelling evidence of a continued connection between the two women via the court, aristocratic service, and family. Given the transaction of the book between Eleanor and Elizabeth, it seems likely that they were on friendly terms of acquaintance, at the very least, and the 'pretty female fashion' of giving books as gifts between women of the court was by this time well established: 'Elizabeth Woodville, Elizabeth of York, and Margaret Beaufort all wrote graceful messages in various books of hours they gave to their female courtiers.'[46] In giving a book to Elizabeth Woodville, Eleanor acted within an established framework of courtly women bestowing inscribed books as gifts to one another.[47]

As well as this connection, other evidence in the manuscript suggests that the Woodvilles received BL Royal MS 14 E III from Eleanor before her death in 1486, and allows us to make some further suggestions about its owners and readers. In their *ex libris* marks in the book, Elizabeth Woodville's daughters, Elizabeth and Cecily, each call themselves 'the kyngys dowter' – the king's daughter. Their father, King Edward IV, died at the palace of Westminster on 9 April 1483.[48] After this date the two girls would no longer have technically

44 Ibid. Date of Eleanor's death suggested by Fleming, 'Haute family'.

45 Meale, '"... alle the bokes that I haue of latyn, englisch, and frensch"', p. 140.

46 Erler, 'The Book of Hours as *Album Amicorum*', p. 505.

47 The book took a rather circuitous route to Elizabeth considering her family connection to John, Duke of Bedford – the book's first English owner was her mother Jaquetta de Luxembourg's first husband. Elizabeth's mother was married to Bedford for two years and five months before he died in Rouen in 1435.

48 Rosemary Horrox, 'Edward IV (1442–1483)', in *Oxford Dictionary of National Biography* (Oxford: OUP, 2004). Online edition, September 2011: http://www.oxforddnb.

been the king's daughters, but rather the king's sisters, before becoming the king's nieces when Richard III was crowned king on 6 July 1483.[49] If Sir Richard Roos's will was proved on 1 April 1482, then this is the earliest possible date that Eleanor would have received the book. Does this suggest that she inscribed the book before passing it on fairly hastily – within a year – when it was then also signed by the two Woodville girls within that same year, before 9 April 1483 (and possibly by their aunt Jane in that period, too)? This seems a hurried set of transactions. There is also the possibility that Elizabeth and Cecily may still have considered themselves the rightful king's daughters even after Edward's death.

Supporting this idea is the evidence that they signed themselves as such in another manuscript after their father Edward's death. Princeton Garrett MS 168, the *Testamenta de Amyra Sultan Nichemedy* ('an account of the funeral of the Turkish emperor Mohammed II'), was produced for Elizabeth and Cecily's brother, Edward, Prince of Wales, sometime after 12 September 1481 (which is the date of the letter it copies), and bound in England by the 'Caxton Binder' in Westminster around 1482.[50] Young Edward's arms are given as those of the Prince of Wales on folio 14v, which suggests the book was given to him before his brief period of kingship (9 April–25 June 1483) and eventual disappearance.[51] Both young Elizabeth's and Cecily's names are inscribed on folio iv (pasted to the front pastedown), along with a statement of their titles: 'Elysabeth the kyngys dowghter boke. Cecyl the kyngys dowghter.'[52] On folio viiir, pasted to the back pastedown, the name of Jane Grey can also be found.[53] If, as young Elizabeth asserts, this book is hers, then it seems likely

com/view/article/8520 (accessed 9 March 2017).

49 Rosemary Horrox, 'Richard III (1452–1485)', in *Oxford Dictionary of National Biography* (Oxford: OUP, 2004). Online edition, May 2013: http://www.oxforddnb.com/view/article/23500 (accessed 9 March 2017).

50 For the catalogue entry for this manuscript, see Don C. Skemer, 'Garrett MS. 168', in *Medieval and Renaissance Manuscripts in the Princeton University Library*, vol. 1 (New Jersey: Princeton University Press, 2013), pp. 383–5, at p. 384. Also mentioned in Meale, '"... alle the bokes that I haue of latyn, englisch, and frensch"', p. 144. I am very grateful to Roger Middleton for bringing this manuscript and its inscriptions to my attention.

51 Skemer, 'Garrett MS. 168'.

52 Skemer, 'Garrett MS. 168'.

53 Skemer, 'Garrett MS. 168'. Meale also suggests that lower down on the same page as Jane Grey's inscription, there 'appears an inscription in drypoint which may read "alyanor"'. See Meale, '"... alle the bokes that I haue of latyn, englisch, and frensch"', p. 157, n. 90. Skemer also highlights Cologny, Bibliotheca Bodmeriana, MS. 168 – an Anglo-Norman manuscript (*Waldef*, *Gui de Warewic*, and *Otinel*) with the signature of Jane Grey. See also K. Busby, *Codex and Context: Reading Old French Verse Narrative in Manuscripts*, vol. 2 (Amsterdam: Rodolpi, 2002), pp. 497, 735. It was suggested to me that The 'De Grey' Hours (NLW MS 15537C) may have borne a connection to Jane Grey in terms of an inscription, but I have not found a signature by her in

that it passed to her after her brother's disappearance (before which time it would have been his book, not hers). If so, the signatures of Elizabeth and Cecily were added after the fact of both her brother's disappearance and their father's death, by which point neither Elizabeth nor Cecily were technically the king's daughters, but his nieces, as Richard III took the throne.

How can this be explained? In the period of political upheaval and confusion following their brothers' disappearance (the famous mystery of the 'Princes in the Tower'), and Richard III's usurpation of the throne, it is perhaps understandable that the sisters might continue to view and define themselves as daughters of the king, given the lack of any other certainty. We might also bear in mind that in 1483 Elizabeth was seventeen and Cecily fourteen, and that being the king's daughters was all they would have known. Undoubtedly there would have been an element of genuine feeling and sentiment involved in these signatures – grief for a recently lost father, and denial at their situation. However, the combination of Cecily and Elizabeth's signatures proclaiming themselves as the king's daughters in both Royal MS 14 E III and Princeton Garrett MS 168 after Edward's death could have another possible motivation: that of political protest. The fact that Elizabeth and Cecily sign themselves the king's daughters in a royal book – that is to say, a book possessing such strong associations of previous royal owners as we have earlier discussed – asserts their royal status.

Should we read these signatures as an act of political defiance? This would certainly be the case if they were written after *Titulus Regius* was issued in 1484, which declared that 'all th'issue and children of the said king been bastards, and unable to inherite or to clayme anything by inheritance, by the lawe and custome of England'.[54] Do these signatures, defining Elizabeth and her sister Cecily as the king's daughters, suggest that they held the new king (Richard III) to be illegitimate? This is a powerful message to have inscribed in the pages of a royal book, and perhaps demonstrates one of the only avenues of protest available to these two teenage girls – now subject to their uncle's rule. Regarding the motives for readers inscribing the pages of their books, H. J. Jackson suggests that they 'must foresee some advantage for someone; so the question of motive resolves itself into another question, *cui bono*? For whose benefit is it done?'[55] In this case, the inscriptions would seem to be for Elizabeth and Cecily's own benefit. The sisters represent both inscriber and addressee – the inscriptions are for their eyes (we can safely assume

this manuscript. It is fully digitised here: http://digidol.llgc.org.uk/METS/ODG00001/physical?locale=en&mode=thumbnail&start=1&ite (accessed 2 November 2015).

54 A full transcription of *Titulus Regius* (1484) is available on the Richard III Foundation website: http://www.richard111.com/titulus_regius.htm (accessed 1 March 2017).

55 H. J. Jackson, *Marginalia: Readers Writing in Books* (New Haven, CT and London: Yale University Press, 2001), p. 82.

they did not mean their uncle Richard to see these signatures), and perhaps even for their own personal dignity. Books can carry political messages, then and now,[56] and can also provide strong emotional comfort: to write a covert message of heartfelt protest in a book's pages is akin to whispering in the ear of an understanding friend, or shouting with frustration into a pillow. It is a moderately safe way to vent emotion, or to tell a dangerous personal or political truth.

Whatever the reason for their signatures as the king's daughters, it is certain that the titles they used for themselves would have changed by 1486 and 1487 at the very latest. Elizabeth married Henry Tudor (later Henry VII) on 18 January 1486 so 'the kyngys dowter' would certainly not have been her epithet once she was the queen of England, or the king's wife, and indeed we do see her signing documents 'Elizabeth the Quene' once she is married.[57] Cecily married Henry VII's half-uncle, John, Viscount Welles, in December 1487, so her title would also have changed from that of the king's daughter by that date too.[58] This provides a definite *terminus ad quem* for their signatures. Therefore the inscriptions by Eleanor, Elizabeth (the younger), and Cecily must have all been made sometime between 1 April 1482 and 18 January 1486.

BL Royal MS 14 E III as family nexus *in extremis*

The presence in this manuscript of two other signatures by members of the Woodville family provides further clues as to dating. As mentioned in the summary of inscriptions above, the manuscript also contains a signature by Jane Grey. Jane Grey was the sister of Elizabeth Woodville and married Anthony Grey, the eldest son of Edmund, Lord Grey of Ruthin, in 1465.[59] Anthony Grey died childless in 1480, but Jane was still alive on 24 September 1485, when she was named in a document specifying the remainder interests in a grant given to her brother Edward.[60] She seems to have died by 1492, as a postmortem inquisition from this year indicates that neither she nor any children of hers survive her brother Richard.[61] This gives us a *terminus ad*

[56] Umberto Eco and Jean-Claude Carrière, *This is Not the End of the Book*, trans. Polly McLean (London: Vintage, 2012), p. ix.

[57] For instance 'Elysabeth ye quene' in BL MS Additional 17012, folio 21r. See Erler, 'The Book of Hours as *Album Amicorum*', p. 507, for a facsimile of this page.

[58] Horrox, 'Edward IV (1442–1483)'.

[59] Rosemary Horrox, 'Grey, Edmund, first earl of Kent (1416–1490)', *Oxford Dictionary of National Biography* (Oxford: OUP, 2004). Online edition: http://www.oxforddnb.com/view/article/11529 (accessed 11 March 2017).

[60] William Campbell, *Materials for a History of the Reign of Henry VII* (London: Longman et al., 1873), pp. 562–3.

[61] *Calendar of Inquisitions Post-Mortem, Henry VII*, vol. I, No. 681 (Richard, Earl of Ryvers). I am indebted to the work of Susan Higginbotham for directing me to these

quem of 1492 for Jane's signature. It is likely that her nieces would also have written their *ex libris* marks by this date, as her signature is located directly beneath theirs, which suggests a temporal relationship between these inscriptions. If the other signature of 'E Wydville' is indeed Elizabeth Woodville's (as discussed above), then her death on 8 June 1492 confirms 1492 as the latest possible date for all the inscriptions to have taken place.[62]

We can assert with some confidence, then, that the majority of the inscriptions in BL Royal MS 14 E III (after that of Sir Richard Roos) took place within a ten-year window: between 1482, when the book was bequeathed by Roos to Eleanor, and 1492, by which point both Elizabeth Woodville and Jane Grey are known to be deceased. Moreover, given the wording of the inscriptions of the two sisters Elizabeth and Cecily (as discussed above), it seems likely that their inscriptions took place between 1482 and 1486. The identical wording for the sisters' inscriptions, and the very similar nature of their hands, suggests that they were written at the same time – perhaps Cecily was copying her older sister's hand. The placement of their aunt Jane's signature just below, with the two siblings' inscriptions above, is possibly even suggestive of the scenario that the two nieces may have penned their marks under the watchful eye of their aunt, who then signed her approval just below. Furthermore, the presence of the signatures of all three of these Woodvilles (the young Elizabeth, Cecily, and Jane Grey) in Princeton Garrett MS 168, also from sometime during this tumultuous period, is suggestive of a pattern of communal literary behaviour – an aunt reading with her nieces. Mary Erler highlights a book of hours with a similar proliferation of familial inscriptions and markings: British Library MS Additional 17012 contains the inscription of Elizabeth of York as queen (mentioned above), as well her husband Henry VII's signature, and annotations by their daughter Princess Margaret (all on the same page), as well as (on the facing page verso) Henry VIII and Katherine of Aragon. There are also signatures and inscriptions elsewhere written by their daughter Mary Tudor; one C (or E) la Baume; Yolande, lady of Savoy; and three courtiers from the 1520s. Erler suggests that 'the inscriptions have multiplied successfully enough that it seems possibly to speak of the development of a new genre. Instead of witnessing to a single relationship between giver and receiver, the book has become a field of messages.' Erler compares this bookish object to the *album amicorum*, 'a booklet inscribed by

sources for Jane Grey. See 'Meet the In-Laws: The Lesser-Known Woodville Siblings', *Ricardian Register* (Spring 2009), 4–14. Available online: http://www.r3.org/wp-content/uploads/2014/03/2009_03.pdf (accessed 2 September 2015).

62 Michael Hicks, 'Elizabeth (c.1437–1492)', in *Oxford Dictionary of National Biography* (Oxford: OUP, 2004). Online edition, September 2011: http://www.oxforddnb.com/view/article/8634 (accessed 2 September 2015).

friends and acquaintances as a memento for the owner'.[63] The inscriptions in Royal MS 14 E III – although not engaging with one another in the same way as MS Add. 17012 – arguably provide similar evidence of association. Though not quite a 'field of messages', the inscriptions nevertheless reveal a community of readers, and whereas such evidence provided by inscriptions is not infrequently found in books of hours,[64] it is rare and precious in books of Arthurian prose romances.

There is an event that falls within this 1482–86 window that would have brought the Woodville women together in close proximity: their time spent in sanctuary at Westminster. From 1 May 1483 to 22 January 1484, just before and during the early part of the reign of Richard III, Elizabeth and her children sought safety for eight months in sanctuary, fearful of Richard III. Earl Rivers and Lord Richard Grey were arrested at Stony Stratford at the close of April 1483 whilst conveying the new king Edward V, and when word of this reached London, Elizabeth and her five daughters 'again took sanctuary at Westminster', along with the Marquess of Dorset and Prince Richard.[65] The Italian humanist scholar Polydore Vergil (c. 1470–1555) dramatically imagines the events surrounding the sanctuary of Elizabeth Woodville and her family in his *Anglica Historia* (first edition dated 1513). After Richard, Duke of Gloucester captured Elizabeth Woodville's son, the prince Edward, at 'Stony Stratfoorth':[66]

> Elyzabeth the quene was much dismayed, and determynyd furthwith to fly; for, suspecting eaven than that ther was no plane dealing, to thintent she might delyver her other children from the present danger, she convayed hirself with them and the marquyse into the sayntuary at Westmynster.[67]

In a moment that highlights the interconnectedness of Eleanor and Elizabeth's lives, Richard Haute – Eleanor's husband – was also captured at this *coup d'état* at Stony Stratford. However, unlike Elizabeth Woodville's kinsmen Rivers and Grey, he was spared and 'lived out Richard III's reign in quiet obscurity', returning to the court after the Battle of Bosworth.[68] Michael Hicks

63 Erler, 'The Book of Hours as *Album Amicorum*', p. 508.

64 Erler, 'The Book of Hours as *Album Amicorum*', p. 508.

65 Baldwin, *Elizabeth Woodville*, pp. 94–5. Baldwin cites Thomas More, suggesting that the family 'did not go into the sanctuary building itself (as they presumably had in 1470), but to "the abbottes place" or apartments'. See Thomas More, *The History of King Richard III*, ed. R. S. Sylvester (New Haven, CT: Yale University Pres, 1976), p. 19.

66 Stony Stratford.

67 Polydore Vergil, *Three books of Polydore Vergil's English history, comprising the reigns of Henry VI., Edward IV., and Richard III. from an early translation, preserved among the mss. of the old royal library in the British museum*, ed. Sir Henry Ellis (London: Nichols and Son, 1844), p. 175.

68 Fleming, 'Haute family'.

claims that Elizabeth and her family took with them into sanctuary 'so much personal property that a breach was made in the walls between the palace and abbey for easier access'.[69] It is certainly feasible therefore that BL Royal MS 14 E III could have formed part of this property.

It is clear that the Woodville family gathered around this Arthurian book – that it functioned as a nexus of sorts (and still does in combining their signatures in one place). This gathering almost certainly took place physically, as the Woodvilles signed – and presumably read – the book together. It arguably may have also taken place mentally and emotionally, in discussions of the book's contents or themes. However, such activities are sadly lost to us. We are left with the tangible evidence contained in the book's pages, which suggests an object that provided a space for family gathering and communion. The manuscript as an object reinforces 'the social connection between giver and recipient, establishing the book as a site of memory, its physical existence recalling various degrees and kinds of invisible links among its owners'.[70] If the Woodvilles did indeed take the book into sanctuary with them, this offers a potentially powerful and poignant new angle to the notion of this Arthurian book as nexus. The next section of this essay will consider how the textual content of BL Royal MS 14 E III may contribute to our understanding of its uses and functions within the Woodville family, particularly if read in sanctuary.

The Arthurian texts of BL Royal MS 14 E III

We have explored the palaeographical and contextual aspects of the manuscript and the ways in which users and owners of the text have interacted with the physical object of the codex itself. However, another important aspect of this manuscript is, of course, its literary content. If the Woodvilles read and inscribed this book during a period of very difficult upheaval in their lives, then what were the ethical and instrumental motivations for reading Arthuriana in such times of *extremis*? What was it about this particular book that might have encouraged their readership and inscription? The first text in this manuscript – the *Estoire* – details the history of the Grail and its initial journey with Joseph of Arimathea and the miraculous occurrences that take place around the vessel. It is mostly religious and miraculous in tone and content, a prequel to the second text, the *Queste.* Whilst still predominantly centred on questions of spiritual purity and morality, this second romance features a cast of familiar knights, as Launcelot, Gawain, Perceval, Galahad, and others set out on their sacred mission to find the Grail. The final text, the *Mort Artu*, portrays the decline and downfall of the Arthurian court and kingdom. This concluding romance of the manuscript hinges around the adulterous affair of

69 Hicks, 'Elizabeth (c.1437–1492)'.

70 Erler, 'The Book of Hours as *Album Amicorum*', p. 505.

Launcelot and Guenevere and the fatal battle between Arthur and Mordred, highlighting the discordant factions within the fellowship of the Round Table, and ending the manuscript on a note of hopeless pathos.

There are very few extant manuscripts that contain all five *Lancelot-Grail Cycle* texts and it is normal to find them in a variety of combinations.[71] Of the complete possible set of five *Lancelot-Grail Cycle* texts, BL Royal MS 14 E III omits the two whose material focuses on Merlin and Lancelot: the *Estoire de Merlin* and the *Lancelot Propre*. These omitted texts contain the most provocative content (for instance the situation surrounding Merlin's conception) and also the lion's share of knightly adventures and battles. The content we are left with in BL Royal 14 E III is rather more religious, and certainly more sober in tone, with the Grail stories highly prioritised. The two romances on this subject comprise the majority of the manuscript, taking up 140 out of a total of 162 folios. The *Mort Artu* is included in an abridged form at the end, suggesting a token effort at cohesiveness and completion of the cycle, but overall the emphasis is undeniably on the Grail material. The main concerns of Royal MS 14 E III and its contents are the religious and moral aspects of Arthuriana.

In his Introduction to the *Prose Merlin*, Conlee suggests that 'the sequence of works in the *Vulgate Cycle* were presented as being historical works, not romances, and at their center they possessed a serious religious purpose'.[72] He goes on to suggest that in these works, 'a great effort is made to bestow upon the events of the Arthur story a fundamentally religious purpose, and also to suggest that the ultimate achievement of Arthurian society, for which only a few would be worthy, is the attainment of a transcendent spirituality'.[73] This set of romances afforded an ideal balance between spiritual comfort and entertaining escapades, and the sobriety of the romances in this manuscript, avoiding all lascivious Arthurian themes, would certainly have been considered suitable for a fifteenth-century aristocratic female reader. Were these texts used for spiritual and emotional comfort during a trying time? Another service undoubtedly rendered by reading books is escapism. As Escarpit suggests:

71 See the other manuscripts of the *Lancelot-Grail Cycle* in the British Library for further examples of combinations: Additional 5474; Additional 17443; Additional 32125; Egerton 2515; Harley 4419; Harley 6340, 6341, 6342; Lansdowne 757; Royal 14 E. iii; Royal 15 A. xi; Royal 19 B. vii; Royal 19 C. xii; Royal 19 C. xiii; Royal 20 A. ii; Royal 20 B. viii; Royal 20 C. vi; Royal 20 D. iii; Royal 20 D. iv. From 'The Prose Lancelot Grail', *Arthurian Manuscripts in the British Library: The French Tradition*: http://www.bl.uk/catalogues/illuminatedmanuscripts/TourArtProse.asp (accessed 25 June 2014).

72 'Introduction', in *Prose Merlin*, ed. John Conlee (Kalamazoo, MI: Medieval Institute Publications, 1998). Online edition: http://d.lib.rochester.edu/teams/text/conlee-prose-merlin-introduction (accessed 1 March 2017).

73 'Introduction', in *Prose Merlin*, ed. Conlee.

'when we hold a book in our hand, all we hold is the paper: the book is elsewhere'.[74] The same is true for us: when we hold a book, we are imaginatively elsewhere. This is a particularly useful aspect of literature for those in confinement, and Arthurian literature is known to have served another spatially restricted contemporary of the Woodvilles: Sir Thomas Malory, who wrote his Arthurian masterpiece using a wealth of Arthurian literature in prison around 1471. Omar Khalaf has also persuasively argued that Elizabeth Woodville's brother, Anthony, 2nd Earl Rivers, may also have taken a manuscript (that had similarly migrated to England during the Hundred Years War) into prison with him before his execution, and likewise inscribed it. Like BL Royal MS 14 E III, MS Bodley 264 contains a cycle of romances (albeit about Alexander, rather than Arthur), as well as a fragmentary poem signed by 'ARiveris' that Khalaf has attributed to Rivers. Khalaf suggests Rivers 'may have written the poem in the time span between his imprisonment and his death'.[75] The example illustrates the uses of literature as comfort and escapism in times of *extremis*, and as a medium upon which to inscribe marks – perhaps as a means of leaving something permanent in a world that may have seemed increasingly threatened and transitory.

Another relevant aspect of the Arthurian romances contained in Royal MS 14 E III is the importance of inscriptions, and the written word. The first illumination in the manuscript after the well-adorned opening page depicts a scribe, presumably in the act of writing the sequence of romances in a pertinent meta-narrative (fol. 6v). This is a particularly technical portrayal – all of the tools of the trade are shown: an inkpot rests to the left of the scribe, who has his attention fixed on the copy text before him, and busily writes with the quill in his right hand whilst the tool in his left hand is ready to scrape any errors from the parchment. Some delicate weights are even depicted, holding flat both the exemplar and the scribe's copy text, so that he can read and write unhindered by closing pages. The artist has also written legible text in the lined pages of the tiny books depicted within our greater book. The scribe is in plain monk's garb, nothing mystical or glamorous at all about him, and his environment is plain and empty, bar an empty table (or an altar perhaps) with a cloth draped over it. (See Fig. 11.6.)

The textual content in this Arthurian manuscript also emphasises the importance of the written word. Echoing the meta-narrative scribal image, the prologue begins by drawing attention to the act of writing. The first line reads: 'The one who, by order of the Great Master, is setting in writing the high and noble story of the Grail first sends greetings to all those men and

74 Robert Escarpit, *The Book Revolution* (London: Harrap and UNESCO, 1966), p. 17.

75 Omar Khalaf, 'An Unedited Fragmentary Poem by Anthony Woodville, Earl Rivers in Oxford, Bodl. Library, MS Bodley 264', *N&Q* 58 (2011), 487–90. Online version: doi: 10.1093/notesj/gjr163.

Fig. 11.6 © The British Library Board. Miniature depicting a scribe, from BL Royal MS 14 E III, fol. 6v.

women who believe in the glorious Holy Trinity …'[76] This direct address to the reader (and women are explicitly included here as potential readers) has the effect of delineating writing as a sanctified act, and also offers the suggestion that the act of writing and reading can transcend time and space – the past author, by reaching out with the written word, has touched readers in the present moment. This may have been a consoling thought to the Woodvilles in their precarious position in sanctuary, having already lost several family members, and with their futures probably seeming highly uncertain. A sense of permanence in the written word may have afforded an attractive alternative to present unknowns. The comfort offered by reading books continues to be

[76] 'The History of the Holy Grail', trans. Carol J. Chase, in *The Lancelot-Grail Reader*, ed. Norris J. Lacy (New York: Garland, 2000), pp. 3–48, at p. 4. All subsequent translations are quoted from this edition.

emphasised in the *Estoire*, as its narrator/writer describes being given a 'little book' in a holy visitation:

> any man who looks often inside this little book, as one should, will win the two greatest joys that exist: joy of the soul and joy of the body. For there is no mortal man, no matter how distressed, if he can see inside sincerely, as he should, whose heart will not be delivered at that moment of all anguish and filled with all the joys a mortal heart can have [...] nor will anyone who has held and seen this little book one time die a sudden death, no matter what sin he has committed in this life.[77]

Again, if the Woodvilles were in sanctuary, the message contained within BL Royal MS 14 E III of the spiritual salvation and even physical preservation afforded by the mere act of reading a book would have encouraged its readers.

Finally, inscriptions feature at pivotal moments in this Arthurian manuscript. For instance, in the *Quest*, there is a detailed examination of the Round Table and its inscriptions on each seat, giving the name of its intended occupant, before turning to the Perilous Seat, with its recent inscription: 'Four hundred fifty-four years have passed since the passion of the Christ; on Pentecost, this seat will find its master.'[78] This, again, gives a sense of timelessness with regard to inscriptions and the written word – ostensibly this all took place several hundred years ago, however the sense of immediacy provided by this inscription is acute. Other inscriptions provide warnings and instructions; regarding the Sword in the Stone, which 'only the world's best knight' can remove;[79] for those wishing to board a magic ship: 'You who wish to enter me, whoever you may be, be certain that you are full of faith ...';[80] against any man drawing a sword from a magical scabbard 'unless he can fight better and more boldly than anyone else'.[81] It is often female 'readers' in the texts who perceive the 'truth' of these cryptic inscriptions, such as Percival's sister,[82] and indeed one inscription on the sword and scabbard explicitly states:

> Let no one be so bold as to remove this belt. No man is authorized to do so now or in the future. It can be removed only by the hand of a woman, daughter of a king and a queen [...] This young woman will call the sword by its rightful name, and me by mine, something no one will be able to do until that time.[83]

77 'The History of the Holy Grail', p. 6.
78 'The Quest for the Holy Grail', trans. E. J. Burns, in *The Lancelot-Grail Reader*, ed. Lacy, pp. 305–64, at p. 307.
79 'The Quest for the Holy Grail', p. 308.
80 'The Quest for the Holy Grail', p. 335.
81 'The Quest for the Holy Grail', p. 337.
82 'The Quest for the Holy Grail', p. 337.
83 'The Quest for the Holy Grail', pp. 338–9.

That the written word can provide not only comfort, but also tangible instruction – furthermore instruction only intelligible to women, and that emphasises the agency of women over that of men – would surely have been a welcome message to the disinherited and illegitimised 'daughter[s] of a king and queen' reading BL Royal MS 14 E III in confinement.

Conclusion

BL Royal MS 14 E III provides evidence of a courtly book-sharing family network of women, suggesting bonds of family and friendship that extended beyond its pages. The inscriptions in this manuscript indicate that it was a nexus around which the Woodville women gathered (physically, intellectually, emotionally) within a relatively brief window of time. The manuscript's Arthurian literature may have offered spiritual and emotional comfort during a period of extreme personal and political duress – perhaps even accompanying them into sanctuary, where it may have provided a source of consolation, entertainment, and empowerment – suggesting the power of reading in times of *extremis*. Furthermore, this book and its inscriptions suggest some of the means available to these women for mitigating the negative situations they faced: using inscriptions as political defiance, literature as escapism and familial bonding, and the inscribing of the word on the physical page as a symbol of permanence in a shifting world.

Index

Volumes Already Published

I: *The Orient in Chaucer and Medieval Romance*, Carol F. Heffernan, 2003

II: *Cultural Encounters in the Romance of Medieval England*, edited by Corinne Saunders, 2005

III: *The Idea of Anglo-Saxon England in Middle English Romance*, Robert Allen Rouse, 2005

IV: *Guy of Warwick: Icon and Ancestor*, edited by Alison Wiggins and Rosalind Field, 2007

V: *The Sea and Medieval English Literature*, Sebastian I. Sobecki, 2008

VI: *Boundaries in Medieval Romance*, edited by Neil Cartlidge, 2008

VII: *Naming and Namelessness in Medieval Romance*, Jane Bliss, 2008

VIII: Sir Bevis of Hampton *in Literary Tradition*, edited by Jennifer Fellows and Ivana Djordjević, 2008

IX: *Anglicising Romance: Tail-Rhyme and Genre in Medieval English Literature*, Rhiannon Purdie, 2008

X: *A Companion to Medieval Popular Romance*, edited by Raluca L. Radulescu and Cory James Rushton, 2009

XI: *Expectations of Romance: The Reception of a Genre in Medieval England*, Melissa Furrow, 2009

XII: *The Exploitations of Medieval Romance*, edited by Laura Ashe, Ivana Djordjević, and Judith Weiss, 2010

XIII: *Magic and the Supernatural in Medieval English Romance*, Corinne Saunders, 2010

XIV: *Medieval Romance, Medieval Contexts*, edited by Rhiannon Purdie and Michael Cichon, 2011

XV: *Women's Power in Late Medieval Romance*, Amy N. Vines, 2011

XVI: *Heroes and Anti-Heroes in Medieval Romance*, edited by Neil Cartlidge, 2012

XVII: *Performance and the Middle English Romance*, Linda Marie Zaerr, 2012

XVIII: *Medieval Romance and Material Culture*, edited by Nicholas Perkins, 2015

XIX: *Middle English Romance and the Craft of Memory*, Jamie McKinstry, 2015

XX: *Medieval Narratives of Alexander the Great: Transnational Texts in England and France*, Venetia Bridges, 2018